KENTUCKY
Remembered

An Oral History Series

James C. Klotter
and
Terry L. Birdwhistell

General Editors

Conversations
with
Kentucky Writers II

L. Elisabeth Beattie, Editor

Photographs by Susan Lippman

With a Foreword by Dianne Aprile

THE UNIVERSITY PRESS OF KENTUCKY

Publication of this volume was made possible in part by a grant
from the National Endowment for the Humanities.

Editorial and Sales Offices: The University Press of Kentucky
663 South Limestone Street, Lexington, Kentucky 40508-4008

04 03 02 01 00   5 4 3 2 1

Library of Congress Cataloging-in-Publication Data
Conversations with Kentucky writers II / L. Elisabeth Beattie, editor: ;
photographs by Susan Lippman ; with a foreword by Dianne Aprile.
         p.   cm.   — (Kentucky remembered)
Includes bibliographical references and index.
Contents: Sallie Bingham — Joy Bale Boone —Thomas D. Clark —
John Egerton — Sarah Gorham — Lynwood Montell — Maureen Morehead —
John Ed Pearce — Amelia Blossom Pegram — Karen Robards — Jeffrey
Skinner — Frederick Smock — Frank Steele — Martha Bennett Stiles —
Richard Taylor — Michael Williams.
         ISBN 0-8131-2124-8 (alk. paper)
    1. American literature—Kentucky—History and criticism—Theory,
etc. 2. American literature—20th century—History and criticism—
Theory, etc. 3. Authors, American—20th century Interviews.
    4. Kentucky—Intellectual life—20th century. 5. Authors, American—
Kentucky Interviews. 6. Kentucky—In literature. 7. Authorship.
    I. Beattie, L. Elisabeth, 1953– . II. Title: Conversations with
Kentucky writers two. III. Series.
PS266.K4C68   1999   99-23215
         810.9'9769—dc21

Manufactured in the United States of America

To my beloved friend,
Marion Kingston Stocking,
my mentor in intellectual honesty,
professional integrity, and personal loyalty

Contents

Foreword

In her preface to this volume, L. Elisabeth Beattie speaks of the "raw reality" of spoken conversation. The verbal exchange, she notes, is rarely as grammatical as the written message, but neither is it as guarded. Clearly, that is a trade worth making, particularly when the purpose of a verbal exchange is to uncover the essential character of one of the two parties so engaged.

The unmasking of the author is, of course, the heart of the matter in each of Beattie's unpredictably eloquent and dependably revealing conversations with Kentucky writers. This latest batch of her tape-recorded tete-a-tetes will enlighten even those among us who thought we knew the writers under her spotlight. Raw reality has a way of coyly creeping (or grandly sweeping) into these informal and informative dialogues.

For example, just as it appears that Beattie's interview with journalist John Ed Pearce is winding down, we hear his voice turn plaintive and his tone melancholy, as he sums up his newspaper career in a metaphor of regret. He leaves us with a scene in which he is rereading old stories filed away in his condo storage room, still liking what he reads yet suspecting that "no one remembers them." With not a little irony, he sums up his journalism career as so much fish wrapping.

For more of the same, eavesdrop on Beattie's conversation with poet Fred Smock. He first defines his childhood and the early influences on his writing in an understated, almost detached way. We get the picture of a boy growing up in an affectionate and supportive family setting, in which his father was a bit distant but only due to his work as a physician. Later in the exchange, however, Smock speaks more candidly about his father, revealing a discovery in young adulthood that he now views as "the only blot" on his childhood. This wounding discovery was not easily healed.

What role do such personal punctuation points play in a discussion of the writing life, a reader might ask. May I suggest they provide the key to the individual writer's creative process. In fact, Smock spells that out in the words he speaks following his comments about his father. With grace and a sense of humor, he puts raw reality into context and gives meaning (as artists cannot help themselves but do) to suffering.

"You have to come to terms with your own limitations and your own losses, and I think creativity is a way of dealing with that," he says. "... I think writing is short of a cure, but I think it is a way to deal with it. It still leaves you with the loss, but at least you've done something with your hands in the meantime."

Humor, it turns out, is the other reality that rewards the reader of these conversations. Sometimes bitter-edged and self-deprecating, as in Pearce's lament about growing old alone: "No one to appreciate the wonderful me." Sometimes delightfully offbeat, as in recent Kentucky Poet Laureate Joy Bale Boone's response to official forms that ask where she, a self-educated poet, received her schooling: "In public libraries." And sometimes sounding as if it were lifted directly from a writer's page, as in this Freudian slip of the tongue offered up by romance writer Karen Robards, regarding her brief fling with college journalism: "Hard news is a little dry for me. But it was a way to make good grades."

The writers interviewed in this collection represent many genres, including poetry, short stories, essays, history, novels, science fiction, creative nonfiction, historical novels, memoir, and romance. What Beattie coaxes out of even the most reserved of the group is how and why they do what they do—their process and their motivation.

Kentucky is a major element in that equation. Whether a writer has adopted the commonwealth or was born here, the association over time with Kentucky's land and culture makes them brothers and sisters on the page, sharers of a common tradition, witnesses to a collective history. At times the connection may seem tenuous between, say, Amelia Blossom Pegram, a South African poet and woman of color transplanted to Kentucky, and this commonwealth's legendary historian Thomas D. Clark, who grew up knowing "ex-slaves" in Mississippi before moving to Lexington to pursue a graduate degree at the University of Kentucky. Yet both speak passionately about the impact that putting down Kentucky roots has had on their work.

Listen to Pegram, who came to Radcliff, Kentucky, as the wife of a military man, and later, after divorcing him, married herself to a lively writing career: "Coming to Kentucky, I don't want to sound as if there is a fate, and that your life is planned ahead, and you have no free will and all that, but I think that a lot of times things happen for a purpose."

For the transplanted writer, Kentucky offers fertile soil. When Louisville poet Sarah Gorham compares her life in Kentucky today to her years on the East Coast, she speaks of the advantages of "being in a small family instead of being in a huge family." For her and her husband, poet Jeffrey Skinner, the move has meant getting "the recognition that we feel we deserve."

Current Kentucky Poet Laureate Richard Taylor, who grew up in Louisville and now lives on a farm outside of Frankfort, says he appreciates Kentucky's "rural beauty" and finds in it a wellspring of ideas for his work. Even Louisville's fantasy writer Michael Williams, whose books are set in exotic places as far removed from the commonwealth as possible, finds himself connecting his work and his home state: "I think my affinities to the landscape are Kentuckian."

In the end, each author Beattie interviews takes a turn at describing his or her creative process. The places where their writing is done. The time of day they work.

The inspirations. The discipline. The motivation. At some point in each exchange, creativity is defined.

Skinner calls creativity "some mixture of gift and hard work … The hard work is writing the bad poems, which I do to get ready for the good poems." Sallie Bingham, who left Kentucky for New Mexico several years ago, proffers the provocative notion that having babies may be the "only form of creativity that the society really endorses, at least if you are white and married." For Lynwood Montell, folklorist, creativity is something intensely personal—a process of "bringing my soul out and somehow putting it on paper."

Perhaps the most poignant comment on the subject, however, comes from novelist Martha Bennett Stiles, who quotes an anonymous writer: "If I knew where my ideas came from, I'd go live there." And if we were Beattie, we'd be sure to take our tape recorder with us.

For the writer who wonders about how her peers do it, or for the fan who is just plain curious, author Frank Steele offers a glimpse of the writer's life that takes the wind out of all romantic notions of the process.

"Some people read the newspaper early in the morning. Some people watch television early in the morning. [My wife] Peg often will get up and play the piano early in the morning. And I get up in the morning and write."

Louisville poet Maureen Morehead speaks of the paradox of writing poems to answer questions and solve problems even though she knows from the start that solutions are not the work of poems. She describes her writing process in spiritual terms: "I use poetry to discover God." Her comment calls to mind another Kentucky poet and author, dead now thirty-plus years, who once said he wrote in order to discover who he was. That, of course, was Thomas Merton, the Trappist monk who lived half his life in Nelson County, the last few years in a hermitage in the woods.

As she has in the past, Beattie has again selected a combination of writers that is as rich and varied as life in Kentucky can be. John Egerton, a Kentucky writer who is perhaps best know these days for his widely acclaimed book, *Southern Food,* is an example of the dramatic range of writers represented in this volume. He's published social history and essays, worked as a magazine journalist and a travel writer, written about food, civil rights and the new South. Egerton's wily description of his own forty-year writing career could be applied to Kentucky writers in general, and in particular to the ones interviewed here by Beattie.

"Writing on so many different subjects," Egerton says, "leaves me pretty much outside anybody's little cubbyhole of definition."

So it is with the writers in this volume. Don't look for definitions or solutions as you tap into their conversations. Look instead for clues to the creative process and you may find, in the margins, where you least expect it, the raw reality of the spoken word.

Dianne Aprile

Preface

Between 1990 and 1993, as director of the Kentucky Writers' Oral History Project, I conducted fifty interviews for the Archives and Oral History Program of the University of Kentucky. In 1996, the University Press of Kentucky published *Conversations with Kentucky Writers,* my first volume of twenty of those edited interviews with authors who are Commonwealth natives or who have adopted Kentucky as their home. This second volume includes sixteen more edited interviews from that ever-enlarging collection. Its publication permits additional voices to enrich the canon with the observations and life stories of individual, influential authors, and to expand the overarching conversation that, bound together in book form, occurs among the entries themselves.

It's always a privilege to spend time with people whose poetry, prose, or creative nonfiction has created for me and countless readers realms of heartfelt intimacy, creative inspiration, and intellectual stimulation rich enough to enhance life's meaning. That is why, prior to interviewing each author, I read that person's published and unpublished writing extensively, if not exhaustively, so that during our tape-recorded conversation a passing observation might trigger a response different from or possibly more complete than any previously recorded or perhaps even articulated remark. It's true that verbal exchanges are rarely as grammatically correct or as formally shaped as essays. Yet the impulsive nature of spontaneous replies often elicits a raw reality masked by more self-conscious, written reflections. Thus, whether the writers in *Conversations With Kentucky Writers II* are discussing their childhoods, their writing habits, or their views concerning the nature of creativity, their comments remain, above all else, unrehearsed and candid.

I hope these private conversations conducted for public use can help beginning writers learn how particular professionals launched their careers; can help educators understand how they might encourage their students' creativity; and can help literary historians record the biographical facts, the significant reminiscences, and the artistic attitudes that, in conjunction with their eras and regions, have fashioned literary luminaries' lives. In addition, I intend my discussions with the writers in this and my first volume of *Conversations* to reveal allegiances and alliances among Kentucky writers that shaped, if not actual schools of thought, at least geographically or psychically linked enclaves of writers whose shared subjects, styles, interests, and values have resulted in significant literary trends and communities.

And, finally, I expect interest in these interviews will extend to audiences whose engagement with writers and writing may not be as much academic or artistic as merely human. For the men and women who herein tell their tales are people whose struggles, good fortune, and occasional setbacks constitute the stuff of stories as powerful as they themselves have concocted or recreated concerning sometimes fictitious, and always legendary, lives.

As I edited, sometimes for the fourth or fifth time, each of these entries from their 150– to 250–page full-transcript girth to a slim twenty or so typed pages, I relived often-humorous and always-intense discussions that my tape recorder had captured, keeping recollections and reflections, even if five or more years old, vital and alive. Working with one transcript and then another, I would take stock, compare notes, and imagine these disparate voices conversing not with me, but with each other, around a table set for sixteen. Even now I can hark back and hear Amelia Blossom Pegram mention what it was like to live in Cape Town, South Africa, and in London, England, prior to cocooning in a claustrophobic Radcliff, Kentucky, caravan. Jeffrey Skinner who, in my mind's eye, appears by her side, then leans across his plate and discusses his life as a detective, a prelude to his creative encounters at Yaddo. From the head of the table Tom Clark chimes in and comments on attending Duke University when it stood, in the 1920s, as a few scattered buildings, prior to its reincarnation as a world-class school. As thirteen literary lives join their chorus, the conversation roars into a real celebration of imagination, of language, and of the transcendent human spirit. Consider this preface your invitation to this confidential gathering. Indulge in the author's tales, enjoy their diverse perspectives and, by all means, enter the conversation.

For awarding me, in conjunction with the University of Kentucky Oral History Program, project and transcribing grants to help fund the work that resulted in this book, I thank the members of the Kentucky Oral History Commission, as well as that Commission's director, Kim Lady Smith, for their continuing support.

I also appreciate University of Kentucky Archivist and Oral History Program Director Terry L. Birdwhistell and Kentucky State Historian James C. Klotter's expressions of confidence in my work; their invitation to me to edit a second volume for their Kentucky Remembered Oral History Series; and their constant, collegial good will.

This book would not exist were it not for the determination of University of Kentucky Oral History Program Assistant Director, Jeff Suchanek, who supervised the often-difficult and always time-consuming transcribing process. Therefore, I thank Jeff for his essential role in this project.

To the sixteen writers who made this book possible by permitting me to talk with them at length, by providing me manuscripts and other materials prior to our interviews, and by responding with grace and patience as I followed up our conversations with queries to check spellings and bibliographical information, I express sincere gratitude.

Additional thanks to Susan Lippman, who supplied the lion's share of author photographs, and to typist Candy Jerdon who, with the help of Judy Akers, assumed the formidable task of converting thousands of transcribed pages, all covered with editorial changes, into a pristine manuscript.

When Dianne Aprile agreed to write this book's Foreword, we both thought she would have several months to do so. But delays in manuscript preparation caused her to write on a deadline that would make most journalists wince. So my heartfelt thanks go to Dianne for her friendship, her professionalism, and her talent that together transcended less than optimal writing conditions and resulted in a memorable, valuable essay.

Every writer would like a live-in proofreader; in my parents, with whom I share a home, I'm proud to acknowledge two. So for their editorial advice and their copyreading skills, as well as for their constant encouragement during this book's preparation and in all of my endeavors, I thank Elisabeth Watts Beattie and Walter M. Beattie Jr.

Conversations
with
Kentucky Writers II

SALLIE BINGHAM

BINGHAM: My name is Sallie Bingham, and I was born in Louisville, Kentucky, on January 22, 1937. My father's name was Barry Bingham and my mother's name is Mary Caperton Bingham. My father was a journalist by profession, and my mother was a housewife. Mother was also very active in education.

BEATTIE: Would you tell me about what you recall about significant family members?

BINGHAM: My maternal grandmother was a great figure in my childhood. Her name was Helena Lefroy Caperton. She was a writer, and she had published two books of short stories. She was also a wonderful storyteller.

Also, my father's older sister, Henrietta Bingham, was a fascinating figure to me. There were many cousins and aunts and uncles, with a very large connection in that time.

I had two older brothers and a younger brother and sister. Two of my brothers died tragically quite young. My elder brother, Barry Bingham, ran the newspaper here in Louisville for many years, and my younger sister, Eleanor, is married and lives here in Louisville and is a filmmaker. Mine was a very special childhood. We lived in a big house out on the Ohio River, about ten miles outside of Louisville. It was a very beautiful place. I learned to appreciate natural beauty there. We had a big house with a lot of what we called, then, servants, and we did some traveling. We often were taken abroad in the summer. I went to a small girls' school here in Louisville called The Louisville Collegiate School for Girls, and I graduated from there in '54. I left for college right away and really did not live in Kentucky after that.

BEATTIE: What was The Collegiate School like, and weren't you at Ballard High School before that?

BINGHAM: I was at Ballard for a couple of years. It was an experimental public school that had some special financing from the students' parents. It was a small school in the suburbs that attempted to put together some new ideas about education, but I left there in second grade and spent the rest of my lower education at The Collegiate School, which was then a small school for girls with entirely women on the faculty. It was an excellent school, very demanding. It had a good athletic program, and Collegiate made a great difference to my life. I was writing stories by the time I was in third grade, and I also took a great interest in history. After we spent a year abroad in 1949, I learned to speak French, and I was also very interested in French.

BEATTIE: In your book, *Passion and Prejudice,* you write that you learned to read by piecing together newspaper headlines while sitting on the floor of your parents' bedroom. Will you tell me about that? Also, I understand you first wrote in a leather-covered book embossed with your name, a book given to you by your father. What sorts of things did you write in that book, and have you kept diaries or journals since that time?

BINGHAM: That book was for writing poems, and I have always kept diaries and journals quite regularly from the time I was eleven.

BEATTIE: You also write in *Passion and Prejudice* that one of your Collegiate School English teachers, Mrs. Alcorn, encouraged you to enter high school competitions. Your story "And the Band Played On" was published by *The Atlantic Monthly* in a pamphlet for students. How did that first publication experience affect your desire to be a writer?

BINGHAM: Well, it was very exciting—a first publication always is—and it gave me the feeling that maybe I could actually exist in the world as a writer. I already existed in my own imagination as a writer, but it's a different feeling when you know there are people out there who might want to read what you have written.

BEATTIE: Do you think it was on the occasion of this high school publication or after the fact that you decided to become a writer?

BINGHAM: No, I had really already made that decision. I don't remember exactly when, but I would say it was certainly by the time I was thirteen. I knew that what I could do was write, and I felt I had a talent, and I also very much enjoyed the process of writing. I was quite introverted, and I enjoyed being alone, and writing was a way for me to understand my experiences.

BEATTIE: Will you tell me about your undergraduate years at Radcliffe College?

BINGHAM: I went there as a freshman in 1954, and graduated *magna cum laude.* It was an English degree in 1958, and it was not easy at first. We Radcliffe students were outnumbered fifteen to one at that time by Harvard students, and there was a certain degree of anonymity and even lostness in the experience of being in those great big classrooms. I had no women faculty at all for the four years I was there, which was alienating. But those being the more negative sides, the positive side of it was that I did begin to read things that I had never been exposed to before, particularly the European writers, and I also began to have an audience in writing classes that were much more discriminating and even critical than I had before.

BEATTIE: I remember reading in your autobiography that you found the male professors at Radcliffe, even the big-name ones, not particularly helpful. Was that because of their "male" point of view, or was it due to their particular personalities?

BINGHAM: It's somewhat in the system in that they were very large classes at that time. The lecturer was removed physically from the students at a podium. It also had to do with the suppression of women, which was so rampant in the fifties, so that often there was not an opportunity to ask a question or to express an opinion.

BEATTIE: You began to publish regularly in the Harvard Literary Magazine, *The Advocate;* when did that start?

BINGHAM: I think they published my first story in 1955, when I was a sophomore. I had applied to be on the board of *The Advocate,* which at that point accepted women only in minor roles, and they rejected me, which was very fortunate, I now think. But they continued to publish my fiction very regularly for the next three years.

BEATTIE: One of your early short stories was published in *Mademoiselle* magazine. Was this as a result of *Mademoiselle's* annual college writing competition?

BINGHAM: Yes, I did win that writing competition, and I went on to work for *Mademoiselle* one summer.

BEATTIE: What was the experience of working there like?

BINGHAM: It was fairly strange. *Mademoiselle* then published good, serious fiction. I think the editor was very interested in fiction; she was very, very, serious-minded about it. But it was basically a fashion magazine, so that a lot of time was spent on going to visit Hélène Rubinstein and getting together with cosmetic representatives for breakfast, and so on. It was very strange.

BEATTIE: I understand you married the editor of *The Harvard Advocate.* What is his name, and what was your life like during that marriage? Also, don't you have a son from that marriage?

BINGHAM: Yes. My first husband's name is Whitney Ellsworth. He went on to found *The New York Review of Books,* and he has also been active in Amnesty International. Our son, who is now thirty-one, is named Barry Ellsworth. We were married for about five years right after college, and we lived in Boston and in New York. Whitney was at that time working for *The Atlantic Monthly,* and I was developing my skills as a writer. *The Atlantic* published two of my stories during that time.

BEATTIE: Will you discuss your life and work during the 1960s? You have written about what a volatile decade that was for you, especially as your brother, Jonathan, died in 1964, and your brother, Worth, died in 1966, and a woman who raised you—whom you referred to as Nurse—died in that same decade.

BINGHAM: I also went through a divorce in that time, and then remarried, and I experienced the birth of two more children, so *volatile* is the word for it. I think it was probably the most difficult decade of my life, except for, perhaps, my childhood. I was writing at that time, the 1960s, short stories almost entirely.

My first book, which was published in 1960, was a novel, but after that I turned to writing short stories, and I had two collections out in the '60s and early

'70s. I was also publishing in magazines, the so-called fashion magazines. Fashion magazines were still running serious fiction then, so that was a publishing market. I was struggling mightily to combine my professional work with raising children and being part of a marriage and of a family. It was extremely difficult. I am very grateful, looking back on it, that my children were as understanding as they were. Two of them are now artists, and I think that's maybe part of the reason why they understood the struggle I was going through. Also, it was wonderful to be able to live in New York, where we could easily get to the museums, get to Central Park, and be somewhat part of life there. So, my life was less isolated than it might have been.

BEATTIE: I understand you divorced and then married another man—also in the sixties—by whom you had two more sons. What is his name, and what was your life and writing career like during that period?

BINGHAM: His name is Michael Iovenko. He is an attorney in New York, and we have two sons. My life in that marriage was really a continuation of what I described before.

BEATTIE: Will you tell me about your three sons? What are they doing now and where do they live?

BINGHAM: Barry Ellsworth lives in New York, and he always has. He is a filmmaker. He started a foundation for young filmmakers called Apparatus, Inc., and he has made seven independent drama films—these are not documentaries—in collaboration with other people. He is a script writer and a director and a cinematographer; he is very, very skilled. He started out as a painter and now brings many of those particular talents to his film making.

My next son, Chris Iovenko, is twenty-five. He is a writer, and he graduated from Vassar, where he wrote fiction. He also is working in film, more from the point of view of writing and acting. My youngest son, Will Iovenko, is twenty-two, and he is finding out what he wants to do in the world.

BEATTIE: Your return to Louisville in 1977—will you tell me about how that came about and what your life was like after you returned?

BINGHAM: I was divorced with three young children, and my father felt it would be easier for me to be living closer to family. That was the primary motivation for my moving back to Louisville. The ultimate motivation was that I had not been writing about Kentucky for about fifteen years, and I was very curious to find those stories again. I thought it would be helpful to go back and immerse myself in Kentucky and listen to what language sounds like here and look at the landscape. And doing so was extremely fruitful. It produced three short novels in a matter of three years after I returned. So, I was really trying to find some material that, as a writer, I felt had escaped me, because I had left here at such an early age.

BEATTIE: You also were working at *The Courier-Journal* after you returned to Louisville.

BINGHAM: I was book editor of the Louisville *Courier-Journal* from 1981 to 1985, so it was about three years after I moved back here. That was lots of fun. It is a wonderful job. In those days newspapers were still running a page of book reviews on Sunday. It was a column, so it meant that I could see my words in print every week, which is unbelievable. That's why people stay in these book review positions. And editing the book page gave me a chance to review many more books by women, which I felt was a crying need, and to use reviewers who were living in this area, rather than depending on the wire service reviews. It was really a lot of fun; I learned a lot.

BEATTIE: Were there other changes you made in the book page?

BINGHAM: I changed its design, with the help of a very talented designer, who was working at the newspaper at that time. I also ran more reviews; I crowded more into the space. I gave the page a definite feminine perspective; in other words, I was interested in addressing issues that are of importance to women.

BEATTIE: Did you make writer friends through that job that have lasted?

BINGHAM: Not really. I did get to know a lot of people in publishing, though, through the central network of book reviewers and also through being a member of the National Book Critics Circle. It was very helpful in that way.

BEATTIE: When did you start teaching at the University of Louisville, and what was that experience like for you?

BINGHAM: I believe I started in '81, and I had never done any teaching before, so it was enormously instructive for me. I was quite terrified and did not know, really, what I had to contribute to students. I started out teaching a very basic composition course, a required course, and went on from there to teach more specialized creative writing courses. It was really illuminating for me—I hope also for the students—in that the students I had were so enthusiastic, often without much background, but very enthusiastic about learning how to write about reading and to talk about writing. I value the experience. I ended up teaching a graduate course in playwriting.

BEATTIE: Would you like to teach again, and do you think teaching would hinder or help your writing career?

BINGHAM: I can't teach regularly because it takes too much energy. What I like to do is just occasionally teach a workshop. I am going to be teaching one in August at Skidmore for the International Writers Guild, a week-long workshop. I very much enjoy doing that, but that is about the best I can do.

BEATTIE: How do you think creative writing should be taught, and what do you believe the nature of creativity itself is?

BINGHAM: Well, you have to somehow inspire writers to read; I think you just start with that. If you are going to be a writer, then you have to also be a reader. These two things can't be separated. Then encourage women, especially, to find their own voices and tell their own stories, which can be quite painful, in that it usually involves some long-held secret.

As to the nature of creativity, I think it is a very freely floating spirit. It is not just contained in writing, or any of the other arts, and it has to do with whether we are ever willing to listen to ourselves, to really accept and honor our own individuality and allow it to express itself in some form of creativity.

BEATTIE: Do you believe creativity is a matter of nature *and* nurture?

BINGHAM: Yes. I think the gift is much more important than the teaching.

BEATTIE: But you think some aspects of writing can be taught?

BINGHAM: You can raise people to a certain level of proficiency, which is useful and even necessary in life. But I think the great writers have to have their own gift that carries them beyond that.

BEATTIE: James Still told me he had been at Yaddo with you once, and Jim Wayne Miller was at Yaddo with you, too. What have the Yaddo or the MacDowell Writers' Colony experiences been like for you?

BINGHAM: Absolutely essential for me as a woman with small children at home. It was really my only uninterrupted time to write, and I tried to make certain that I applied and, I hoped, would be accepted, at least one month out of a year during all those years. It's no longer necessary, because my children are grown. It also was validating because I was there as a contributing member of society, and artists often are not treated with very much respect.

BEATTIE: How many times have you been to writers' colonies?

BINGHAM: Oh, gosh, I don't know. Probably fifteen times.

BEATTIE: When did you start going?

BINGHAM: I started going in 1978.

BEATTIE: I see, and was it mostly to Yaddo and MacDowell, or have you been to others as well?

BINGHAM: No, I have been to others. I have been to the Virginia Center for the Creative Arts and to others.

BEATTIE: You were starting a women's writers' colony here in Louisville, weren't you?

BINGHAM: The Kentucky Foundation for Women was.

BEATTIE: Will you tell me about that?

BINGHAM: The Foundation operates a house in the suburbs here called Hopscotch House. The thought was that it would be a good place for four or five women writers to spend a month in the summer working. I imagine it will simply be writers who are willing to call themselves feminists. The house is used all the time by women's groups for a place to meet.

BEATTIE: Is there any one person who has read all your work before it's been published?

BINGHAM: No, I don't think so. You would be the only one.

BEATTIE: I read it all *after* it was published. When you returned to Louisville, you married Tim Peters.

BINGHAM: That was in 1983.

BEATTIE: Would you discuss where you lived and what you think was important about that time?

BINGHAM: We lived in The Highlands, a residential area of Louisville, and we put together a family, my two younger sons and his two sons, and after a few years we moved to a big piece of land in the suburbs called Wolf Pen Mill Farm. Tim was a contractor involved in building projects, and I was continuing to write and, of course, during that time, I published a memoir called *Passion and Prejudice.*

BEATTIE: In the mid-1980s you founded and funded the Kentucky Foundation for Women. Will you tell me about that organization and its magazine, *The American Voice,* and about how you came to think of the importance of sponsoring women artists?

BINGHAM: I knew from my own experience how difficult it is for women artists to survive economically, and, of course, we know that women artists are not adequately represented either in publishing or in museums and galleries. So, organizing The Kentucky Foundation for Women was an attempt to deal with the oppression of women artists, specifically, by giving grants to individual women who submit proposals, which are passed on by the board, and it was also an attempt to pay women writers who appear in *The American Voice,* which is a feminist literary quarterly that the Foundation publishes.

BEATTIE: The Foundation started in what year?

BINGHAM: Nineteen eighty-six. It was funded by ten million dollars, which came from my proceeds from the sale of the companies that didn't belong to the men in the Bingham family.

BEATTIE: Will you tell me about some of the writers and other types of artists you have sponsored? Are there any you are particularly excited about having sponsored?

BINGHAM: I turned over the directorship of the Foundation a year ago, so I am a little more out of touch with it now than I would have been. I am still on the board, but I'm no longer involved in the day-to-day activities.

One of the photographers, at that time an Appalachian photographer that we gave a grant to, I believe in '87, is a woman named Wendy Ewald, who just won a MacArthur Foundation grant. We were able to help a young professor at the University of Kentucky named Kathleen Blee with a book that was recently published, called *Women and the Ku Klux Klan.* We have also been able to help the careers of three opera singers. The best-known of them is Marilyn Mims, who needed money in order to get to New York to continue her career. There is a local chamber music group called Ars Femina, which we helped to start. That ensemble has resurrected music by women from centuries past and plays it. Also, the Foundation has helped fund a local women's band named Your Girlfriend, which got their start-up money from us several years ago and has continued to be very successful. We have collaborated with Appalshop on several films and have also helped underwrite the costs of some other very impressive films by women who were doing their work in Kentucky. We have supported the efforts of a lot of visual artists; probably most of our grants go to visual artists—a lot of painters, sculptors, some craftswomen, wood carvers, a puppet maker. We have been involved in a variety of theatrical productions, both bringing productions to the state from outside and helping playwrights to find an audience for their work either in or outside of the state.

BEATTIE: A number of the writers I have interviewed have told me how instrumental the Foundation has been in their being able to continue their own writing.

BINGHAM: Yes, sometimes that's the crucial factor. If you can get ten to fifteen thousand dollars to buy yourself a year's time, it may make all the difference in being able to start or finish a product.

BEATTIE: Absolutely. Would you comment on Kentucky writers whom you admire and on other writers who have influenced you?

BINGHAM: I don't tend to divide people by category, although some of the writers I admire do live in Kentucky, Sarah Gorham being one of them. There are a couple of writers who are very firmly rooted in this landscape who, I think, are extraordinarily talented. One of them is Denise Giardina. I tend to read almost entirely or ninety percent writing by women, and the women who influence me tend not to be contemporary writers. I don't know quite why that is.

BEATTIE: Who are they?

BINGHAM: Well, it's changed over the years. I started out being very influenced by nineteenth century British writers, particularly the Brontes and, in fact, I had wanted to write my senior thesis at college on the Brontes. I went on to be much more influenced by American twentieth century writers. Willa Cather has been enormously important to me, as has Katherine Porter. The women poets who are probably doing the strongest writing today, like Adrienne Rich and essayists like Carolyn Heilbrun, are very, very important to me, as are, of course, the women who are doing the ground-breaking biographies now. There is just such an enormous richness of writing by women now; it is quite extraordinary what's happening. But my influences tend to be writers that I have discovered a little earlier in my career.

BEATTIE: I'd like to ask you more about your own writing. In your book, *The Way It Is Now,* and in your story, "August 9th at Natural Bridge," your last sentence reads, "It seemed to her that she would never be safe again." When did you first feel that you would never be safe again, and do you feel you have found that safety now?

BINGHAM: No, I certainly haven't found that, and I don't really expect to find it. I don't think it's findable, certainly not for women in this society. I think I felt that very early, probably by age three or four. I don't look on that, though, as being entirely negative. I am not certain that feeling safe is really my goal.

BEATTIE: Maybe, when I say *safe*—I'm taking your word here—I am not looking at or thinking about something that is definitive, or a state that's safe as opposed to something else, but perhaps I mean *states,* in the sense that you are on a psychological or spiritual track that makes sense to you.

BINGHAM: Oh, yes. Well, that's a different interpretation. I think it took me, really, until my early forties to feel that way, and that particular feeling of safeness comes from an internal sense of security of having some idea of what you are trying to do, of what action you want your life to take in spite of many frustrations. That probably is the only real sense of safety. Before my forties, I thought it was my fault that it did not make sense. I didn't have a political framework growing up, and the unhappiness that I saw and felt seemed random and inexplicable.

BEATTIE: There is a character in this story ["August 9th at Natural Bridge"] named Shelby, just as there is in your most recent novel, *Small Victories*. Also, the name *Louise* shows up as a protagonist's name in *The Touching Hand*, in "Please, No Eating, Nor Drinking," and in "The Visit," as well as in *Small Victories*. The name *Tom* occurs, too, in your story, "The Need," as it does in *Small Victories*. I'm wondering if there is any significance to this repetition.

BINGHAM: Well, I haven't been consciously aware of that. I haven't been particularly attuned to names, and I think that's something I probably need to work on. I never really associated names with character. Names don't have a great deal of relevance for me.

BEATTIE: I wonder if there are subconscious similarities there, because there are qualities in the characters that are similar.

BINGHAM: There may well be connections that I am not consciously aware of, but I think it's largely because I simply have not been very sensitive to names. I would almost as soon call characters X, Y, Z. It just is not something that makes a great deal of difference to me. It may be connected with the fact that I don't remember names frequently. Names just don't seem to me to have very much symbolic importance.

BEATTIE: That's interesting. That's just the opposite of what Sena Naslund said about the importance to her of naming things.

BINGHAM: Yes, and, of course, there is a strong feminist implication in terms of naming aspects of reality. I am not certain that naming the individual, though, is the same thing.

BEATTIE: The other day, when I heard you read from *Small Victories* at Western Kentucky University, you started by making an eloquent statement about Tom in that book, about what he stands for. Will you discuss that?

BINGHAM: Actually, I've been just thinking about that in the last few days. This young man in *Small Victories* is floundering, really going down. He has not yet found his true vocation in any sense of the word, and he begins more and more to be an example of the state of pre-vocation when there is such a sense of urgency and undirected energy and isolation and huge psychological suffering. I think sometimes that really is not the beginning, but the end, for people in life or for characters, in that for any number of reasons they never find their vocation and life becomes impossible and something else is chosen. I think it's crucial to understand that, because so often we, in this country at least, have very little tolerance for the floundering that everyone goes through, but that artists go through to a particular degree and probably for a longer time. It is very rare to find an artist who is truly in tune with her vocation in her early twenties and even in her late twenties. It's something that takes a long time to accept and develop, even though all the inklings may be there.

BEATTIE: I am interested in the fact that you write in *Passion and Prejudice* that you have been able to return to the church after having stayed away for so many years, because your spiritual focus has shifted, or it's *become* yours instead of someone else's, perhaps. Would you comment on that?

BINGHAM: Yes, that's very interesting. I grew up in the Episcopal Church, and I was devoted to aspects of it, but it is very alienating for a woman to be in such a male-dominated setting where the references are always to a male God, and the priests are always male priests. So, I had to, in a sense, seek out women who were practicing in the church. The church has become, again, a great resource for me, and it has become central to me. I would be glad to see some more progress made, I would be glad to see some more women up there by the altar, and I would be glad to hear some more female pronouns—or at least gender-neutral pronouns—and I think that will come. I think there is always a terrific struggle when you are embedded in a hierarchy and bring about that kind of change, but there are a lot of women involved now, and I think it will come.

BEATTIE: Is it still the Episcopalian Church you are talking about?

BINGHAM: Yes. I can't tell you quite why.

BEATTIE: In your story, "The Big Day," a wife waits for her husband to come home from war, and nothing, emotionally, is as it should be. One of the clear messages in your early fiction is that the events of the world, or of the world of our particular experiences, astound to the point of numbness, and we are all terrified to reveal or even to feel our real feelings for fear that, if we do, the only world in which we know how to function at all will crumble. Will you comment on that?

BINGHAM: Oh, that's a very, very good summing up. I think that's particularly true of the fiction I was writing in the '60s and early '70s, when it seemed as though women were encapsulated in situations, particularly inside the family, where there was really almost no opportunity to change behavior or attitude. Since then with women going into the work force and becoming both economically and emotionally independent, I think there is a good deal more sense of hope or possibility, which I think is beginning to turn up also in my writing.

BEATTIE: How do you view the evolution of your vision as a writer?

BINGHAM: I think I began very close to despair, and I have often felt writing literally saved my life, because if the despair is bearable, then you can do something with it. I have become increasingly hopeful over the years because of external changes in the society, because of learning more, and also because I have such a great feeling of our fortitude as human beings, particularly as women.

BEATTIE: Do you see that reflected in your work more?

BINGHAM: Yes. I think my work is always a little on the dark side, but recognizing the dark side is one of the things I am most interested in doing, because we need hope—realistic hope—not delusions, not romance.

BEATTIE: I see some humor in your work, too.

BINGHAM: Some humor. Yes, that's a great help. I think humor is precious, sheds wonderful light, so that's something I hope to encourage in myself and in my writing.

BEATTIE: Have you been able to discover things about yourself through your writing that you haven't been able to discover in other ways?

BINGHAM: Absolutely. In fact, I sometimes think it's the only way that I discover anything about myself.

BEATTIE: Will you discuss your novel, *Small Victories,* and how you view the characters in that novel?

BINGHAM: Sure. It was written in the late '70s and concerns primarily the two sisters, as you know, Louise and Shelby, and the whole question of the passionate commitment that women feel for each other, particularly when there is a great need. Shelby desperately needs care and love and understanding, and Louise really rises to the occasion to the point where the relationship becomes somewhat obsessional, and there is a question of whether it really is for the best for either of the sisters. I think that's what fascinates me about that relationship: is this really now a full-blown obsession, which is in itself fascinating, or is it still a healthy expression of mutual affection and care? I am always intrigued by those kinds of relationships.

BEATTIE: I can see that recurring theme in your work, and also your writing does address the question of how do you tell the difference.

BINGHAM: Exactly, exactly.

BEATTIE: That difference is not just in what people say, and it is not necessarily in what they do, because the observer has to interpret what they do.

BINGHAM: Yes, indeed. It is very complex. I think we often find, with writers who are men, that they are trying to make the distinction between lust and love and the confusions therein. But with me and with a lot of other women writers, I think the confusion is between a sense of duty and love, that point at which obligation takes over.

BEATTIE: I think you are one of the writers who earliest wrote about that theme, not just in terms of marriage, but in terms of women dealing with children. It was rare in the '60s and '70s for even women writers or feminist writers, if you could call them feminist at the time, to talk about children as being obligations, but that comes out clearly in your writing.

BINGHAM: Absolutely. It does come out clearly. It's still not written of very much because, of course, it's a great American myth. Children are supposed to be wonderful, and we all are supposed to love children. I think it's really only since people have begun to talk about child abuse openly that we realize the deep ambivalence. I think this is true for everyone, because children place terrific demands on us, as they must and should. Particularly artists, and people who are following another path, find themselves very divided and tortured, really, by these demands. I wish more was written about women and children. Grace Paley is one of the few people who writes about that subject consistently, and often in terms of community, which is interesting in itself.

BEATTIE: It has been interesting to me, in asking writers about the nature of creativity, that two or three have said that they think creativity is not feminist, but feminine, in nature, and that they believe the drive to be creative for men comes out of the fact that men can't have children.

BINGHAM: That is an old-fashioned, male point of view. I think there is some delusion in that. We'd all like to think, I guess, that that was so, but the experience of giving birth is full of contradictions and certainly full of creativity, on a certain level. But, on another level, it's so controlled by outside forces that I wouldn't say it is creative at all. Well, maybe it is the only form of creativity that the society really endorses, at least if you are white and married.

BEATTIE: You've told me you've just learned that two companion novels to *Small Victories* will be published within the next four years. Will you discuss those books, and are they already written?

BINGHAM: Yes, they were written in the late '70s and early '80s. *Small Victories* was written first, and the second book was written in the following year, called *Matron of Honor.* The third one was written a couple of years after that, *Straight Man.* Although no characters reappear from one novel to another, there is a Shelby, and it is a man this time. In *Straight Man,* the protagonist is named Shelby, which is kind of interesting.

BEATTIE: Very Faulkneresque. He has his Quentins, you have your Shelbys.

BINGHAM: Yes, and I think there is some meaning in that the geography is the same, in that they are all set in the Border South, and the emotional geography is also the same. *Matron of Honor* deals with a pair of sisters in their twenties, and it is set in the '60s rather than the '50s, trying to come to terms with their differences, a very different set of differences, but still within a rather rigid framework of a day given over to a wedding. *Straight Man,* which is told from the point of view of a professor at a southern university, is about the bursting apart of that framework, when this man falls in love with a woman, a hitchhiker he picks up on the road. I think, in all three novels, there is this sort of accordion feeling of great pressure forcing people closer and closer together, and then something explodes, and the whole apparatus stretches out and gets much bigger, at least temporarily. But you always have the feeling that the same pressure will begin to force people into a smaller range.

BEATTIE: We have talked about your being able to understand things more through writing than by any other means. Have you also been able to come to terms with your own life through writing and make decisions through your writing that you had not made, or had not realized you made, until you had written them?

BINGHAM: I don't think I have been able to make decisions; however, I think my writing has cast a very different light on decisions that I was either going to make or had already made. In other words, I don't think I actually learned how to decide through writing, but certainly my writing cast a different light on issues with which I was dealing and, often in a rather frightening way, would illuminate some decision I had already made, or thought I had made. My writing certainly has helped me to come to terms with my fate or my destiny and to accept the uncertain nature of life and to really appreciate how much happens that we can't possibly control or predict, and some of that is very, very positive. I am constantly astonished by the wonderful people or events or feelings that just appear out of nowhere, in my life, that couldn't have been planned or invented. I think that's something that is rather like the fictional world, in a sense, where things do appear out of nowhere and people are made out of air. I also believe, if you had been committed to writing as I have for thirty years, you really do begin to understand what it means that life is short and art is long.

BEATTIE: I see composites in so many of your characters made up of what I know of your autobiography, of your life—brothers and grandparents and self and parents rolled into one character—or events from several lives making up one character, and I am wondering if the interesting perspective of two or three generations depicted in one character corresponds to things that you believe have literally occurred between generations or among generations in your family?

BINGHAM: Very interesting. Of course, what you realize, I think, may be a little more visible with me because of writing the memoirs. That's why a lot of writers really don't want to write a memoir or an autobiography, because it becomes a sort of shorthand for their fiction. But I often feel, too, that writers appear at a moment when there are so many unresolved issues, either in a family or, perhaps, within a certain area, and it is our duty to begin to try to understand, not only the last ten, fifteen, twenty years, but perhaps the last five or six generations where there has been a lot of sort of blind acting, unconscious drives that were never analyzed. It is as if there is a huge amount of material that someone has got to understand, finally, or attempt to understand, because this blind force can't just continue to roll down through the generations.

BEATTIE: It seems that you are able to come to terms with events in your own life, in your fiction, by taking characters from life that may have had different viewpoints and by combining them in one character and by having that character come to an understanding of the dichotomies battling within that character.

BINGHAM: Yes, interesting, very interesting. I am a great believer in fairness and understanding. But having said that, there is a remorseless quality, I think, too, in my writing, which I prize, because sometimes when you say fairness and understanding, it sounds like a kind of bland evenhandedness.

BEATTIE: What writing are you working on now, and what work do you have planned for the future?

BINGHAM: I'm finishing up some writing. I have a collection of short stories that's a year old called "Southernmost Point." I am about halfway through rewriting this collection and, at the suggestion of an editor, I am writing a framing story for the beginning and the end of this collection, so I hope it will be ready to go out by the end of the summer. I also have an Afterword to write for a short novel that's being published this next spring, called *My Case for Love*. It is being published by Permanent Press, a small press in Long Island. The publisher there suggested, and I thought very wisely, that this very dramatic story needed an Afterword, a look back from the point of view of the character. So I'm working on that. Once that is cleared away, which won't take very long, I have three new ideas boiling around in my head. Possibly one of them is a play, although I am not really sure and, I think, I'll write two short novels, or they may boil down to two short stories.

BEATTIE: Do you have a preference concerning in which genre you write?

BINGHAM: I love short novels, two- to three hundred pages. That form gives me a latitude that the short story does not. The short story—now I feel a little differently about it than I did in my thirties and forties. It's hard to find enough space in short stories for the complexity that I want, so my tendency is towards the longer forms now.

BEATTIE: Have you ever had any inclination to write poetry?

BINGHAM: Yes, I have written poetry all my life. In fact, I have a collection of poetry that I intend to work on some this summer. Playwriting is, for me, the most difficult genre in which to write, because theater is collaboration, which is very exciting, but difficult.

BEATTIE: You recently moved from Kentucky to New Mexico. Will you discuss that move and your plans for your new life there?

BINGHAM: A writer needs to be anonymous in order to observe, and it had gotten to the point where it was just simply too difficult for me to be anonymous here in Louisville. That was my primary reason for relocating. I'm also fifty-five, and I think it is a great idea to pull up stakes and try something new.

BEATTIE: Do you think a geographical change will alter the sense of place in your writing? A literal sense of place figures strongly in the work of many contemporary Kentucky writers but, in your writing, as in that of others, that sense of place seems far more interior and psychological than geographical, even though you do refer to Kentucky or New York or Asheville settings. Would you agree with that?

BINGHAM: I think I have a strong feel for place, but I don't think that it has much to do with what I actually write. It has more to do with creating characters that are very uncomfortable in a certain place. I am now interested in writing within the framework of the West. You probably remember D.H. Lawrence's writing in the West. It's something I am not ready to do, and I don't know when I will be ready to do that, but the West is very interesting, particularly for women, in the sense of adventure and expansiveness and danger and so on. My hope is that I can also incorporate those senses in my writing. I am also very interested in getting to know enough about the South American countries so that I can use that in some way. I have a long-time wish to live in Europe, probably in France, and use that, also, as a setting. In fact, I just finished a short story called "Sargasso" that's set in Normandy.

BEATTIE: Is there anything that I haven't asked you that you think is important for people to know about you?

BINGHAM: I think it's important just to say again that we writers are gifted with patience and perseverance, which is really what is needed. The talent is something over which we have no control, but once you decide to really devote yourself to your talent, and that takes a long time, nothing really is going to get in the way, even though life may become extremely difficult, particularly for women who have many economic problems to deal with, as most women do. But nothing will really get in the way once that decision has been made.

BEATTIE: I am wondering if you have continued to write ever since you made the decision to become a writer?

BINGHAM: Yes, the only times when I did not write were the first couple of months after each of my three children was born. That decision was practical but, also, it was the only time that I really did not want to write. In fact, the thought of writing frightened me considerably.

BEATTIE: Why is that?

BINGHAM: Oh, I thought maybe I would never want to write again. I imagined that with giving birth I lost an enormous part of myself. But that did not happen; it was, I think, a central biological and psychological pause. After each child was a few months along, the desire to write came back, along with a little sleep.

BEATTIE: What are your writing habits?

BINGHAM: Usually, I write five days a week. I get up early, 6:30 or 7:00, and I get straight to writing. I don't read the paper or look at television or talk on the phone. I immediately go to whatever it is I'm writing, and I always have several projects going, so I am either rewriting or writing or dealing with some aspect of writing. I work for four or five hours, and then I knock off and get outside for a few hours, and that's really my routine. I generally don't work on the weekends. The only significant change in the last thirty years is that I am now beginning to be able to write when I travel, which I never used to be able to do. Since I travel a lot, it's important for me to be able to keep that going, because after a month or so without writing, I really am beginning to lose my sense of who I am.

BEATTIE: You can work on several writing projects simultaneously?

BINGHAM: I need to get one project through the first draft and then, I may, for many reasons, work on another project before I get back to the original one and get it through a second draft. I think it's probably quite helpful; it gives me a little more perspective. But I don't interrupt one project to go on and work on something else, usually. I write a lot and I write pretty fast, so I never have needed to grind out a certain number of pages. It's been more a question of not allowing everything to interrupt and interfere. I don't answer the phone when I am working.

BEATTIE: I think there are so many women artists of all kinds who can't make that decision because of their fears of hurting or upsetting other people's needs or schedules.

BINGHAM: Then it is really because they haven't yet been able to make a commitment. The phone is only a symbol, really.

BEATTIE: What advice would you give to new writers?

BINGHAM: The best advice I have ever been able to come up with is to try to write what you are afraid of writing. If there is one nagging detail or one nagging story that you thought about off and on over the years, but you always think, "Oh, I musn't write that; I couldn't write that," then that probably is the roadblock, that's the thing that needs to be written before anything else *can* be written.

June 21, 1992

Since moving to Santa Fe, New Mexico, in 1991, Bingham has published three novels, as well as poems, short stories, and essays, which have appeared in such journals as the *Louisville Review, Southwest Review,* the *American Voice,* and the *Connecticut Review and Conscience.* Bingham teaches workshops in the writing of memoir under the auspices of Recursos de Santa Fe, and she is a founding member of Santa Fe Stages.

BOOKS BY SALLIE BINGHAM

After Such Knowledge. Boston: Houghton-Mifflin Co., 1959.

The Touching Hand. Boston: Houghton-Mifflin Co., 1968.

The Way It Is Now. New York: The Viking Press, 1972.

Passion and Prejudice. New York: Applause Books, Inc., 1991.

Small Victories. Cambridge, Ma.: Zoland Books, Inc., 1992.

Upstate. Sag Harbor, N.Y.: Permanent Press, 1993.

Sleeping with Dionysius. Freedom, Ca.: The Crossing Press, 1994.

Matron of Honor. Cambridge, Ma.: Zoland Books, Inc., 1994.

Straight Man. Cambridge, Ma.: Zoland Books, Inc., 1996.

Joy Bale Boone

BOONE: I was born Sylvia Joy Field and then, when I married Garnett Bale, I became Joy Field Bale. When I married George Boone, I became Joy Bale Boone. It's difficult for a woman, you know.

BEATTIE: Where and when were you born?

BOONE: October 29, 1912. I was born in Chicago, Illinois, right there by the lake.

BEATTIE: How long did you live there?

BOONE: Well, till I was about five, and then my parents moved to Evanston, which is still Chicago, really—just a suburb. I was there until I was twenty-one, when I married Garnett. Garnett and I were in New York about two years, then in Louisville one year. Then we were in Lynch, Kentucky, for a little less than a year, a coal mining town in Harlan County. Then we came to his home in Elizabethtown, where he practiced medicine until he died. So I really have been a Kentuckian way over fifty years.

My father was William Sydney Field, and my mother was Edith Maude Overington. They were born and grew up in England and married there, and came to this country on their honeymoon. They became residents. My father was a dentist, as his father and his brother were. I was born a Chicagoan, but I have a jillion English cousins, and I visit them and they visit me, and it's really very nice.

BEATTIE: Would you also tell me about grandparents and other family members, such as aunts and uncles, or brothers and sisters?

BOONE: Well, you see, I didn't know any grandparents, because they were all in England. I knew one aunt. She came over to America. She called me Joy and that's all I've ever been called.

BEATTIE: How long did your parents live?

BOONE: Mother was in her early eighties and Daddy was in his late seventies when they died. Mother died in the early 1960s, and my father in the late 1950s.

BEATTIE: What about brothers and sisters?

BOONE: An older sister, who's still living, lives in the Chicago area, and I had a younger sister, who died in her forties. She committed suicide, and that's a hard thing to get over, you know. You just can't believe someone was that desperately unhappy, I suppose, and that you didn't know it.

BEATTIE: Were there just the three of you?

BOONE: Three girls, yes.

BEATTIE: What sort of childhood did you have?

BOONE: I guess I had a happy one. I have a lot of memories that are nice, but I remember being kind of lonely. And, well, my older sister was enough older that we were never really on the same wavelength.

BEATTIE: How many years older was she?

BOONE: Five to six. When we got to Evanston, it was a little better because I was big enough to ride a bicycle, and that was rather fun. Oh, I guess I've got lots of happy memories. But I'll tell you I've had a lot more fun since I've been grown. And the older I get, I think the more I enjoy it, because everything begins to relate to everything else.

BEATTIE: Where did you attend school and what was it like?

BOONE: Well, I started at kindergarten, at what was called Chicago Latin School. And I remember loving that, because I remember planting seeds in little pots that they'd have on the windowsill, and then the seeds would grow. But we moved to Evanston soon after that, and I went to the public school for maybe two or three years, and then I went to Roycemore School for Girls, through the twelfth grade. It wasn't parochial in any way, but you wore uniforms and really got a great classical education. But they didn't do anything the way the public schools did with what they called Domestic Science. Consequently, when I married, I really had to learn. Mother never cooked. I did know how to make toast, so I put peanut butter on it when friends spent the night, and we'd have a midnight snack in the kitchen.

BEATTIE: Did your mother have a cook in the house?

BOONE: Yes. Those were the days when you had much more help. We had live-in help, you know, and we had a third floor. It was an interesting house there in Evanston, a Frank Lloyd Wright house.

BEATTIE: Did Frank Lloyd Wright design the house for your parents?

BOONE: No, not for my parents. They bought it. It was about ten years old when they bought it, I think. It was a fascinating house.

When I graduated from Roycemore, Mother wanted to spend the winter in Florida, and she, of course, wanted me to go. My poor father got left almost every winter. Mother would go to Florida or California. I really wanted to go to the University of Chicago and be a journalist. But Mother's will prevailed, of course, and she said, "Well, you can go to school in Coral Gables. I'll get a cottage there."

Well, I went down there and I saw that college. I know it's changed a lot. Remember, this was in 1931. It looked like a country club to me. I was serious-minded and was very interested in writing, so I said I wouldn't go there.

So, I went to a little weekly paper and I still remember the man who ran it, Mr. Francis. He was so nice. I asked Mr. Francis if I could work there. He said,

"What experience have you had?" Well, you know, none, and I was pretty young. He said, "Well, why don't you come and work about two weeks, and we'll see if it works out. If it does, I'll hire you and start paying you."

It was wonderful, and it gave me my opportunity. I worked there and really, after a week, he paid me. Then, after about a month, he said, "How would you like to go over to our sister paper, *The Miami Beach News,* in Miami Beach and be editor?"

BEATTIE: You were right out of high school with no other school experience?

BOONE: That's right.

BEATTIE: And this was also your first work experience?

BOONE: Yes. So, goodness, this just sounded marvelous, and Mother was great about it. She said, "All right, we'll move, we'll get an apartment over at Miami Beach." So we did, and for the rest of the time I was there, which was about seven or eight months, I had the responsibility of the paper. I really learned layout. I did a lot of interviews, and a lot of famous people came to Miami Beach in those days. I used to go to parties where George Gershwin played. That was marvelous. And Bernard Baruch came down a couple of times to visit, and I was interviewing these people. It was heady stuff, but I had enough grim responsibility, like getting the paper out, without too many errors.

BEATTIE: Was this a daily or a weekly paper?

BOONE: A weekly. Oh, I could not have handled a daily, I'm sure.

BEATTIE: How did you know what to do as an editor, with no previous newspaper experience, even reporting experience, except that brief experience in Coral Gables?

BOONE: I really don't know. I had one reporter who'd do the news and then we had a common typesetter, printer, for the two papers. So, once I got it all pasted up and ready, why, they took off with it.

BEATTIE: That's a learning experience that would be hard to find today. What did that experience do to your aspirations to become a journalist?

BOONE: Well, when we went back to Evanston, then I was able to get on *The Chicago Daily News,* which is now, of course, defunct. I was on the Woman's Page, or Women's Page, whichever they called it. I did headlines there.

Then, I met Garnett Bale, who went to Northwestern Medical School, and was a Kentuckian. We married in eight months. Thus ended my newspaper career, because it was, of course, the Depression. We married in 1934 and went to New York, and I needed to work because, in those days, they did not pay an intern anything. I got jobs there. But I was not foolish enough to try for a newspaper job. My goodness, there were great newspaper people out of work at that time. But I found little jobs and kept myself going.

BEATTIE: When you were in New York, did you live in Manhattan?

BOONE: Right down East Seventy-ninth Street, between—it sounds snazzy—Madison and Park Avenues. But what it was, was an old brownstone that had been a fine place, but now was a rooming house. So anyway, that was fun.

BEATTIE: How old were you when you married?

BOONE: Twenty-one. Then, after that, we went to Louisville, and by then I was expecting our first child, so I didn't work anymore.

BEATTIE: Why did you come to Louisville?

BOONE: Because Garnett was a Kentuckian and Dr. Hart Hagan, who was one of the surgeons in Louisville, wanted Garnett to come back.

BEATTIE: Was your husband's family from Louisville?

BOONE: He was born in Louisville, but really they lived in Elizabethtown more than any other place. So, we were back in Louisville, and then it was the Depression still. The U.S. Coal and Coke Co., a subsidiary of U.S. Steel, had their coal mining camp in Lynch, Kentucky, in Harlan County. They kept five doctors, and they offered a position to Garnett.

BEATTIE: Where did you live in Louisville?

BOONE: On Baxter Avenue. In the Highlands, quite close to that big cemetery [Cave Hill Cemetery] there.

BEATTIE: What year was your baby born?

BOONE: 1936.

BEATTIE: Which child was this?

BOONE: Shelby, my oldest son. I have four boys and two girls, and Shelby's the oldest.

So, anyway, we went to Lynch. It was the time of John L. Lewis trying to unionize all the camps, and the heads of this camp were scared to death of unions. It was a weird experience. But oh, it was great. I had this baby. I didn't want anything else.

Well, we stayed a little less than a year, because it really turned out to be a dictatorship. How much was the fault of U.S. Coal and Coke, or how much was the fault of the chief surgeon, I don't know. He was a terrific egoist. I won't try to give you all the examples, but we were told after we got there that we weren't to associate with anyone but the other doctors and their wives. There were five doctors and only one other was married. That was kind of limiting.

Well, this was beginning to get to us. We were being part of something we didn't quite understand. So then one day one of the miners had a daughter, eight, nine years old, who developed appendicitis. He took her to the town of Harlan, where there was a surgeon who had a very good state-wide reputation. This miner knew about him, and he took his daughter to the best. When the chief surgeon at Lynch found out about it, he immediately had the miner fired. So when Garnett found out about it, and we talked about it, we decided we couldn't stay at a place that did things like that. It made us part of it. So we left and went back to Elizabethtown and really settled in and started being like normal people again.

BEATTIE: Did your husband join an existing practice or did he start his own?

BOONE: He started his own. Then World War II came, and he was a flight surgeon for about four-and-a-half years. So there went everything again. By then we had four children: Shelby; Barbara's the second child; Darryl, another girl, is the third one; and then Richard. Then there was World War II. But after Garnett came back from World War II, we said, "Well, we're awful lucky; we have two girls and two boys, and we'd better leave it at that." But we really wanted six. And the next child has proved, in his lifetime, how determined he is. He came along, and that was Bradley. Two boys, and then we thought, "He'll be worse than an only child, six years younger than the youngest of the four," and so we said, "Let's just make it six after all." So then we had Phillip, and that makes the sixth. And it's been a wonderfully happy thing, because they really all like each other and they're close and fun. So having six was right for us. They're all decent, self-supporting, nice people.

BEATTIE: How long did you live in Elizabethtown?

BOONE: I guess we went there at about the end of '37, and I left there in '75. And, I would like to say that I had wonderful help there. Her name was Mabel. She came before my last two children were born, and she was with me over thirty years, and she never failed to come. We buried her last summer. My children were always so good to Mabel, but she'd been good with them. You knew, when Mabel said something, she meant it. She had real dignity and a rollicking sense of humor.

BEATTIE: When you lived in Elizabethtown, did she work for you exclusively?

BOONE: Yes. Came every day except Sundays. While there, I was working pretty hard trying to get the town integrated. And [Walter] "Dee" Huddleston lived there then, and between us, we really worked hard. We'd got every restaurant in town except one integrated. And, oh, I was so thrilled. Dee was a senator from Kentucky, and he was in charge of the radio station there. I was crazy about Dee, and he was just a good civic person, who took a lead in those things. I remember Garnett and I went to Frankfort and marched with Martin Luther King once. We were just citizens who felt something should be done about this.

BEATTIE: What else did you do in terms of integrating Elizabethtown?

BOONE: We did have Mabel buried in what was the white cemetery. There was a separate place for blacks there for years. But I happened to own Garnett's and my plots, which we were not using because we both had willed our bodies to U of L [University of Louisville] medical school. That's where Garnett went and where I'll go. But I hadn't sold the lot. So, I thought, Mabel would like that, and she didn't have anything. But that was my children's idea. My daughter, Darryl, said, "Shelby and I think that Mabel would probably like to be buried in the plot where there are others of the family." And I said, "Oh." You know, that *did* come as sort of a surprise. And Darryl said, "Look, Mother, you integrated everything else in town, you might as well integrate the cemeteries." So I said, "Mabel, would you like to be buried in the cemetery there?" She nodded her head and smiled real big. Yes, she certainly would. So that was fine. Then she told me one day she wanted to be cremated. So that was fine. I mean, Mabel was really right with things.

BEATTIE: Would you say that those efforts of yours in integrating Elizabethtown were among your first efforts in community service, both in Elizabethtown and in the state?

BOONE: No, because I think it was 1944 when I started the League of Women Voters in Elizabethtown. Then I was state president of the League in '48, into '50 or '51. I served on the City Council once.

BEATTIE: What would you say was your greatest contribution to the League?

BOONE: I had two babies while I was state president, and that convinced a lot of people there's no reason you can't be in the League and work.

BEATTIE: What other statewide activities have you been involved in?

BOONE: There are so many of them. I was president of the Mental Health Association of Kentucky for a while. And I'm still serving on the Comprehensive Care Center Board for the Pennyroyal area. I served on it in the Lincoln Trail area, too, but then, of course, I left Elizabethtown. I served for nine years on the Kentucky Council on Higher Education, for about nineteen years as editorial board member of the University Press of Kentucky, and now I'm chairman of the Endowment Committee for the University Press of Kentucky. I was president of Friends of Kentucky Libraries for quite a few years. I'll say I can't remember them all. Whatever seemed interesting to me I did, and one thing leads to another.

BEATTIE: You say your first husband passed away. When was that?

BOONE: June 22, 1972. He had an inoperable brain tumor. He died at sixty-four. It seems terribly young. He found out he had, I think it was, three months to live, and he knew, being a physician, that he would be paralyzed on one side, probably go blind, certainly have no control over his own use of his body, and so he just never took any food or liquid after that. The children and I, when we realized what he was doing said, "We really admire what you're doing, but tell us quick if you change your mind." He just shook his head. The doctors and nurses all cooperated. He died naturally of starvation.

BEATTIE: So you only knew about his impending death for a few months before he died?

BOONE: A few months. Garnett and I had had Living Wills since they first came out, and we'd both willed our bodies to the medical school. See, Garnett died nineteen years ago, and we'd had a living will at least ten years. Now people are beginning to talk about them, you know.

BEATTIE: How long was it before you married your second husband, George Boone?

BOONE: Well, I'd known him for years. He and Garnett and I were good friends, and my children and all liked him a lot. Three years. And, oddly enough, he didn't know it, but he proposed to me on my Garnett anniversary, June eleventh.

BEATTIE: What year was that?

BOONE: Seventy-five. We married in August.

BEATTIE: And he is an attorney?

BOONE: Here, in Elkton. This house you're in was built by his family in 1815. Now, this front part was added in 1837, but the back part, the original part, was built in 1815. I met him right in this house. *He* is the one who is interested in politics. My goodness. He served in the legislature for a while, the state legislature.

BEATTIE: Your writing is what I want to really talk about next, but you mentioned being a member of the editorial board of the University Press of Kentucky. What years were you a board member?

BOONE: In '64, maybe, it started. And then, as I say, I'm a chair of the Endowment Committee for it now. I went on the board when it became the consortium. It had been University of Kentucky Press, and I think it was the second consortium of university presses in the whole country. So now it's the University Press of Kentucky. It was the same year I got the Sullivan Award from the University of Kentucky for being an outstanding citizen of Kentucky, and I think I'm the only person who ever got it who hadn't gone to U of K [University of Kentucky] or even had a college degree, you might add. I think my citation says it's for civic work and for befriending education. And in E-town I had done quite a bit of, I don't know if you'd call it teaching, but, you know, kids who weren't getting along too fast, disadvantaged children, blacks in many cases, in the earlier years. I used to give quite a bit of time going and tutoring them with their reading. I do quite a few poetry sessions for college and high school and even primary school students, whenever I'm asked. I love to do it. And, gee, the response is good and it's wonderful for me, too. I really am lucky in having a lot of enthusiasm. Of course, I think that's a big ingredient. But I think people respond if you're crazy about your subject.

BEATTIE: I think you're right. What would you say was your greatest interest when you were on the consortium of the University Press, or what do you think your greatest contribution was?

BOONE: I'm not really sure I made much contribution, except I was the one person on it who wasn't an academic, and I could kind of say a few things they wouldn't say, and I think I gave them a laugh or two now and then. The Board's made up of a consortium of people. It started out being all the public universities, but now private ones belong, too. Even the Filson Club is a member. And, of course, they send mostly their history and English professors. I enjoyed that very much.

BEATTIE: Will you tell me about your publication *Approaches,* now the *Kentucky Poetry Review?*

BOONE: I'd love to. I was president of Friends of Kentucky Libraries at the time, and I told Margaret Willis, who was state librarian, that Kentucky really interested me, and I felt sure there had to be a lot of people writing poetry in Kentucky, but you didn't hear about them. The only poetry you got, by Kentuckians, was in various university or college publications that did fiction and essays and had the stray poem in there, too. I told her I would just love to find out about poets in Kentucky and do an anthology. So she spoke to Mary Belknap Gray, who was extremely wealthy and extremely interested in libraries, and who was on our board, and she told her what I wanted to do. And Mary said, "Oh, I'll underwrite it. I'd be glad to."

So, I got started. And I like the idea of how I found out where poets were, through public librarians. They know who in their little area writes poetry and who takes out poetry books. So I did that kind of corresponding and got names of a lot of them. Then I wrote to them and asked if they would contribute. Of course, I wasn't paying for the poems—but poets do not object to having their poetry published—and got an anthology together.

So Mary Belknap Gray never had to give me a cent, because the first printing sold out. In fact, we made some money. Many of the poets who were in the anthology wrote to me and said, "Isn't there some way we can go on sharing our work?" So I spoke to my friend, Lill Parrish. I said, "Would you be willing to help?" "Oh, yes." So we started *Approaches*. I named it that because I feel a poem is an approach. It's an approach for the writer, and for whoever reads it, to a new feeling, or an old feeling, a new way to feel about an old feeling. And, well, our first edition was pretty pitiful. I don't mean our first edition was poor in the poems we got, but we got a moonlighting printer. You should have seen that miserable little thing. We did it over. Even *we* couldn't stand it. The subscription price for a quarterly was just one dollar, so I don't think anyone would have felt gypped, but I couldn't stand it. If you can't read a poem, you're insulting it.

So, we went on. The first Endowment of the Arts came to Kentucky. I mean it was Kentucky's first. That must have been about '66 or '7. It was really the Endowment for the Arts. Anyway, William Hull was the first director, and he came to Elizabethtown. We had a Lively Arts Series by then. Oh, that's a great story, and I got to go back to newspaper work for a little while with that. For *The News Enterprise* I did a Lively Arts page once a month. I did the layout, and oh, I had more fun. Anyway, to go back to *Approaches*, William Hull had come down to see something about our Lively Arts series, and I was on that board, and I had him and some others in for lunch. He called me up later, a few days, a week or so, from Frankfort, and said, "The next time you're in Frankfort, would you come by my office? I want to talk about the poetry magazine." Well, I found the time to get to Frankfort pretty quickly. And he said that he was very impressed with our poetry magazine and that the Endowment for the Arts would like to offer us a grant for a year, if we would let their artists redesign the cover. I got the message. And if we would go to a better printer. Well, wonderful, you know. So, they actually gave us a grant. I think it was for three years. The magazine became better looking. Oh, and he said they would have nothing to do with the editorial work, we'd be perfectly free.

But, when I was going to marry George, I knew I couldn't be editor from down in Elkton. So, I asked Wade Hall if he'd take over, and he was glad to. But see, when I started *Approaches*, it was meant to encourage Kentucky poets. Yet after our little magazine started, there was such a proliferation of small poetry magazines in Kentucky, you can't imagine, and some of them still exist. But Wade had been on the board a long time, and was certainly well-qualified as an editor. He wanted to open the magazine up to poets outside of Kentucky. Well, I'd edited the thing for twelve years. You know, anything he wanted to try then was fine. He also wanted to carry reviews now and then, and essays, so he renamed it *Kentucky Poetry Review.* I don't like the name as well, but it serves a purpose, and it's still going great.

BEATTIE: When you started the magazine, did you try to get representative poets from all over the state in each issue?

BOONE: No, we just published it according to the poems the editorial board chose. Oh, we'd have long discussions, you can imagine. If some of us liked one poem especially well, and others didn't, we had quite a time. But, eastern Kentucky really has had more poets than any region in the state, which I think is interesting, the mountain people. Then I'd say Louisville next. Western Kentucky never has sent in many. Well, of course, you can't judge today, with famous poets from other places in it.

I've got to tell you about the Robert Penn Warren Center. I feel that that's one of the most exciting things.

BEATTIE: You are still directing it?

BOONE: I'm head of the committee, and the Center has grown so much, I just can't get over it. I think the best thing we did, besides getting started, was to appoint an advisory board. Now, this board is to do nothing but meet once a year, when we have our regular April celebration of Robert Penn Warren, and give us ideas. They're all bright. Most of them are authorities on Warren. There are a few who aren't, but they are such creative thinkers. Well, I was scared to death at first, because we were really asking important people. And, of course, they're appointed by the president of Western Kentucky University, but he takes the suggestions from us. So many have written books on Warren. There's James Justus, from the University of Indiana, and Alexander Heard from Vanderbilt, and "Bo" [James] Grimshaw from the University of Texas, and Cleanth Brooks is on it, as is Warren's daughter, Rosanna Warren. They're all so special, it's bad to mention just a few out of fourteen.

BEATTIE: Will you talk about the Center itself, what it's purpose is, when it was started, and where it is?

BOONE: It's at Western Kentucky University. We have what we call a War-ren Room, a very nice room with Warren things set about. The really valuable things, we were told right away, really should be under security and good environ-mental conditions at the Kentucky Museum. Riley Handy's head of that, and he's on our committee, too. We have a rare edition of "Blackberry Winter," the one children's story Warren ever wrote; you can hardly see that anywhere. But if some-body comes to do serious research they, of course, are given access to that. Our purpose is to have more and more people know about Robert Penn Warren and understand him, and for his influence to go farther.

BEATTIE: Did you know Warren?

BOONE: Oh, yes.

BEATTIE: What was your relationship to him? When did you know him?

BOONE: It started through poetry. But I had dinner with him once. Well, I mean, I was at a dinner, and I was lucky enough to sit beside him. You'd think we would talk about poetry, wouldn't you? We were there about an hour-and-a-half, and all we talked about was education. I'm afraid people are going to forget what a great teacher he was, because he's such a great writer and, really, I think he cared as much about education as about writing.

BEATTIE: I want to ask you about your own writing. When did you become interested in creative writing?

BOONE: I don't know if you'd say you become interested, or that writing is just a form of expression. I think I was eight or nine when Mother saw a poem I'd written, and quickly got it in the church bulletin, the Episcopal church in Evanston. And, you know, it's pretty pitiful. I'd guess you would call it inspirational, but I was a child. I think I've always written little poems.

BEATTIE: Was this something that started in elementary school or high school, or in school did you particularly like English—reading and writing?

BOONE: Yes, it's the only thing I really ever did any good in. I was always good in English. I spent too much time with it to be good in other things, I think. Looking back, I almost wish I'd been a better student, and then I think, why do I wish that? No one could have enjoyed literature the way I have all my life. I used to go to the public library there in Evanston and you could check out as many poetry books as you wanted. Now, that says something, doesn't it, because you could only take three of any other kind of books. "Oh, take all the poetry you want." I remember walking home with my arms just aching, just full of poetry. And I'd work late at night in my room, typing. I'd type all my favorite lines and paragraphs, sometimes whole poems. Poor Mother thought I was doing my homework.

BEATTIE: This is other poets?

BOONE: Other poets, yes, but I'd be writing at the same time. I've got, I think, seven flimsy notebooks full of all that poetry that I saved.

BEATTIE: It's wonderful that you saved it.

BOONE: Yes. I'd love to have time to go through it sometime, really. So, it's always been my love. I don't remember ever thinking, "I'm going to write poetry," or "I'd like to write poetry." And I'm still doing it. People, now that I've gotten older, sort of annoy me when they say, and a few do, "Do you still write poetry?" *Still* write poetry.

BEATTIE: Did you mostly educate yourself in reading and appreciating poetry?

BOONE: Yes. You know how you're always getting forms for things? One recent one where it said, *education,* I wrote in "public libraries." Oh, those days are gone, aren't they, of really wonderful public libraries when they didn't have to worry about funds being cut and books being so expensive and everything? I guess

I have to say I'm self-educated except, you know, I've audited a few classes. But I read a lot and I hear a lot of good lectures. But I will say I got an extra-good background.

BEATTIE: Were you writing poetry from the time you were eight?

BOONE: I would say so. But really, I didn't start saving it probably until I was about eighteen or nineteen, and since then I've written a lot. I don't know how many [notebooks] I've got of my own poems, but that doesn't tell you much, anyway. I think I'm now writing in the seventh one, but some are big, and some are little, and some have two poems on a page, and some poems take three pages.

BEATTIE: Will you tell me about your two books of poetry?

BOONE: Well, one of them is a collection that Wade Hall really took the lead in. Wade said, "Joy, do you just have one copy of all your poems?" And I said, "Well, yes, as a collection." He said, "Well, would you dare risk leaving it with me while you're in England?" I was going to be gone six weeks. "I'd just love to look at it all." I said, "Oh, yes," because I knew he would take good care of it. And what he did was, he got three other people to select poems from it, and he put them into a book, and then he told me when I got back. I got to pick out a title, *Never Less Than Love,* which I still think is a fun title.

So, that was one. Then, after Garnett's death, a friend of mine—she hadn't known Garnett, but she hadn't lived in E-town long—was a very scholarly type, Chinese history, actually. She said everything I told her about Garnett made her think of Cassius Marcellus Clay. She said, "What you ought to do is write about Clay and see if that would help you get out of things." So I did a narrative poem about him. And I say the Robert Penn Warren Center has been as much fun as I've ever had, but writing *that* was, too. That was more fun, to write about just one thing and change the meter and the style.

My daughter, Darryl, told me the other day, "Mother, you've got to get together some of your favorite poems of the last twenty years and have them put together." I said, "Oh, Darryl," And she said, "Well, I want to do it." I said, "Well, it costs some money, you know." And she said, "I want to do it." So my children are on me now, all of them, to do that, but I haven't started yet. It won't be any job. I think my poems have changed quite a bit since I've moved down here, which is interesting to me. The atmosphere is different. This house is great for writing. You know, you feel certain things.

BEATTIE: How do you think your poetry has changed since you've moved down here?

BOONE: I think I write more about places. And, I'm sorry to say, fewer love songs. I love short little love songs, or love poems. I've done a few here, but they almost have to come to you unbidden. You don't think about them. A few I've really liked have happened here.

BEATTIE: Do you have a favorite poem of yours?

BOONE: No, but probably if it came right down to it, I might have six or eight favorites. The hardest poems to write, for me at least, are about people I love. And yet, I think maybe my best few are about them. My poems are not so much directed toward them, as much as those people are *in* them, if you know what I mean. There's one called "The Supper," about after all the children had left. That's a great favorite with people, and it is with me. Then there's one called "Kiss Both Hands." One of my granddaughters—when she was little, my daughter Barbara was going to stay with her for a few days while her parents went away—and Barbara told me later, "You know, before they left, Darryl said, 'Now, Barbara, when you put her to bed you have to kiss both hands.'" And I thought, "Well, of course." And I wrote one about that. People seem to like that poem especially well. The last poetry session I did over at the Glasgow campus of Western Kentucky University, all the people in the class wrote to me after. That was wonderful. And the poem that I'd say most of them liked was about my father. That's odd, isn't it?

Within the last few months I decided I wanted to write about the house in which I grew up. In fact, I seem to be in a memoir kind of prose-poem period. So, I wrote about it. It's fairly long. And I reread it after I worked on it for a week or two. It's about my parents, mostly, though they're not mentioned, and you might not realize it, if you read it. So, it's funny how it comes out. You really *are* writing about people you love, but it's not, should we say, so noticeable.

BEATTIE: How do you compose your poetry? Is it usually at one sitting, or over a period of time?

BOONE: I'd say over a period of time. A few come so blithe and easy. But when I say a period of time, I mean weeks. I'm not talking about months or years. And I always write them out in pencil first. By the time I get to the typewriter, I'd say they're two-thirds done. But then you make changes in lines. I don't know if you write poetry, but I love the ones that come already written. But they're little ones.

BEATTIE: That brings up another question, one that people often ask me. And that is, because your background is so similar to mine, in terms of being a journalist and a poet, people see those as two entirely different approaches to writing, or to life.

BOONE: They really are.

BEATTIE: But do you see them as complementing each other?

BOONE: No, I see them as just about as opposite as you can get.

BEATTIE: What about the close observations that you have to make as a journalist?

BOONE: Well, now you're right. A poet has to observe things closely, and a journalist darn well better. But then, you're more confined to facts. Journalism is about facts more, and poetry is about feelings more, but they're both about truth, now that you put me on it. Because, you know, poetry is imagery, more than what actually happened, but it needs to be as true as the journalistic fact. With me, of course, poetry came first. But just all kinds of writing I've enjoyed doing. It seems I really have to write. So, it could be letters, it could be poems, it could be a feature story. I wish I had had an opportunity to write essays. And, as you know, book reviews. Now, when I was young, in my teens, I wrote a little short review of every book I read. Like maybe no more than three or four lines.

BEATTIE: Just for yourself?

BOONE: Just for myself. When I was in Elizabethtown I wrote to the book editor at *The Courier,* who was Mary Bingham, and said that I would like to review books. Well, of course, she didn't know me, but she wrote back and said, well, please tell her what kind of books I was most interested in and write her a long letter about why I wanted to review. She sent me my first book in 1945, so I've been reviewing for them a long time, haven't I? And I did that because it was something I could do at night after the children were in bed. It didn't take me away from home, and yet it really kept my mind going. So, I don't know. I guess there's been a cause for everything, but next to the people I love, any kind of writing has been what I love. I get hungry for it.

BEATTIE: What about short stories?

BOONE: Never been able to do a good one. I think I've done a few. I'll tell you what I'm not, I'm sure not plot-minded. Give me a fact or two, or let me meet a person, and I could write endlessly. But I can't make up a story line. I have thought in my, I guess, conceited moments, you'd have to say that I might have been quite a good writer, a good poet maybe, if I didn't do so many practical things, too. I mean, you know, if there's anything that interrupts the creative flow, it's working with something practical, like the League of Women Voters, or the American Heart Association. But I like to do that, too.

BEATTIE: Don't you think, really, that such civic work energizes you to write more than if you had not done those things?

BOONE: That's probably true. I really get very excited about people. I really don't regret anything I've done. George and I are way too busy now. But I must say, we each enjoy what we're doing. We're not ready to give up, yet. And I keep thinking, "Golly, when I get old ... " Well, I don't know when I think that's going to be, because I'm really there, but I don't feel it. And I think, "When I get old, I'm going to do more reading, I'm going to do more writing. I want to do this, I want to ..." you know, and I probably never will.

BEATTIE: You've alluded to enjoying conducting writing workshops in the schools. Are you still doing that?

BOONE: Yes. You know, Western Kentucky University gave me a nice feeling a few years ago; they made me an adjunct professor in the English Department. So that's part of the reason I get asked to do that. Talk about energize! Why, I come out of those classes just ... You know, I can't imagine, then, why everyone isn't excited about poetry. Such interesting things come up. This last one I did, I usually don't read my own poems, because I don't like to, but they expressly asked if I'd do a class reading my poems, and then discuss them. I do think it's interesting how different poems mean different things to various people.

I read one that I wrote to my mother, just a few years ago, a little poem. My children have always called her "Emo" for her initials, Edith Maud Overington. So I called my poem "Emo." Well, when I got through reading it, one woman said, "Is your family Jewish?" And I said, "No. I don't believe there have been Jewish people in it." She said, "Well, I wondered, because in Yiddish *emo* means mother." Isn't that amazing? I lived all these years, I never knew that, and I have quite a few Jewish friends. None of them ever mentioned that. And here my children had called her that for a perfectly sensible reason. And the name of my poem to my mother is called "Emo."

BEATTIE: In conducting creative workshops or classes or seminars, how do you think they should be run?

BOONE: Well, I'll make a confession to you who teach. I don't think you can teach creativity, cause if you want to know all those things, it's all there in *The Encyclopedia of Poetry*. I said, "I think the best poems make their own music, not being confined in a form." Though of course, the sonnet form's fine. However you want to do it. But *I* say, a poem I love, you may not like at all. Don't bother with it. There are more poems than anyone will read, but the one that speaks to you, the one that has a line or two in it that'll be with you the rest of your life without even trying, *that's* your poem.

It's a very open thing. I'm sure your traditionalists would disapprove of me terribly, but, to me, the thing is to let people know poetry can be a wonderful part of their lives. And you can read a poem before you go to sleep, you can read a short one while you're waiting for someone to pick you up. If you write poetry, you can write it in your head while you're driving and try to capture it again when you get home. Sometimes you do, sometimes you don't. But just to excite people about poetry is important, because I feel people who don't know poetry are missing so much. I don't pretend to be an authority, because I'm really not. I'm an enthusiast. I'm a cheerleader for poetry.

BEATTIE: You've talked about how moving to this house changed your writing; what do you think about moving to this state? Of course, it's hard to say how your writing has been affected when you don't know how it would have been otherwise, but is there anything about Kentucky that you think has inspired particular things in your writing?

BOONE: Well, of course, this sounds almost a cliché to say, the beauty of the nature, because I'm really not much of a just-descriptive writer; I like to have some thought or feeling in it. But it's hard not to be writing about Kentucky. Mother always said Kentucky was more like England than any state she'd ever been in, and it really is, the wonderful green and the gentle rolling part. I think the Knobs are absolutely fascinating.

So, I would say the physical attributes of Kentucky have affected me. I came when I was so young, but I've wanted to say more about Kentucky than I ever wanted to say about Chicago, though I love Chicago. But maybe that was my age. What did happen down here in Elkton, there's a certain ... hmm, what to say without sounding foolish? A certain mystic quality, or almost a spiritual quality, to a house this old. The fog, *that* affects me in Kentucky. You know, I never knew til coming here that when it's just low over the ground, they call it "witch's breath." This is really rural country. One day I sat at the kitchen sink, and I could see out over the pasture, and the fog rolled in slowly, daytime fog. The fog became people to me. They were all the ghosts of this place. I wrote this poem, it's a long one, and when it was completed—oh, that took quite some days and some work. When I reread it in its finished form, I really sounded like another woman from the kind of person I am. It was written as if by a woman who'd lived here maybe a hundred years ago. Odd things like that happen here. So, that's about all I can say. There are several poems like that that I wouldn't ever have expected to write, and probably wouldn't have, in a more urban situation. Now, of course, this house is right in the city. It's a village now. But, you know, it once was a big plantation that stretched for miles, and I think a lot of that spirit's still here. My study's on the second floor at the back of the house, and I look out, and I could be in the country. So, it's a whole new experience for me.

I feel very fortunate to have had a different experience late in life. I wouldn't have chosen to do without Garnett, but since that happened, I think I'm very fortunate that I could make a whole new life, too, and bring the old with me. Of course, the children are part of the other marriage, but I think anyone's really lucky who later on can have a whole new experience. The people here are different. They have their old traditions and customs. And I feel, and I find out that it's true ... I felt from the beginning a kind of violence here, as if it's underneath. Now, I find this is the part of Kentucky and Tennessee that was considered the most violent. There's a whole book written about it, by a scholar. But you feel those things. There's a gentleness and there's a violence, and the people who live here, I think, worship the past, which I think is too extreme. I don't think you should forget the past, but, you know, if your great-grandfather amounted to anything, you're still great. Now, this is ridiculous. I mean, you should make your own greatness. I have a friend here, who said something so good, because she's an outsider, too. She said, "You know, when he talks about. . ." so and so's people— she was talking about her own husband's family—"I haven't learned yet whether they're living or dead." And that is the truth. I mean, the dead are just as important around here as the living.

BEATTIE: Maybe more, in some cases.

BOONE: And everybody's related. I told George, I said, "George, a stranger comes in this house and always leaves as a cousin." They always find someplace, generations back, where they tied in. And that has a charm.

BEATTIE: He's related to Daniel Boone?

BOONE: Through Daniel's older brother.

BEATTIE: I hate to tell you, but I'm related to Daniel Boone through George Boone, another of Daniel's brothers.

BOONE: See, what did I tell you? You leave as a cousin.

June 10, 1991

Following an illness, Boone moved to Glasgow, Kentucky, where she continues to write poetry and book reviews. On May 22, 1997, Governor Paul Patton awarded Boone the designation of poet laureate of Kentucky, a two-year, honorary appointment.

BOOKS BY JOY BALE BOONE

Never Less Than Love. Louisville, Ky.: The Kentucky Poetry Press, 1972.

The Storm's Eye. Louisville, Ky.: The Kentucky Poetry Press, 1974.

THOMAS D. CLARK

CLARK: My name is Thomas D. Clark. I was born on July the 14th, 1903, in Louisville, Mississippi, same as Louisville, Kentucky. My father's name was John Clark. And my mother's name was Sallie Bennett Clark. My father was born in 1876 and my mother in 1881, both of them just after the Civil War. They had vivid memories of what people had told them and what had gone on in the South. I remember people talking about the battles. We had relatives who were in the Civil War. They remembered the freeing of the slaves—that is, stories of the freeing of the slaves—and of Reconstruction and the general reorganization and re-creation of the South. The Clark family had a few slaves, very few, that had belonged to other families. There were some of them that lived on our place associated with our family. I knew them quite well. As a matter of fact, I knew two Congo slaves that had come over just before the outbreak of the Civil War. There was one of them who lived on our place, Aunt Betsy Harper, who had been sold in slavery from Kentucky and belonged to this famous Harper family, the distillers here in Kentucky. I knew a lot of ex-slaves. My mother was a schoolteacher. I went to school, to her classes, until about the sixth grade, a one-room school. She taught from the elementary grades, certainly not beyond eighth grade.

My people were of English origin, my Clark family. They came to Rhode Island and settled in Providence. The brother of my forebear was old Dr. John Clark, who was very influential in the organization of the Rhode Island Plantations. That man had only one child, a daughter. His brother, my forebear, moved down to Virginia, down into the James River Valley. And I had three ancestors who were in the Battle of Yorktown at the surrender of Cornwallis. They lived at Prince Edward County, Virginia. My immediate forebear moved down to Anderson County, South Carolina. But that was just a momentary stop. He had four sons who went on out to that Choctaw Indian country in Mississippi in 1834 and settled down at the headwaters of the Pearl River. And that's where my family has been ever since.

BEATTIE: What did your father do for a living?

CLARK: He was a cotton farmer until the day of his death. He died just short of his eightieth birthday and left a very fine field of cotton ready to be picked. As a matter of fact, I was in England at the time he died, and I had to go home and make arrangements to get that cotton picked, the last crop of cotton on that farm. And it was a good crop.

BEATTIE: How long did your mother live?

CLARK: My mother lived twenty years, at least, after that. I'm not sure of the year she died, but it was approximately 1970. She was, I believe, ninety-six years old at the time of her death. I have five brothers and sisters, one dead; there are four living. I'm the older. I have one brother who lives in Denver, Colorado; one brother lives in McAllen, Texas; and two sisters in Mississippi.

BEATTIE: Do you remember anything about your grandparents?

CLARK: I don't remember my Grandfather Clark; he died the year I was born. But my Grandmother Clark lived to be somewhere in the neighborhood of ninety-five years of age. I remember her quite well. She was of what they call Dutch extraction. Her maiden name was Cagle. Her people came from East Flat Rock, North Carolina, the little village made famous by Carl Sandburg. They sold their land to George Vanderbilt and moved out to Mississippi. Her father was a major figure in the little town. He gave land to the Baptist church, which is still there. And he and my great-grandmother are buried inside a little iron enclosure, which he made himself. He was a blacksmith. And when Garrison's Raid took place through that town, it went right by the door of his shop. He had a son who was a bugler for Nathan Bedford Forrest.

My Bennett family came from Charleston, South Carolina. They followed the land frontier into the Pearl River country. But my great-grandmother Bennett died in Louisiana. They moved on across the Mississippi River. I obviously never knew them. But, yes, I knew my Grandfather Bennett quite well. He died when I was a senior in high school. He was a very successful farmer. Everybody in that community grew cotton.

BEATTIE: What was your childhood like?

CLARK: I had a happy childhood. It was rural. We didn't have a lot of material things; we were very limited in that respect. But we had the whole wide open world in which to grow up, with creeks nearby where you could go fishing, swimming. We had neighbors of our age, and we enjoyed those associations.

BEATTIE: You talked about going to your mother's school, being taught by her. What was school like?

CLARK: I have her certificates, I have her school records, and she was paid, as all Mississippi teachers were, or Kentucky teachers, a very low salary. She taught in a one-room school in my father's community—that's where she met my father—right across the road from the big, double-log house that my South Carolina ancestor built. It was a Carolina-type house. She taught one-room school there and met my father. Then later, after we moved on to a second farm that we owned, she began teaching school on that farm. After that, she taught in two or three different locations. I was quite pleased when she lay a corpse; some of her old students came to the funeral. Well, she never forgot anybody. My mother had college training. She went to a school called the Southern Female College at West

Point, Mississippi. She was a woman with a keen memory, and she read. That, I think, had as much influence on me as anything. She read all the time and remembered what she read, too.

BEATTIE: Did she read to you a lot?

CLARK: She did. I remember one time—I suppose if we had any image of Abraham Lincoln, it was of the "Black Abe" image, coming up in that strong Confederate atmosphere. But I remember she read Mrs.—I believe it's, E.D. [Emma Dorothy] Southworth's *Ishmael,* that had to do with Abraham Lincoln. It was just a thinly veiled biography of Lincoln. I can remember quite vividly how interested we were in that story.

My grandmother had a fairly large library, for a southern cotton farmer, and we had books. My whole life, some way or other, I've been associated with books. I've been in an atmosphere where books were very important.

BEATTIE: What about in elementary school or high school? Do you remember reading or history emerging as special interests for you then?

CLARK: Yes. Certainly, in high school, I was interested in history. I remember I went to a boarding school. In those days Mississippi had only a limited number of high schools, and the legislature created a system of high schools called agricultural high schools, designed largely for the benefit of rural boys and girls. Those schools had associated with them the dormitories where you could board very cheaply and go to school for a minimum expense. I went to that kind of school. It had a small library. I came up in that very strict religious atmosphere, if you can call it religious. We were Methodist.

BEATTIE: Did the school have the same atmosphere?

CLARK: Yes. It was just simply an extension of the home and community. I remember that some reading was taboo—and it appeals to my sense of humor, even yet. *Huckleberry Finn* was on the no-no list. And I read it. I read it at night under the bedcovers in the dormitory.

BEATTIE: Was it as exciting as you had anticipated?

CLARK: It was. Oh, I spent my life reading. One thing that had a little impact, we subscribed to some magazines and newspapers. They were weekly or tri-weekly papers. *The Commercial Appeal* of Memphis and *The Atlanta Journal, The Atlanta Constitution*—I read those papers. My father was not a book reader, but he read the newspapers constantly.

BEATTIE: Had he gone to college?

CLARK: No. Very few people in that community had gone to college.

BEATTIE: What about your interest in writing? Did that develop in school, in your younger years?

CLARK: I suppose it did. My mother was an imaginative woman, and I had, maybe, an inborn curiosity. I really can't tell you. I was interested in writing in high school to the extent that I undertook to organize a student newspaper. We had no money, had no facilities, and we did actually publish some things in that little county weekly newspaper. I think we got out—once or twice—a little published sheet of school news. Must have been pretty elementary, whatever it was. I had the bug, and it's hard to say just when and where you picked up that bug.

From my sixteenth birthday on, right after World War I ended, the boll weevil hit that part of the South hard, almost bankrupted the cotton farmer from Texas up through Alabama. And, during those years right after World War I, the boll weevil was a severe menace. The farmers had not made a transition over to other types of field crops, or diversified farming, and everybody was in the same boat. I got a job for my sixteenth birthday on a dredge boat, and I spent two years on that boat. We were digging a canal in the headwaters of the Pearl River, a drainage canal. I got sick and tired of that mud, that grease, and that dredge jerking around. A boy had brought some books on board that boat, and I got excited at those books. I decided that that was not the life for me. I wasn't going to spend my life among water moccasins and mud and drilling miles of holes in that roaring dredging machine.

I went to what's now Mississippi State University thinking that they had a preparatory school. They did have, but they had discontinued it. They would not admit me, obviously, to this state college. I learned about this school that was on the same little railroad, and I went there and was admitted. Choctow County Agricultural High School at Weir, Mississippi. I was admitted on Friday. I went back to my home and got ready. On Sunday, I went to that school. I think they never asked me how much schooling I'd had. That never entered into my consideration. I was weighing around 190 pounds at that time and, of course, on that dredge I'd developed into a pretty strong lad. They were interested in my playing football, and I did. For four years I played football. I entered school on Monday and played football on Friday against a team from Koscusko, Mississippi, a much larger town and a school that should have had a much better team. We won that game. We didn't win them all, but we won a fair share of them.

BEATTIE: Did you play football all the way through high school?

CLARK: All the way through high school. Played the position of right guard. When they needed a substitute center, I played in that position. I can hardly think of that now, but I did play four years.

BEATTIE: Then what happened?

CLARK: I did not want to go to Mississippi State; at that time it was called Mississippi A&M (Agricultural and Mechanical) College. I was not interested in agriculture or engineering, either. I wasn't good in mathematics, and I'd had my fill of agriculture. As a matter of fact, at school they required me to take four years of agriculture. That was potentially a training ground to turn farm boys and girls back on the land. There was nothing back on the land for me, because the boll weevil had taken care of that. And being a southern boy from a small, southern rural community or town, there were only about three professions open. One was law, the other medicine, and an engineer came along once in a while. But that was not a flourishing profession. I chose to study law. There was only one school really open for that, and that was the University of Mississippi, "Ole Miss."

I entered the University in the fall of 1925 thinking I was going to law school, but I never got near the law school. I met a very interesting man, a man who was to have a tremendous personal influence on my life, Charles S. Sydnor. I never had but one course under him, and it had very little to do with my interest in history, almost nothing. It was British history. But I had numerous conversations with him. He was a young professor, just out of Johns Hopkins, and he was on the rise as a young professor. And I turned to history. I did not have a lot of history at the University of Mississippi, but I came away with the interest.

BEATTIE: How did you develop that relationship with him?

CLARK: More or less accidentally. I saw this young professor in the hall of that old Lyceum Building there, which had been so prominent in national and international news, and I began talking to him and just developed a friendship which endured to the end of his life, an intimate friendship.

I had another professor in freshman English, a man named Arthur Palmer Hudson, who came from precisely the same background I had and from pretty close to my home community. He was a very difficult professor; he was rigid rather than difficult. He took those Mississippi boys and girls who had poor high school backgrounds—he had a poor background himself—and he drilled hard on them, correcting their speech or their writing, their intellectual development. Students undertook to dodge his courses, because they thought he was bloodless. Well, I had to take his freshman English, and he did something that taught me a lesson that I used in my own teaching. He required us to write a paragraph, a daily paragraph, of something that challenged your imagination. Anything you saw or anything that crossed your mind, whatever, write a paragraph about it. And I did. I turned in a paragraph every day. A lot of them are published. I have in my desk drawer back here [Lexington residence] those things that were published. He published a weekly sheet called *The Freshman Theme Review,* in which the better ones were published and the poorer ones were also published.

BEATTIE: Were they pointed out as the better ones and the poorer ones?

CLARK: Yes. And thank God I never got one in the poorer ones. There were a lot of poorer ones published, and they were horrible. But I do know, in my case, that was a real stimulus.

I also, right from the start, became a reporter on the college paper, and I remained a reporter until I left "Ole Miss." I was associate editor of the college paper, and that was a wonderful experience. As a matter of fact, that almost led to a course of my life. In the latter part of my days on that paper, I reported on the Chancellor's office, and I got to know the Chancellor. One day I was walking across the campus and met him, and he said, "I've been looking for you." He said, "I've been to a meeting," evidently of the Southern Association of Colleges and Secondary Schools, "and I met Dr. Frank McVey, president of the University of Kentucky. And he asked me to have one of our boys make an application," and I did, and got that little two-hundred-dollar scholarship here. I went three years to the University of Mississippi, and then I lacked a quarter of having my work completed for my A.B. [Bachelor of Arts] degree. And they permitted me a very unusual thing; they permitted me to go to the University of Virginia and finish work for my A.B. degree. And I came here [Kentucky] from the University of Virginia.

BEATTIE: Why did you go to Virginia?

CLARK: I had an uncle who was on the staff at the university, my mother's brother; he was superintendent of schools in Albemarle County, and he didn't think I was getting a good education at Ole Miss. He wanted me to come to Virginia. I'll have to do a little bragging here. He didn't think I could do the work at the University of Virginia. He had a supercilious notion about Mississippi and Mississippians, despite the fact he'd come from there. And I went to work. I had a double challenge; one was not to let my university down and the other was not to let my uncle down. But, most of all, not to let *me* down. When I got my final grades, he went with me. I was uncertain about what kind of a record I had, and I knew that if I had a poor record I was going to a get a stern lecture. But I had an all-A record from Virginia, and that startled him. He offered to send me to medical school. If I'd go to medical school, he'd pay all my expenses. We were walking down that colonnade there on the lawn at Virginia when he said that, and I said, "No. I'm positively not medical school material. I have no interest whatsoever in studying medicine. I'd make a miserable doctor."

When I came here to the University of Kentucky, I was committed to going on in the field of history. But when I got off the train down here [Lexington] on September the 14th, 1928, I had no more idea of what was to become of me, of where my life might wind up, than the porter on the train. But I did get a glimmer of the future in history, several vistas. Number one, I concentrated strictly on the field of history, and that cultivated a further interest. The second thing, I became aware, at least, of the literature in the field of history. I became aware of what it meant to do research in history. And I became aware, also, of some of the personalities in the profession of history, some of the old lads who were the great men of their time.

I heard James H. Breasted, the famous Egyptologist, deliver his presidential address that December. Well, I didn't know how significant that would appear to me later on, but I look back on it and think what a wonderful opportunity that I was present at the American Historical Association when a panel discussed Ulrich Phillips's *Slavery*, the central theme in southern history. I sat just barely in front of him, where I could see him, and I heard his reply to that discussion. That was a monumental moment in history, and I talked with him. He gave me some advice about my master's thesis. My thesis was trade in livestock, slaves, and hemp between Kentucky and the lower South. And that was in Phillips's area of interest. I met other people there who, later on, I came to know fairly well. But, for a young boy who had never been north of the Ohio River and who was just beginning to get into the profession of history, that was a marvelous opportunity. Later on, I used to see young graduate students come along, and I never forgot the moment when I stood in their same shoes and could appreciate what they were seeing. Fortunately, the American Historical Association at that time was relatively small, and I could meet people there. I remember hearing a professor at the University of Iowa say his salary was so low that he was living in a house so small that he had to go outdoors to put his britches on. Well, that was not an encouraging fact about going into the profession. But, once I got through that year, I was committed to the profession.

I think life is made up of a great many fortuitous circumstances. In doing that research I had got myself familiar, in an elementary way, I suppose, or a cursory way, with the resources for historical research in this region. I went home. I had not graduated from the University of Mississippi. I graduated here [University of Kentucky] one day with a master's degree. I got on the train and rode to Oxford, Mississippi, and got there just as the commencement line was going. I was the last man on the totem pole going into the chapel, and I got my A.B. degree. I didn't spend much more than a couple of hours on the campus of the University of Mississippi on that trip. I went home, not knowing precisely what I was going to do that summer. I thought, as the train pulled out down Water Street, a blind [dead end] street here in Lexington, that, if I ever see this place again, it'll be too soon. I was not real happy here that first year. I found Kentuckians rather difficult. I had come from a very friendly, free, and easy southern atmosphere into this mixture of Bluegrass snobbery and mountain reticence, and I couldn't quite reconcile myself with either. I got a telegram asking me to come back, to make a calendar or a catalog of research materials within easy, accessible distance to the university. I spent that summer doing that.

I got a fellowship at Duke University. I went to Duke University and, well, let me come back just for a moment to that experience here during the summer of 1929. I became familiar with the resources in the state library, and the state historical society library, Transylvania, and over at Georgetown, and the Lexington Public Library, and some of the other resources. In that round I discovered that Centre College had a magnificent serial set of the federal documents and publications, a thing that was to benefit the University of Kentucky in the future greatly. I did not know anything about Duke University, except just what I'd read in the newspapers. I remember quite distinctly, in a course on education at the University of Mississippi, the old professor mentioned the fact that a rich person had endowed a school in North Carolina to be called Duke University. That's almost all I knew about Duke University. I made application there without knowing anything about the professors. And I entered there in September of 1929. They had produced, up to that point, only one Ph.D., a man named Ralph Flanders, who spent his life at New York University.

I entered Duke University in those very, very interesting transitional years, when it was growing out of being a small, religious, Methodist school, Trinity College, and trying to become a major university. They had books stacked up in there, the basement of the Trinity College Library, just in windows. They were furiously building their library. They had rebuilt Trinity College, and that's where

I lived the first year and had classes. They were building that grand campus, their West campus, on that grand design of an English university, really, with that gothic limestone. There was a real fermentation there. There was a real stirring, an intellectual and physical stirring. That was an exciting time to be there. My major professor was so busy building the library that I formed almost no real personal association with him. I never did, as a matter of fact, although I owe a great deal to him.

BEATTIE: Who was this?

CLARK: William Kenneth Boyd. He was a man who never published much. He was too busy building the foundation for Duke University's history department. He was head of the Department of History.

I was at Duke University less than two years for my doctorate. I took my generals in March, I believe, of 1931, and I accepted a job teaching at the University of Tennessee in that quarter. That was not my first teaching experience. My first teaching experience was in what's now Memphis State University, in the summer of 1930. But I taught that spring quarter at the University of Tennessee. And, just by the grace of God, I got this appointment here. I was appointed here [University of Kentucky] by the president, not by the Department of History. President McVey, in his own personal hand, wrote me about my appointment. I came to the University of Kentucky to help develop a library and also to be an instructor in the Department of History. My wife-to-be was on the library staff at Duke University. She had graduated from Greenville Woman's College, which is now Furman University.

BEATTIE: What was her maiden name?

CLARK: Elizabeth Turner. And she went to Simmons College in Boston in library training, and she got a job in the new Duke University Library. That's where I met her. Graduate students and librarians were thrown into close association. We were married in 1933, not long after I came here to be on the faculty.

These were Depression years that I'm talking about. These were hard years in which you fought like a tiger just to hold on. I don't think people realize how biting and pinching the Great Depression was and what grim futures faced young academicians. I know many a time I walked with one or two of my classmates up that long walk going into Duke University, the main drive, worrying our heads off about where we were going to get jobs, where our lives were going to wind up. But, I came here, as I said a moment ago, thoroughly dedicated to the profession of historian, and I've never turned back on that. I've never had any desire to be anything else *but* a historian. And I came with a deep appreciation that it was one thing to stand in a class and peddle secondary information. It was an altogether different thing to get out and do some original work yourself. And I had, I suppose, that yen to write, and I did.

BEATTIE: I know you can't tell how much comes from your own personality and how much doesn't, but did you have professors that felt the same way, who did a lot of original research?

CLARK: Yes, I had professors who did original research. But, like all my experiences with academic colleagues, I had a lot of professors who talked a good line but never delivered much. But I had some—Sydnor, for instance—who was a distinguished historian who wrote some landmark books. Here at the University of Kentucky, when I worked on my master's degree, I did not have a single publishing scholar. None of the professors I had published anything.

BEATTIE: Which was more typical in those days than now.

CLARK: That's right. It's almost impossible to say just exactly what kind of bug bit you and why. But in doing that survey here, on literature in this region, I saw so many potentials for writing and research. I still do.

BEATTIE: That project was fortuitous in launching you and your writing career, wasn't it?

CLARK: Very much, yes. When I came to Lexington, I already had the bug to write from that experience on that student newspaper and from the writing in courses that I had, and then from going to graduate school for my doctorate. I wrote a long, dull dissertation on the building of railroads in the South prior to 1860. I published two books, *The Beginning of the L&N* and *A Pioneer Southern Railroad from New Orleans to Cairo.* But I lost interest in railroad history almost immediately and turned my interest to a thing that I've never departed widely from, the western movement in American history. I got interested in Kentucky because, when I came here, eventually I had to teach Kentucky history and there was no textbook. And I got busy and prepared a book, or started that book, [*History of Kentucky*], back in 1932. Published it in 1937. And it's gone through, what, four or five editions? I don't know how many. It's out of print now.

I got that off and also wrote an elementary book, *Exploring Kentucky,* which was used for many years in elementary school. But my real interest set forth on the writing of a book that got wonderful reviews and would have had a real good sale had not the paper shortage of World War II killed it dead in its tracks. That was *The Rampaging Frontier.* I see that listed in bibliographies all alone, and that book went through, oh, two or three, maybe four, editions. Then, I had so many interests and saw so many things that could be done.

BEATTIE: You were how old when your first book was published?

CLARK: I was thirty years old when I published my first book. I was thirty-five years old when the Kentucky history was published.

BEATTIE: Of the more than twenty books you've authored and edited, do you have a favorite?

CLARK: No, I don't, really. The railroad books I look on with a great deal of tenderness, because they were my first books. I'd do them differently now, if I were doing them. But, that goes with the trade. I enjoyed doing the river book *[The Kentucky],* which got marvelous reviews, and it's coming back into print. Certainly, I enjoyed writing *Pills, Petticoats and Plows,* which has gone through I don't know how many editions. It's still in print. I guess I'll go to my grave with people remembering that, about as much as anything I've ever done. Of course, my big book, *Frontier America,* I'm glad I did. *The Emerging South,* I did that book just at that feverish moment after *Brown vs. Board of Education.* And *Kentucky, Land of Contrast,* I think, is a book that I will never be sorry I did. And, oh, you don't have favorites. You do these books and it's like a woman who's in this constant state of pregnancy. You get rid of one and there's another one in the womb.

I want to mention something that I did, and I think it will outlive me. I hope it will. I edited that six volumes of *Southern Travels (American Exploration and Travel Series),* which, I think I can say, with some modesty, is an important work. The University of Oklahoma Press agreed to publish that, and the Rockefeller Foundation gave us some seed money. I spent one whale of a lot of time on that. There was a lot of creative writing in that six-volume work. I think a lot of people think of my writing, and they don't realize that that book is there. And then, of course, a back-breaking job—oh, my Lord, an enormous, challenging job—was that four-volume history of Indiana University *[Indiana University, Midwestern Pioneer].* But I must not have done a good job on that, because I have yet to have had a complaint about it. I know there's something wrong with it.

BEATTIE: Is there a book you would like to have written, but haven't?

CLARK: Oh, yes. Yes, sirree, there's a book I would have liked to have written. That is a *big* book. I would have liked to have written a big book in American history, a seminal book. I think I would have liked to have written a book that would have been a landmark, national book, a book that would have had a tremendous national impact. I would have liked to have written a book, for instance, of the scope and stature of Dumas Malone's *Jefferson and His Time.* I would have liked to have written a book of the stature of Phillips's *Life and Labor in the Old South,* or a biography of the distinction of Bob [Robert] Remini's *Andrew Jackson.*

BEATTIE: When you write your books, who are you primarily writing for? Historians or lay people or both?

CLARK: Never for historians. I've stayed away from that. That's an abomination in the sight of God, historians writing for historians. That's digging a corpse up out of one grave and burying him in another. No, I have an interested reader in my writing. I've always seen some faces across the typewriter, just ordinary people.

BEATTIE: So you have an audience in mind.

CLARK: That's right. I think an historian has an obligation, not to his profession. If you're writing a professional book, like compiling a professional book like *Travels in the Old South,* you do have a lot of people in mind, the users of all sorts, seekers after information. But in writing *Pills, Petticoats and Plows,* I had two people in mind. I had the person who had a sentimental, emotional view of the rural South, and I also had in mind a very important chapter in southern development, and that is that old furnishing system that sustained the southern agrarian system and southern society after the Civil War. In *The Southern Country Editor* I had in mind the influence of the editor on the development of the southern mind, and the southern reaction to political issues, economic issues, the source of information, and the source of entertainment, the development of viewpoints of the southern population, and I was writing back to those people. I was writing back to the readers who, again, were agrarian, rural-oriented. And if the historians found them useful, so be it. But I wasn't writing to the historians. A lot of historians *do* write to historians.

BEATTIE: Are you working on any writing projects now? Do you have any planned for the future?

CLARK: Right now I'm up to my eyeballs in this editing of the Bradford notes, with a deadline that would kill a mule. In 1826 John Bradford, first editor, first newspaperman in Kentucky—publisher of *The Kentucky Gazette,* which came out on August the 11th, 1787—was also a pioneer. He was very actively engaged in many of the events in Kentucky development from 1775 down to the time of his death in 1830. He was an active participant, an active viewer of the scene. Certainly, as a newspaper editor, he was a very active viewer, but he'd been a land surveyor; he'd been a soldier. He had been at all kinds of political things. He was chairman of the Board of Trustees of the town of Lexington, who welcomed Issac Shelby to Lexington when Shelby became first governor of Kentucky, and they organized state government here. I'm sure, without having documentary proof of it—and I doubt that's available or ever was available—I'm sure that Bradford read Jefferson's notes on Virginia. I'm sure he was influenced by those notes. There's just too much internal evidence of that fact. He started in September of 1826 publishing notes in *The Kentucky Gazette.* He had resumed editorship of that paper. And, in many issues, he published sometimes a column of reminiscent or historical material. Sometimes he quoted from documents; sometimes he quoted from notes that people had given him. He says that he had at hand a great many notes. [Humphrey] Marshall's *History of Kentucky* and [John] Filson's history are just about the only published sources he had available. He gives a good insight in those notes into the almost day-by-day progression of the Anglo-American settlement of this region, and a very monstrous conflict, the Indian conflict. He's almost obsessed with the Indian conflict. And that requires a great deal of looking into corroborating sources. Not original sources for Bradford, but corroborative sources to see that Bradford is on track with his information. He was obsessed with the idea that future generations would not appreciate the hardships of the pioneers. And [Daniel] Boone, [Simon] Kenton, or all those people that contributed to the [Lymon] Draper manuscripts, the Draper sources of information, were obsessed with the idea that future generations would not appreciate their monumental accomplishments. That thread runs throughout, and I'm getting that ready for publication in the bicentennial year.

One thing I have done, I have been involved heavily in the production of this encyclopedia of Kentucky history [*The Kentucky Encyclopedia*], contributing eighty-some articles and writing the overview article. That was a monumental writing task itself. On Sunday morning, if I'm still around on that day, I'll be eighty-eight years old, and an eighty-eight-year-old man doesn't even buy green bananas. He can dream of doing another book, but getting it done is another matter.

BEATTIE: What do you get out of writing that you don't get out of teaching?

CLARK: God knows what you get out of writing. I don't know.

BEATTIE: Other than publication.

CLARK: There's a mean wench in your life when you become a writer. I think this must be generally true of every writer, that you never quite reach that point of satisfaction. You're always dissatisfied with what you've done. Maybe there is no such thing as soul satisfaction. There's always a feeling of inadequacy. And I've been dogged by that feeling.

BEATTIE: What about when you re-read books that you wrote years ago? Are you able to read them objectively?

CLARK: Yes. You have two reactions to your own books. One is, "I wish I could do that all over again." But when you say that, you must remember that several books have gone under the bridge, and you've matured in perspective and new sources of information have been uncovered and are now available, which were not available to you. My *History of Kentucky,* for instance. Look at the slender resources I had in 1931, compared with the resources you have now. State Archives have been developed. The State Historical Society has improved its collection enormously. The Filson Club has grown. The University of Kentucky, at the time I started, could not have supported the writing of a chapter, let alone a book. Or look at the Special Collections now. Enormously important now, not in existence then. Look at the books that have been published since then, biographies of Boone, biographies of Benjamin Logan, biographies of Simon Kenton, for instance, or the special books that are opening broad vistas that were not then available.

BEATTIE: Have you changed some of your points of view, then?

CLARK: Yes, I have. I hope I've grown intellectually over these years. I would look at the Kentucky political system with a great deal more maturity, I think, than I had then, and a great deal more understanding. I would look at the development of constitutional government with some new perspective. I would look at the role of women, for instance. Women were enormously important. There were pioneer women who made major contributions. There were women all along the line. The state couldn't have existed without the contribution of women, but I would treat them in the context of Kentuckians, or of the collective society. And I would look at slavery differently. I would look at the contribution of blacks differently, not segregating them and treating them as an unrelated part of the whole. They were part of the whole structure, and I would try to treat them as they fitted into that.

BEATTIE: Do you believe a lot of the movements now, which are ostensibly intended to achieve equality, actually segregate more?

CLARK: I think so. I think, as I read these modern works and see these reactions, we're fabulists, and I think we're creating a segregated extreme on the one hand, where we didn't treat those things as fairly in the past as we should have. We're going to the extreme, on the other hand. I've always thought there was a sensible middle ground on which to stand. I would not want to be interpreted in this interview as being anti-feminist or racist, because I certainly am not. I used to say to my classes, "Young women, one of you can make a whale of a reputation if you'll get busy and write a good book on women." And, doing this editing of these Bradford notes, I came on so many references to the role of women that the pioneering movement never could have succeeded without women. And I say that very conscientiously and, I hope, from the perspective of basic source knowledge. But I'm not an extremist. I've always been, I hope, a middle grounder. I'm not anti-Indian. The Indians had a point of view, and that's one thing I have to deal with in this Bradford thing. We wrote the history, but the Indians had a point of view, and it definitely must be presented, and I'm going to try to present that viewpoint as honestly and as faithfully as I can. It's hard to be objective. That's the greatest challenge that a writer of history faces, I think, is being objective, being comprehensive and objective. I've had three students that justified my going into the field of teaching, those three alone. I think Harry Caudill, in his *Night Comes to the Cumberlands,* wrote a book that any author would be proud just to fold his hands on and rest on that laurel. Harry wrote other books, *Theirs Be the Power* and *The Moguls,* and these whimsical little books, *The Lord and the Miner [The Mountain, the Miner and the Lord],* that's not a whimsical book. But Harry awakened not only Kentucky, but a nation, to a situation that's as pressing this morning as any issue in Kentucky could be: Appalachia. Oh, downstream there's another seminal author. I disagree with him, always, but I admire him enormously. He is a seminal person. He's always pursuing beyond an unrealistic dream, [Henry David] Thoreau and the land: Wendell Berry. Wendell Berry is an important seminal author, and he's contributed mightily to the literature of this period. In his way, John Ed Pearce has made major contributions. I look back—had all three of those boys in class, and they are people that Kentucky can be proud of.

We've come light miles away in the literature, but we've got light miles to go. There's no history of agriculture of the state. There's no good history of women in the state. George C. Wright has made major contributions in the field of black history in Kentucky. There is no history of the horse industry, which right now is in deep trouble. Or, there's no history of the cattle industry in Kentucky, and it's just crying to be done. There's a need for a good history of transportation. If you want to be specialized, just write about the highway system alone.

BEATTIE: In terms of education and of how history should be taught, I was wondering how you feel about writers who not only tell what actual historical figures were doing in the past, which they verify factually, but what they were thinking and how they were feeling.

CLARK: Let's go back to something that you're introducing here. The dedicated historian is dedicated to trying to find the truth, trying to establish as much of the truth as he can, be it favorable, palatable, or unpalatable. Historians should not have any morals whatsoever, should be thoroughly immoral in their attitudes. In this sense, the historian's not there to pass judgment; let St. Peter do that. He's there to try to find what the facts were and to interpret those facts with as much intelligence as he can muster. He's not there as a moral judge sitting in on the case. Yet, he has an obligation not only to dig up the facts, but to organize them in some fashion so that they'll have some chronological significance, some sequential significance, or some intelligible consequence. He can never reconstruct a scene. You can't reconstruct the last hour, in my opinion. But you don't have to eat all of an egg to know whether or not it's a good egg. In the use of documents, in the use of personal correspondence, and in the use of editorial comments, all sorts of sources, you can pretty well construct what happened in a reasonable form that will give you a sense of the flow and of the course of human events. It would be a very foolish historian to write and say, "These are the facts, this is what happened," and say it with a conclusive position. He doesn't know.

BEATTIE: You're even talking about some things that might be in the realm of fact, as well as in the realm of human nature, or in the realm of human psychology.

CLARK: That's right. I'm speaking of getting into the minds and the thought processes of individuals. The places where people reveal most intimately their thoughts or, at the same time, conceal their thoughts, be it said both ways, are in personal letters and diaries, diaries that are kept with no view to publication. Beware of a diary that's written with a view to publication. Sometimes in speeches, newspaper interviews, what not, you get an insight into the proceedings. But you know when you're dealing with proceedings of organizations of all kinds—political, governmental, religious, any kind—you oftentimes are dealing with facts that have been accomplished, and what you have to do is go behind that to see what influenced the arrival at those facts. The historian can only do the best he can. It depends on how sound his own judgment is. Maybe his moral attitude is toward handling those facts, or how conscientious he is.

BEATTIE: At least one school of biography tends to say not only was Daniel Boone or Napoleon or Lincoln or whomever it may be, not only was he here, but this is what he was feeling when he committed a particular action. You wouldn't endorse that school of writing.

CLARK: No. You don't know whether their digestive system is out of order, you don't know whether they are depressed in mind, you don't know whether they were over-optimistic or over-jubilant about something. There are all those things. You're not a psychologist, and a psychologist is not God. I want to touch on one source that a historian has to work with. He would be woefully handicapped did he not have a newspaper press. But no historians have ever yet really come up with a good sound answer as to how substantial a newspaper is as a source of information. Yet we depend on them, we quote them, and I've seen many a newspaper reporter come and go, and I've seen them make all kinds of blunders. You know what they said was not true. And they'll tell you they have to grab a story and run. They don't have time to go behind all these things; they're space confined and time confined. And politicians. You take a speech of a politician, it may be that's what he thought, but it may be just the opposite. He may be obscuring everything he can.

BEATTIE: We talked about, when you were going through school, your being asked to write about history constantly, and so many students today are only asked to fill in the blanks or circle multiple choice questions for historical factual knowledge without reflecting on what any of it means.

CLARK: I never knew whether I was a good teacher or not, but I used to go to class and hold this up and say, "That's the one thing that makes a difference between you and a monkey."

BEATTIE: The pen.

CLARK: That one instrument right there. That's the thing that challenges your mind to write intelligently, cohesively, or comprehensively. But, most of all, writing is stating as clearly as you can your thoughts.

BEATTIE: And would you say it's important not only to write the facts about what happened, but to write an essay somehow reflecting on those facts or interpreting them and making some sort of sense of them?

CLARK: If you write something, number one, students have to be able to state their thoughts in some form or other—something they've maybe never done before, something that would reveal to them possibilities they didn't know they had. Second, you've got to have some information to write about. That necessitates your going and digging up something. And the third thing, you have to undergo review in the matter of instruction, if the professor's conscientious. Then that student should get the benefit of criticism. And finally—and this is one of the things connected with authorship—there's the joy of having expressed yourself. And, later on, you don't have to get somebody to write a letter of application for you, you don't have to get somebody to tell you how to dig up facts, you don't have to get somebody to tell you how to write something, some instructions or what-not. They don't have to tell you the joy that comes with the labor of writing.

I think one of the things that maybe takes an author on is the fact that there's some soul-satisfying thing about writing. I'm quite serious. That's one of several means, possibly, but that's the one major means of drawing an individual out intellectually. That's the one way to mature the intellectual process. As a professor in the classroom, I never gave one of those damn, so-called objective tests. That was bull of the first order. I never gave those. I just abhor that kind of thing. That's one of the reasons we're in the mess we're in in education today. In every course where this could be applied, I never let a student get out without writing a paper, a paper of length, because I was trying to develop in them some originality, some skill at applying knowledge. Knowledge isn't worth a damn if you don't know how to apply it. Another point I want to make is, in the teaching of history, you're always dealing with youthful minds in school, people who've had no experience, or not much experience, who have not much perspective. All their perspectives are anticipatory, not back looks. And the best you can do is to stimulate in them an interest that will grow in the future. I used to tell my students, "What I'm saying to you now, these facts won't mean a whole lot to you, ever, but we have to deal with them in order for you to get a sense of what's happened. But, as you grow older and become more mature, the challenge of learning something about the past will grow, will become greater.

BEATTIE: Either in teaching or in writing, what have you found interests people in history who may not have been interested in it before?

CLARK: Oh, I think the human incidents. I think a good teacher of history will never forget the humanity of the subject, and a little touch of humor helps. It's a lubricant that helps things along.

BEATTIE: Are there trends in writing about history now, on the national or international scene, that you'd like to comment on?

CLARK: Yes. I think these young historians are going haywire right now. Maybe I'm looking at it from an age-old perspective that's out of date. Maybe I'm an archaic historian. But I think we're generating books just by the hundreds, literally by the thousands. I almost don't go to the professional meetings anymore, but I recently went to the one in Louisville, and the publishers were there with literally thousands of books. Who in the name of God is going to read all of these books and, *if* they read them, would they pay mind to them anyway? And the libraries are just being stacked tight. I was in the stacks yesterday, just rows and rows and rows of books. I wondered who takes those books down and reads them. They're there. They're not out. That's self-evident. I think our young historians are taking an adversarial position. They're crusading right now—women, Indians, blacks, urban dwellers. We're shifting over from an age of old agrarian historians or agrarian background to urban historians.

BEATTIE: So instead of sweeping histories of the continents or cultures, you're seeing compartmentalized, ethnocized histories.

CLARK: Quite true. And all the colleagues that I've talked with seem to be disturbed in the same way. In correspondence that I have with old colleagues, they're disturbed about it. The journals are just full of this stuff.

BEATTIE: How much of that do you think is the fault of, or the cause of, universities and colleges that force people to publish or perish?

CLARK: Oh, I think that it's like injecting cancer cells into the academic system, that publish or perish. May I make a personal reference here? I obviously, desperately, needed to get an advance in salary, because I started at a very low salary, and my economic situation for years was just touch-and-go. I always wanted to be promoted, and one way to do that was to establish yourself as a scholar. But I would hate to think that that was the only objective I had for writing. I think I could say, with a fair degree of truth, that I had an urge, really. You don't write books, you don't sit down those long nights and long days, and you don't forgo the things that ordinary human beings do—you don't go to plays, you don't go to musical events, you don't go to amusement parks—you don't do all those things, you don't go tearing around and still write books. You just can't do it. And if your only objective is getting promoted and advancing your economic situation, that would be as empty an objective as I can imagine. I do not remember two things. I do not remember ever really being concerned about tenure. I just don't have any recollection of that. Nor do I remember when I got tenure. And I just barely remember when I got promoted from instructor to assistant professor, after about four or five years service, which was an unusually long period. Then I got promoted to associate professor in a rather short time. And, just by circumstance, I was made professor when I was made head of the Department of History. As a young professor, I was promoted to a full professorship. I had not been concerned about that. Then I was promoted to distinguished professor, and that was something I had never anticipated. They just created those ten professorships and I got one of them.

BEATTIE: Talking about all the thousands of books being generated each year, is there any way of your knowing, because nobody could possibly read all these, their general quality? Do you think their quality has gone down, or do you think they are good, scholarly works?

CLARK: Oh, I think the young historians are better researchers than we were. We were diligent, but they have more time. Universities have research funds, and younger professors are not teaching the heavy loads that we taught. And they have better libraries, better facilities. Take, for instance, these copying machines. I went over yesterday and took some notes in ten minutes that once would have taken me three hours. I can just dash them off like that. And microfilm. You can bring the world to your desk in microfilm.

BEATTIE: And you don't have to travel as much.

CLARK: That's right. In gathering notes for *Pills, Petticoats, and Plows,* I traveled thousands of miles and, in gathering materials for *Southern Country Editor,* I traveled—heavens above, I have no knowledge how much I traveled. Or in doing that travel series, I traveled a lot in connection with it. And all my other books. *The Kentucky River,* I traveled an astonishing number of miles for it. I know nothing about computers. Everybody tells me those things are wonderful, but I'm too far gone to get into that. But the facilities are just so much. Imagine a young instructor in 1931 in a university that had a library that had almost just nothing, really—just imagine setting out to be a historian in that kind of situation.

BEATTIE: Even though it's easier today to have materials sent to you from anywhere in the world, and ostensibly you're able to write a book in your own home without ever leaving it, do you think that people who do this may also lose something from not traveling to sources?

CLARK: Let me point out that when I left Washington, D.C., doing research on my dissertation, they were just breaking ground for the National Archives.

BEATTIE: So you preceded the Archives themselves.

CLARK: That's right. And only since 1958 have we been in business with the State Archives in Kentucky. If I were a young historian, I'd certainly go to the National Archives and work. I worked in the Huntington Library twice. It was marvelous. The Library of Congress, oh heavens above. You never know when you'll turn the page what's going to turn up on the next page. You never know what's going to stimulate an idea.

BEATTIE: And also, being on site helps you find things that have been catalogued incorrectly, on occasion.

CLARK: That's right. There's nothing like turning that page yourself. I like to feel it, smell it, see it. Microfiche, that's sort of an hygienic process.

BEATTIE: What about not just the quantity of books being turned out today in history, or the quality, but what about trends in writing styles? Not that everybody is writing the same way, but do you have anything to say about that?

CLARK: I have mixed feelings about the quality of writing. Some of these young historians write in a pretty dead, static style. Not many times do you come on a book now that has real literary quality.

BEATTIE: To what do you attribute that?

CLARK: To graduate training, graduate seminars. Too many fleas have be-gotten fleas, and too many professors were trained in the old methods of get the facts, drag them in, and stake them down as best you can.

BEATTIE: Do you think there's a fear of adding style to writing? That add-ing style would somehow detract from the scientific nature of the beast?

CLARK: I'm sure that's a lot of it. Too many graduate seminars, too many stylistics, too many *Chicago Manuals of Style.*

BEATTIE: What incident or historical occurrence in the past decade or so do you think will emerge as something very significant in the future? I know there are millions of them, but something that you think may not have been covered the way it should have been.

CLARK: Oh. You threw me a curve there in that last statement. There are a lot of areas that need investigation. I think in the twentieth century we've had a lot of writing. The library's full of the impact of world wars changing the course of American civilization, of all civilization. I think one of the things that'll be impor-tant is the international position of history, writing from the world viewpoint. I think we'll go on writing in the field of civil rights, looking at the application of the Bill of Rights on the Constitution, on the due process of law. I think an area, which is a frontier indeed, is the urbanization of American society, or world society. Then, two big topics that will figure prominently in the past and in the approaching future, one is communication—instant communication—and the other is the distribution of world products in an effort to make sure all the people on this globe somewhere or other have just basic food to put in their bellies. Those, I think, are important things.

BEATTIE: I also wanted to ask you about your writing habits. Do you compose longhand or on a typewriter?

CLARK: I can do it both ways. But, generally, I have a lap board and I sit down with that across my lap and rough it out in longhand. Then I take a typewriter and rough it out some more. Then I begin the refining process and the cutting and adding. I go through five or six drafts before I'm satisfied.

BEATTIE: Is there a certain time of day that you work, and do you work regularly on one project, or on several at the same time?

CLARK: I snatched desperately for sixty years for time. I should be at that lap board right now. I write at night a great deal. Fortunately, I'm not temperamental. I take it as it comes, and I can lay something on my desk and go teach a class and come back and pick it up. But I have the ability to sit down and stay with it once I get started. I have determination to get it done. That's what it takes. And I have, I hope, but I sometimes question this, pretty good research ability. But, sometimes, when I come on things that I should have known fifty years ago that are brand new to me, I wonder if I'm just plain stupid.

BEATTIE: I doubt it. What advice would you give an aspiring writer?

CLARK: Put his pants on, sit down on them, and stay down on them.

BEATTIE: Just write, huh?

CLARK: Sure. Don't wait for the muse to come sit with you, because she's off flirting with somebody else. Get a topic well-formulated in your mind first, then explore—explore, explore, explore what the sources are and what side you might be able to use. Then begin taking those notes. Take those notes, notes, and notes. Half of them you may throw away, but who knows? There may be one bit of knowledge there that will mean a whole page to you. I just accidentally came on a line day before yesterday that gave me an entirely new perspective on this thing I'm doing.

BEATTIE: What was that?

CLARK: That possibly John Bradford was stimulated to do his notes by Jefferson's notes in Virginia. I don't know why I felt just plain dumb when I read that. I should have thought that in the beginning. But, you never know, one thing leads to another. I said, a while ago, you never know what the next page you turn will reveal to you. And there's a certain excitement of the hunt. I get a thrill out of searching for things. I would say, just concluding this, that there's always a yearning in an author's heart that he write a better book. And he doesn't know how to do that, really. Some books come off better than others. I take deep satisfaction in having tried. And I take deep satisfaction in having taught. When I meet old students now, just to have them greet you warmly, those reactions are cheering. And I take deep satisfaction in having had a career as a historian. If I had that choice to make now, I'd make the same choice. I have no regrets in that respect. I wish I'd been a better teacher, wish I'd been a better author. I wish I could have done more things.

July 12, 1991

Clark's wife, Elizabeth Turner Clark, died on July 30, 1995. On November 29, 1996, Clark married Loretta Gilliam of Lexington, Kentucky. Since 1991 Clark has continued to write and publish. In addition to the publication of his *History of Clark County,* in 1996 Clark had published by the University of Oklahoma Press a new edition of *The Old Southwest, 1795–1830, Frontiers in Conflict,* a book Clark co-edited with John D. W. Guice. In 1997, at the invitation of the directors of the Center for the Book at the Library of Congress, Clark participated in a panel discussion honoring the sixtieth anniversary of the *Rivers of America Series.* Annually, at events throughout Kentucky, Clark continues to be honored as the Commonwealth's pre-eminent historian.

BOOKS BY THOMAS D. CLARK

The Beginning of the L&N: The Development of the Louisville and Nashville Railroad and its Memphis Branches from 1836–1860. Louisville, Ky.: Standard Printing Co., 1933.

A Pioneer Southern Railroad From New Orleans to Cairo. Chapel Hill: The University of North Carolina Press, 1936.

A History of Kentucky. New York: Prentice-Hall, 1937.

The Rampaging Frontier: Manners and Humors of Pioneer Days in the South and the Middle West. Indianapolis, Ind.: Bobbs-Merrill, 1939.

Pills, Petticoats, and Plows; The Southern Country Store. Indianapolis, Ind.: Bobbs-Merrill, 1944.

Travels in the Confederate States (American Exploration and Travel Series). (general editor). Norman: University of Oklahoma Press, 1948.

The Rural Press and the New South. Baton Rouge: Louisiana State University Press, 1948.

Travels in the Old South. (3 vols.) (American Exploration and Travel Series). (general editor). Norman: University Press, 1950–1959.

The Southern Country Editor. Indianapolis: Bobbs-Merrill, 1948.

Travels in the New South (2 vols.) (American Exploration and Travel Series). (general editor). Norman: University of Oklahoma Press, 1962.

Indiana University, Midwestern Pioneer. (Four Volumes). Bloomington: Indiana University Press, 1970–1977.

South Carolina: the Grand Tour, 1780–1865. (editor). Columbia: University of South Carolina Press, 1973.

Off at Sunrise: The Overland Journal of Charles Glass Gray. San Marino, Ca.: The Huntington Library, 1976.

Agrarian Kentucky: That Far-Off Land. Lexington: The University Press of Kentucky, 1979.

A History of Laurel County: An Account of the Emergence of a Frontier Kentucky Appalachian Community into a Modern Commercial-Industrial Rural-Urban Center. London, Ky.: Laurel County Historical Society, 1989.

Footloose in Jacksonian America: Robert W. Scott and His Agrarian World. Frankfort: The Kentucky Historical Society, 1989.

JOHN EGERTON

EGERTON: I am John Walden Egerton, and I was born in Atlanta, Georgia, on June the 14th, 1935. My father's name was Graham Egerton. He was a traveling salesman, sort of a Willy Loman character, Tennessee born, lived most of his life in the South. My mother's name was Rebecca White Egerton. She was from Cadiz, Kentucky. Her father was a miller in Cadiz. She went to college at Sullins College in Bristol, Virginia, right on the Tennessee border. I was the fifth and final child to come along. By the time I was born, in 1935, the family was in Atlanta, but they had lived in probably a dozen different places in those thirteen or fourteen years.

BEATTIE: What can you tell me about your grandparents?

EGERTON: I had an interesting two sets of grandparents. On my father's side, my grandfather and grandmother both died in the '20s, so I never knew them. He was an Englishman. He was born in Bombay, India. His father was in the British Civil Service and lived for years in India; my grandfather was born there in 1862. He ended up trying to go to medical school at Edinburgh, Scotland. He couldn't make the grade; he flunked out. At the time, the English novelist Thomas Hughes—who was a member of Parliament and a social reformer—was involved with some people from Boston in trying to found a colony in America that would serve as a kind of a symbol of the reunification of Britain and the United States after the Civil War. Thomas Hughes ended up coming to east Tennessee with a group of these investors and buying a piece of land in a county up on the Cumberland plateau and starting a colony there called Rugby, which was named after *Tom Brown's School Days,* a private school he went to in England, The Rugby School. My grandfather was one of the early settlers there. He came there as an eighteen-year-old boy to help build that Christian socialist colony in east Tennessee. Like most utopias, it fell on hard times. The remnants of it are still there as a little restored village. But, back in those days, it struggled through hard times, and essentially closed within a few years. As an ongoing community, it pretty much ceased to exist around the turn of the century.

BEATTIE: What did your grandfather do after that?

EGERTON: He came west, eventually to Dickson County in middle Tennessee, where he studied law under a lawyer, and then eventually went to the law school at Lebanon, Tennessee, called Cumberland Law School. He got a degree and was a practicing attorney for a good number of years. He ended up in 1913 going to Washington to be a solicitor in the Navy Department. My grandmother was a Dickson County farmer's daughter.

Now, on the other side, my mother's parents were both natives of Trigg County, Kentucky. Both of them were old families there that went back several generations, back to around the beginning of Trigg County in the 1820s. My grandfather, the miller, was a wonderful man. He was an inventor. He came up with all kinds of wonderful gadgets that he created—fish traps and tools of various kinds. He was a builder and a dreamer.

BEATTIE: What about your brothers and sisters?

EGERTON: My oldest sister died before I was born. Then I had two more sisters, who are still living now. I have one brother, Graham Egerton, who's nearest my age. He's a stockbroker in Baltimore. He lived in Kentucky for quite a number of years before he moved.

BEATTIE: Would you tell me about your childhood, where it was spent, what it was like?

EGERTON: We moved to Cadiz when I was a month old, from Atlanta, so all of my childhood years are associated with Cadiz and Trigg County, a little farming community in western Kentucky, maybe a thousand people at that time. Wonderful place to grow up, the kind of place where you could get up on a summer morning and eat a good breakfast and tell your mom goodbye and get on your bicycle and be gone all day.

BEATTIE: What do you remember about your elementary school days?

EGERTON: I went to the Cadiz Grade School for six years. Actually, I skipped the second grade, because I had what was diagnosed as tuberculosis and was ordered to stay out of school and stay at home and rest, which seemed like an impossibility then and now.

I had pretty wonderful childhood years in school there. I remember some of my teachers very fondly, people who gave me encouragement. Mrs. Grace Hall in the fifth grade was one. And Mabel Sexton was another one. They were local women in the thankless job of "school marm" to a bunch of unruly kids who didn't know much and learned by accident maybe more than any other way. It wasn't a terribly good school system.

BEATTIE: Did you have a favorite subject?

EGERTON: I was always interested in reading and writing. Those interests did start pretty early for me. That year I missed school, when I was in second grade, my mother—in a desperate effort to find something to occupy me—came up with the idea of creating a newspaper that she would mimeograph. She had a little mimeograph machine that she did the church bulletin on. So we designed a newspaper that was essentially gossip from the kids at school, who would come see me after school and tell me what was going on. I would write it up and put it in this paper. It was great fun, and I sent those issues back to school and all the kids loved it. Of course, it had my byline all over it, and I got totally consumed by the egotistical love of seeing my name in print. By the time I was in the sixth grade, I was writing for the *Cadiz Record,* which is the local weekly. I started writing up the high school football games.

BEATTIE: To have a sixth grader doing it is pretty unusual, isn't it?

EGERTON: It didn't seem unusual at the time.

BEATTIE: You must have been a good writer at an early age.

EGERTON: No, I read *The Courier-Journal,* and I knew how Earl Ruby wrote sports for *The Courier-Journal,* and I just blatantly imitated and stole all the cliches and the adjectives and whatnot. Even if I didn't understand them, I used them. I did it through high school. I did the student annual and all that, so, by the time I got out of high school, I had pretty much figured out in my own mind that that was what I most enjoyed doing. But I couldn't articulate in any formal sense what that meant.

BEATTIE: Did you enjoy reading as well?

EGERTON: Yes, I liked to read. That year I was sick, my grandmother read books to me. There was a wonderful book called *Ungava Bob.* It was sort of a *Call of the Wild*-type book, Canadian wolves and dogs and trappers and all that stuff I thought was wonderful. I loved reading that.

BEATTIE: Did your parents read to you as you were growing up?

EGERTON: Yes, both of them liked to read. My father liked to read and, I think, would have liked to have written, too.

My mother enjoyed reading. She was so busy trying to raise a family pretty much on her own, because my father was gone so much. Reading was a luxury she didn't have much time for. So, I did well to get through the usual childhood books. I certainly wouldn't say that reading really defined my character in those early years.

I went to Western Kentucky University right out of high school, for a year. That was right at the end of the Korean War. At the end of that year, I was pretty uncertain about what I wanted to do, and I had an English teacher at Western, Justine Lynn, who was a sister of Mabel Sexton, who had been one of my high school teachers. And Justine was a wonderful woman. She inspired me to write and do more with words. She got me more interested in reading and writing, and I think of her as someone that I owe a real debt to. But at the end of that year, I didn't know what I was doing there or why I was there, and it seemed to make sense for me to go ahead and get my military obligation over. So I went ahead and volunteered for the draft and went into the service. I graduated from high school in '53, so I spent the next year at Western and in '54 went in the army, and spent two years in the army.

I was in Germany most of the time. I had a clerical job. I ended up writing a little history of the regiment I was in. I traveled a lot and I enjoyed that, saw Europe. I came back in '56 and went to UK [University of Kentucky], where I remained for the next four years and got a couple of degrees. I got a B.A. in what was called a topical major. I was in the J [journalism] school mainly, but not in the journalism curriculum. I was taking some PR courses. My degree was in Public Relations. It involved a special kind of tailored curriculum that included some history and some philosophy and other liberal arts courses, as well as journalism. English, of course. And I finished that degree in '58 and stayed there and worked in the PR office for a year and then for the Kentucky Research Foundation for a year as a writer and editor. I also got a master's degree in political science during that time. So, by 1960, I quit being a student for good. I got married in '57 to Ann Bleidt from Trigg County. We'd gone to high school together. We had courted a little bit in high school, but went to separate colleges. She went to Centre [College in Danville, Kentucky]. We got back together after I got out of the service, and we got married a year later. We were in Lexington till 1960. Our first son was born there, Brooks Egerton, in 1959. I was doing this PR job and then writing other things at the Kentucky Research Foundation. They had an overseas program with Indonesia, and I worked in that program as a staff person.

BEATTIE: Did you feel as though any of the writing that you were doing in those jobs prepared you for any of the writing you'd do later?

EGERTON: Sure. Experience always is helpful. I wasn't at all sure what I wanted to do in those years. I knew that I didn't want to be in PR, but it was a good place to start.

I got a chance, though, in 1960, to go to a new university in Florida [The University of South Florida in Tampa] that was just in the process of being built. I would have been twenty-five years old then. I heard about the place and I was intrigued by it, and I wrote the president a letter and expressed my interest in a PR job there, and I got invited down for an interview. They offered me a job as head of the news bureau, and I grabbed it. We moved there in August, 1960, from Lexington, and stayed five years. I was director of what's now Public Relations and Publications. I did a lot. It was a great job, because I ended up being the speech writer for the president, and the university was involved in a lot of controversial stuff having to do with a legislative investigation into Communism and immorality and all this other crap that people in the legislature thought was present there. I'm not certain that a lot of the anti-Communist fervor, in the South, particularly, wasn't a thinly disguised anti-black, anti-integration impulse. People just sort of assumed that if you were for integration, you must be a Communist.

The University of South Florida opened in the fall of 1960 with its first class and, if I'm not mistaken, there was one black student in that first class. So the university was the first Florida university to desegregate. In the middle of all of that I got to write a lot, but as time went on, I came to realize that my original instincts about not wanting to be a PR man were still true. I wanted to be a writer and not an administrator.

In 1965 I had an opportunity to go on a long trip to Africa. I'd had an automobile accident in the first year I was at South Florida, and I was in the hospital for seven or eight months. The university held my job for me while I recuperated from this. I had that period of time, though, to read and reflect and write. I read a lot during that time, more than I ever had in my life. I got really interested in the South and in social issues, and I came to realize, after dabbling a little bit with fiction, that what I really wanted to do was to write nonfiction. I started free-lancing magazine pieces during that time.

BEATTIE: What sorts of pieces were they?

EGERTON: They were mainly feature pieces, nothing very significant in those early years. But I took this trip to Africa. That came about because, when I recovered from this accident, one of the things I had done during all that recuperation time was to read a lot of Albert Schweitzer. I was really interested in Schweitzer as a person, not as a theologian or a musician, which he also was, but just as an individual. I wrote him a letter and asked him if I could come over there and see him. I figured that I could free-lance some articles if I took a big trip. And I got a letter back from him saying, yes, I could come to see him. So, I decided to go. My sister, Mary Higgs, "Skip" Higgs, was a missionary in Rhodesia, and I decided I would go and spend a little time with her family. I just plotted out an itinerary that included getting me as close as I could figure out how to get to where Schweitzer was. I ended up getting that close, but no closer. I could not find a way to get where he was. I found a bush pilot who would take me there, but he would not wait for me. So I wouldn't know how to get out. I lost my nerve, and I've always regretted that I didn't do it. I was gone about six weeks. But I wrote a lot of pieces during that trip. One article was on the political situation in Rhodesia, which was very touchy at that time. I went to New York and made the rounds at magazines, leaving my articles with people I didn't know and who didn't know me. And miraculously, four or five of those pieces got picked up and published.

BEATTIE: How many did you write in six weeks?

EGERTON: Well, I had one long piece that I had written, this political piece, and I sold it to *The Atlantic Monthly.* That publication was fatal for me, because it just absolutely thrilled me to death. It was not a byline piece, it was in the "Atlantic Reports" in the front of the magazine. But they paid me three hundred and fifty dollars for it, and I thought, "This has got to be the right way to make a living." I never looked back after that. But I've never sold a piece to *The Atlantic* since then. I sold some other pieces to *The Christian Century* and I can't remember who-all, and then some newspapers, *The St. Petersburg Times* and *The Courier-Journal,* during that time. That really changed my thinking a lot, and I thought magazine writing would be great.

It happened that in Nashville there was, at that time, a magazine called *Southern Education Report,* which was a project funded by the Ford Foundation to report on school desegregation in the South. It was written by a lot of journalists and academics, and those were the areas that I had my main interest in. I contacted the man who was the head of the project when I came back from Africa, and he subsequently hired me. So that summer of '65, we moved to Nashville, and I went to work for that magazine. The magazine went through another incar-nation, but I remained essentially there working from 1965 till '71. I was a staff writer for the magazine. I was also free-lancing during that time for such publica-tions as the *Nation* and the *Saturday Review*. I got in some pretty nice magazines during that time, and it was all of that that led me to think that I could make it on my own. I became a contributing editor to the *Saturday Review*, so that was kind of a break point in 1971, when I left my job and started free-lancing full-time. At that time I went to work for the Nashville organization called Southern Education Reporting Service. It had originally published a newspaper tabloid monthly called *Southern School News*. Then it went to a magazine format with something called *Southern Education Report,* and that was when I went to work for them. A few years later, it changed the name to the Race Relations Information Center and published a magazine called *Race Relations Reporter.*

BEATTIE: While working on that publication—and it sounds as though it ties in with situations you had to deal with at the University of South Florida—were you honing topics of interest to you, in terms of race relations and social history?

EGERTON: Absolutely. I wrote my first book while I was still working for that organization, a book called *A Mind to Stay Here.* It's a collection of profiles of southerners who had a mind to stay in the South and try to work things out when the South was in the throes of so much turmoil. Several of those pieces in the book were pieces I wrote for magazines before I did the book. That was some-thing else that prompted me to quit my job and take up the free-lance trade. I really hoped that I could continue to write books as well as magazine pieces.

BEATTIE: The reception for your first book must have been good.

EGERTON: If I had listened to that, I wouldn't have done it. That book didn't do much. It only had one printing, I think, of about five thousand copies. It sold those, but they never reprinted it. I didn't make any money to speak of out of it. But, you know, you're blind to that kind of stuff. I kept thinking, "I know a lot of people." I was doing a lot of education reporting and I'd made a lot of contacts in education, so education writing was a big part of what I did and what I felt I could continue to do as my bread and butter income. Then I could do these other things on the side. By the time I quit, I was thinking about working on a book that eventually materialized in '74, *The Americanization of Dixie.*

BEATTIE: Will you talk about the origins of that?

EGERTON: Well, again, its contents were essentially journalistic. I had pieces that I'd written for somebody else that set me to think about that theme of the South as a place that was becoming less identifiable, both for better and worse. The South seemed more like the North, and the North more like the South, for better and worse. It was basically an idea book, as opposed to a subject book. I don't know if I make that distinction clear or not but, to me, some books originate as ideas, some books are strongly the exposition of an idea, and some are just following your nose, or an unfolding event, or a person's life, or something like that. The content is dictated by external things. But an idea book is something that you've got to dope out in your head, somehow. You've got to construct a whole system of thinking about something that you can defend. *The Americanization of Dixie,* the idea that I tried to develop in there was that the South was disappearing, it was changing in ways that cheered me and in ways that grieved me. And that conflict that I felt about that seemed to me to be almost in itself a part of the conflict of the South. It was always a schizophrenic place, of two minds about everything.

Of course, the South has not disappeared, but I still think that the idea that I tried to develop there was basically a correct idea, that the South was and is changing in ways almost beyond recognition, yet it still remains very much an identifiable place. That book had the same unfortunate publishing history as the first one, though. It didn't make it into paperback, it didn't make it into a second printing. It got me a certain notoriety as having coined that phrase, "the Americanization of Dixie." I ended up years later, when Jimmy Carter got elected, being interviewed on television and even by foreign journalists because I was identified with that phrase. But in terms of the book itself having any successful life, it didn't.

BEATTIE: Were you able, from the books and the magazine articles and whatever free-lancing you were doing, to totally support yourself?

EGERTON: Yes, I always managed to do that. I've had good years and bad; it's a real roller-coaster thing. But one way or another, I kept enough work going. I wrote an awful lot of magazine stuff in those years, just scores of pieces.

BEATTIE: When did you start writing regular columns for the *Atlanta Journal and Constitution?*

EGERTON: It was quite a long while before I did. I had several things that came along before that. After publishing *The Americanization of Dixie* in '74, the next book was a little book I did for University of Tennessee Press, called *Visions of Utopia,* which is about Rugby, and some other places in Tennessee. That was published in '77. That was a book that the Press came to me and asked me to do as part of their bicentennial series on Tennessee history. Just a little hundred-page book. That was fun, and it was a diversion, and it really kind of got me into history in a way that I had not been before. And, by that time, I had drifted pretty far out of writing about education. *The Saturday Review* had had a special magazine called *The Saturday Review of Education,* and I was a contributing editor to that, but the magazine went under.

BEATTIE: I imagine your political science background always had you interested in history.

EGERTON: Yes, I always had had an interest in it. I never took a course under Tom [Dr. Thomas D.] Clark at Kentucky, and I always regretted that I hadn't done that. I've subsequently come to know him well, and admire him greatly, not only as a fine historian and writer in his own right, but as a great nurturer of other writers. He's a real treasure, that man.

So, by '77, *Visions of Utopia* came out. I was really interested in history then. In '76 I got the germ of the idea for this book, *Generations*.

I met an old woman on an old plantation in South Carolina, a woman named Sue Alston. She was a black woman who had been born and raised at Hampton Plantation on the coast of South Carolina. She was a hundred and something. She didn't know exactly how old, maybe a hundred and five. I happened on her by accident. I went to the Hampton Plantation, having read a little article in the paper that it was being restored, and the University of South Carolina was going to try to preserve it, open it up. I was on vacation, and I went over and looked at it. It's a wonderful, old, three-story frame house sitting back under the live oaks, just a great place with all kinds of history. I was talking to the person who was in charge of it. He told me about Sue Alston, who lived nearby, and he said that the University had sent all these historians and scholars down there to document the history of that place. He said they had gone over and talked to Sue Alston, but they didn't stay very long. They said that she was interesting, but it was all hearsay and that what she had to say just was not really going to help them. I went to see her, and it helped me a great deal. I mean, they were fools not to see what a treasure she was. She had a great memory. She had a gift for telling stories. I sat on her porch for about an hour and taped an interview with her. It was, I think, maybe the most spellbinding hour I ever spent with another person. She took me by the hand, so to speak, and gave me a guided tour of a century. It was spectacular. She inspired me to come up with this idea.

Basically, I constructed a hypothetical model of a couple who were near a hundred who had their wits about them and good health, good memories, who still lived close to where they had originated. They had had lots of children, and the children had had children, and so in this one, self-contained family, there would be over a hundred people. That was the basic idea. And the more near the middle I could define that family—white, middle-class, mainstream religion, Republican or Democrat, not members of splinter groups and not members of fringe churches, and not people with unusual occupations—the more the family would symbolize the center of our national experience. That idea was born on Sue Alston's front porch in 1976.

BEATTIE: Had you thought about writing anything about her?

EGERTON: I thought about it, but I decided that it would not work for several reasons, one of which was that her husband was not living. I didn't have the other half of the family that I felt I needed. I wanted to find somebody nearer the center of the country, too, nearer the geographical center, not in the Deep South. So I avoided looking in South Carolina, Georgia, Alabama, Mississippi, Louisiana, and moved more to the Upper South and looked in Tennessee, Kentucky, Missouri, Arkansas, and Kansas. I spent about six months trying to find somebody.

BEATTIE: How did you go about doing that?

EGERTON: I wrote a lot of letters to people I knew in different places and told them what I was looking for, and asked them to look in their weekly papers for people having fiftieth wedding anniversaries, or sixtieth, that kind of thing. I just sort of put out my feelers to inquire.

The following year, '77, I got invited to be a journalist-in-residence at Virginia Tech. and to teach a course in magazine writing and to go on doing my writing. It was during that year that my brother, who lived in Elizabethtown [Ky.], sent me a clipping out of *The Courier-Journal* about Burnam and Addie Ledford. I think [*Courier-Journal* columnist] Bob Hill wrote the piece about happening on these people out of his travels, and he wrote a little feature piece about what good storytellers they were. So, I got a couple of names out of that column and I called them from Virginia. One of the Ledfords' daughters was there, and she answered the phone. She was real suspicious of what I was trying to do, but said she'd ask her daddy. He was pretty deaf, and I could hear the conversation. She said, "Papa, there's a man on the phone from Virginia wants to talk to you." And he said, "What about?" She said, "I don't know. He said he wanted to come see you." He said, "Well, tell him to come on. Just tell him don't come when the Wildcats are on TV. And tell him he better hurry, 'cause I won't be here much longer."

I went in, I think, March of '78 to see them for the first time, and that began an experience that went on until this book came out in '83. I had to do a lot of other stuff during that time, but that was always near the front of my mind. I stopped in the middle of that to write another book about Nashville, a bicentennial history of Nashville, which I wrote in 1979. That was an interesting project. It was a commissioned assignment. I was hired to supervise the research and to organize the design and layout and to do the writing for that book. I had a lot of help in getting the material together. Then I wrote it and essentially put it together.

BEATTIE: This is the book called *Nashville: The Faces of Two Centuries*?

EGERTON: Yes. It was kind of amazing, really. We started in January of 1979 and in November of that year we passed out the copies of the book.

BEATTIE: Meanwhile, you say you had already finished *Generations*.

EGERTON: I had written a draft of it. I thought I knew exactly what I was doing. I wrote a draft, in the midst of which I discovered I was doing it the wrong way. But I decided to go ahead and complete it in that way. What I did was, I wrote it as a third-person story, the whole thing. I was not in it. I was invisible and detached from it, and the story essentially gave equal time to the generations.

I was so confident that it was going to work that I took the first draft to New York, and I literally went in person to one publisher after another. People were good enough to talk to me, and I was able to get in to see a lot of people, but I could not get anybody interested in that book. Everywhere I took that book people ended up saying to me, "It's a good idea, it's a nice story, but nobody's going to buy this book."

BEATTIE: What were the publishers' reasons?

EGERTON: Well, nobody knows who these people [the Ledfords] are. They're all anonymous people. They're nobodies. I was totally discouraged by that, and didn't know what I was going to do with my manuscript. I just came home and put it away and wrote the Nashville book. I had to completely separate myself from it, so I left it alone for a while.

When I got back to writing magazine pieces I used to put—in the little author's note at the bottom of the page, you know—"Egerton's working on a book about a Kentucky family" or social history of whatnot. Kind of like little fortune cookies, trying to get somebody interested. And Ken Cherry called me from UK [University Press of Kentucky] and said he'd like to see it, and I showed him that manuscript. He liked it like it was. When he said he was interested in it, and offered to publish it in its original form, I decided to go ahead and publish it with the University Press of Kentucky, but I wanted to rewrite it, so I did. It came out in '83, and it's still in print. They still sell some. I sold the paperback rights to Simon & Schuster, and I sold a Japanese translation. Of course, *Generations* was another idea book in the sense that I had the idea of what to do, what I wanted to do, long before I met the Ledfords.

There's a KET [Kentucky Educational Television] half-hour documentary that I made with a guy from Arkansas, who kind of fell in love with the book and got interested in it and got me involved with him. He's a filmmaker-video person. We went to the Ledfords' homecoming one year and made a video of it. That documentary aired before Burnam died. He saw it. It must have played in the fall of '82.

So *Generations* came out in '83, and I guess the next thing I did of any major consequence was the food book.

BEATTIE: *Southern Food?*

EGERTON: Yes. That was another idea I'd been carrying around for a long time, that I'd like to do a book on food. Food was such a natural way to look at the South, you know, and it just absolutely made for the kind of social history I enjoyed doing.

Out of the blue I was notified that I had received a Lyndhurst Prize. The Lyndhurst Foundation in Chattanooga—which is Coca-Cola money—started, in about 1980, giving two prizes a year to writers, mainly, but also to some other creative arts people. It was a large financial prize for three years, in recognition of my body of work. That was like manna from heaven for me. Suddenly, I was going to get twenty-five grand a year for three years to keep up my work. Having that cushion, I decided this was a time for me to do something risky. So I pulled out that idea about doing a book on food, and spent several months really trying to conceptualize a book. And of all the things I've ever done, that probably is the only one that really turned out exactly as I imagined it. I knew what I wanted in it, and I knew how I wanted it to look, and that's exactly the way it turned out.

I tried to get an agent to help me sell that book. I'd never had an agent before, and there was a woman in Atlanta named Caroline Harkleroad who was then doing literary agentry. I talked to her and she was interested, and she sent out a query letter to about twenty-five publishers with that idea in it. I think five or six of them even bothered to respond at all. And, of those, there were maybe three that really seemed interested enough to want to pursue the idea, and one of them was Ann Close at Knopf. She's one of the best editors. She's a native of Savannah. She understood this book immediately; it did not have to be translated for her. She was not a food editor, she didn't do cookbooks or anything; she did fiction and nonfiction. But this idea really appealed to her. So we struck up an acquaintance and a relationship that led, within a few months, to my producing an outline and a little bit of what subsequently became the introductory section. And on the strength of that I got a contract from her to do that book. So in the fall of '87, my wife, Ann, and I started out on a series of road trips that ultimately amounted to about thirty thousand miles of travel. We spent a year visiting restaurants and trying out recipes.

BEATTIE: What about the social history in *Southern Food*? That looks as though it took exhaustive research.

EGERTON: A lot of library work, a lot of reading and searching for books and whatnot, building up a great collection of cookbooks and food books. In the fall of '85 I started writing the book, and it took me about a year to write it. It came out in the summer of '87. Writing on so many different subjects leaves me pretty much outside anybody's little cubbyhole of definition.

BEATTIE: Although you seem to have been defined more from that book and your subsequent book, *Side Orders,* as a food writer.

EGERTON: Which I was not and never had been. And won't be, subsequently, because I'm not going to write any more books about food.

BEATTIE: But you have written food columns for magazines.

EGERTON: I've written columns. Essentially, what happened was, when I wrote that book and the book came out, the book did right well and it got great critical reviews. The book review people liked it, but so, too, especially, did the food people, and that was what really surprised me. I didn't expect that to be the case, but I got some lavish praise from people who are professional food writers. As a consequence, all of these magazine assignments started coming to me and, for the first time in my career, I found getting assignments to be easy. *Food and Wine* and *Travel and Leisure* were calling me up saying, "Would you do this and that and the other?" If I had wanted to suddenly transform myself into a food writer, I could have done it, I think, and gotten away with it, at that point. I wanted to keep doing some food writing, and I did. I had a lot of material left over from the food book that I wanted to use, and people were writing to me, sending me ideas and information about restaurants and all that. So I came up with the idea of writing a column, and I self-syndicated the column to, I think, eight papers in the Southeast. My original idea was if I could build up a clientele of thirty or forty or fifty papers, this could become my sinecure. This would be my bread and butter, so to speak, and I could do other things. But I never could get that many papers. I couldn't compete with the big syndicates that sell columns for three, four, or five bucks apiece, because they deal in such volume, and I was trying to get twenty-five bucks apiece from my papers. Then the *Atlanta Constitution* got interested in my column, and they not only bought into running the piece on Sunday, but they agreed to buy my old columns and run them, which I was amazed at. They essentially ran all the old columns that had already run in these other eight papers. *The Constitution* carried those for about a year and a half. By that time, I'd used up most of my ideas. I knew that I didn't want to keep doing this forever. I spun off that *Side Orders* book from the columns and magazine pieces on food that I had done. I was pretty much ready to get out of the food game by then.

BEATTIE: For *Southern Food,* you'd won the International Association of Culinary Professionals Book of the Year Award.

EGERTON: Yes, the Book of the Year Award for the best book on food.

BEATTIE: People also termed you "The Mouth of the South" and "The Southern Homer."

EGERTON: I really got kind of a level of notoriety from doing that that I never have had from any of my other writing. Ann still says I ought to go back to doing the food columns. We had so much fun doing that, traveling around, and I still get called.

BEATTIE: What do you think is the most significant aspect of *Southern Food?*

EGERTON: It gave readers all those literary allusions, the excerpts from books by and about southerners, about the South. You can look through all that marginalia and you see how much food has been in our literature, and you don't even think about it until you just start looking. And every durn writer we've ever had, just about, at some point or another, gets off on the subject of food. It is a way of saying how important food has been. Then, that book also gave people who are really interested in food a good bibliography, which is something no cookbook gives them. It gave readers a narrative overview of the food in southern history, which didn't previously exist. It gave them some ideas about traveling and where to find places to eat. Finally, *Southern Food* gave readers about a hundred and fifty classic old southern recipes that demonstrate, I think, why southern food is so good.

BEATTIE: What is the story of your "hemorrhoid comic book?"

EGERTON: I knew a woman in Atlanta, who used to live in Nashville, and I saw her at a cocktail party some years ago. I can't remember exactly when this was, but it would have been in '82, '83, '84, somewhere in there. She and a friend of hers had started a publishing company, producing medical patient information —reading material. You go to a doctor and you're sick, and you've got some exotic disease, here's a book on it, you know. You go to the hospital, you're going to have open-heart surgery, here's a little book. It's written at about fourth-grade level, it's got cartoon characters in it, it's just a simple, straight-forward little hand-holder. This woman was telling me about how well these publications were doing, and I said, "I got a great idea. You ought to do a book on hemorrhoids by somebody who's had the surgery and lived to tell about it—a survivor." They loved the idea.

They created a little cartoon character called "Little Rhoid." He's got a little scarf around his neck; he's a real debonair-looking character. I wrote them a little comic-book-worth of copy about this phenomenon, hemorrhoids, and what to do about it called *The Bottom Line*. It's still in print. Sells a few hundred copies every year. I've gotten many a laugh out of it.

In a more serious vein, I collected a bunch of my magazine pieces in a book last year that LSU [Louisiana State University] published, called *Shades of Gray*. They're pieces that I had written over about a twenty or twenty-five-year period. They're mainly southern pieces. A lot of them have to do with race. They all have to do with people or events, which seem on the surface to have a sort of simple, understandable explanation, but when you kind of get underneath, you find all these subtleties. Hence, the title: *Shades of Gray*.

BEATTIE: I've read that you've been working on a book about the relationship between blacks and whites from the end of World War II until the early 1950s. Are you still working on that project?

EGERTON: Yes, I really am. It's changed shape quite a bit. It's now about the years from 1932 to '54, starting with [Franklin D.] Roosevelt's election and going up to the Brown versus Board of Education decision of the Supreme Court. I'm nearing the half-way point of getting a draft of it written. I've been working on it off and on, but mainly on, for nearly two years. It's going to be a great, big book, too big right now. I'm worried about how big it is. I've got to trim it down somehow.

BEATTIE: What is your basic thesis?

EGERTON: There are several themes that I'm trying to keep running. Basically, the book attempts to take the belief of most people, that the civil rights movement began in 1954, and turn it on its ear. It really began a long, long time before that. The generation before that is what I'm dealing with, twenty-two years. I'm dealing with people who were southerners, and who faced the dilemma of race in this society—what they thought about it and what they came to believe about it and how they divided in their beliefs. So, it's about liberals and conservatives, and integrationists and segregationists, and whites and blacks, and men and women, and exiles and live-in southerners. It's about that twenty-two-year period all the way from Washington, D.C., to Texas, and it's just vast. I'm trying to assimilate all that material.

BEATTIE: How are you organizing the book?

EGERTON: It has four big sections. It's more or less chronological. It has a big section that deals with '32 to '38, and that section really has a whole lot about pre-'32 stuff in it, also. And then there's a section from the beginning of '39 to the middle of '45, the end of the war. That's about where I am now. Then the next big section is really where I started out thinking I wanted to be, and that was right after the war, up to 1950, and then the last four years.

BEATTIE: You talked about going back to the Roosevelt administration. In what ways is that administration influential in your thesis?

EGERTON: It was during the Roosevelt years that blacks from the South—and whites from the South, too—went in big numbers to work in Washington in various government agencies. The programs of the New Deal, though they were not originally pointed at the racial problem in America, had the effect of addressing that problem through the back door. If you took up, for example, the issues of poor farmers starving and needing homesteads, and you wanted to start a federal agency to create homesteads for farmers, you couldn't get very far before you had to deal with black farmers. Every program—agriculture and business and social security and youth and health care and education—right on down the line, had a big impact on the South and a big impact on blacks. One of my theses is that the South in those years was to the rest of the country very much like blacks were to whites. It was sort of a stepchild, poor relation—unwanted, shunned, full of self-doubt and insecurity and bitterness and all the rest. I'm using those parallels a lot all the way through.

The other thing is, I started with a question—with an idea—that became the basic idea. And that is, if everything else in the whole wide world was changing when World War II ended, why didn't the South change? Why didn't it change on its own? Its people were changing. Its men had been fighting in the war, its women had been working in the factories, its blacks had gone North and gone everywhere, the South was coming out of the Depression and it was reaping the benefit of new technology with jet airplanes and air conditioning and all the rest. All of that was accepted. People understood that it was going to be a different world. So why didn't they go ahead and make it a different world racially and just get it over with? They had to do it, and I always felt like they knew they had to do it, but southerners couldn't face it. I think that's basically true.

When I started interviewing people and I asked them what their reaction was to the Brown [Brown v. Board of Education] decision in '54, I was greatly surprised—I still am, really—at how many people, almost everybody, whether they're liberal or conservative, whether they were glad for it or sorry, were shocked that it happened. They expressed astonishment that this was the decision. It stunned them. Yet I go back and read all that was in the papers, and integration was being talked about. I mean, southerners knew it was coming. Everybody knew it. For years they knew it. Ralph McGill was writing columns saying, "Some day it's going to be Monday." Monday was Supreme Court decision day, and every time there was a lynching or something, he would write these columns saying, "We'd better get going here because we're going to face some coercion, and it's going to be terrible." But even he was not pushing real hard for that change to happen.

BEATTIE: Do you think this resistance to change was mostly a response to the real South that would be changed, or to altering the romantic notion about the South that southerners have held, but that has never really been true?

EGERTON: Well, we've always been suckers for self-delusion in this region. And, in the 1950s, self-delusion was epidemic in the South. A lot of people were hung up on that. But I think, really, maybe the majority of people, blacks included, just looked at integration and they just thought, "It's just unthinkable that these people are going to change, it's just unthinkable." So, they didn't think about it. They just went on hoping that separate would somehow be made equal, which is what everybody talked about for a long time. I think that probably integration never would have happened if it had not been for the Supreme Court and the black rebellion, Montgomery and all that followed, the growing realization that hundreds, thousands, of blacks in the South would no longer submit to that, that they would rather die in jail, that they would rather die in the streets than to have their rights denied them. That, plus the courts and, eventually, the might of the federal government, were what it took. Short of that, we never would have done it. We would have kept on saying forever, I think, "Well, yes, maybe it's a good idea, but not now."

BEATTIE: As exhaustive a project as this sounds, are you planning any follow-up book to cover the years beyond Brown versus Board of Education?

EGERTON: I'm not going to write on this subject after this. There are lots of good books about the years since Brown: *Parting the Waters, Simple Justice,* David Garrow's book on Martin Luther King. And Fred Powledge has a new book, *Free at Last.* There are some wonderful books about the civil rights movement. This is the one I want to write, and when I get through with it, I'm going to go do something else. Knopf is going to publish this book.

BEATTIE: What about future writing projects? Do you have any in mind after this?

EGERTON: Well, I always keep lists around of things I'd like to do some day, and usually the ideas that I end up writing books about are ideas that I've been carrying around for a long time. I guess in that bag now I have a few ideas of things that are really unformed. Something, maybe, about England that would help me to tie in the story about my grandfather coming here in 1880 to help form a colony in this country. I'd kind of like to write about that. But that would be mainly a book about England, I think, more than it would be anything else. A kind of contemporary social history of social phenomena in England. Oh, I've got other ideas of things about old people. I'm interested in old people. Travel. On-the-road kinds of books. I like to think that the writing I do, almost all of it, fits this sort of "journey of discovery" notion—that you have an idea that you want to pursue, and it takes you somewhere, and along the way you gain certain insights. The lines between fiction and nonfiction and journalism have blurred a lot in recent years. I heard Shelby Foote one time talking about his approach to writing, and it fits my thinking. So, I use his description for what I like to do. He said he noticed that most academics come at writing by saying, "Here's a subject I'm interested in; as soon as I know everything there is to know about it, I'll write a book." And he said, "My approach is to say, 'Here's a subject I'm interested in; I think I'll write a book about it and see how much I can learn.'"

June 2, 1992

Speak Now Against the Day, The Generation Before the Civil Rights Movement in the South, Egerton's book about race relations in the South from 1932 to 1954, published in 1994, won the Robert F. Kennedy Book Award, the Ambassador Book Award of the English Speaking Union, and the 1995 Southern Book Critics Circle Award. In 1996 Egerton assumed the role of senior correspondent for *The Tennessean* in Nashville, and in 1997 he spent a semester at the University of Texas in Austin as senior lecturer in American Studies. Since returning from Texas Egerton has resumed his career as a freelance writer.

BOOKS BY JOHN EGERTON

A Mind to Stay Here. New York: Macmillan, 1970.

The Americanization of Dixie. New York: Harper's Magazine Press, 1974.

Visions of Utopia. Knoxville, Tn.: University of Tennessee Press, 1977.

Nashville. Nashville, Tn.: PlusMedia, 1979.

Generations. Lexington, Ky.: University Press of Kentucky, 1983.

Southern Food. New York: Knopf, 1987.

Side Orders. Atlanta: Peachtree Press, 1990.

Shades of Gray. Baton Rouge, La.: Louisiana State University Press, 1991.

Speak Now Against the Day, the Generation Before the Civil Rights Movement in the South. New York: Knopf, 1994.

SARAH GORHAM

GORHAM: My legal name is Sarah Gorham Skinner. My professional name is Sarah Gorham. I was born March 30, 1954, in Santa Monica, California.

My mother's full name was Kathryn Aring Gorham before she got divorced, and then she remarried and her new husband's name was Morton. She was called Peg. My father's name is William Gorham.

My mother had a degree in literature from Stanford University and Wellesley College; she studied with Yvor Winters. She worked as the director of the Montgomery County, Maryland, Association for Retarded Citizens. My father has had a variety of government positions, but he's currently president of the Urban Institute, which is a research think tank that he founded twenty years ago.

My mother's side of the family, I think, has more literary interest for me. My great-grandmother, in particular, was a poet. Her real name was Clara Homann, but she published under the name Clara Prince, and she wrote early-1900s sort of poems. You know, very little old ladyish poems. But she did found a magazine called *The Wisconsin Review of Poetry,* and I have old copies of this. She was also on the board of *Poetry Magazine* and of the American Academy of Poets. I think they moved around a bit, but Wabatosa, Wisconsin, was basically where they lived. And I think, at one point, my mother judged one of the poetry contests for the magazine, when she was still Kathryn Joan Aring.

Then my grandmother, Edna Aring, also had an interest in poetry. She liked limericks and wrote limericks constantly, but she was a self-taught woman. She had a great interest in literature, and she's the one who gave me *The Magic Mountain*—in German, I might add.

My mother's sister, Nancy—she's now Nancy Graham—worked for the Teacher Corps and the Peace Corps, and so did my uncle, the man she married. Her daughter, my cousin, Nan Graham, is one of the editors-in-chief at Penguin. She's Salman Rushdie's editor, and she's also Don DeLillo's editor.

And, on my father's side of the family, my grandfather died in his sixties; I didn't know him too well. He was a business man. All I know about what he did is, he worked with stocks.

And my grandmother was a very tenacious, funny—Faye was her name,

Faye Gorham—and stubborn woman, a wonderful little old lady, and she lived into her eighties.

BEATTIE: What about your sisters? You have four, is that right?

GORHAM: Four sisters, yes. I'm the oldest. My sister Nancy's the next one down; she's now consulting. She started out as an editor at *Who's Who.* My sister Kim is a special education teacher in Montgomery County, Maryland, and she has a family, too. And my sister Jenny is a writer. She's a science writer. She's worked at *National Geographic* for a number of years, editing and writing for them, and then she took off on her own. She's also free-lancing now. She's involved in a series of essays—she's trying to put together her own book right now—but she's published chapters, and I've got a whole string of her books. This one, *The Curious Naturalist,* she edited. She's been very successful. I'm very proud of her. My youngest sister, Becky, is profoundly retarded, and she has had probably the most influence on my life of all my sisters, just in terms of what I write about.

BEATTIE: What sort of childhood did you have and where was it spent?

GORHAM: I spent seven years in California; I don't remember a whole lot about that. I went to nursery school and kindergarten there. Then we moved to Omaha, Nebraska, for one year. I don't remember a whole lot about that, either. Then we moved to Georgetown in Washington, D.C., and I grew up there. It was a wonderful place to live.

We walked to school and I spent six years in the same elementary school. I was involved in a triangle of friends that was very painful for me as a child. I was extremely adept academically. I always got straight A's and never had to work very hard, but I was more interested in social stuff, you know, and in getting a boy friend. In fact, in kindergarten I was interested in boys. I started keeping a journal in sixth grade, and I still do. I didn't keep my sixth grade journal, but I did keep my eighth grade journal.

BEATTIE: Do you reread it?

GORHAM: I do, and it's what you might expect from an eighth grader. This is important, too. I spent two years in the public school system, which was going through the beginning of busing, and it was pretty explosive, so my mother and father decided to send me to private school. I went to Burgundy Farm Country Day School, and they happened to have an extraordinary seventh and eighth grade teacher, who was a natural scientist. And, basically, he taught us everything we needed to know about botany and ornithology. And I mean *everything.*

BEATTIE: Do you remember that teacher's name?

GORHAM: John Trott, and he was one of the most important influences on me. My interest in the natural world has remained since then. Almost everything I learned from him has stuck with me, and I've used it in my poems, over and over again.

BEATTIE: That attention to detail is very important for a writer.

GORHAM: Yes, as are the specifics about flowers and about trees and birds and knowing what they do and what they are and having a healthy respect for them. I'm, hopefully, passing that on to my kids, too, now. So, he was a really important influence on me.

Then I went to public school for a year. And then I went off to Switzerland for two years. It was an international school run by a woman whom my aunt had gone to Wellesley with, Natalie Luthi, and it was a very small school, about a hundred and twenty-five kids, grades K through twelve.

BEATTIE: Where in Switzerland?

GORHAM: In a valley called the Goldern, [in Benese Oberland,] the German part of Switzerland. It was a very tiny little town in the Alps, a beautiful setting. I attended tenth and eleventh grades there. This place was a hard work place. That school really taught me a sense of discipline and responsibility, and I came back much changed. I was fluent in German by the time I got home. But also, Natalie Luthi, who taught the English classes, really gave me the best education in writing that I could have gotten—a very firm foundation. She spent an entire year taking us through a research paper from the notecards and the reading up to the final version. That was just indispensable. Everybody coming out of college these days doesn't know how to write, but I had that head start, and that made an enormous difference.

BEATTIE: Did you experience any homesickness?

GORHAM: A little bit, towards the end, and that's why I ended up coming home for my senior year.

BEATTIE: This science teacher that you had earlier in school, did he cause science, instead of English, to emerge as one of your favorite topics in school?

GORHAM: He did. It stuck with me. But the two went neck and neck, because Natalie also taught Shakespeare, and she gave us the best education in Shakespeare.

Then I went back to Washington, and my parents had moved to Bethesda, Maryland, at that point. My parents divorced, so it was a good thing that I came home for my senior year; plus, I got it together to get into college. I wouldn't have been able to visit college from Switzerland, so that was important.

BEATTIE: Where did you go to college?

GORHAM: Well, let's say I ended up at Antioch College, and I think I chose Antioch because I flipped through a catalog and I liked the photographs. I really didn't make the kind of decision that students these days do. I just sort of went there.

I started out as a botany major and I took two or three natural science courses. I took biology and ornithology, and I took a Shakespeare class from Eric Horsting, which was also another important turning point, because I loved it, and that sort of reconfirmed my interest in literature. And I wrote poetry all along, ever since high school, mostly for therapy.

I came across Anne Sexton when I was, I think, a freshman in college, and

I loved her. I think I chose her because she wrote love poems. I was such a romantic and so anxious to find a boyfriend, you know. So, this attracted me to her. I wrote Ann-Sexton-look-alike poems for about a year, and submitted these to an advanced poetry workshop. I had never taken a poetry workshop before. And poet Ira Sadoff was teaching this advanced poetry workshop. He wasn't going to let me in the workshop based on my work sample, but he had heard from other faculty members that I was a hard worker, so he let me in. And I'm glad he did, because it changed my life. That was an amazing class, because James Galvin was in that class, Laurie Sheck, Jean Day—I think I'm probably forgetting a couple of people—Steven Cramer, Stuart Dischell. Those are five people. Six people in that class out of twelve now have at least one book. I mean, these were real poets, and they were writing real poetry back then, too. But it was a tough class; Ira Sadoff had us write three poems a week, and we read two volumes of poetry a week and responded to them in our journals. I took this very seriously and, consequently, I took a lot of risks in my work and moved forward very quickly. And I made the biggest progress. I didn't save anything from that workshop, but I discovered what metaphor was and how to clean up my act a bit. So I took that workshop, and then I just was hooked on poetry. I knew that this was going to be it.

BEATTIE: What do you think was particularly good about Sadoff's teaching?

GORHAM: He was demanding and he was very opinionated. He knew what he liked, and I think that beginning writers need that. I think that, when you're flailing about, you don't need someone to tell you, "Oh, you can just write whatever you want; just write." He wasn't afraid to criticize, and it came across.

I became a literature major. I hung onto ceramics as a balance. I've always sort of reached for balance and have been very sensible in that way. Ceramics was my minor.

The other thing I should probably mention is that Antioch has a work study program, so six months out of the year you are on jobs all over the country. And one of my jobs was working as the assistant poetry director at the Folger Library in Washington, D.C., which, once I got past doing the secretarial stuff—I was really impatient with that—was a good experience. I got to meet some poets.

I taught kindergarten at the Columbia Nursery School in New York one year. I loved being in Manhattan. It was a good job. It paid pretty well. I lived with some friends in New York and was able to take a course at the New School with Daniel Halpern. And that was also an important influence, because he pushed me into different directions because he had different ideas and, you know, Ira Sadoff had been *it* for me. But he introduced me to the work of Robert Desnos and Elizabeth Bishop, especially the sonnets of Elizabeth Bishop, and he introduced me to John Berryman's work, too. He told me to go in Berryman's direction, because it is much more disjointed and quirky than what I had been writing. And that was an important piece of advice. I also went to museums every weekend. I had a cultural sort of brainwashing in New York. It was wonderful.

Also, at Antioch, I worked on the staff of the *Antioch Review* for two years, and on the staff of the *Seneca Review,* which Ira Sandoff had been publishing out of Antioch, and that was also a great experience.

BEATTIE: Did you start mailing out your own poems at that time?

GORHAM: Not until graduate school. But the *Antioch Review* published my first poems. It's a good magazine.

I applied to four graduate schools, and at that point there were not a zillion MFA programs. Montana, Columbia, Irvine, [California], and Iowa were it. I got accepted at all four places, and I came up with a really good work sample to submit to those places, largely because of my combined work at Antioch and also at the New School in Manhattan where I did some good writing. But Iowa was the only place that gave me money, so it was just an economic decision, and it's also, you know, the big place for creative writers to go. So, I went there, and a number of my classmates from this one poetry workshop went with me—Steven Cramer, Stuart Dischell, Jim Galvin, and Laurie Sheck. All of them were in the same class, and we wound up at Iowa together.

My first year at Iowa I studied with Bill Matthews and Louise Gluck. It was a very difficult year for me. Iowa's big time, and there are sixty poets and four faculty members, and there's a lot of ego running around. There's sort of this necessity to make a mark.

My first year I was very lonely. I was living alone for the first time, in an apartment, and it was a loud apartment. There were a couple of co-eds who lived above me who played rock and roll music until 4:00 in the morning, so I didn't have any sense of inner peace, and this is where I was supposed to be writing. I did not write very much. I was intimidated.

My second year was better. I think, by that point, I had made a circle of friends, and most of us were sort of on the outside. We weren't the inner circle of poets, and we didn't produce regularly, but we were happy together. I also met a fiction writer whom I ended up living with for a year, and for a while that relationship was happy. His name was Chris Anderson. He got an NEA [National Endowment for the Arts] grant the year that he left, and I haven't heard from him since, so I don't know what happened to him. But I'll tell you who my graduating class was; Jorie Graham was in there, as was Rita Dove. Now, we're talking Pulitzer Prize here. Gee, Jane Miller. She was an example of somebody who gained a lot from the workshop. Gosh, who else? Jim Galvin. Lots of people, you know, who ended up getting books—Linda Gregerson, Sharon Bryan.

BEATTIE: Were you there for a total of two years?

GORHAM: Two years, yes. And gradually, the second year, I started to write. I produced very workshoppy poems. They were very safe, very controlled, very clean, very cold.

BEATTIE: Do you feel that they were different or improved in any way from your Antioch poems?

GORHAM: They were more of the same, probably, but probably even colder and even cleaner. At this point, and this is probably something that I could talk about now, I subconsciously started to assume a male persona when I was writing. I did not write in my own voice. I did not know what my voice was. I had been fed mostly male models. You know, back in the '70s there were a number of really important women poets—Sandra McPherson; Louise Gluck, certainly; Tess Gallagher; Linda Gregg—and I read these women voraciously, but the ultimate majority of poets whose work I studied were men—William S. Merwin, Robert Bly, Allen Tate—and this was where I thought the answer lay, so I wrote in that direction. I don't blame myself for that. I was very young, and I think that part of one's early writing career should be an attachment to mentors, an attachment to trying out different kinds of voices until you figure out which is yours. I think that now at Iowa the focus is to find the original voice more than to produce the polished poems. At least, the work I see coming out of there now is much more sparked and quirky than at the time we were there.

BEATTIE: Did you find anyone that you were best able to work with at Iowa?

GORHAM: Bill Matthews was the most generous towards my work. I worked a short time with Louise Gluck but, again, I had maybe one or two private sessions. Her instinct with my work was to hone it down. She's a very spare writer. And she also was a very strong influence on me, and I think it's taken me most of my life to shake her syntactical tics out of my work. But Bill Matthews has been generous to me continually. He wrote a blurb for my book. He spent some time with me, and I'm really grateful to him.

But, the other important thing that happened that second year is that I sent out my first submissions, and I got amazing acceptances. I thought this was what it was going to be like for the rest of my life, too. I had a poem taken by *Antaeus.* I had four poems taken by *Plowshares.* I had a poem taken by *The Nation.* I was a finalist in The Discovery Award. And I think I had a couple of other publications that year. They were major publications.

I did teach, though, for two years, and I loved that. I taught Introduction to Literature for one year, and then the second year I taught Dramatic Literature, and it was wonderful.

BEATTIE: What did you do after the Workshop?

GORHAM: Well, I wanted to teach college, but I did not get a job teaching college. I had written no books. So, I got a high school job, at an alternative high school in Englewood, New Jersey. It was sort of set up like a college instead of a high school. And I did not write for two years. I burned out very, very rapidly and, the third year, I took a workshop in the City [New York] just to sort of try to revive my inner life again. I took one with the poet Ai, who was not a very good teacher, but at least I was getting in there and talking with people about writing again. I was getting up at 5:30 in the morning that third year, writing for an hour, and then going to school. The school deteriorated rapidly. I quit in February of my third year there. I applied to three or four artists' colonies and basically became a colony groupie.

I traveled from colony to colony, my parakeet in my front seat. I went to the Virginia Center for the Creative Arts for a month, and then I went to Yaddo for two months. I got into Ossabaw in Georgia, but didn't end up going there, and I also got into the Helene Wurlitzer Foundation, but I didn't end up going there, either. So I just bopped around from place to place. I started to scrape my writing back together again. And at Yaddo I met Jeffrey Skinner.

I forgot to say that the other thing that happened in my third year of teaching was my mother died, during the summer of 1980, and I think that was the real instigating factor for me, in terms of making a change in my life. I knew that I was being eaten alive by that school and, in fact, I remember sitting on my couch in my apartment, and the windows were all frosted up, and I wrote on them the words "Help me! Let me out!" So, I took off.

BEATTIE: How did your mother die?

GORHAM: She had cancer. She was diagnosed in January of 1980, and she died in July, so it was a very rapid decline.

BEATTIE: When did you write your "Mother Series" of poems?

GORHAM: Not until 1985. I kept a lengthy journal throughout her illness. We were all at home, all my sisters and I, and she was at home. We had a nurse come in. My mother was giving and open about her dying up until the very end. I think that made it much easier for all of us. I think the only problem was that the four of us competed with each other to take care of her, to do things for her, and to feel useful. I tried to get some of that—not the competition, but the necessity to do something—into one of those poems, "Washing Her Hair." So I basically kept a journal through that period, but I wasn't able to write the poems for four years. Once I wrote the journal, I went back to read it and the poems almost came verbatim from the journal. I was very happy to discover that I had just been very objective and honest and straightforward, and I paid attention to the detail when I was writing in the journal. So, I could just pick up whole sections of those passages and put them into the poems, and they came out, like, one a day for five days. Those were the best poems I've ever written, really.

BEATTIE: You talked about having kept a journal since sixth grade. Do you find that many of your poems come out of journal entries?

GORHAM: They all do. The journal writing is part of the process. I write several ways. My journal is both a commonplace book, in which you pick up sections of things that you are reading and write them down, and a place to free associate; I do a lot of that. I also record day-to-day stuff—observations. I think description, for me, has always been a way into a poem.

BEATTIE: When do you write in your journal?

GORHAM: It's the start-up process. I get my cup of tea, I come up here [Gorham's home office], I sit down, I do a little bit of reading, and then I write in my journal. That's the first thing I do.

BEATTIE: So, it's in the morning, not at the end of the day.

GORHAM: At the end of the day I'm too tired. The only time I have quiet is when the kids are gone, too. So, yes, it's in the morning, when I'm fresh.

BEATTIE: Do you write poetry after writing journal entries?

GORHAM: Yes, that's usually the way it starts. Let's see, going back to Yaddo, I was working on an elegy at Yaddo for two months, and I ended up saving maybe one or two of those poems. I wrote thirty of them. But I didn't save very much. I was not writing well. But I met Jeffrey. We had a whirlwind courtship, during which time he told me he wanted me to have his kids, and I said, "Oh, okay."

BEATTIE: Did he ask you to marry him first?

GORHAM: No, he didn't. He was still married at that point.

BEATTIE: Probably a good thing, then.

GORHAM: Yes. He didn't want to tell me that, but our time together at Yaddo was ideal, it was wonderful, it was responsibility-free. It was great fun.

BEATTIE: Was he there for exactly the same period of time that you were?

GORHAM: Yes, and there was a whole group of us that got to be very fast friends and hung out together and went to the halls to dinner together. We had a great time. And then I drove Jeffrey home from Yaddo, and I realized that this man had a lot of the same values that I did, and I had gotten to know him for a couple of months, and I thought he was worth taking a risk on. So, I moved in with him, and I ended up getting a job at the University of Bridgeport very quickly, a freelance writing job, so that was a very smart move.

BEATTIE: Was he separated at the time?

GORHAM: He was separated. He told me once we got back that he was just separated, not divorced, as he had told me at Yaddo. I'll forgive him that little lie. That's one of those casual lies.

BEATTIE: Going back to Yaddo for a minute, how did you find that experience, other than meeting Jeff?

GORHAM: Oh, it was great. I've been there three times. Anyway, each time is different. But, as you know, for a woman in her late twenties, it was wonderful. It was being treated as royalty. Iowa was just the opposite. I was a peon at Iowa; I was scrambling to get on the little ladder of success. And then, when I was teaching, I was not a writer. I had to bury that part of myself. But at Yaddo I received the gift of writing time, the gift of meals three times a day, the gift of hanging out with other people who are more established, and the gift of being treated as an equal.

BEATTIE: Also, anybody who goes to Yaddo is considered to have arrived.

GORHAM: Yes, that's true. So, it came at a really good time in my life, having just been through nine months of grieving over my mother's death. It was a real boost.

BEATTIE: What kind of writing did you do the first time you were there?

GORHAM: Like I said, I worked on my elegy. They were not very good poems. They were sort of vague. They had all the trimmings of good poetry, but none of the core.

BEATTIE: The style but not the content?

GORHAM: The style but not the content. I wrote a poem called "A Photograph of My Mother" in which I talked about everything around the mother in the picture—talked about the grass, the trees, the birds, the hay, the barn, but not about the mother. And that, I think, epitomizes the problem I had. I had not reached the soul of my voice—my subject matter—even though my mother had died. I was too afraid to touch it directly. That came later.

So, Jeff and I lived together a year; we got married at Yaddo a year later, in the rose garden. Everybody who had been our friends at Yaddo when we met came up from all over the country to Saratoga, and we rented the Adelphi Hotel, which is this nineteenth century hotel. We had the whole hotel to ourselves, every room in it. We had a reception in the Adelphi, and then everybody hung out in those gorgeous lounges and went to the races after the wedding. Everybody had a wonderful time. Our Yaddo friends comprised the little core of what we called "the kiddy table," which consisted of eight or nine people. Laura Cunningham, she's a playwright—a fiction writer—she was there, as were several really wonderful artists. And then we went back to Connecticut.

We went on a honeymoon to Europe—to Switzerland and Italy—and I conceived my first child. So I was pregnant for the next nine months. And Laura was born, and with the birth of Laura began the discovery, or this sort of narrowing in on my poetic voice. Writing time—I now looked at it as sort of the only time in which I could salvage my ego and my sense of self, and I could only do this for three hours on Tuesday and three hours on Thursday. Monday, Wednesday, and Friday I worked my regular, freelance job. So I had an extremely condensed period of time in which to get some work done, and I just started to write as a woman, not as a man, anymore, and I became more interested in women's work, and I started reading only women's work, and I really haven't abandoned that since then.

BEATTIE: To what do you attribute that sudden change?

GORHAM: I think to my having become a mother. I think the other thing is living with Jeffrey. We are both poets, and a lot of the themes in my work are the kind of fine line we walk daily between being and not being, and I think that women face this in a marriage. Married men do, too, but not as often, because I think they are defined by their careers more than we are. And I had to redefine myself. I wasn't going to write like a man anymore, because I was living with a man who wrote like a man, and that would make two of us.

BEATTIE: So you think it was a subconscious switch due to your feeling of competition?

GORHAM: A little bit and, also, too, I needed to reforge my identity.

BEATTIE: I was wondering if your finding your poetic voice had anything to do, as well, with the Women's Movement?

GORHAM: I didn't discover the Women's Movement until I got here [Louisville]. There's a really strong sense of women's community here, and I think that

that's where that came from. No, this was just a fledgling voice beginning to cry out in the wilderness.

BEATTIE: Or from Connecticut. And the freelancing you were doing at the university was what?

GORHAM: I started out doing feature stories for their alumni magazine and for the newspaper. I did four of those a month. That lasted a year, and then they hired me as the information director for the Women's Athletics Department, so I was a sports information director. This meant going to basketball games and baseball games, and they wanted the women athletes to be recognized. I didn't know anything about sports. It was trial by fire. I didn't know what a free-throw was. I didn't know what a foul shot was. I didn't know anything. But there's a sport's lingo, and once you figure it out, it's really easy. I had a difficult first year, but then I got hold of it, so it was fun for a few years. Then I quit that job because I got tired of going to the games. They weren't a winning team, ever, so it was really boring; it was hard to come up with positive stories, you know. So I joined the staff of a bank and did their employee newsletter for a year. I made some good money.

BEATTIE: You talked about the transformation in your poetry at that time. What sort of poems did you start writing, and how did this new influence manifest itself?

GORHAM: Just to give you an example, "My Car Slides Off the Road" was a poem that I wrote at Iowa, and it is a very clean and crisp poem. But, first of all, the last two lines are stolen, and it really doesn't say a whole lot about my soul at all. It's interesting; I've had two other poets then steal lines from *my* poems.

BEATTIE: Who were those stolen from?

GORHAM: Theodore Roethke. "Everything I Love is Near at Hand," is a sort of a version of his "In the Far Field." I'm not sure you're supposed to admit those things directly, but people do it all the time, and if you're going to steal, you might as well steal from somebody great, like Roethke. But this was the poem that was published in *Antaeus,* and I think my "Mother Poems" were a real turning point, and those were some of them. "Mirror" was another one, which directly talks about my experience with Laura, my daughter. This was written maybe a year after she was born. Let's see, "Walking Stick" was another one. What you have here, then, are more direct emotional statements. "... I think spirits move like this—/ clinging to a parallel world, invisible/ except when they fall, startled to our side./ I watch, a nervous child, completely uncritical." Then these childbirth poems at the end. "Spice," which is a love poem, "Bundled Roses," as well, which I wrote for our wedding. Jeffrey wrote, "On the Failure of all Love Poems," and I wrote "Bundled Roses." I think my poems became more directly autobiographical, which now is very unfashionable. I think those poems I wrote soon after Laura's birth are slightly risky, but I think recently I've been taking more risks than I did even then. I think I still had a lot of the standard material to shake at that point.

BEATTIE: What about your other child? When was she born?

GORHAM: Laura was born in '83, and then Bonnie was born in '85. Then, a year after Bonnie was born, we moved to Delaware. We took an enormous risk. Jeffrey just couldn't get a teaching job, and he quit his business position and moved down to Lewes, which is where my father owns a beach house. My father offered this to us. He said, "You can pay me a hundred dollars a month and you can live there." So, we mustered up all our savings and went down there and just took the year to write. During that year, Jeffrey got an NEA [National Endowment for the Arts] grant, so we had a little more money to spare. And, also, a writing professor who was teaching at Salisbury State College went on leave, so Jeff took his position the next year. And then that year Jeff applied to U of L [University of Louisville], and we moved here. That was a very difficult year for me.

BEATTIE: The year you were in Delaware?

GORHAM: Yes. It was difficult because Jeffrey was doing so well. He won the National Poetry Series. He got an NEA grant. The volume of his writing was extraordinary. He finished *A Guide to Forgetting* in two years, and that's a brilliant book. I think it's a wonderful, wonderful book, and I'm not surprised at all that it won the National Poetry Series. I was still sort of struggling into my own. I'd gotten a number of good publications, and I had won a Connecticut Commission on the Arts grant, so that was a big boost, but I didn't have a first book yet, and here he was, coming along with his second book. I was starting to send my book around. It was a finalist everywhere and, in fact, at Wesleyan University Press, it made the top three. They ended up publishing Dean Young's book; they didn't publish mine.

So it was a difficult year. I think that, until you get your first book, you really haven't made it, and I was feeling that very deeply. I did a lot of good writing, though. I wrote "Circles," I wrote "I'd Go Back," I wrote "Snow Melt," and a number of other things that have been prize-winning poems.

BEATTIE: You were continuing to publish in little magazines?

GORHAM: Yes, I was doing pretty well with that. Not as well as I'm doing now, but pretty well. Just a little tad, now and then. But I did go for a whole eighteen months with no good news, and you need the feedback. You write in such isolation when you leave school that you need it, you really do. Or *I* needed it, anyway.

BEATTIE: Did you find it difficult having another poet in the house, either in terms of conflicting work habits or in terms of feeling professionally competitive?

GORHAM: Well, ninety percent of the time it's wonderful. We have the same vocabulary. We actually work on each other's work. He is absolutely an incredibly good critic of my work. He can look at a poem of mine and say, "This is what you need to work on; this is what you need to fix," and he's right. I can't tell you how good it is. It's better than having a teacher. And the same things goes vice versa, too, although he tends to produce more finished poems. When he doesn't, when there's something at risk there, I can nail it on the head, and he'll change it. But I came up with the title for his first book and things like that. It's a real partnership in that way. And we discover books, and we pass each other materials. We also have a playful competition, in terms of imagery. While we were at the beach, we found a collection of stuff that we discovered was named Mermaid's Purse. And he says, "Oh, I got that. I got that. It's mine." I wrote a poem called "Starfish" in sort of this race to include a metaphorical object in my work, because we live the same life, although our inner lives are quite different.

Two important things happened in Delaware that year. One is that we started going to the Episcopal Church. I was not raised in any religion at all; my father is Jewish and my mother was Lutheran, and that meant nothing. And the church was in a real small town, a wonderfully warm and welcoming little place, and we became very active and very involved with the people there. That has had a big influence on my work, too, in that I started looking outside the autobiographical, and looking outside the self to the spirit. I was just starting to scratch the surface of it with "Wind Tunnel." But then spirituality became a shared interest for Jeffrey and me, too.

The other thing that happened is, my book was accepted, finally, at Galileo Press. I decided to send my manuscript there because, number one, they're a very visible press; number two, they do beautiful books; and number three, they published a lot of the people I went to school with, and I knew that they treated their authors very well. There were six hundred manuscripts and they picked mine.

BEATTIE: Are you able to find enough time to write?

GORHAM: Well, that's probably another negative part of the fact that we're both poets. Instead of being understanding of the other, saying, "You need more writing time today than I do," we are both quite selfish about our writing time. It's a grabbing game, and we fight like dogs and cats about it. I think that you have to have a real stubbornness and arrogance to keep doing this silly thing that we call writing poetry, you know. And that's where it comes from. But we've worked out a pretty good balance. I think we've been lucky, because Jeffrey's had the whole year off because of a fellowship from the Howard Foundation. That's been really good for him. Then he has his summers, of course. And he's been able to get course release time so that he can write during the year, too. And then, when the kids are in school, I can write, although I've had to set up a freelance business, too, because our income went up for a while, and now it's going down. You know how hard it is to make it on one salary.

BEATTIE: I'd like to ask about your first book of poems, *Don't Go Back to Sleep*. In those poems it seems to me you discover and articulate the miraculous and the mundane a lot, such as in your poem "Sampler" where you write, "Everything I have lived through,/ I will view in my daughter's posture." You also draw the ironic parallel between things intimate and infinite. Do you agree with that, and how do you view that book and the development of your personal or poetic vision?

GORHAM: I think that's a very, very accurate observation. I do see a relationship between the physical details of the world and the larger abstract world. One thing I strive for in my work is the relationship of the abstract to the concrete and the miraculous and the small. I think that's why I became interested in the "Chinese" series and the "Empress" series, because of the relationship of metaphor to their daily lives. Everything is metaphorical to them. They don't pick up a spoon or a straw or put down a piece of brick without some ritual that points to tradition and to the larger picture. Their writing is that way, too. I think what poetry can do at its very best is to explore the mundane, to cause people to look at it again and not to become numb to it. So yes, I think that's a really accurate observation.

BEATTIE: I particularly like your poems "Wind Tunnel," to which we were referring before, and "The Architecture of the House Wren." Will you comment on how they relate to your spiritual beliefs?

GORHAM: "Wind Tunnel" is the first poem I wrote about the spiritual life, and it's the first long narrative poem I've written, too. It's supposed to describe a journey through the romantic tendencies of one's spiritual life to the basic idea, which is that a true spiritual life requires discipline, that faith is this type of pattern sculpted out of time, step by step, Sunday by Sunday. Each visit to the church, each service, is not going to be a miraculous event, it's not going to reaffirm your faith over and over again. It is simply going to open the door, inch by inch. But it's necessary to be there in order to make it happen, just like it's necessary to sit down and write, even though you don't feel like writing, because you have to keep the door open. I think, also, my second book is about the conflict between living a true spiritual life, which requires basically that we dissolve the ego, that we break into a kind of formlessness, that we surrender our will. And the opposite of that, which is the formation of a self, and of an ego, requires that you build all those things that you have to dissolve. It's a real conflict in one's life, and I sort of feel like I'm walking that boundary line.

BEATTIE: And that you have to keep both sides of it intact.

GORHAM: Yes. And, you know, sometimes I live on the ego side, and other times I live on the non-ego side, and it's hard to decide which way to be when. I think that comes clearer as you get older. But this is the struggle of the second book: what do you do to establish your existence on earth? I mean, what is the right thing to do? Is it to build up details? Is it to build a nest like the wren in one of my poems does—and collect things—to make pots, to make poems? Or is it our responsibility just to dissolve those things and to prepare for the final nothingness?

BEATTIE: Or can you only dissolve through doing those things?

GORHAM: Right. Well, I have to say that, when you're writing well, you're out of yourself, and that's the only time that that's the case. It's not the only time; there are times in church that I'm out of myself.

BEATTIE: You also go, periodically, on retreats to the Abbey of Gethsemani, near Bardstown, Kentucky, don't you?

GORHAM: I've been there a couple of times. I haven't been able to go as often as I'd like.

BEATTIE: What is that like, or how is that experience for you?

GORHAM: It's not entirely positive. You see, the monks there believe that this life is preparation for the next life. Well, that's one thing they believe. Death is a real, constant presence there. But their faith is uplifting, and you're given a tremendous amount of solitude. Looking inside yourself is not always a great thing, but I've had some very uplifting experiences there. I like the discipline of attending church service seven times a day. I like to punctuate the day that way, instead of the way it's punctuated now, with kids' schedules and mealtimes and things like that.

In my poetry I've always been concerned with foreshadowing. And again, that's the view of the macro and the micro. I point out in my poem "Irises" that the longest petal of the iris is the petal that is going to die first. It is going to wither and fall. And I compare it to my hand, but of course my hand is just the balcony of my death, and the beginning of the iris's death is also the beginning of my death. I have a more recent poem in which I talk about holding on to a particular detail, that occurs now, that perhaps will bode for something in the future. You can also call that hypochondria. You know, if you get a scratch or you feel your heart skip a beat, you think, "Oh, God, does that mean I'm going to die of a heart attack?"

BEATTIE: I see it having to do with connections, though, too.

GORHAM: Yes, looking for that sense of relationship and order.

BEATTIE: In your poem, "The Death of Saint Claire," you write, "My whole life comes to this place." Are you referring to an external as well as to an internal place?

GORHAM: Yes, I am. That poem was written twenty years ago. I don't know where that poem came from. But that's a macro and a micro, it's a gathering of things.

BEATTIE: We talked about the Chinese culture paralleling the poetic vision. Would you comment on this?

GORHAM: I think that, when you use details from the physical world, they're saturated with meaning. But that is a poetic process. And the Chinese do that very well. I often will see something physical before it becomes language. I'll see a black iris before I'll understand what that black iris is supposed to mean.

BEATTIE: I've become very aware of writers being primarily vision or sound-oriented in their writing and in their approach to it.

GORHAM: I think I'm definitely that way, vision-oriented. That's why description is a way into a poem for me. I'll look at something and it's the act of writing it down and looking at it very carefully and very precisely that brings out the truth, the insight, instead of the insight coming first. Although, when I put my book together, I really didn't have any sense of what its theme was. And I think that, as time has gone by, my themes have become much more crystallized and much more clear to me, so that I will know exactly what I want to write about. I'll try to find my way to the poem from there. But that usually isn't successful. Again, I have to start in a small place and move to the larger picture, although, as time has gone by, I think my obsessions have become more clear.

BEATTIE: Would you talk more about your book of poetry, *The Dragon's Lullaby: Sonnets to the Last Empress,* and comment on the symbolism, both in those sonnets and in the culture?

GORHAM: That book was triggered by Bernardo Bertolucci's film, *The Last Emperor,* by the opening scene in which the Empress is wheeled out into her death chamber, and she's lying on her deathbed with a black pearl in her mouth. I saw those first three minutes of the film and then I did not see the rest of the film. I left. I liked it so much, I was so startled by it, that I said, "I want to write a poem about this." I wrote something called "The Dying Empress." This is the last poem in a series, which I've already thrown away. I wrote that poem the next morning, after I saw the film at night. It was a perfect triggering subject for me, because where the Empress was is what the Tibetans call Bardo, which is the transition between death and rebirth, or it's got a larger meaning now, which basically means any place of tremendous change, any time of tremendous change or transition. And I think that this is where the Empress lived a great deal of her life; I imagined that she lived this way, anyway.

In the beginning, she was very ambitious. I think that she desired to be an Empress from very early on. At least, in my work, I'm going to talk about it in that imaginative way, because I really care very little about the historical truth. There were so many repressive forces at work, and I think that her life became a struggle of balancing. You know, "Do what they tell you to do," and "Do what I want to do," and it's in that kind of conflict, of back and forth, of "Stay where you are," and "No, I want to go here." Then, once she became Empress, there became the issue of the role of being a mother to her child and being a ruler, and those roles required very different kinds of being. One required a great deal of abject cruelty. Cruelty was the way that you did things then. Being a mother required nurturing. And then, finally, at the end—hopefully the series resolves this conflict—there's a sense of forgiveness. Then the last poem in the series, "Dancing With the Empress," brings me into the picture, too.

BEATTIE: Do you feel that her life is parallel to your life, with you being a writer and a mother?

GORHAM: Like I said, I think that we're asked to make decisions every single minute of the day between being and not being and, as a mother, you certainly realize this. You know, when do I give in and allow my child to do this, or when is it better that I do it myself? Or when do I demand that I be a writer, and when do I give in to my husband? You're asked to do this over and over again.

BEATTIE: In your poem "Bisecting a Water Lily" that appeared this spring in *The American Voice,* you write, "Call it longing or balance or compensation,/

but I believe everything completes itself,/ even in detachment." Will you comment on that comment, if you will, on your visions?

GORHAM: You know, my comment is a loaded comment, and it comes from two different places. The word *compensation*—actually, the poem sort of came together after I had read an essay by Ralph Waldo Emerson called "Compensation," which talks a lot about balance and polarity. It's a wonderful essay; I love Emerson. If there's anybody who has influenced my work, it's Emerson. But the word *compensation,* the notion of compensation, comes from that detachment and the necessity to separate yourself from the loved one in order to complete the whole. Detachment is a password in the Twelve-Step Program. It's a way of getting yourself through crises, removing yourself emotionally and focusing on yourself. So, that's what that is about.

BEATTIE: The newest, as-yet-unpublished poems you've allowed me to read seem stronger in their vision, or perhaps bolder, than some of your previous work. Do you see that, and will you comment on your current work and on future projects you may have in mind?

GORHAM: Well, I hope that is what is happening. I mean, I feel that that's happening. Like I said, I think I've defined what I'm writing about and what my purpose is, and in my work I now get to the point a lot quicker.

BEATTIE: It seems that the voice behind the poems is now stronger.

GORHAM: Yes, it's more confident. I think, in general, I'm more confident. I think that publishing this book, *Don't Go Back to Sleep,* made the difference, and I've had a lot of success in magazines since then, and I'm ready for my second book. But, also, I just sort of know what I want to say now and, at the same time, I want to take more risks. I'm anxious to break out of what I think my other influence was, which is Louise Gluck. I'm anxious to not sound like her anymore and to really amplify my voice. Sometimes I think when you become more defined in your themes, there's a danger of repeating yourself, and I think I've become much more obsessive in my recent work. Polarity obsesses me. Also, the sense of having to sacrifice one's integrity, both in a physical sense and a moral sense, over and over again, that's become an issue. Just what does it mean to be here? How do you establish yourself in the brief time that you have? And I don't mean that career-wise. But I've become so obsessed with it that I sometimes think that these truths are being reduced to trivialities, or to banalities. But I think that the truths are universals, and the reason why they are universals is they have relationships to huge areas of our lives, to many different areas of our lives. But I think that that's normal, and that's a risk I have to take.

I also have to say that I'm reaching farther, in terms of detail, in my work. I said at one point in my journal, "I really want to write a poem that's like a sideshow, that has a sort of bizarre and quirky, quixotic language and sound in it," and I listed a bunch of words. I listed *gold tooth.* I listed the word *tabernacle.* I listed the color *scarlet.* And I ended up writing a poem called "Casual Lies."

BEATTIE: Something else that struck me about your new work was that there seems to be an insistence in it, a call to action, instead of merely a summation.

GORHAM: A definite move from the passive to the active. I think that's definitely true. And I think that that has tied in also with becoming more feminist as I get older, realizing this [Louisville] is a wonderful city for that. Women are respected here. I have lived in so many other places in which the women I saw were the wives of lawyers, you know. I've just written three new poems that I'm really happy with. I had a very good writing year this year. I think that I like to see my poems as cranky.

BEATTIE: Cranky?

GORHAM: I'm a very cranky person, and I'm impatient, and I want my poems to reflect that, to be true to my character. I think my first book is a real quiet, submissive book. I mean, I have things to say in there, but it's a passive book. And I'm not afraid to show that I'm a little cantankerous.

BEATTIE: Do you think living in Kentucky or in Louisville has affected your writing in any way?

GORHAM: I think living in Louisville has. I love it here. Like I said, I think there's a strong feminist community, and the Kentucky Foundation for Women has been instrumental. It's a small state. It's not like the East Coast. It's sort of like being in a small family instead of being in a huge family. On the East Coast, you're drowned. I mean, you're just lost, there are just so many people there, and there are so many people doing the same thing. Here, there are fewer of them, so Jeffrey and I get the recognition that we feel we deserve. That's delightful; that really does help. So, I'm very grateful to this state for that.

May 18, 1992

Gorham's chapbook, *The Night Lifted Us,* co-authored with Jeffrey Skinner, appeared in 1991 from Larkspur Press. In 1994, her manuscript *The Tension Zone,* published in 1996, won the Four Way Books Award in Poetry, judged by Heather McHugh. Since her interview, Gorham's poems have appeared widely in such magazines as *Poetry, The Kenyon Review, Ohio Review, Georgia Review, Southern Review, Missouri Review, Ploughshares,* and *Poetry Northwest,* where in 1990 she won the Carolyn Kizer Award. Other awards include grants and fellowships from The Kentucky State Art Council and The Kentucky Foundation for Women. Her work was anthologized in *A Formal Feeling Comes: Formal Poems by Contemporary North American Women* (Story Line Press, 1993) and *Love Poems by Women* (Fawcett, 1990). In March 1994, Gorham founded Sarabande Books, Inc., a small press devoted to the publication of poetry and short fiction. Gorham serves as President and Editor-in-Chief. She has also worked as a Kentucky Artist-in-Residence, teaching poetry to elementary school students throughout the state. She recently edited a special all-poetry edition of *The American Voice.*

BOOKS BY SARAH GORHAM

Don't Go Back to Sleep. Sparks, Md.: Galileo Press, 1989.
The Night Lifted Us. (with Jeffrey Skinner). Monterey: Ky.: Larkspur Press, 1991.

The Tension Zone. New York: Four Way Books, 1996.

Last Call: Poems on Alcoholism, Addiction and Deliverance. Co-editor with Jeffrey Skinner, Louisville, Ky.: Sarabande Books, 1997.

Lynwood Montell

MONTELL: My name is William Lynwood Montell, and I was born on February 18, 1931, in Monroe County, Kentucky, in the Rockbridge Community. My mother was Nellie Hazel Chapman Montell, and she was born on the same homeplace that I was. My father was William Guy Montell. He was born all of three miles away. My dad's people were storytellers. My mom's dad was a story-teller, too. He would get my brother and me aside, usually one at a time, and he would just love to tell us stories.

BEATTIE: Do you attribute that background and those stories to your choice of a career as a folklorist and to your choice of subject matter for your books?

MONTELL: Yes, I do. Let me begin by saying I joined the navy in 1951 and I took three or four Armed Forces Institute correspondence courses leading to the notion that I wanted to be a forester when I got out of the navy. That didn't pan out at all. But I did, early on, even before I got out of the navy, decide that I wanted to be a horse doctor, a veterinarian. And when I got out of the navy in the fall of '55, I went to Campbellsville College one year in the pre-vet program and then transferred to U of K [University of Kentucky] and did two years there. My last semester at UK, which was at the end of my junior year, I was taking all kinds of "ology" courses, as well as a chemistry course. I didn't like it at all, and I knew that I was in the wrong field. So, I prayed one night. I said, "Lord, if you'll just get me out of this semester with at least a C standing, then I'll get into some field that I like." I really did. So I got out of those courses with a respectable standing and went into history and studied under [William] Clement Eaton, at U of K, and under Dr. Tom Clark. When my first book came out, by the way, Dr. Clark wrote me a letter and he said, "Lyn, that's just the kind of book that we professors always hope our former students will write."

BEATTIE: And this book was *The Saga of Coe Ridge*?

MONTELL: Yes. I got into history because I loved human beings. Then, because of financial difficulties, my wife and I—we had two kids—moved back to Tompkinsville. My wife's name was Ruth Evelyn Jackson Montell. She was working as a lunchroom dietitian. I was commuting to and from Western Kentucky University, and I eventually began teaching at Temple Hill, and while commuting I was taking history courses. The more I got into history, it just turned me against the pedantic way that many historians back then approached the discipline.

It just so happened, the last semester I was at Western, D.K. [Donald Knight] Wilgus, who was teaching at Western then, moved on to UCLA [University of California at Los Angeles] and founded the folklore program there. I was looking through the catalog for an elective course to finish out my schedule, and I saw under the English department a course titled The Ballad. I enrolled in The Ballad. I didn't know what it was all about, but it wasn't more than two weeks until I knew that I had found what I was looking for. And it wasn't long after that that D.K. got a notice from Richard Dorson, head of the Folklore Institute of Indiana University. Dorson had managed to get funding from the feds [federal government] to get five National Defense Fellowships for the study of folklore. So I applied for one of those five NDA [National Defense Education Act] fellowships and got it. I began my doctoral study at Indiana, then, in the fall of '61. At Indiana I was able to study human beings through their expressions, through the folklore. I continued in my study of history, but it was a different thrust in history. I got into social and intellectual history. Then I studied another field at the Ph.D. level—cultural geography. All of these were letting me get at what I loved most of all, and that is people. But the folklore, I think, is what it was that let me see that I could really apply the things that I had grown up with and actually make a living at it. Oral historians and folklorists have a common ground now, with cultural anthropology. By golly, even historians are coming into the fold.

BEATTIE: You grew up without electricity, and you attended a one-room school. I assume there were several classes being conducted at once in one room and all taught by the same teacher. Did the older students teach the younger ones, too?

MONTELL: Yes, they did. I not only went to the Rockbridge Elementary School, but then my last two years I walked an equal distance in the other direction and finished up at Maryville School, another one-room school. Both of these schools were taught by, naturally, one teacher. I had both male and female teachers. I'm still persuaded that there has never been an educational system any better than the one-room school. Now when the conditions were overcrowded, as they sometimes were in earlier times, with sixty or seventy kids in one room, it would be hard to maintain discipline, let alone teach anything. I'm very philosophical about this, but I'm very persuaded I'm right; the good thing about the one-room school is, when you are a little fella, then you hear the older ones during their recitations. You don't understand what it's all about, but you're hearing the youngsters as they begin to learn. So, constantly, you're being reinforced. And did the students help the teacher back then? The answer is yes. It was not uncommon for students, because they didn't go on to high school, by and large, to finish elementary school, what we called grade school, then just drop out. But it was also not uncommon for both fellas and gals, after they graduated from the eighth grade, to stay on three, four, and five years in the eighth grade, as nothing more than teachers' assistants.

BEATTIE: Did a particular subject emerge as a favorite for you early on, and when did writing become something you enjoyed?

MONTELL: I don't recall writing, but I recall I've always had an avid interest in spelling. We were taught, of course, to spell phonetically. I was a very good speller and always have been. In terms of writing, I never felt confident with my writing skills until I got into graduate school at Indiana University in the early '60s.

BEATTIE: Was there another subject in elementary school, other than spelling, that you particularly liked?

MONTELL: I always liked history. I liked reading. We wouldn't refer to being in the second grade and the third grade, but we'd refer to being in the third reader and the fourth reader, and that would be synonymous with the word *year.* I loved to read and, as a matter of fact, I got sick, I don't even know what was wrong with me, one year there, and I stayed out of school a while. My mom, she always liked to read as well, so she was tutoring me at home. I was able to totally skip the second grade, and I wasn't sick that long. The teacher just had enough insight to see that I would probably be dragging if I did stay in the second grade. So, he promoted me on to the third grade, but my mom had been letting me read to her every day.

BEATTIE: Did she read to you much when you were a child?

MONTELL: Yes. And my dad did, too. As a matter of fact, that brings up a very wonderful family memory, and that is, when I was in the old ancestral homeplace, every Friday we got *The Grit* newspaper. It had a magazine section to it containing stories. I always looked forward to Friday nights, and this, I think, influenced my life, really. My mom, on Friday afternoons, would clean the lampshade on a big reading lamp that we had, getting things ready for that night, see. Then, while she would sit there and crochet or maybe quilt, my dad was sitting there reading to all of us out of *The Grit* magazine section. My brother and I slept together then, and we would be in bed, just lying there, taking in every word. I recall Zane Grey's story, "Twin Sombreros." There are several stories that I can even recall the names to right now, just because my dad read them to us.

Then, when I got a little bit bigger, I started delivering *Grit* newspapers to some of the neighbors; I was on horseback. I quit when I got dragged off my horse by a dog once. But, my mom and dad, they didn't go to high school. As a matter of fact, they both went probably through the sixth grade, and that was quite an achievement then, even. But they were both very sharp individuals. Both were good readers and encouraged their children.

I think, too, that I can attribute my interest in sense of place (and this is in one of my books, probably the book *Killings,* where I talk about the cultural geographer Carl O. Sauer, and he was at Indiana just for a semester when I was there. He was from Berkeley, actually, already retired) to the time he had commented, in a class that I had with him, that if he had his academic life to live over, then he would choose as a study area one small sub-regional area and he would go into that area and look at everything that human beings placed on the cultural landscape—you know, fences, road patterns, field patterns, houses, outbuildings. He said, "I would document what's there, then I would go back every fifteen years and document all over again, and I would look for changes and ask *why.*" That not only challenged me, but it gave me an opportunity, because I was at Campbellsville College soon after that, and Sauer's philosophy gave me an opportunity to also adopt what was essentially my home region, about forty counties in Tennessee and nine or ten in Kentucky, as the upper Cumberland region. Although people will say, "I'm a Kentuckian," or "I'm a Tennessean," culturally, there just simply is not a difference. State is not nearly as important as county. So, those of us in that whole upper Cumberland region, especially if we grew up in a rural area, would say, "Lynwood, where are you from?" I wouldn't say, "Tompkinsville," and I wouldn't say, "Tompkinsville, Kentucky." I would simply say, "Monroe County." We shorten it, actually, to "Roe County," you see, and I think this is typical of people of the upper South, especially. They identify by county and not by county seat. After homeplace, after the land that you identify with as your family farm, then community is the next construction. It's almost as meaningful as family, the community in which you grow up. As a result of that, then, if a young man from, let's say, Stone Town or Mt. Gilead or Cyclone were to come into Rockbridge for the purpose of dating one of the local gals there, then he just might get rocked or stoned, you see. Because everyone felt like they needed to guard their home community. It was territory.

BEATTIE: What did that mean in terms of people from outside moving in or marrying in a county, over generations?

MONTELL: Well, it took place. But there wasn't much moving in. It was inbred up until essentially the 1930s and '40s. People left the area. They moved to Muncie and Indianapolis and Fort Wayne and Gary and Chicago and Detroit. Typically, they moved out, and it wasn't that they moved to Detroit, married someone there, and then brought that spouse back to Rockbridge. That just did not happen. Now *why* it didn't happen, I really don't know. Whether they just didn't want to come home again or whether their spouse wouldn't hear to it . . . that's the way it was until the 1930s. But then when people began to get pick-up trucks and cars, and when a lot of people began going to high school, especially around 1940, '41, '42, then it was fairly common to marry from across the county, but not until then.

BEATTIE: You were one of the few from your immediate community to go to high school. Why was it that you went and where did you go?

MONTELL: I really don't know how to answer your question, *why* did I go? A livelihood from farming, I think I recognized the fact that it was beginning to phase out. I really hadn't thought about it until you asked that question. As to where I went to high school, a man who lived north of Rockbridge three miles from Cyclone, he had an old bus. It was his private bus. Back in that day and time, if you rode a bus to school, you paid. We paid three dollars a month per head. But this bus did not go to the Tompkinsville School; he took students to Gamaliel. We split Tompkinsville right down the middle and went on below eight miles to Gamaliel on the Tennessee line.

BEATTIE: It was a choice, then, which school to go to?

MONTELL: Oh Lord, yes. I mean, they were just thankful to get you in *any* school. I went to Gamaliel for three years and then we transferred to Tompkinsville because my brother wanted to play basketball up there, and he was a good player. So, I graduated from Tompkinsville in 1948. I've got to admit that during my first two years in high school at Gamaliel, I made virtually straight As, and when I saw how easy it was, I began to back off some and just didn't study as I should have.

After high school in Tompkinsville, then I went immediately to Andrew Jackson Business University in Nashville. I thought that that might be the career that I would carve out for myself, working as an accountant. I was in Andrew Jackson for probably ten or eleven months and got some sort of certificate and then went to Bowling Green and took a job in a bank at a staggering salary of one hundred and fifty dollars a month. Now, that was in nineteen hundred and fifty. I saw there was no future whatsoever in the banking business. So I joined the navy.

I did get married in Bowling Green to a young woman—Betty Lois Cherry from Smiths Grove, Warren County. It shouldn't have ever taken place, because it wasn't more than five or six months later that she came in one day and announced to me that she had filed for divorce. I was still only eighteen years of age and frankly didn't know what a life in this world was all about. So soon thereafter I made overtures to Ruth Evelyn Jackson, whom I had dated my last year in high school. Then we married, and we were married twenty-seven years. She's the mom of my only two children, Moniesa and Brad. Moniesa was born in January of '54, and Brad was born in December of '56. Brad now is an investment counselor in Shelbyville, and he has two sons. My daughter is married to Jack Wright. She's working now in the health department on campus at Western Kentucky University. Otherwise, she was raising three boys. Her husband is in the construction business.

BEATTIE: You were saying you were married for twenty-seven years. Did you get divorced?

MONTELL: I got divorced, yes, but another person came into my life, Barbara Allen.

Together we wrote one book, *From Memory to History,* but we've collaborated on numerous other things. Barbara and I got married in nineteen and eighty and were married for ten years and one month or something like that. We were very happy for ten years, or close to it, and then Barbara reached a mid-life crisis. She had turned forty-four and, ever since she turned forty-four, she was dreading forty-five and almost fell apart at the seams just in anticipation and dread of it. So she just decided, even before she turned forty-five, that she wanted to start life all over again. She moved to Wyoming just to be out West. We were divorced, then, in July of '91.

I had retired early from Western Kentucky University, at age fifty-nine, and I had gone to Notre Dame where Barbara was department head, and I was teaching part-time and loving it. I mean, I could write and still retain contact with the academic world and with students. You know, as I know, students keep you young. I tend to identify with my students, really. Then, after Barbara announced her intentions that we would break up, and after we did, I came back to Kentucky. I went to Dean Ward Helstrom at Western and I said, "Dean, I would like to come back and teach one course. Is that possible?" So, Helstrom says, "Well, yes. There's no problem with that." He said, "You're a senior folklorist and we don't have one right now in the program." But he said, "Will you come back as acting department head for one semester as well?" I agreed to it. About two weeks after I took over as interim head, the dean asked me if I would go on acting as department head through the spring term of '92. I said, "Well, why not?" Then it wasn't very much longer after that that he came to me again and he said, "I want you to be department head for the '92–'93 school year." I went back in on Monday morning and I said, "Here are the four provisions that, if you agree to them, I will agree to go on for one more year as interim head of the department." The first provision was "You will not ask me to serve after the '92–'93 school year." So what I'm going to do is go ahead through this academic year as interim head, and then go back to full-time retirement, but under the optional retirement program, which means I will teach half-time and draw thirty-eight percent of my full salary plus full retirement benefits. And I will still have telephone and mailing privileges.

BEATTIE: We started talking about your starting college with a business school. What happened after that, in terms of your college education?

MONTELL: I went from the business school to the banking career to the navy, and I spent four years in the navy. After I got out of the navy, I enrolled immediately in Campbellsville College. I went there for one year. That was in '55 and the spring of '56.

BEATTIE: Is there any particular reason you chose Campbellsville?

MONTELL: Yes, simply because Ruth Evelyn had graduated from there when it was a junior college. She just loved it and I did, too. Later, I went back there as a teacher, and then I became dean for a while. Anyway, I put in one year at Campbellsville, then transferred to UK in the pre-vet program and, as I say, because of financial reasons, transferred to Western. Before graduating from Western, I taught for a year and a half at Temple Hill High School in Barren County. It is now part of Barren County High School. But Temple Hill was a wonderful, wonderful situation. I loved the kids and they loved me. I taught a course in citizenship and then American History. I graduated form Western Kentucky University with a major in history and with a minor in Spanish and in geography. It was there, during my last semester at Western, that I took this course on the ballad. Then it was because I was in that course that D.K. Wilgus had passed on to me the fact that he had news that Indiana had these five National Defense Fellowships. And I applied for one and got it. It was thirty-three hundred dollars a year. Ruth Evelyn did not have to teach. When I got my first job then, in the fall of '63, I went back to Campbellsville College simply as an assistant professor of social sciences. I taught a folklore course, too. But my salary was sixty-three hundred a year. That was good money.

BEATTIE: Prior to talking more about your first jobs after graduate school, may we talk about your graduate school experience? Did you take courses from any of the eight people who made Indiana one of the outstanding folklore programs in the country?

MONTELL: Yes. Although I grew to somewhat disrespect him later on in my career, at the time I just really venerated Richard M. Dorson. He probably had the name of being the leading folklorist in the country. His interest was history and folklore, you see. Early on, after I had accepted the NDEA fellowship for Indiana, he asked me, "Well, what will you do for your dissertation study?" And, my God, I didn't know, you know.

As a little boy growing up I had heard of Coe Ridge, and it was always in fear and trembling, because these stories drifted out about the bootleggers and all of that. I know it scared me, what I had heard about it. So I thought, "My God, how interesting it would be to actually capture these stories on tape, about the Coe Colony, both from blacks and whites." So I said, "Well, I would like to collect the stories about this"—back then we called it Negro—"I would like to collect these stories about this Negro colony, and test the validity of the spoken word." And Dorson loved it. He just loved my master's thesis, which I had done on supernatural narratives told by blacks and whites in the Cumberland River country.

BEATTIE: Was that the precursor to your book *Ghosts Along the Cumberland?*

MONTELL: Yes. That's what really gave me the idea for *Ghosts Along the Cumberland.* So I presented my master's thesis containing my analysis of the storytelling traditions, along with a lot of these narratives that people had told me. And Dorson, just as it was, hugged it to his chest and loved it. He signed it, as the chair of the thesis committee.

BEATTIE: After you'd taken your graduate school courses, which area of folklore emerged as your specialty or as your favorite?

MONTELL: That's very easy to respond to, and that is simply the historical legend, because early on I was just enamored, not only by the context in which these stories were told socially, but by the content as well. I just wondered, you know, how people are able to retain the historical core of truth in these stories. And not only that, but I was just fascinated by the content of them. They're wonderful stories, as you well know. I had amassed numerous Civil War legends, and legends about the Cumberland River, supernatural legends. Look at virtually any supernatural legend, let's say a ghost story; it's amazing how much historical content it possesses. Take away the supernatural part of that story, and you've still got a very good description of a house, you see. You've got a good description, many times, of what the furniture was like, at least in the room in which the appearance was made. I've been tempted, even, to write an article about the historical content of supernatural legends.

BEATTIE: How about the psychological content?

MONTELL: As I tell my students, whether this is really true or not is not really the important thing. It's the fact that the storytellers believe it to be true, and the fact that they're going to structure their lives in accordance with what they believe to be true.

BEATTIE: At least a part of it is true—the psychological, emotional aspect of a story.

MONTELL: That's very true, and there are many historical legends that are full of truth that historians would debunk. For example, Abraham Lincoln. It is carved in stone that Abraham Lincoln was born near Hodgenville, you see. All history ascribes that to him, that he was born there. But, the truth of the matter is, his parents' generation lived either in what is now Clay County, Tennessee, or in Cumberland County, Kentucky, for several years. By several, I don't mean just four or five, but I mean numerous years. And Abraham Lincoln's father was the first county court clerk ever in Cumberland County, Kentucky, which was carved out in 1796, I think. Now, you go to the visitor's temple in Hodgenville, to Lincoln's shrine there, and there's a map of the Lincoln family's journey westward. It does not even show Cumberland County, Kentucky, as being a part of their westward trek. There are local legends that say that Abe Lincoln was born in what is now my home county of Monroe, when it was then part of Cumberland County. There was an old black woman, Jean Bedford, and she was still living when I was a little boy. She died at age 114. I never heard her say this, but she always maintained—she called her her "Mammy," her mother—she said, "My mammy always said that she *nussed* little Abe Lincoln when he was a baby." And there was an old banker, Price Kirkpatrick—and this is on tape—he told me that, and I didn't see the letter, but he said, "I've got the letter in a lock box, and it was written by Abraham Lincoln's father after they moved," (to, I guess, LaRue County), "and the letter written back to this old man's grandfather, old Price Kirkpatrick's grandfather.' And in the letter there was a postscript, and it said, 'And little Abe is better now.'" Now, old man Kirkpatrick would not have known of this little baby had they not at one time lived there, you see.

BEATTIE: Why is it, then, that history hasn't adopted that?

MONTELL: I don't know, but you don't change history once it's been carved into stone; you don't change it. And I wouldn't touch it with a ten-foot pole.

So, anyway, I'm interested in historical legends like that. The things, I guess, that I'm interested in more than anything else are family stories and community stories. Family stories that give one—it's a term I think I coined—generational bonding. You see, I know, for example, why my great-great-grandfather Strode, not James K. Strode, but his daddy, I know why he was named "Pick" Strode. When he was a little boy, it is said that he could pick up more brush from a freshly cleared new ground than any of the other fellas his age. Somehow, even though people are dead in your family, their memories live on, and this is the generational bonding I'm talking about. Through family narratives, the generations live on. It's not only the land, then, if there's a generational continuity in the land, as there is in my case, but it's the bonding that takes place because of the narratives that the family continues to tell about these family members. And it's something else, and I'm sure you've observed this. But in my culture, at least, people don't do this now, but at one time, in my grandparents' generation, if there was a family photograph made and maybe a spouse of one of these family members was deceased, the survivor is holding a picture of the spouse in his or her hands. That person is not dead, you see.

BEATTIE: You are currently chairman of the Kentucky Oral History Commission. Did you have a role in founding that commission?

MONTELL: Actually, my role in founding the Kentucky Oral History Commission was simply in an advisory capacity. I don't know, actually, when I did come onto it as an active commission member. But I've been appointed now by some four or five governors, at least. I'm so proud of this organization, because we're the only state that has oral history as a line item in the state budget. We won't be, I guess, after our merger with the Historical Society, but we will still have control of our own budget within the Historical Society.

BEATTIE: I'd like to talk more about your academic and then your publishing career.

MONTELL: I stayed on and made full professor at Campbellsville College before I left in 1969 to go to Western. Not only did I make full professor, but I had also, in 1966, achieved—I started to say "to the highest status," and yet I never liked it, I never have liked administration. But I became Academic Dean in '66, and then in '68 they elevated the title to Vice-President for Academic Affairs at Campbellsville. Then I went to Western beginning in the fall of '69, leaving Campbellsville only because there was a newly emerging folklore program at Western, and I wanted to be a part of it. At Campbellsville I taught one course in folklore, but I saw no future for it there. So, I moved to Western and immediately was stuck with the job of assistant dean of the College of Liberal Arts. I kept that for one year and gave it up. A year later, I was able to spearhead the graduate folklore program's coming into existence. Folk Studies was a separate program under the Vice-President for Academic Affairs from about '71 to '76, and then we had grown enough, with five full-time folklorists on faculty, that they gave us departmental status. So, we became the Department of Folklore and Intercultural Studies. Actually, it was just the Department of Intercultural Studies, now that I think about it. I was coordinating programs in Folklore and Afro-American Studies and Asian Studies and European Studies and Latin American Studies. Then the person who was Vice-President for Academic Affairs gave his job up, and he took everything from me except Afro-American Studies and Folk Studies. But I was department head all the time until '82. Then Western, as all state institutions, went through a serious financial crunch, and any department that had fewer than ten full-time faculty members had to be subsumed within a larger unit. So, we lost identity. English wanted us and thought they would get us, but we had come out of English and we knew we didn't want to go back. So, as it happened, modern languages—they were called foreign languages then—had only ten full-time faculty members, and therefore their existence was tenuous. So they came courting and we went courting. We married foreign languages, and it came out the Department of Modern Languages and Intercultural Studies. I was coordinator of Folklore at that point, not department head. In the meantime, I had made full professor back in the late '70s at Western, and I taught until 1989, when I retired.

BEATTIE: I've wanted to talk about your being known for your use of oral history sources in the study of local history and culture. What drew you to oral history as a technique or as a source?

MONTELL: It was when I responded to Richard Dorson that I wanted to do this study of these historical legends. At that time, until I began researching this, I really didn't know that there was something called Oral History. Then I ran across the name of Allan Nevins from Columbia University and read some things that he had written, some articles as well as his book. I just became enamored with the whole concept, knowing full well that the experiences that I had grown up with, and that my people had grown up with, would never see print unless I took it upon myself to do something about it. I don't view myself as being the creator, although creativity is at work in producing a book, I'll grant you that, or an article. But I think where I pride myself, and this is not a boastful statement, but I hold the ability to draw people out and to let them articulate their emotions and their experiences in a narrative framework. I'm letting them create, as it were, and this is what pleases me very much. So, I have always, in terms of what I've published, looked upon myself as being the person who can make others' experiences articulate to the world at large.

BEATTIE: But your creativity may just be that vision, the vision of the possibility of this particular community, that everyone else who drives through it has forgotten, and it may be your saying, "Wait a minute. This is special because . . ."

MONTELL: Well, you may be right, and I appreciate your saying that. But I have a very strong commitment not only to write about local people and local things, but to write *for* them, and I write for them in a non-jargonistic way. The thing that I pride myself in is that I write in terms that my subjects can understand. If they've got a sophomore education in high school, they can read what I write.

BEATTIE: So, your audience is not the typical audience for which most academics write?

MONTELL: That's exactly right, and I pride myself in that. I'm always hopeful that the academic sector will appreciate and read what I write, but I don't write *for* them.

BEATTIE: I know that academic audiences do read what you write and have valued what you write and have used your books as models. *The Saga of Coe Ridge* I remember as one of the first oral histories I read when I was getting a degree in oral history, in the mid-'70s, and it's still used as a model. So, obviously, it is not just *still* around, but still around and revered. I think it's the rare writer who can have that bridge between or among audiences.

MONTELL: To move from *The Saga of Coe Ridge*—because I do want to tell this—my book called *Don't Go Up Kettle Creek,* the title for that book was not my choice. That was the Press [University of Tennessee Press]. I wanted to call it what is now the subtitle. I wanted to call it *Verbal Legacy of the Upper Cumberland.* But the Press thought . . . well, I call the title cutesy. The Press thought that a cutesy title might help to regionalize it and sell it. So the Press asked me could I somehow pick out a title that would maybe help to sell it, to regionalize it. So I was reading through some of my transcripts and I came across this story that this fellow John Stone had told me, about how he was the cub pilot on a steamboat, and the captain had turned the boat over to him, and the captain was taking a nap. And John Stone, the young cubber, had turned up a little river there near Selina, Tennessee, and had missed the main channel of the Cumberland, and he ran aground. He woke up the captain, and the captain wanted to know what was taking place. The young cubber, John Stone, told him he had missed the main channel. So the captain got him back in the main channel of the river and headed north, and the captain looked at him and he says, "Now then," he says, " young man, don't go up Kettle Creek." That was the next major tributary up the river. John Stone died a week ago tomorrow, at age ninety-three. His daughter called me and said her dad had always thought so much of me, because I'd quoted him several times. I'd made his experience articulate, you see, known to the world at large. He just loved me, she said, so she called me about him being dead. And the way it worked out, I could not go either to the funeral home or to the funeral, because I had so many meetings that I had to attend. But I sent flowers. Then the granddaughter called me after the fact to say that she wanted me to order her a copy of that book, because they used *Don't Go Up Kettle Creek* in their eulogy of this old man at his funeral. See, here he was, he had achieved immortality. But not only through God, you know, but because of this book. I think that thrilled me more than anything that's happened to me in a long time.

BEATTIE: It brings your sense of place full circle.

MONTELL: Oh, you'd better believe it. Whenever your work is mentioned at a funeral—now *that* did something to me. And then this *Singing The Glory Down,* I was at the Kentucky State Singing Convention this past Friday night in Bowling Green. And the daughter of a man whose picture is in that book, and who had a very well-known group, she's a very sick woman, in her late thirties, I would say. She's had nine surgeries now, and she was going into surgery again on Monday after I met her on Friday. She came to me and she was bawling like a baby, because it had meant so much to her to read about her daddy. And of course, you see, she had followed in his footsteps, she had been a singer, too. She said, "I want you to know," and tears were just running down her cheeks, she said, "I want you to know, I'm taking that book into surgery with me." She says, "They may say I can't do it, but I'm going to do it. It's going into surgery with me."

BEATTIE: So now your *books* have some strange senses of places, too.

MONTELL: Oh boy, I'm telling you. So, I called her then after her surgery, I called her on Tuesday to see how things were going. And, lo and behold, she didn't have a malignancy as they had anticipated. She hadn't taken my book to surgery, but she did have it on her bed, back in the room.

BEATTIE: You've published, I believe, seven major books and you're about to publish the eighth.

MONTELL: I don't know the honest to God number, I really don't.

BEATTIE: Well, I believe that's it. Do you feel that your drive to produce these books derived as much from a desire, or from a need, to *write* as from a desire to *record* history?

MONTELL: Yes, I do. I think I write now out of compulsion. I need to do it because, as I say, I still feel young. But there is so much ahead of me that I see that I still want to do that I want to just give it every ounce of energy I have. I just don't take time for anything but my research and writing. Or preparing, you know, for presentations that I give from here to there.

BEATTIE: Yesterday, at the annual meeting of the Oral History Association in Cleveland, Ohio, you participated in a discussion of Kentucky writers' attitudes concerning the nature of creativity. So, I'll ask you: What do you think the nature of creativity is?

MONTELL: Well, I had intended to ponder that, because I had never thought about it. But I think, to me, it is two things. Creativity, first of all, is the ability to draw the best out of the people I interview, to really help them make themselves totally articulate and to get their feelings and emotions on tape. I mean, to get their content as well as their emotions on the tape. But then, in all honesty, and I can't articulate this, but creativity, secondly, to me, is somehow bringing the inner soul of me as a human individual, bringing my soul out and somehow putting it on paper.

BEATTIE: Those things are the results of creativity and they are manifested in your work and your writing. But do you think creativity comes from a drive you were born with? You've just talked about a drive or a compulsion. Or do you think this somehow developed environmentally?

MONTELL: It developed environmentally. But, as I look back now, I realize that Lynwood, the little boy, I was always a little bit different from my playmates. One of the things I delighted in doing was sitting down with a Sears and Roebuck catalog or the Montgomery Ward catalog and looking through—see, they sold books back then—the book list and really just dreaming of the day that I could afford to buy books like that. My mom, for Christmas, she would usually buy me—and they didn't cost much back then—but she would usually get me a book or two. Then I would sit down and read them, or maybe she would read to me, you see. But, as I look back, I realize that I think I had the making of this in me all along. But quite frankly, I had assumed, when I got out of high school, that I would go to Indianapolis and get a job and go to work on the assembly line, because that's what everybody did, you see. And what led me into business school, and consequently on into college, ultimately, I don't know. I guess we would say it's fate. I'm the first Ph.D. ever from my home county. I only know of a couple of others before me who even taught in college, out of my home county. So, I don't know, there's just something intuitively in me that just led me on.

BEATTIE: But you believe that it wasn't just your training in academics—being encouraged to publish or perish—that made you desire to write?

MONTELL: No. Because neither Campbellsville nor Western had the publish or perish policy. And Western is not even there yet, as a university. They like for you to have a book if you're going to go up for promotion, but the truth of the matter is, many people get promoted without a book. So there's something inside Lynwood that drives me. Whether it's a creative spirit that I can't articulate, I simply don't know. But something pushes me, and I love it.

BEATTIE: I believe that nonfiction writers can be as creative as fiction writers; nonfiction is simply another form. And maybe the creativity is realizing, as we talked about earlier, that those lives about which you write need preserving and your creation is showing their worth in another light, another sense.

MONTELL: Yes, and the thing that I would like to do—and I'm going to try my luck at it soon—I want to do a children's book. And you know what I'm going to use in order to do that? Historical legends. You see? To show this thing of generational continuity. Maybe I'm starting, as I do get older and realize that my days are numbered down there someplace, maybe I'm starting to feel what I have referred to all along as the sense of the urgency of history. I've had informants who I could sense that in them, you see. And I think I'm starting to sense that. So what I want to do is to leave not just the books that I've written, but I want to leave something even for younger children to take hold of.

BEATTIE: That would be a nice circle, from your looking at catalogs and wanting books, to your writing a book for your own grandchildren.

MONTELL: And I guess, really, my grandchildren are the ones I have in mind. I want to show youngsters that there is continuity and that it's something worthy of their hanging on to.

The truth of the matter is, I have so many family narratives, on both sides of the family, that I'm tempted to try my hand at something new for me, also, and that is to actually create a novel. In other words, creative writing based on legendary fact. There's all kinds of work yet to be done. What I want to do next, I think, is to do just simply a collection of narratives of historical legends, if you please, the storytelling situations in which they occur, the extent to which people believe in these, and then to evaluate, to the extent possible, just how true they are. But I want to do another *Ghosts Along the Cumberland,* only not in the supernatural vein this time, but just in a plain historical legend vein.

BEATTIE: If you would, I'd like you to discuss, from a researcher's point of view, exactly how you conducted your historical research for *The Saga of Coe Ridge* and why your methods were, when the book was published, and still are, considered seminal?

MONTELL: I think, first and foremost, this was the first study that I know of, at least, of a black rural group after the Civil War. So, it's important in that regard. But in terms of my research methodology, well, I'm going to be totally honest with you. Nobody in folklore had ever done this before, in terms of using the spoken word in order to reconstruct the historical record. And the greater paucity of formal records I ran into, the more I realized that this just had to be done. I mean, more of this needed to be done. At the time I did this, my God, nobody was out there interviewing the grassroots people, let's face it. And especially not members of a black community. I was interviewing in order to simply get onto tape the historical record. The more I did it, the more I realized really and truly what a great thing I was doing, because I was giving these people a feeling of dignity, because they couldn't get over a university person "being interested in me."

There's one old man, his name was Arnold Watson, a white man, in Cumberland County, Kentucky. I went to him, I was interviewing him for my *Don't Go Up Kettle Creek* book. I typically don't interview the first time around for but about an hour and a half, because people, if they're not accustomed to the tape recorder, get a little fidgety. But I somehow sensed that he wanted to talk. I knew he did. So I let the first interview of him go for about two-and-a-half hours. And, finally, he was getting tired. He was an old, old man. Finally, I said, "Mr. Watson, I need to go home and listen to these tapes, because I'm sure I'll have questions that I'll want to come back and ask you about for further information." I said, "So, let me go ahead and excuse myself now," I said, "You're tired." I said, "I'll be back." And he leaned forward and he looked me in the eye and he says, "Hurry back. I'm an old man." I went back three weeks later and interviewed him again for about two hours, and then in about two months that old man was gone. Now, he sensed the urgency of being able to talk about the things that he loved to talk about most. And his granddaughter, about five years ago she called me and said, "Do you still have those tapes that you made with Granddaddy?" She said, "As far as we know, you're the only person who has his voice on tape. Could we have copies?" She said, "We'll be glad to pay anything you want." I said, "You won't pay me anything, and I'll furnish the blank tapes and I'll send them to you." I'm not always that benevolent, you know, but she was so nice about it. That's another way you touch people.

I'm co-editing a new book series called "The Ohio River Valley." That's for the University Press of Kentucky. I'm also editing for the University Press of Mississippi a Folklife in the South book series. Too, I'm working on a book about the Woodland Peoples of the Northeast. I'm already under contract with the University of Indiana Press to do a volume for them. I'm really excited about these projects. I've got to stay young.

BEATTIE: You're under contract to stay young.

October 17, 1992

In December, 1993, Montell re-married Ruth, the mother of their two children. She died unexpectedly of sudden heart failure on May 16, 1995. Two years later, June 21, 1997, he married Linda Embry, a native of Sweden, Edmonson County. Montell's research and writing efforts have produced thirteen major books; he is general editor of four additional volumes. He is presently working on three other books, including one on African Americans in the Upper Cumberland region of Kentucky-Tennessee.

Since 1993, Montell has served as historical/cultural consultant for Mammoth Cave National Park, Filson History Club, and Tennessee Historical Society's "Eden of the West" project, as well as for Russell County's "Vision 2000," a cultural/economics project. Additionally, he has conducted numerous oral history workshops in Kentucky and Tennessee. Montell was initiated as a member of Phi Kappa Phi in 1993, an organization that considered him for its Scholar of the Year Award in 1994. In 1994, he was portrayed as one of the three "Kentuckians Who Make A Difference" by McMillian/McGraw Hill Publishing Company. That same year, the University Press of Mississippi recognized Montell as one of its leading authors.

BOOKS BY LYNWOOD MONTELL

The Saga of Coe Ridge: A Study in Oral History. Knoxville, Tn.: University of Tennessee Press, 1970.

Monroe County History, 1820–1970. Tompkinsville, Ky.: Monroe County Press, 1970.

Ghosts Along the Cumberland: Deathlore in the Kentucky Foothills. Knoxville, Tn.: University of Tennessee Press, 1975.

Monroe County Folklife (editor). Tompkinsville, Ky.: Monroe County Press, 1975.

Kentucky Folk Architecture (with Michael Morse). Lexington, Ky.: University Press of Kentucky, 1976.

Folk Medicine of the Mammoth Cave Area (editor). Tompkinsville, Ky.: Monroe County Press, 1976.

From Memory to History: Using Oral Sources in Local Historical Research (with Barbara Allen). Nashville, Tn.: American Association for State and Local History, 1981.

Don't Go Up Kettle Creek: Verbal Legacy of the Upper Cumberland. Knoxville, Tn.: University of Tennessee Press, 1983.

Killings: Folk Justice in the Upper South. Lexington, Ky.: University Press of Kentucky, 1986.

Singing the Glory Down: Amateur Gospel Music in South Central Kentucky, 1900–1990. Lexington, Ky.: University Press of Kentucky, 1991.

Upper Cumberland Country. Jackson, Ms.: University Press of Mississippi, 1993.

Kentucky Ghosts. Lexington, Ky.: University Press of Kentucky, 1993.

Mysterious Tales from the Barrens (editor). Glasgow, Ky.: Jett Press, 1994.

Black Life in the Barrens (editor). Glasgow, Ky.: Donneley Printers, 1994.

Bob Dudney's Recollections of Yesterday in Free State and the Tennessee Upper Cumberland (with Nancy Keim Comley). Gainesboro, Tn.: Jackson County Historical Society, 1996.

Kentucky Ghost and Witch Stories From the 1930's (with Trudy Balcom). Nashville, Tn.: Express Media, 1997.

Always A People: Oral Histories of Contemporary Woodland Indians (with Rita Kohn). Bloomington, In.: Indiana University Press, 1997.

Maureen Morehead

MOREHEAD: My name is Maureen Podshadley Morehead, and I was born on March 28, 1951, in St. Louis, Missouri. My father is Dr. Arlon Podshadley. He is a professor at the University of Louisville. He teaches in the Dental School. My mother is Callista Mahoney Podshadley, and she also is from Illinois, and she has been a homemaker all of her life.

My mother's parents I never knew. Her father died when I was about one or two years old. I know things about him that I use in my poetry. For example, he fought in World War I and was injured by chlorine gas and suffered with lung problems for the rest of his life. Her mother died when she was about two or three years old, giving birth, but her father remarried. I always knew his second wife as my grandmother, and she lived until about four years ago. My mother has a sister and two brothers.

My father's father died when my father was thirteen years old. He was hit by a drunk driver on Christmas Eve. He was a mechanic, and I know that he was an inventor, because my father is very proud of that fact, and he, too, invents dental equipment. His mother lived a long life. She just died a few years ago, and we were very close to her.

BEATTIE: What about aunts and uncles? Were they very influential in your life?

MOREHEAD: Actually, no, because we always lived so far away from any relatives. My father, because he wanted to be a college professor, went where the job was, and so most of my relatives are either in the North or East or in California, so I don't know them very well.

BEATTIE: What about brothers and sisters?

MOREHEAD: I have four sisters and we are still all very close. They are all younger than I am.

BEATTIE: What sort of childhood did you have and where was that spent?

MOREHEAD: My earliest childhood I don't remember much of; I mean, we moved a lot. I remember from about age four on when we settled in Springfield, Illinois. Before that my father was in the Air Force, and he just made a lot of stops, and he set up a practice in Jacksonville, Illinois, and he was in practice until I was in sixth grade. I was probably about ten or eleven when he moved us to St.

Louis where he went back to graduate school and specialized in one area of dentistry, and then his next stop was the University of Kentucky where he helped to set up the Community Dentistry Program. I remember that vividly because he would take us into eastern Kentucky, and that was my first glance at another part of Kentucky. Wolfe County, he worked in. Then, after he finished, I guess he was at UK [University of Kentucky] four years, and then he accepted a position at U of L [University of Louisville]. And so, we have been here ever since.

My mother was a very strong Roman Catholic, and I had a strong Catholic upbringing, even though my father wasn't. He converted later on in life. I did not go to Catholic school, but I went to religion classes every single week. I knew the Baltimore Catechism backwards and forwards and have a lot of guilt and stuff like that. I understand sin.

BEATTIE: Are you still a practicing Catholic?

MOREHEAD: I am since my son was born; I left for a while and came back.

BEATTIE: Where did you attend school and what was it like?

MOREHEAD: I attended public school in Illinois, and I remember it was very, very strict—what they call now traditional school. There were no special programs, except for one, and that one was a writing program. They would take three or four kids out once a week and we would write stories and poems, and I was encouraged in elementary school.

BEATTIE: Had you exhibited some sort of proclivity for writing?

MOREHEAD: I must have. I probably had language skills, or I could read when I went to school. I can remember wanting to write poetry from the time I was a very young child. I probably scored well on language tests.

BEATTIE: Did your mother or other people in the family read to you?

MOREHEAD: Yes, they read to us. I remember reading *Alice in Wonderland* before I went to school. And my mother says that I could memorize the books and pretend that I was reading them back to her before I went to school. So language was important to us, and reading was important to us.

The worst part of my school experience was all that moving we did. I went to three different junior highs—and that's a horrible time, too—in three years. I don't think my parents quite realized how hard that was on me at that particular time. But I do remember my father—it was my senior year in high school—commuting to Louisville so that I would not have to miss my senior year. By that time he knew what it meant to us. But that was really hard. I remember being very lonely and, you know, there were just hardly any kids and friends and so forth.

BEATTIE: Because you were selected for this special language arts experience in elementary school, did writing emerge as your favorite subject?

MOREHEAD: Yes, it did. I was getting a lot of positive feedback. In elementary school I liked everything, and I remember even excelling in math. But that didn't stay; I don't have a propensity for math at all. But I love music, too, and I think I could have been good at music, if I had been encouraged that way. Then I loved science in high school, but girls didn't think that way in those days.

BEATTIE: Do you remember favorite teachers along the way, teachers who encouraged you in English?

MOREHEAD: Yes. In fact, I have written a poem that's in one of the series I'm working on now about this particular English teacher who was a major influence. She was a ninth grade teacher in Social Studies and English, and she just had absolute enthusiasm for language. She would talk so rapidly when she was analyzing stories for us, she got so excited about it, and I loved her. She was a really assertive, strong, powerful woman. I mean, it was ninth grade and in junior high. She introduced me to the power of literature. We read a story called "The Scarlet Ibis" in her class, which, just three years ago, I taught for the first time to a ninth grade class. They had the same kind of reaction. Some of the kids that I had were just actually blown away by that beautiful little story. And she started teaching me about similes and things like that, so she was very important. I still call her sometimes. She lives in Lexington, but she's no longer teaching.

Other than that, I was in advanced-type classes, and I didn't have an accurate notion in high school about what other people's high school experiences were like. We were very elite and we were taught new critical principles by our teacher, who had gone to Vanderbilt, and I had a really good background. It was almost like a college experience in high school, in English. Small classes, good discussions.

BEATTIE: Were these classes tracked according to students' abilities?

MOREHEAD: I wasn't tracked in math, but I was tracked in English. They made us think critically. That's when I started to think that the poem was all that matters. You know, forget about the life of the writer and all that stuff. Next year I will be teaching at Manual High School.

BEATTIE: I know it's now a trend for teachers not to analyze anything for students. How do you feel about that?

MOREHEAD: Well, what I try to do is to guide them to learn how to analyze. I try to teach them the questions to ask, and until they are able to ask those questions and answer them, I work with them. I don't answer them all, and I never tell them that I know the answers. But I give them the questions, and we answer them together. I did something interesting this year, though. At the end of my little modern poetry where we analyzed other people's poems, I had a couple of honors classes, and I gave them some of my poems to analyze.

BEATTIE: Did they know they were your poems?

MOREHEAD: Yes, and they had a ball with them. They made meanings out of those poems that I had not intended, and that was just fine. They thought my poems were much more complex than I ever did. They really, really got into it; I was really proud of them.

BEATTIE: What grades have you taught in other schools, and are you going to be teaching the same ones at duPont Manual High School?

MOREHEAD: The last two years I've just taught seniors, and I have sponsored the school newspaper. But in my seventeen years in Jefferson County Public Schools, I've taught everything from the seventh grade to twelfth grade, and next year I am going to be in a different type of program. I am at Manual because I have proposed to do a dual-credit U of L class in creative writing with Sena Naslund. So, we are going to teach creative writing at Manual together. I am also going to be teaching journalism, and then I'm also teaching senior English.

BEATTIE: What was your own education like beyond high school?

MOREHEAD: Well, I went to U of L, my father was teaching there, and that was part of the deal, our tuition was paid. So I went to U of L back before it was a state school, and I was there for about three years.

BEATTIE: What year did you start there?

MOREHEAD: I started there in 1969, and then I transferred to Western Kentucky University because I was madly in love with the man who is now my husband, and I finished at Western, and then we came back and both got teaching jobs in Louisville, and I started immediately on my master's at U of L.

BEATTIE: What year did you marry?

MOREHEAD: We married in 1974.

BEATTIE: What is your husband's name and what does he do?

MOREHEAD: His name is Robert Byron Morehead, and he is a teacher in the Jefferson County Schools. He teaches geography and health and PE [physical education], and he was a football coach for many years in the system.

BEATTIE: So, when you came back from Western, you were married, and that year you started at U of L on your master's?

MOREHEAD: I spent a year at Western working on my master's while he was finishing his degree. Then we came back to Louisville, and we both got jobs that year, so while I was teaching in the public schools I got my master's. I did that in my first two years of teaching, while I was teaching in the middle school. After two years in the public school, we moved back to Bowling Green. He finished his master's and coached on the college team to see if maybe he wanted to do that, and he did his master's, then, at Western. Then I took correspondence courses toward my doctorate. And when we came back to Louisville the next year, I took a full load at U of L toward my doctorate and finished the course work, and then decided I either had to go back to Jefferson County or quit my job. So I went back to Jefferson County. Then there was a six-year period between finishing my course work and going back and writing the dissertation.

BEATTIE: And this was a creative writing dissertation?

MOREHEAD: Yes.

BEATTIE: With which professors did you work?

MOREHEAD: Just Sena Naslund in creative writing, because she was the only one there in the creative writing department. Of course I took all those literature classes for both the master's and the doctorate, and then I switched over to rhetoric and composition; I had to, when they changed the program. So, I have a pretty general background in English because of everything that was required.

BEATTIE: So, your Ph.D. is in rhetoric and composition?

MOREHEAD: Yes, with a creative writing dissertation.

BEATTIE: I see. And were you teaching during that six-year interim?

MOREHEAD: Right, teaching at Central High School and Doss High School.

BEATTIE: And you have one child from your marriage, is that right?

MOREHEAD: Right. His name is Robert Clinton—we call him Clint— and he is ten years old; he is going into the fifth grade. He is a nice little boy, he really is.

BEATTIE: Have you been able to write at the same time that you have been teaching during the school year and, during the six-year interim before you finished your degree, were you continuing to write?

MOREHEAD: I always write, but not very much when I am also teaching, not very much at all. Part of the reason that I took leaves of absence to work on degrees was because that gave me more time to write. So even though I was studying for the comprehensive exams or working as a graduate assistant, I still got more time and I still had more energy than when I teach in the public schools. One thing I did that was really incredible to me was I took a semester off. U of L gave me some full-time teaching about five years ago, and I taught a year and then I taught a semester, and then I took an entire semester off before I went back to the public schools, and I wrote thirty poems in three months. I need to write during periods of time when I'm not doing anything else.

BEATTIE: When you teach creative writing, I am wondering how you think it ought to be taught.

MOREHEAD: I use the method that Sena Naslund uses, because I think it is a wonderful way to teach creative writing. I always begin by teaching my students what a good piece of writing is, by using examples and so forth, by having them discover what makes a piece good.

BEATTIE: So, really, you teach writing in conjunction with analyzing literature?

MOREHEAD: Right, I do. And then I think reading is absolutely essential. You have to combine the reading and the writing. In fact, creative writing, even if you don't come out of Sena's workshops or mine being a wonderful writer, almost everybody is an excellent reader, if they take it seriously, because you have to look at things so closely. Also, the person you are criticizing is sitting across the room from you, and you want to be fair to that person and as honest as you can be. Then the workshop part of it's great, because the writer has a real audience. That's a rare opportunity for a writer, to get feedback.

BEATTIE: Are you able to teach using the workshop method at the high school level?

MOREHEAD: I have not been able to because my classes have been so large, and also it is expensive. I would have to provide copying. But that's how we are going to teach the class at Manual; it's going to be a smaller class. I've always wanted to teach composition using the workshop method, and if I did an English 101 or 102 class again at U of L, I believe I would try it.

BEATTIE: Would you comment on what you think the nature of creativity itself is?

MOREHEAD: I think that it's being able to use the imagination to solve problems and to discover things, which is what I try to do in my poetry. I don't even try to do it; that's just what happens, and that applies to all kinds of situations. You just figure things out when they don't seem like they can be figured out.

BEATTIE: Do you think creativity is something that can be taught, or do you think it's a mixture of nature and nurture or one or the other?

MOREHEAD: I think it probably is a mixture, but I'm not sure. I know it's a nurturing, though. I am sure it can be nurtured and encouraged.

BEATTIE: Will you discuss your publishing career?

MOREHEAD: I was published in high school in the *Kentucky English Teachers' Bulletin,* which is rather interesting now, to me. That's, I think, the first place, which showed again that my teachers encouraged my ideas. Then I published in *The Thinker* at U of L, the student magazine. Then, as a graduate student, when I started working with Sena Naslund, I started publishing in more natural places. First, the state. The first place I published was in *The Kentucky Poetry Review,* then called *Approaches.* And there were some other magazines in the state—*Twigs* and *Wind* and *Pegasus.* Then I just started sending things out to other areas, and they started picking them up around the country. That was, of course, wonderful, because if you don't get that encouragement along the way, you stop. You need that, so I guess maybe the first place was the *Kansas Quarterly* and then the *California Quarterly* and *The American Poetry Review* published some poems—and *The Iowa Review.*

BEATTIE: I am interested in your having had Sena Naslund for a teacher for so long when she is mainly a fiction writer. I don't know if you have experimented with fiction. Have you?

MOREHEAD: Yes. My short stories look like long poems.

BEATTIE: Did you find Sena helpful to you as a poet, with her working in another genre?

MOREHAD: She is a good creative writing teacher, period. Sometimes she even says that teaching poetry is easier for her than teaching fiction writing. She has your paper in front of her and, when she likes things, she puts little checks, and when she does not like something, she puts little xs. I was straining my eyes to see where the xs were. She started out really being critical in showing me what was good and what wasn't, but from the very beginning, in comparison to everybody else in the class, my work was just absolutely simplified—overly simplified and amateur and immature. From the very beginning, she encouraged me. She has always said that I'm good.

BEATTIE: And you thought you were not as good as the other students?

MOREHEAD: Oh no, I was sure I wasn't.

BEATTIE: But she must have been sure you were better?

MOREHEAD: I don't know if she did; she just thought that there was something there worth nurturing. I have had students I teach in that way, and I have had students who want me to be more critical, and I can be that way. But I think more students than not need you to be positive. Of course, you can be gently critical, too, without hurting their feelings. I read a lot of poetry; I think my teachers of poetry are the people I've read.

BEATTIE: Whom do you most admire of the contemporary poets?

MOREHEAD: Of the contemporaries? My very, very favorite poet is Sharon Olds. And I like Maura Stanton an awful, awful lot. And Bruce Weigl's Vietnam poems, I think they are just wonderful, and Gregory Orr and Molly Peacock. I haven't had much time to focus on those people since I quit teaching creative writing at U of L, but I still get *Poetry* and *The American Poetry Review,* and I try to keep up to some extent with these people.

BEATTIE: What about Kentucky poets and other Kentucky writers? Are there any you most admire?

MOREHEAD: I love teaching Bobbie Ann Mason's fiction, both on the college and high school levels. The kids really, really get into that. Her short stories were fun to teach on the college level. Of course, Marsha Norman is wonderful, although I haven't taught her, but I definitely admire her as a writer. I would love to have time to really read Kentucky literature.

BEATTIE: Do you find yourself reading as much fiction or nonfiction as poetry?

MOREHEAD: No, I have always read more poetry, and it's mainly because of time. I don't have as much time as I'd like to, and when I do have time, I always think that I should be writing poetry or planning lessons.

BEATTIE: Do your English-teacher colleagues at high schools treat you any differently because you are a poet, in terms of wanting you to teach more poetry in your classes?

MOREHEAD: No, but one of the really sad things about high school teaching is that we are totally isolated from one another. It takes years to be in a school to even get to know the other teachers, much less to know what they are doing in their classrooms. However, when my book came out last year, some of my friends bought it.

BEATTIE: Was this their first experience with your poetry?

MOREHEAD: Right. They really don't know very much about what I do, the other English teachers.

BEATTIE: Probably a good thing, to be able to lead a couple of different lives.

MOREHEAD: Yes, it's very interesting, it is, and they all have their lives, too, that I know nothing about, and that's just the way it is.

BEATTIE: What about your methods of composition? Do you set aside specific times or days or hours to do so many poems or pages at a time?

MOREHEAD: I only do that when I have time to do that. I'll give you an example. I'm planning after I teach this two-week course that I start tomorrow to block out some time for writing. Over Spring Break I gave myself an assignment to finish some poems I had started because my publisher promised to publish another book, and I had these poems. So, I was determined to finish them, and I did nothing else but work on these poems over Spring Break. So, when I have periods of time, I do set time aside to write, and I have plans for what I'm going to write.

BEATTIE: Do you get up at four a.m.?

MOREHEAD: I used to do that because I wanted to and I was young; I can't do it anymore. Sometimes poems, though, just come, and they are gifts. I always have assignments in my head that I like. I know, for example, that I am going to finish a group of poems that I started about twelve years ago called "The Map Woman Poems." I am going to work on those this summer, and I am going to write some angel poems, which will have a music motif.

BEATTIE: When you write a poem, do you write it in longhand or do you write it on a word processor?

MOREHEAD: I write it in longhand first; I always print it and do some revising and type it in on the word processor, which is wonderful. I just learned how to do that about three years ago. That saves so much time, you know. I believe that it is part of my process that I have to see the poem in my own handwriting first.

BEATTIE: Your book *In a Yellow Room* is divided into five sections starting with "The Laura Poems" and ending with "The Purple Lady Poems." Would you comment on the growth of your voice in these sections?

MOREHEAD: The voices go from a young woman to an older woman, or a less-mature to a more-mature woman, even though "The Laura Poems" and "The Purple Lady Poems" were written at the same time. "The Purple Lady Poems" are still evolving. I wrote another "Purple Lady Poem" this year.

BEATTIE: By evolving, you don't mean those same ones, but additional poems?

MOREHEAD: Yes, additional poems have been written. The first group, "The Laura Poems," are confessional. I try to make "The Purple Lady Poems" more mythic.

BEATTIE: Do you find that you revert when you are writing to how you felt at different stages of your own life?

MOREHEAD: Oh, yes, yes.

BEATTIE: So, maybe that has something to do with the voice change? Maybe you were the poet taking yourself back to another time?

MOREHEAD: That could be. But it's funny, when Frank Steele wrote about "The Purple Lady Poems," he said they were much more gritty than the "Laura Poems." I know I have to think about that. It was a whole different feeling that I had when I was writing them and, of course, "The Laura Poems" are about growing up and accepting the fact that you are an adult and you have decisions to make and so forth, and "The Purple Lady Poems" were somewhere—I do not know where they came from, they came from the air, you know. I'll tell you who *did* influence me; it was Anne Sexton with her serial poems. I was mesmerized by Anne Sexton. She taught me, number one, I could write about being a woman coming out of that traditional paradigm. And she taught me that I could use wild and crazy images.

BEATTIE: But yours are much more hopeful.

MOREHEAD: That's what poet Ruth Stone said. I showed Ruth Stone some poems a long time ago, and that's what she said. She said Anne Sexton could have never written some of these poems because of that fact.

BEATTIE: You just referred to Frank Steele's essay, "Voice as Evolvement: The Poetry of Maureen Morehead." He writes, "The voice in Morehead's poems is only rarely bitter revengeful. Its gravidity comes from the imaginative structure of the poems themselves, a structure grounded in the relationship between problems and solution." Would you comment on that?

MOREHEAD: I think that we use language to come to terms, to figure things out, to answer questions. And I really do think that that is the primary motivator of my writing. I am much, much more concerned with audience now than I used to be, maybe because I'm older and I know people are really reading the stuff, and I feel a responsibility to say exactly what I mean and to get my message across.

BEATTIE: Steele also states that a factor distinguishing your poems is your proclivity for compounding figures of speech, a kind of sequencing of the metaphors, as it were. He refers to you as a list maker, and he comments that your lists are also a feature of your technique. He writes, "The poems achieve complexity by centrifugal associations and the complexity is then visible on the page." Do you agree with Steele, and how conscious were you of the development of your style or technique?

MOREHEAD: I think what happens to me is that imagery became so important that the poem, for me, became an image. And one image was not sufficient to get the meaning across, so I started using multiple images. And I don't think it was conscious. I don't. Steele pointed some things out that I had not consciously realized, although I know that I make lucid images just to try to get— in a way, it's like the multiple voices in a novel. But to see the whole thing, you need to see it from a lot of different perspectives. I think that's what I do with images.

BEATTIE: You have written, "My artistic vision seeks the form that implies process. This form is not processed, however each of my poems has a difficult paradoxical texture." Would you discuss that?

MOREHEAD: I think that poems, while sometimes they propose to answer questions to solve problems, they simply don't, you know.

BEATTIE: They just point out the problem.

MOREHEAD: Raise the question, pose the problem. So what happens is, you have a feeling that there is going to be an answer. And I think that's why I write sequences so much, because in a larger group of poems I can work toward answers. I don't have to solve the problems in one poem. Or I let the reader do it, you know, after reading a group of poems.

BEATTIE: You talk about Anne Sexton being a poet that influenced you, and also I've read that Emily Dickinson was another influence. I especially see the similarities between your voice and Anne Sexton's, when I read your poetry. Will you discuss how those poets have influenced you, and also reflect on which other writers—poets or fiction writers—you admire?

MOREHEAD: Emily Dickinson: the obvious is her use of language. She teaches you that one word can mean twenty different things. You know, the ambiguity of language. But the not-so-obvious thing to me, and the important thing to me, is that she used language "to hold her senses on." I really do believe that. She needed to write to get through the experience of living and to work toward an understanding of things. Those are a couple of reasons that she is so influential and so spiritual, too. Her quest for the meaning of death and God, those are all really appealing to me. She is a major influence.

There were some men who were influences, too, because when I was an undergraduate I didn't read any women poets. I was reading mostly the modern men. The men I was reading really startled me. How do you imitate Thomas Stearns Eliot or Ezra Pound? They are wonderful, they are incredible, and I did learn from them. I especially learned, I think, a sense of structure from Eliot. And William Butler Yeats, the music of Yeats ...

BEATTIE: I understand that you recently completed a sequence of poems and titled them "Martha Jones Poems," based on the diaries of Kentucky women during the Civil War. Will you discuss those poems and their origin?

MOREHEAD: The period of time that I had to write was three months. I went to The Filson Club to see if I couldn't find anything over there to inspire me, and I found these diaries, letters, and photographs of Martha Jones and her family. She kept a diary from 1860 to '64. She was from Versailles, Kentucky, and she and her husband had a farm, and they had horses and a nice house, and they had four children. I think they had five and one died, and she just kept a daily account during that period of time. The '64 diary was very sparse, because she was afraid, at that point. She was a Confederate and Confederates in Kentucky, at that time, were under suspicion. And her husband was killed and she did not write very much after that. But the diaries are incredible, filled with details. I was one of the first people to see them. They were fascinating, so I took the diaries and my imagination, and I took lives from the diaries and added some material and organized things and wrote those poems. I think they are powerful poems. I love them.

BEATTIE: Are they a mix of fact from the diaries and your fiction?

MOREHEAD: I tried to keep them as historically accurate as I could. When I fictionalize, I don't think it is distorting history. I might just be adding some other things that she did or thought. The truth is, where I added was where

I interpreted how she might be feeling or thinking, because the wonderful thing about the diary is that she did not do that, she did not interpret anything. She just told what happened, even when her husband died.

BEATTIE: I was wondering whether that had to do more with her personality, or with her upbringing as a woman at that time?

MOREHEAD: That was just her concept of what a diary was, just recording what happened during the day. But, see, I found another such diary since then. There is a diary in the Kentucky Museum down in Bowling Green, and this woman was younger. Her name is Josie Underwood Nazro, and it was much more difficult to make something out of her diary. Her experiences were not as poignant, they were not as tragic. These poems are going to be published together with stories by Pat Carr, and her stories are also based on Civil War diaries.

BEATTIE: How did you decide to work with Pat Carr? How did that come about?

MOREHEAD: I went down to Bowling Green for a poetry reading and I met her and she told me she was working for a publisher on some short stories she had written. And I said, "Well, why don't you call John Moremen?" He is really interested in the Civil War, and I knew her stories were about that, and so she called John, and John got hold of her stories, and his concept was to put my poems and her stories together. Pat was agreeable, and I think her stories are wonderful, so I am really excited about it.

BEATTIE: You talked about poems that you are writing now. What are they?

MOREHEAD: The series that I have been working on is about a woman who is under a lot of stress. We call it "The Two Stress Poems." They are very autobiographical. That seems to be easier to write now, when I don't have much time. But they are bizarre—even more so than "The Purple Lady Poems,"—and they deal a lot with violence and the crazy world. The closest feeling that I've had to "The Two Stress Poems" was watching the movie *Grand Canyon.* You know how there was so much violence in that movie, but there is so much violence in the world and, at the same time, people go through and try to have hope and try to survive and so forth. I think that's what the poems are about. My protagonist in the poems is also a teacher and she is married and she has children and she is trying to figure things out.

BEATTIE: So many of your poems seem to be part of a series. Do you start off with one or two poems, or do you start off conceiving the series and then writing your poems?

MOREHEAD: "The Laura Poems" and "The Purple Lady Poems" just evolved that way. Then I realized how that form seems to fit. I can't set it all in one poem. Now, I conceive a poem as a series instead of just single poems. I still write single poems, too, but I like to have a series going, also, because I know I have something to work on.

BEATTIE: Frank Steele writes that he believes that with "The Martha Jones Poems" your poetry is undergoing a change in voice. Will you comment on that?

MOREHEAD: I think he is right. Where he is really right is when he says that the poems that are more autobiographical are becoming simpler and more conversational. I am not sure if it is because of the reasons he gives; he says I am losing the New Critical baggage, or maybe it could possibly be the influence of people like Sharon Olds. I think that her writing is deceptively conversational. Her poems seem so easy, and they are not. I am really attracted to that, and it seems to me I'm also becoming more conscious of an audience.

I'll tell you something I did. I wrote a poem about AIDS, which was published in *The Thinker Review* this year. I actually wrote this poem in school the day Belinda Mason died. I said to my students, I told them about her—"We are going to write today about AIDS." I had really good students, so they sat there and they wrote and wrote and wrote, and I wrote a really rough draft of this poem, and then the next group came in and I said, "We are going to write about AIDS," and I revised the poem. I worked, then, at that poem—revising and revising and revising and revising for the next two or three months, and it was a totally different poem when it came time to decide what to give *The Thinker.* A lot of people who have read it, they understand that the first time through it captures how I was feeling that day. The second poem is more beautiful, I think, and much more crafted. But this less-sophisticated poem does what a poem is supposed to do about that subject, so I am changing. I guess you might well say that I felt really amateurish in Sena Naslund's class, and I have always been afraid of people thinking that my writing is too simple, but I am not really afraid of that anymore. I don't usually deal with politics and social issues in my poetry.

BEATTIE: In the poems I have read in *In the Yellow Room,* you are dealing, certainly, with human issues and individual issues and, in most cases, with issues pertaining to women.

MOREHEAD: Right.

BEATTIE: How do you feel about being called a women's writer as opposed to a writer? Do you think of yourself that way?

MOREHEAD: I don't think of myself that way as much now as I did years ago when I was first writing, but I do know that everything I write comes from my perspective, which is that of a female writer. When I read a man's poetry, I think, "I'm reading how this man perceives things," and when he reads mine, he is reading how I perceive things. And I really believe men and women perceive things differently. You can learn something about the way we perceive things by reading each other's work. I think women, particularly, enjoy my writing. But there are some poems that men enjoy more, too. I doubt if you have heard the poem "A Woman Remembers Hiroshima," which is a poem that appeals as much, I think, to men as women. It's really lonely not having anybody to bounce things off.

But, on the other hand, I don't think I'm influenced too much by anybody anymore, and that's probably good. People can give you useful feedback—they always can—so I probably should be in a writers' group. It's been all right to have just Sena Naslund as a teacher, because I think I am really particular about who I want to listen to. Maybe I am just protecting myself. I had students when I was teaching on the 500–level at U of L, too, that I would have loved to have read my poems, and sometimes I asked them to because they were such incredibly good readers. I trusted their advice. I especially enjoyed teaching those upper-level classes, and I especially enjoyed teaching the people who come back to school after a career or after raising their children. I'll tell you something that Sena Naslund and I were talking about just a couple of days ago. Sena always helps me clarify things. There are important things that she feels sustain her that she writes about, and they keep her buoyed up, and visually she sees that as a vertical picture. And she said she sees mine as a horizontal picture. I am constantly asking questions and reaching points—sustaining points—such as family, nature.

BEATTIE: And those points might be the conclusion of a series?

MOREHEAD: Yes, a series, or they might be an answer to a question which, down the road, gets asked again. And I have to find the answer. But she sees my vision as more horizontal, and my journey is the quest. I felt that was really revealing about both our writing. The art itself is sustaining for me; it is something I have to do. I would probably be doing it even if nobody read my poetry.

BEATTIE: You're talking about writing poetry as a personal quest, and also you are talking about having returned to the Catholic Church. Do you see your poetry as a spiritual quest that parallels your religion, or do you view your poetry and your spirituality as separate entities?

MOREHEAD: I think that I use the poetry to discover God. I really do, and I haven't discovered God yet. I like going to church, and the ritual—we go to a nice church out in the woods—and it has good music, and the priest is nice, but I still haven't rediscovered God yet, and I'm going to use poetry to do that. That's the end of the quest, I think.

June 14, 1992

Recently, Morehead has completed the poems for her series based on the Stations of the Cross, as well as her poems dealing with teaching literature to contemporary students. In her poem, "The Interview," a group of students ask Hester Prynne questions to help them understand her story. In addition to her writing, Morehead continues to teach full-time at Louisville, Kentucky's, duPont Manual High School where she also acts as advisor to the school newspaper and literary magazine.

BOOKS BY MAUREEN MOREHEAD

In a Yellow Room. Louisville, Ky.: Sulgrave Press, 1990.

Our Brothers' War (with Pat Carr). Louisville, Ky.: Sulgrave Press, 1993.

JOHN ED PEARCE

PEARCE: My name is John Edward Pearce. It was John Edward Pearce, Jr., but when my father died I dropped the Jr. I never liked to be Jr. I was born in Norton, Virginia, in 1919, September the 25th. My father published and edited small-town newspapers. My mother's name was Susan Leslie. She was from Tazewell, Virginia, and her father published the newspaper there in Tazewell. After he died, her brothers took it over. She had another brother who was editor of the Norfolk *Ledger-Dispatch* for a while; newspaper work sort of ran in the family. My father's paper was called the *Coalfield Progress.* It's still published.

BEATTIE: I imagine you learned a lot about the newspaper business from your father.

PEARCE: Well, it's the way I got into college. In the late summer of 1937 I accompanied a friend of mine to Lexington where I met a man named Dave Griffith, who asked me why I wasn't in college, and I told him honestly I had no money. I was working for Swift & Company in Norton at the time. And he said, "Why, if you're willing to work, you can work your way through. About half the boys here are working their way through." I came back later and he said, "It's a shame you can't run a duplex press. We're getting a new press over at the shop. I could give you a job that would pay your way through school." And I said, "Well, I can run a duplex," which wasn't entirely a lie. That was during almost the depth of the Depression, and it was not considered bad form, much less a sin, to lie in order to get a job. As old Colonel Sanders once said to me, in explaining how he lied to get a job on the railroad, it wasn't bad to lie and get a job. What was bad was to lie and get a job and then not be able to do it. I couldn't run a duplex press, but I knew the theory of printing presses, and, within a short time, I was running the press fairly well. And that's how I got into college.

BEATTIE: What were your years growing up like?

PEARCE: My Grandmother Pearce lived in Pennington Gap, Virginia, a strange little farming town not far from the Blue Diamond coal fields where my uncle was, Doctor Clarence Chilton Pearce. He was my favorite human being on earth until he died when I was fourteen. When I was a child I'd often go and spend time in the summer with my uncle who lived in one part of town and with my grandmother who lived in the other. They both pampered me, I imagine, spoiled me. I played. There were a lot of boys around, and a great deal of the time we'd spend up in the hills around the town, or on the little river that ran east of town. We'd fish, swim, climb hills, throw rocks.

I had two brothers and I had four sisters. Certainly, a large family. I was right in the middle. There were three older and three younger. I was never terribly fond of my brothers and sisters. I accepted them as, well, as part of life. It was like loving parents. Everybody said, "Oh, don't you love your mother and father?" I guess I did to the extent that normal little boys love their parents. I think it was the attitude of children in my day to stay away from grown people as much as possible, because they always had foolish things for you to do that you didn't want to do, and they were always keeping you from doing what you *did* want to do. They were always afraid for you to go in the river; you'd drown. Climb trees, you'd fall out and break your neck. Things like that.

BEATTIE: I remember a column you wrote about your mother. It seems to me that you indicated that she let you find your own way in life.

PEARCE: I think if there was a good influence in my life, it was my mother. She was a kindly but hardworking little woman. She didn't have an awful lot of time to spend on any one child, having seven of them to take care of, and we were never wealthy. We were always comfortable. But she worked. She was a hardworking woman. She was very bright. I have an idea that my mother chafed at domestic cares. What she wanted to do was run the newspaper, and she did a better job of it than my father. My father was often away. He would go places to start new ventures, most of which failed. And, while he was gone, my mother would take over the newspaper and straighten it up and have it running well by the time he got back in time to mess it up again. But she was rather strict. She'd come from a strict, tee-totaling, Baptist family, and she brooked little nonsense, but she was a happy person. And she was a cultured person. She had gone to the Female Academy there in Tazewell.

Our home always had lots of books. From the time I can remember, they would always subscribe to boys' magazines for me, *Youth Companion* and *American Boy.* I always got books at Christmas time. We always had music in the family. I was about the only one who didn't play an instrument. I don't know why I didn't want to; I've always regretted it since. But we had the old Victrola, and we had classical music, always.

My mother loved flowers, she loved growing things, and she instilled that in me, I think. All my memories of my mother are very fond. As I say, she was not a great one for laying on of hands or for expressing affection, but I never doubted it; I always was aware of it. She didn't have a whole lot of self-confidence, I think.

BEATTIE: It sounds as though your mother was more of a detail person and your father was the big-idea person. Would that be accurate?

PEARCE: I'm sorry to say that my relations with my father deteriorated about the time he should have become important to me. I think my father was always very fond of me when I was a small boy, and he wanted me to do well. He tried to give me advantages, send me off to summer camp, send me off to private school—things like that. But, during my teen years, we broke too violently, and we were never close after that.

BEATTIE: What about your early education? What was that like?

PEARCE: We were not poor, but during the Depression we didn't have any money. My father went broke in 1930. He had done very well and established a chain of newspapers in North Carolina, and we lived awfully well then. Those were very happy years. But after he lost the newspapers we moved back to Norton where we owned an office building and a home, so that we could have a place to live, anyhow. Those were very hard years, but my mother always told me, "As long as you have good manners, keep clean, and make your grades in school, people will know you're nice people." And we were always expected to make good grades in school and to keep clean. Actually, I was always threatened if I didn't. I didn't appreciate that. I tried, but I was always threatened with punishment if I made B's And I didn't make a B, I think, until I was about in fourth grade.

BEATTIE: What happened when you made the B?

PEARCE: I got threatened again, I guess. My parents made a mistake with me. They sent me off to a private Baptist school when I was in the fourth or fifth grade. And when I came back home they skipped me a grade, and that was a terrible thing to do to a boy, because I skipped fractions, and I never caught up. Before then, math had just been another subject. After that, it was a nightmare, and I think they didn't understand why I wasn't doing better. I didn't know fractions. But I made good grades and, with few exceptions, I liked my teachers pretty well.

BEATTIE: You talked about your mother getting you magazine subscriptions. Did you like to read as a child?

PEARCE: That's all we did. I'm so grateful, so thankful, that there was no television to vulgarize and trivialize life, to rob us of imagination and initiative. All of us boys read. We used to get together on rainy days and swap magazines. We had piles of them, stacks of magazines. And, at Christmas time, if I could get two Tom Swift books or something like that, that was a big deal. It just never occurred to me not to read. And I've often tried to recapture, to recollect, the reasons. I imagine it was seeing everybody else read. In the evening, my father would read the papers. I'd go up to my grandfather's when he'd come home, and he'd go into the parlor and sit under that lamp with the tassels around the edge of it, smoke his pipe, and read the paper, and we weren't supposed to bother him. And my mother would sit out on the porch in the afternoons and read. I'd see my older brothers and sisters reading. And, long before I went to school, I had my little books out, *Baby Ray Had a Cat* and *Baby Ray Had a Dog*. Idiotic Baby Ray. And I would worry my poor mother to death, "What's this?" "What word is this?" I could read pretty well before I went to school.

BEATTIE: Did she teach you?

PEARCE: No, *I* taught me. Well, I just kept asking, you know. And she'd sit with me, I guess, and tell me the sound of the letters. I must have been in the very early grades when my family got a set of *Compton's Picture Encyclopedias.* And that was a wonderful thing for me. I just read those encyclopedias, just devoured them. They gave me a smattering of knowledge all around, and I think that was helpful.

I imagine our schools were no better than they should have been. I remember that in high school one year we had to cut back to eight months because they simply didn't have money to run the schools. Those were very desperate years. An awful lot of children dropped out because they were needed to work at home or because they could see no future in education. It was tough to stay in school. When I was a sophomore, I went to school a half day and worked half a day in the printing office downtown, the newspaper office, just to help my family. I was fifteen at the time. I didn't like that. It seemed to set me apart from my friends and to make me feel inferior, having to work. But I did it.

BEATTIE: Did your brothers and sisters do the same thing?

PEARCE: Well, they didn't do that, but my older sister, Rose, went to college, got a teaching degree, and came home and started teaching in a little coal camp down the road from Norton, and she helped my mother. Then, when I got out of high school, I went to work for Swift and Company meat packers there, a fascinating and terrible job. It was a brutal introduction to life-in-the-raw for a seventeen-year-old.

BEATTIE: Going back to high school for a minute, what was that like? Did you have a favorite subject in high school?

PEARCE: No. I sort of liked Latin, and that's weird. I liked English. I liked history. Again, I sometimes had trouble with solid geometry and chemistry. But I lacked incentive a lot in high school. Our home life was difficult. My father was in a state of collapse. After he lost his business, he just sort of, as I say, collapsed. I was afraid that I wasn't going to have a future, that I wasn't going to be able to go to school—to college or to anything. Not that these were unhappy years. I had a good time in high school. I went out for football and basketball and made my letter, though I was small. And I was fairly popular. I was the president of my class three years out of four. And, by the time I was fourteen, I was becoming interested in girls. We had wonderful girls there. We had a fine group of people, when I look back on them—unusually nice boys and girls.

BEATTIE: Did you start writing on your own in high school, or did you think that was something you might do in the future?

PEARCE: No. The only time I ever did writing was one time when the local newspaper held a contest. You were supposed to write an ad for one of the local businesses and submit it. My mother wrote an ad for one of the businesses there in town and gave it to me to take down to the newspaper office. So, I sat down and I wrote a couple myself, you know, and I took them down. I won first prize, and Momma won second, and I won third.

BEATTIE: What did she think about that?

PEARCE: Oh, she was delighted. Really tickled. And the first prize, as I recall, was ten dollars-worth of groceries, or something. That was a big deal. Third prize, I'm afraid to say, was a pair of women's shoes.

BEATTIE: Which you gave to your mother, I presume?

PEARCE: She got the shoes. No, I didn't think anything about writing. I had a good memory. I could memorize things very well. I had always had a vocabulary. That came from reading.

I was always very concerned with girls. I had a normal boyhood, is all I can say. I never did anything very bad. I didn't do anything especially good.

BEATTIE: When you worked at the meat plant, how long did you work there?

PEARCE: About fifteen months.

BEATTIE: And you did their bookkeeping?

PEARCE: McNerney was the bookkeeper. I'd help him out. I'd ride the trucks sometimes. Help load and unload meat from the coal camps, and that was exciting.

BEATTIE: When was the first time you were in Kentucky?

PEARCE: When I was five or six, we moved from Norton. My father sold the paper, and we moved to Pineville. He started a paper in Pineville. Why he did that, I don't know. Then, when I was about twelve, he sold the paper in Pineville and we moved to North Carolina. That was the nicest time of my life, I think. He bought a paper there and expanded it. And we had a beautiful home. And Rutherfordton was a lovely little town. It wasn't far from Lake Lure and Chimney Rock, not too far from Asheville. Beautiful area. Very happy time.

BEATTIE: How long were you there?

PEARCE: A couple of years. When everything crashed, we moved back to Norton where I went to high school and worked and then left.

BEATTIE: Why did you decide to leave? Where did you go after the meat plant?

PEARCE: I went to college. There were two out of my crowd, two boys, who hadn't by then gone to college, and I was one of them. And it really gave me a feeling of inferiority, being somehow lower class. The other kids would come home at Christmas time, and I almost died every time they came home, because they were speaking a different language, they were wearing different clothes, the world was opening up for them, they were having new experiences, and I was stuck there in that dirty little coal-and-railroad town. I could see no future ahead of me. I was desperate, almost. My mother knew this. She was very sympathetic. She later told me how much she regretted not being able to do more for me during those years. I didn't expect her to. I knew how things were.

But the Swift & Company experience was interesting, and it was probably valuable. I saw a rough side of life. We were down in what you call Little Italy, at the east end of town, full of coke ovens and railroad yards and whorehouses, and it was a fairly violent place.

BEATTIE: You must have been even more grateful then, when you went to college, seeing how you might have had to live otherwise.

PEARCE: The first time I went to Lexington, it was with a young man named Sagaser Kash who was from Carlisle, Kentucky, and who had gone to the University, graduated, and come to Norton to work on the newspaper. He dated a girl who lived across the street from us, a friend of my sisters. And one time he said to me, "You want to go down to Lexington this weekend with me?" And I said, "Yes." We caught the L&N (Louisville and Nashville) out of Norton and got into Lexington about 4:30 in the morning. We walked up Limestone to the University, just as dawn was breaking, on a late summer morning. I thought it was the most beautiful place I had ever imagined in my life. Lexington was everything that I had wanted. I made up my mind then and there: "God, if there is some way, I'm going to come here and go to college." I always wanted to go to college. I thought it was a glamorous life. I didn't have any great goal in going to college, but I wanted to be a college boy.

BEATTIE: Was it the F. Scott Fitzgerald image you had of the college boy?

PEARCE: Yes. That was the whole thing. I used to read the college stories by Thomas Beer and they excited me. I wanted to be a fraternity man and wear nice clothes.

BEATTIE: Did you earn enough money on your job to pay the tuition to go to college?

PEARCE: When Sag Kash and I went up there, I went back home and remembered what Dave Griffith had said to me: "You can go, you can get a job, you can work your way through." I had a few days coming to me at Swift, so I hitchhiked down to Lexington without telling anybody where I was going. For three days I just walked the streets of Lexington asking anybody who I'd bump into on the street if he had a job. And I couldn't find one. On the last day I was running out of money. I was staying at the Drake Hotel, which cost me a dollar a night, which was a lot of money. On the last day I gave up, and I went out on Richmond Road, East Main Street, and started hitchhiking. I hitchhiked all afternoon without catching a ride. And about four o'clock I said, "Well, I can't get out of here this afternoon," so I went back to the Drake Hotel one more night. And I called this man named Griffith and I said, "I did what you said, and I'm damned if I can find a job." And he said, "Well, come out here and talk to me." I went out, and that's when he said, "It's a shame you can't run a Duplex press. We're getting a new one in next week and I could pay your tuition through school."

It was a good job. I ran the printing press that printed the student newspaper two nights a week, starting around eight to ten o'clock, and worked usually through the night, getting off anywhere from four to six in the morning, which made it very hard to go to an eight o'clock class, I can tell you.

I had other jobs. I soon found I could get other jobs. A couple of fraternities rushed me. I was very excited about this, and wanted to join, and did.

BEATTIE: Which one?

PEARCE: Pi Kappa Alpha, a good southern fraternity. Boys from home had recommended me; they were Pi Kaps. I told them quite honestly at the fraternity house, "I don't have any money. I'd join, but I don't have any money." One said, "I can get you a job," and he did. He got me a job at Keeneland, working on the pari-mutuels fall and spring, and it was a very good job. Paid eight dollars a day and, really, that was good. And you'd work three days a week, you know.

One of the most interesting jobs I had was working at the Paddock Restaurant. When I was in high school, I worked at Norton Pharmacy there at home, as a soda jerk, so I knew how to handle a soda fountain. I went from there and I'd work on the sandwich and salad board in the back and then sort of run the place. It was a lot of fun, too. It was interesting as it could be. I made a lot of friends.

If I had been content to work and go to college, I could have gotten through easily. I was vain and I was a little silly, like most young men are at seventeen, eighteen. And I was very conscious of women. I wanted to look good to women. I wanted to date. I saw very early in my stay at UK that wearing an ROTC [Reserve Officer Training Corps] uniform wasn't going to cut it, that the men who handled themselves with confidence and were looked up to on the campus were good dressers. They dressed well, they belonged to fraternities, they went to nice places. So, I was determined to do that, too. I spent a lot of money on clothes. I spent money on girls and whiskey. And I spent money on fraternities and dances and had one hell of a fine time. I just enjoyed it more than I can tell you.

BEATTIE: Did you write for the school newspaper?

PEARCE: Yes. And I not only wrote for, but owned, the magazine. There was a young man named Vogel, as I recall, who took over the humor magazine, and when he left school he copyrighted the name. He had got in a lot of debt and sort of dropped it. The graduate manager of publications came in and said, "If you'll take over that magazine and pay the debt on it, you can have it and see what you can make of it." So, for about eighteen months, I ran that magazine. It was a mess, really a terrible magazine. I'm ashamed now to look at it. But, I made money, and I was always out shucking and jiving and trying to get along.

And I dated wonderful women, some of whom I still know. And they were the nicest women. Two of them died recently, and it hurt. I loved to dance. The first thing I bought when I got some money was a tuxedo, and when I was a sophomore, I bought tails. I got my clothes tailored a lot of times; that was big stuff. I was always in debt.

Lord, we'd work in the summer time. I don't know how I survived. When I got through college I weighed 132 pounds. Half the time I didn't have money to eat on, but I had money to drink on. I liked to date town girls because, while they were upstairs, I'd go in the kitchen and eat.

BEATTIE: What about academics? What did you major in?

PEARCE: Well, I started out in journalism, and I can't tell you why. I just sort of drifted into it. At the end of the first semester of my sophomore year, the head of the journalism school said to me, "John Ed, you could be a good student and you could be a good news writer, if you didn't think that you knew more than your professors." I thought about this for a while. And I said, "You know, he's right; I *do* think I know more than my professors." And I *was* right. With the exception of Willis Tucker, I was a better writer and I knew more and I was brighter than the teachers in the journalism department who were there.

BEATTIE: How do you think you became a good writer?

PEARCE: Well, I'm a facile writer, not a good writer. But I decided right then, "I'm not going to waste any more of my time here, and I'm wasting it." I was. Lord, I remember we had a course called Typography, in which we learned type faces, and we learned how to set a stick of type from California case. A total waste of a college man's mind and time. I was working too hard for that. I got out and went over into political science and enjoyed it. I just took courses here and there. I didn't expect to get a degree. I didn't care. I wanted the college life and I wanted to get enough education so I could get a job somewhere. And I was offered jobs. I didn't worry about it too much. I was having too good a time.

I was always hanging around the newspaper office. I wrote a column for the paper, I edited the magazine, things like that. And there were three of us who lived in this ratty apartment over on Upper Street. It was a wonderful place. We had a little efficiency place and we'd ask girls up and play music and make tea and have whiskey. Had good times.

Then I met Harry Williams, who was a stringer for United Press. It wasn't then UPI [United Press International], it was just United Press. He had a lot of strings like that, and I worked into this. I got a job writing for the downtown papers there, writing specialty stuff and features, and I got hired by them for special editions. I remember I worked for a couple, one on horses, one on tobacco. I went around to the radio station. I heard they were looking for somebody to write two news broadcasts a day, local news. I went around and got that job. Nobody else wanted it. Sometimes I'd write the news and then I'd give it over the air. Then, when Harry left town, the UP took him to Columbus, Ohio, and I inherited his job. I was a full-time newspaper man, and I was a senior in college. I was working far more than I was going to college. But a lot of us did that. We didn't worry about the degree so much. I was hoping to stay in college long enough to get the degree, but, if I got a job somewhere else, I'd leave without it.

Then the University announced that those of us who were drafted in the last half of our senior year would be given our degrees, if our work was satisfactory. So, I took my midterms and stayed on, hoping to be given a degree. And I was going to be drafted. I was examined and declared 1–A, which surprised the hell out of me. I thought that I was too skinny and meek to be taken as a soldier. But I was basically sound, and they said, "No, you're 1–A." This scared me almost to death. The idea of taking up a gun and facing other men who had guns was not my idea of a good way to stay alive.

I was down in the federal building over there in Lexington one day, gathering feature stories for my news broadcast, when I went into the navy recruiting office there to see if any weird enlistees had signed up or anything. And this chief said to me, "Hey kid, they're going to draft you." And I said, "I know." And he said, "Don't let them do it," whereupon I delivered what I still think was one of the greatest straight lines in history: "How can I keep them from it?" He grabbed me and yanked me through the door, showed me a poster of a man standing there in navy whites and an officer's cap, a beautiful man. "Be a navy flier," he says. I said, "Gee." He said, "Sign here."

Well, that was it. And I never regretted it. I then went into the navy for four years. When I came back to Lexington everything had changed. I didn't have any jobs and I couldn't get any jobs. Women had most of the jobs. And, of course, women are better at newspaper jobs a lot of times than men, so they weren't about to hire me instead. Nobody remembered me. I was out at the University one day and Margaret King said to me, "There's a woman down at Somerset named Williams who wants an editor for her paper. Her husband died and left her a newspaper, and she doesn't know what to do with it." So, I went down there and got the job running the *Somerset Journal.*

It sounds ungrateful now, and ungracious, in a way, to say how much I disliked that job, because Mrs. Williams was a wonderful lady and she was very nice to me. But it didn't pay anything. I had gotten married, I had a little daughter. I needed the money. I didn't like Somerset and Somerset didn't like me. I can see now that I was far too brash, and I was far too radical for a very conservative, farming, Baptist, mainly Republican county. They didn't like my way of thinking, they didn't like my editorial page, and they just thought I was a loud-mouthed smart aleck, which I was, of course, to a degree. But I was trying to give them a good newspaper. And immodestly I will say I *did* give them a good newspaper. This was evidenced by the fact that the Kentucky Press Association, in its annual meeting in Lexington, gave my paper, as I recall, about thirteen first prizes, for everything from best editorial page to best front page and all that business. I won all these prizes, which showed me I was doing a good job. I was not appreciated and I returned the lack of appreciation.

BEATTIE: When had you gotten married?

PEARCE: In my last year in the navy. I married a girl named Jean McIntire from Middletown, Ohio. I had known her in college. In the summer of my junior year, before I was a senior, I followed her suggestion and went to Middletown and got a job in a paper factory, for the summer. It was a funny job. It paid well, and it taught me a lot. I think it taught me a little humility, if anything ever did. We'd always looked on factory workers as lower-class laborers. They were bright, they were witty, and they were wonderful guys. I worked on what we called the milk press, making milk cartons. And they helped me. I don't know why they were so generous with me. I didn't know anything, and they showed me how to do the job. They were patient with me when I made mistakes, and we became very good friends. I learned a lot that summer and had a big time. I met a lot of nice kids there, most of them from Ohio State University, and they thought that I was weird, being from Kentucky.

BEATTIE: You got closer to your college friend then, who became your wife?

PEARCE: Yes, we were already sort of informally engaged. It was a great mistake; I'm very sorry about that. And I went back to UK and newspaper jobs.

BEATTIE: What was your major role while you were in the navy?

PEARCE: I was on a seaplane tender most of the time. I had jobs here in the States but, after I got to sea, that was my job. And, I was also an officer. I had good experiences. And, let me tell you, the day I joined the navy was probably the greatest stroke of luck in my life. I wasn't a very good officer. If I'm ashamed of anything in my life, I guess it's the fact that I wasn't a good officer, because I didn't try. I was looking for a way to live through World War II and get back to my work, and get back to the life that I had loved so much there in Lexington, not knowing that when I got back it would be gone. Well, I didn't do my best. I was awfully seasick, and that hurt my efficiency. But, the navy was very good to me, if I wasn't good to the navy. And after the war, after I moved here, a friend of mine talked me into going back into the reserve, and I stayed in the reserve thirty-one years. And it was terribly valuable to me. I saw the world and many different kinds of duty, all of them educational and, usually, fun.

BEATTIE: What kinds of things did you do as a reserve officer ?

PEARCE: I was in every war. I went to Vietnam, and we used to go to training duty. I'd go over to Norfolk where I was a speech writer for the admiral. One time I was assigned escort officer duty for VIP's out of Washington and Norfolk, and I took them all down to the Caribbean, to Puerto Rico. I got duty out in Alameda, California, in San Diego. Gee, really, these are vacation spots. I got extended training duty in the Mediterranean with, I believe, it was the Sixth Fleet. I was assigned as public relations officer to Admiral Hopwood on his final tour of the Pacific, his final inspection tour. We went everywhere from Indonesia to Japan and China to Taiwan. It was my first trip to most of these places, and it whetted my appetite so that I went back when I got a chance. I can't think of any duty that I got that wasn't, as I say, educational and pleasant. I was one time based out of Guam; I went to Saipan and places like that.

BEATTIE: Before you were a reservist, when you were in the navy for four years, where did you go during that time?

PEARCE: I caught a ship out of South America. We were on enemy submarine patrol down there. We were transferred very shortly, I'm sorry to say, up to Boston, and put on that North Atlantic run. Oh, I was so cold. I don't like cold weather; I've got thin blood. Then we got the run from Norfolk to Casablanca to England. Most of the time we weren't tending sea planes at all, we were carrying bombs and torpedo heads and octane for the planes, a very combustible little cargo. Made *me* nervous; I don't know about the rest of them. It was very good duty. We had nice quarters aboard ship; the food was good.

BEATTIE: When you got out of the navy, you came back, and you were working in Somerset, right?

PEARCE: I worked in Somerset. Went over to Lexington for that KPA [Kentucky Press Association] meeting and won a whole lot of prizes. And I got a note from Barry Bingham, Sr.: "I'm sorry I missed you in Lexington."

Funny thing, Herb Hillenmeyer, whom I had known in college, came down and said to me, "Hey, let's go out and play some golf." I said, "All right." I didn't want to go down to this place where they were handing out prizes. So, we went out to Lexington Country Club and played golf. When I got back everybody said, "Where were you? You won all these prizes and Barry Bingham was looking for you." I stifled the impulse to kill myself. But, when I got back to Somerset, I had a letter from Bingham saying, "I'm sorry to have missed you. If you're ever in Louisville, please drop by and let's talk newspapers."

Well, I managed to be in Louisville very shortly. I was fascinated by Barry Bingham from the moment I met him. He was sort of what I wanted to be. He was so debonair. He was so polished. He was so graceful. He had such a wonderful way of expressing himself. He was so articulate, he was so beautifully dressed. Everything about him was admirable, I thought. And I'd think, "Lord, I'd like to be like him." I never did get to be like him. But, I kept sitting there waiting for him to offer me a job. I thought for sure he was going to offer me a job. I was praying. I thought, "If there's a God in heaven, if God has any decency about him, he'll see that I get a job." And Barry didn't say a word.

I stumbled out of there and slumped back to Somerset, really a very unhappy person. That was not a good year of my life. And the next Monday morning, as I recall, I went to the post office and there was an envelope from the *Courier-Journal*. I tore it open and it said, "We have an opening for an editorial writer. Would you be interested?" Oh, Jesus. I came to the *Courier* and stayed forty years. It may have been a mistake. I had two good opportunities to leave and didn't take them because of implied assurances from Barry, which didn't work out.

BEATTIE: Assurances that you would be in a different position?

PEARCE: Yes, that I would be editor of the paper. I was offered a job by *Time* magazine. A friend of mine became national editor, and he offered me a job to come to New York. On another occasion, a friend of mine was an important official in the Jack Kennedy campaign. And when Jack won, Jim Wine, who became an official in the State Department later, wanted to establish a public relations firm, of course doing political work, in Washington, with an office in Frankfort. And he wanted me to join him. It may have been a mistake not to. But each time Barry would say, "Well, we never make a commitment for the new job, but I've never had anyone in mind for editor but you. And, if you'll stay, I'll give you a raise." So I stayed. You know, when the time came, Barry Junior took over the paper. Barry Junior and I never got along. He did not like me and I didn't respect him. Our relationship was not good. But I left the editorial page when Barry Junior came in, and went to the *Courier-Journal Sunday Magazine*. That's the best thing that happened to me on the *Courier-Journal*.

BEATTIE: And that's when you started writing your column?

PEARCE: At first, I didn't. I wrote feature stories for the magazine and I wrote a county series. I wrote thirty-five articles on counties. That was an extremely interesting project. We often had need for one page of copy. It was hard to find a good, one-page feature to fit into the ad layout, and I wrote a little column that was really an expansion of an editorial I had once written. Every time we had a blank spot, I'd write a filler. And the little fillers became very popular. So one time Irene Nolan, who was features editor, she and Geoff Vincent and somebody else called me and said, "How would you like to turn that into a weekly column?" And I said, "It's all right with me." So, they put my picture up there and started running it as a weekly feature and it took off. Then I got a little unhappy about it, because it cut into the writing I could do about other things, such as counties. They said, "No, we'd better not have a column and a feature by you in the same edition, so just write the column." And that's all I was doing. That kept me busy about a day or two a week. I was doing a lot of sitting on my hands, really, and I didn't like it too much. But the column proved pretty popular.

BEATTIE: When you started with the *Courier,* what were your assignments and what was your title? What sorts of things did you start writing and how did that progress?

PEARCE: Well, I'll tell you a funny thing. I spent a little time over in Frankfort, familiarizing myself with the state legislature and the capitol and doing a little reporting from there. Then I came back and started writing editorials. And I remember, at an editorial board meeting, the first one I attended, Barry said, "Well, you know I've been looking for a young Kentuckian to start writing about his home state," and I said to myself, "Keep your big mouth shut." He didn't know for some time that I wasn't a Kentuckian. I wasn't going to tell him. But I wrote editorials, especially on Kentucky. Barry was awfully good about that. He thought that we should have direct personal knowledge of the things we wrote about. So I did a lot of reporting while I was editorial writing, and I went with reporters a lot. I would write editorials from the scene and send them in. I traveled all through the state and covered a lot of stories—the TVA [Tennessee Valley Authority] developments in western Kentucky, a lot of the strikes and coal mine troubles in eastern Kentucky, floods—things like that. Very interesting.

BEATTIE: A little while ago you were talking about the *Courier Sunday Magazine* folding. You said that was due to lack of major department store advertising, basically.

PEARCE: That was what I was told.

BEATTIE: Do you think eliminating the magazine was a mistake on the part of the *Courier?*

PEARCE: Well, I imagine it was not a financial mistake. But the Binghams did a lot of things that wouldn't make money that they thought were essential to a first-class newspaper that would give Kentucky first-class service. The Binghams were willing to take a very small return on investment in order to make the

Courier-Journal a prime newspaper. But, of course, the people who came after, weren't. Actually, as soon as Barry Senior stepped off and Barry Junior., took over, it was obvious that the quality of the paper was going to suffer, if only because the children were becoming adults, and they wanted more money. Barry Senior then stepped in and sold the paper.

BEATTIE: Did you think any of that could have been prevented?

PEARCE: Sure, it could have been prevented. It was an idiot's delight. There was simply no excuse for what happened.

BEATTIE: What do you think of the *Courier* since it's become a Gannett-owned paper?

PEARCE: I work for it. I sell them a column and they pay me pretty well. But it is not what it was, of course. It would not have been, regardless of who owned it. Television had cut into its revenues and its influence too much. Even before the *Lexington Herald-Leader,* in its improved state, started taking away their eastern Kentucky and southern Kentucky circulation, the *Courier* had been forced to draw in because of the cost of distributing the paper. It lost money on every paper it sold east of Frankfort and west of Bowling Green. It just pulled in its horns and didn't try very hard to sell papers out in the hinterlands. And the *Herald-Leader* got so much better. I also write a different column for them. John Carroll took over that paper ten years ago, when Knight-Ridder came in. John Carroll was sent there as editor. I had known his father very briefly, Wally Carroll, who was with the *New York Times.* John Carroll was like Barry Bingham, an excellent man, a man with a lot of class, and one of the most likable people I ever ran into. He really made that *Herald-Leader,* I'll tell you. Really shook it up and got in a whole lot of good people. He called and asked me to have lunch. I was so taken with him, so impressed. He said, "I know you have good contacts with the *Courier-Journal* and that you probably have a feeling of loyalty, but if you should ever want to leave them, I'd like to make you an offer for your column." And I said, "All right."

I kept in touch with him. And, once, I said, "Well, why don't I just write another column for you?" And he said, "I don't think the *Courier* will let you. I don't think that they will let you write for both papers." And I said, "Well, I don't think the *Courier's* got any say about it. If they don't want to buy my column, they don't have to, but I'll write for whomever I please." And I started writing for the *Lexington Herald-Leader.* I signed a contract and I had dinner that night with Irene Nolan, my managing editor at *The Courier-Journal,* and told her we had agreed on a contract. And I told her, "I'm going to write for the *Herald-Leader.*" Well, she protested strongly. But, I said, "'Yes, I'm going to write for the *Herald-Leader.* And if you don't want to buy my column, of course, I can't force you to do it. But I don't see that I'll be any less valuable to you." And I'm not. The overlap in the circulation is relatively minor. I don't see any conflict there at all. But David Hawpe [then-editor of The *Courier-Journal*] was very angry about it, and he wrote me a very angry letter. "Do the right thing." And I replied as briefly as possible,

"Let's don't let emotion enter into this; this is a business proposition." I have never spoken to him since.

Writing for both papers has been a very happy arrangement for me, because it gives me what you might consider state-wide exposure. I get a lot of requests to speak out of it—usually for nothing—and I won't do it. I used to speak for anybody who needed a speaker. I don't do that anymore. I'll speak for two thousand dollars. I'm not going to speak for less; it's too much work.

BEATTIE: You've written about your mother as a person for whom sense of place was particularly important. Do you share that same feeling of sense of place, and do you feel an affinity for Kentucky or for a specific locale in the state?

PEARCE: One reason I regret my divorce . . .

BEATTIE: When did you get divorced?

PEARCE: Well, the first time, I divorced in 1953. My first marriage didn't last very long.

BEATTIE: You had one daughter by that marriage?

PEARCE: Two. The second time I was divorced was in 1971 or '72.

BEATTIE: Who was your second wife?

PEARCE: My second wife was a woman named Virginia Rutledge, who was from Louisville. We have three daughters. She still lives out on Blankenbaker Lane, where we lived when we were married.

BEATTIE: Do your daughters live in town?

PEARCE: Oh, I've got daughters all over the place. Got one in Danville, one in Fort Myers, one in Lexington, one here.

BEATTIE: You were starting to comment about sense of place. You said when you got divorced . . . .

PEARCE: Since I was divorced I've moved around from one place to the other, and finally I bought this condominium on Cherokee Parkway where I live now. But, you know, the children don't come home at Thanksgiving. I don't have a tree at Christmas. My father died long ago at a fairly early age, and my mother died about nine years ago. By that time she had moved to North Carolina to be near my sisters. They'd sold the home in Norton, so I didn't have a home to go back to. And I hadn't established a home, except for my condo. Strange, I still refer to Norton as home, but it isn't. I go back there and everything has changed.

BEATTIE: Since you've lived so much of your life in Kentucky, do you feel like a Kentuckian?

PEARCE: More than anything else. I always draw back somewhat from patriotism. I have loved many places. I loved San Francisco. I wish I had enough money to go there and live in the Huntington Hotel for the rest of my life and look out over the bay. I love Boston, Cambridge. In '58 I got a Nieman Fellowship to Harvard; it was maybe the best year of my life. It was just the most intellectually exciting, rewarding year.

BEATTIE: How did you get that Nieman? I know you have to be nominated by your paper. How did you spend that year?

PEARCE: I listened to lectures. I didn't study anything much; I listened to lectures. I just took every lecture I could. I figured I could read books after I got through. I took a course in comparative religion. I took a course in economic history, political history, constitutional law, constitutional development, all those things. Creative writing, poetry. What a good class that was. What a good year.

BEATTIE: Do you prefer living in Louisville to Lexington?

PEARCE: I used to like Lexington better, but like everything, including me, it changed. It grew too much and it changed too much. I could live in a lot of places, I think, and be happy.

To a degree, I'm sorry I didn't remarry. I'm afraid now it's much too late, and that I'm too set in my ways. I've lived alone for so long that I have such a rigid routine of my own. I don't think that any woman could ever adjust to it, but I don't particularly like to live alone. I wasn't a good husband. I was a pretty good father, but I was not a good husband, I'm afraid.

BEATTIE: How long have you had your office here at the Starks Building?

PEARCE: Going on seven years, I guess. I moved from the *Courier* right over here.

BEATTIE: Are you here every day?

PEARCE: Six days a week.

BEATTIE: Will you talk about your books?

PEARCE: The first time I wrote a book, I wrote a novel that was published by Viking. An embarrassment. That was in 1950. Then I did a commercial work, a company history, for Brown-Forman Distillers, called *Nothing Better in the Market,* for which I was paid very handsomely. Working for Brown-Forman was a shock. It was the first time I'd worked for people who paid money. They paid me wonderfully and treated me wonderfully, and it was a pleasure to write that history. The third book I wrote was called *The Colonel,* a biography of Colonel Sanders of Kentucky Fried Chicken, published by Doubleday, which surprised me. It was a pretty good book, and I thought it would sell marvelously, and it didn't. I thought it was a good movie, but nobody picked it up. I was disappointed in that book. I then collected some columns and called it *Seasons.* That sold well, especially here in Kentucky.

When Bert Combs was running for governor, I wrote speeches for him and wrote in general. I had started out, at Barry Senior's request, working for Wilson Wyatt, who was general counsel for the company and a personal friend of Barry's, and he ran for governor against Bert Combs in the primary and against Harry Lee Waterfield. There were three of them. And Barry said to me, "Do you mind helping Wilson out a bit?" I said, "No." I was always interested in politics, anyhow, and liked to get out of the office and get out of the editorial-writing rut. So, I wrote for Wilson. Then he and Bert saw that if they both continued running, Harry Lee was going to win. So, with the help of Earle Clements, they came to a compromise, and Bert ran for governor, Wilson for lieutenant governor. I just drifted over to Bert. I thought he was strange, a hillbilly, and he talked funny. He had that old mountain accent. I thought, "God, this is going to make a weird governor." And I learned better. He was the best governor I've ever seen. That mountain accent cloaked a tremendously bright man, a great brain. My association with Bert Combs was one of the happiest associations in my life. I became very fond of him. He became probably the dearest friend I had in the world.

One day he called me over when he was in Lexington, and he said, "I want you to do something for me. I'll pay you well. I want you to write an account of my administration so I can put it up for my grandchildren. I want them to know what their granddaddy did." So, I started researching it, and I wrote and wrote. One time he gave me a thousand dollars, as I recall, as a downpayment on it. I said, "No, don't. I don't want to be obligated by money. This damn thing is going to expand. This is getting to be a book." I took the little book I had and gave it to Ken Cherry over at the University Press, and he gave it to Malcolm Jewell. And Jewell said, "This is part of a book. This has got to be expanded." So then I started in and I wrote the book called *Divide and Dissent,* which was the best thing I ever did, I think, by far. I am sorry it didn't sell better. I was hoping it could be adopted in schools, because I think it is a valuable bit of Kentucky history. It's a bit of Kentucky political history. I don't think that historians took it too seriously because, for one thing, a newspaper man wrote it, and they don't think highly of journalists. At that time, I was still on the *Magazine.* One day a friend of mine, Rich Nugent, a photographer for the paper with whom I worked on a lot of the county articles, and with whom I like to work, said to me, "I've got this boat over on the river. Let's talk Pope into a story on the Ohio River, a pictorial text." And Pope said, "Yes, that would be great." So, we took off. We thought we were taking our vacation. We went up to Ashland and followed the river down to the Mississippi. All the shore of the Kentucky. And, boy, it was a lot of fun. And, for me, it was quite informative. Rich had been on the river a lot; I hadn't. I had been through locks a couple of times, but this was a totally new experience. It was educational, and it made a nice magazine article. We found out later we weren't on vacation at all; we were on an expense account and we were working. We thought, "Ahha!"

It wasn't long before John Morgan of KET [Kentucky Educational Television] came in and said, "We saw that magazine article. Let's make a documentary." So, we made a documentary for KET, the first one I ever did. And *that* was a new experience, and, of course, *that* was very educational. It was hard, pretty hard. And it proved very popular. KET kept running it and running it and running it.

Then Ken Cherry of the University Press said to me, "How about making a book out of that? This time, let's start at Pittsburgh and go the full length of the Ohio." So, Rich and I got a new boat, had to pay a lot of money. As a result, the book was not profitable, because we spent it all on the boat, which Rich still has. I don't want the damn boat. I don't particularly care for the river. And I don't particularly care for power boats. I like the ocean and I like sailboats. But we put out the *The Ohio River* book. That was the last book that I had published. Now I have a new collection of columns and essays and so forth, and I am trying to find a publisher. I've been turned down a couple of times. They say it doesn't appeal to the general public. I think they may be right. The New York publishing set wants more guts. They want more sex, more violence, more action than a bunch of rather ruminative recollections afford.

Here's a book on Kentucky feuds. I've been working on it for about three years. Not full-time, of course, but working quite a bit on it, I must say, and it's proved to be very hard.

BEATTIE: In what way?

PEARCE: Impossible to research, records are so poor. I'm going a lot on word of mouth. And every time I get one word-of-mouth account, I will get another one that contradicts it. So I don't know what the truth is, and I'm very nervous about this book. I think people will tear it to pieces. Ken Cherry wants to publish it. John Moremen, a local man, has started a thing called Sulgrave Press. He's publishing local and Kentucky authors. He has asked me to write my memoirs. He asked me to write an autobiography, but I wouldn't do it. I think that an autobiography is more revealing than I want. I'd like for my private life to stay private, to a degree.

BEATTIE: Yet in many ways your columns *are* autobiography.

PEARCE: To a degree. I may write the memoirs. That would give a selectivity, and it would let me keep my private life private. One reason that I want my private life private is that I've been married twice; neither marriage was successful. I am friendly now with one of my former wives and not unfriendly with the other; I just don't have any relation at all, which is the best way. I would not want to write anything that might embarrass them. I wouldn't want to write anything that was critical of either of them. And I feel that, to be honest, I'd have to be critical. I gave up everything I had in the world. Everything I couldn't put in the back seat of a Volkswagen beetle, she got.

BEATTIE: You were saying earlier that, in some ways, you wish that you had gone into magazine writing at some point after you started working for the *Courier.*

PEARCE: More creative writing. I find now that I can't write fiction. I really think that's because I wrote nonfiction for so long. In about 1948 or '49, I had a friend at the paper named Buddy Atkinson, B.M. Atkinson, Jr. He wrote a thing called "Downdrafts" for the *Louisville Times.* He and I got to be inseparable friends. He was a wild man. But at the time he was writing for *Collier's* magazine—short stories—and he was writing a thing called the short-short story, a one-page short story. He had an agent, so I sat down and wrote a short story and sent it to his agent. And he wrote me a little note, and he said, "You write well, this is a good story, and I think I can sell it." The next thing I knew I got a wire from him. He had sold it to the *Saturday Evening Post.* That was the first short story I ever wrote. From there I took off; I wrote short stories for everybody. And he sold them to GE [General Electric] Summer Theater, to Studio One, to *Ladies' Home Journal.*

Then things changed. I don't know why life can't stay the same when it benefits me and pleases me, but it always changes on me. And the *Saturday Evening Post*, of course, was highly formalized. You could just lay your story out and sift in different characters and different backgrounds and write it again and again and again. And, in those days, five hundred dollars for a short story was a lot of money. See, this was around '50. I got seven hundred and fifty dollars for the first story, and I was up to about two thousand dollars a story when they changed hands and changed style, and I was out. I never got back to it. I wish I had persevered and tried writing novels and tried harder. I never studied the form. I never really put my mind to it the way I should have.

BEATTIE: It sounds as though you were incredibly successful, for someone just starting out. You never had to experience rejections?

PEARCE: No. I was always facile. I am not a deep person. I've been inconsistent and I have a tendency to do foolish things at times.

BEATTIE: Do you think of stopping?

PEARCE: The thought of having nothing to do frightens me. I think that you must have something in life to do. You must have some reason for getting up in the morning. Somebody should be requiring something of you; otherwise, you have no reason for being here. I have had so many friends who retired who were dead within eighteen months, and I don't think I'd last much longer if I had nothing to do.

BEATTIE: Aren't there books you would like to write?

PEARCE: No, I don't think so. I would like to make a connection with some publication and write travel articles for just enough to pay my travel. If I do that, I think I would never stop; I'd just go from one place to another. I like to travel. But I'm thinking seriously about Costa Rica. I have enough money to live comfortably there. Now, if I retire here, I will have to watch it, have to watch my money. I hate that. I hate watching money. I don't want money to control my life.

BEATTIE: Do any of your daughters write?

PEARCE: My daughter in Fort Myers, Florida, does. She's a free-lance writer and she's a public relations person. She writes commercial writing. She's always been something of a problem. But she's fond of me. My daughter in Denver also likes me, likes to be around me, likes my company, likes to go out with me, and likes to sit and talk. And the daughter in Fort Myers. The others don't seem very fond of me. But the wild horse down in Fort Myers, she likes me.

BEATTIE: Is there anything that you would like to write more than anything else?

PEARCE: I wish I *could* write. I wish I could write a good novel. I wish I could write poetry. I've always wanted to write poetry and I've never seemed to have a feel for it. One reason I regret not having money is that I've always had to consider money in writing. I just haven't had the luxury of writing for pleasure or for self-satisfaction; I've had to write for income. But I think any man who has put five daughters through college has achieved something in life.

I have never thought of myself as a writer. I have always wanted to *be* a writer. At the same time, I have always resented, more or less, people like Sallie Bingham who consider as writers only those who write novels. And I know a few people who consider people writers only when they write poetry.

BEATTIE: Or any type of book. It doesn't matter how bad the book, it just has to be a *book*.

PEARCE: Yes, that's true. But I think that you should write books. They will live after you. What you write for newspapers really does wrap tomorrow's garbage. I regret that at times. I have two or three hundred magazines in my storage room at the condo. And sometimes I'll get a half a dozen of them and look through and see the things that I have written in the past, and some of them I truly like. And some of them I think *were* of value; they show some insight into the subject. No one remembers them. There's no record they were ever there. The *Courier* doesn't even keep me on file anymore.

BEATTIE: Except you do have collected columns.

PEARCE: Well, I wrote for forty years, just about every day of the year. I wrote an average of four hundred articles a year for twenty-three years. I wrote an average of one a week for seventeen years. Thousands of articles, columns, editorials, profiles, book reviews. God almighty. There's no trace of them. They're not on file down there. I don't have copies. I never kept copies of my work. That was stupid, wasn't it? But I never thought of it as something you kept; it was a way to make a living. That's why it's a good thing to write books.

BEATTIE: Well, from that perspective, it's true. It's just kind of sad that there is such a perception, I think, that if it's not a book, it must not be quality writing. Ascribing to that, I think, is a little phony. What are your writing habits? Obviously, you have this office here, so you, I would guess, do most of your writing here and not at home.

PEARCE: I tend to write the columns on Tuesdays and Wednesdays.

BEATTIE: When you come in to your office to write your column, do you know in advance what you're going to write about?

PEARCE: I think about it at home, usually at night, and make notes. Then I come in here and, I'd say, seventy-five percent of my ideas turn into columns. Sometimes the idea just isn't substantial enough to carry a whole column, and I have to abandon it. But once I get an idea, and it's a good idea, it doesn't take me long. I write fast. And I can write two columns a day, if I get two good ideas. I usually come in at nine, sometimes a little before. I go on out to the Colonnade [Cafeteria] and get a sandwich, an egg, or I get a sausage sandwich, something like that, bring it up here, make my coffee, and sit down and read my paper and eat my sandwich. Then I read my mail. I don't do much before noon. Often, I'll have phone calls to make, to answer. Then I'll go to lunch about noon, come back about 1:30, and I'll write, then, until about 6:30 or 7:00. Go home, fix dinner, read a while, and go to bed.

BEATTIE: I see you have a word processor here, but you also have notes in longhand.

PEARCE: The longhand stuff I do at home, or in motels, wherever I'm staying.

BEATTIE: So your actual writing you do on the word processor?

PEARCE: Oh, yes. I make an awful lot of typos on the word processor, the touch is so different and the keys are spaced differently than the old typewriter that I wrote on for forty years. So it hasn't been easy in that respect. I have to do a lot of rewriting just to catch the typos. But, it's a wonderful improvement. Oh, a word processor is just a beautiful way to go. A lot of old-timers say no, they won't lower themselves to that mechanical form. Well, hell, the typewriter's mechanical.

BEATTIE: I'm wondering what you think the nature of creativity is.

PEARCE: Well, of course, there's one of the mysteries of human nature, why one personality, one intellect, creates such images and another simply doesn't, because I imagine we all feel pretty much the same things, to varying degrees. We all want pretty much the same. We have the same loves, and the same regrets, the same ambitions, pretty much. I might have been a better writer if I'd suffered more. Almost everything I recall about my childhood was fun and exciting and pleasurable. I lived very close to nature all the time when I was a boy. And I love being out in nature, around the river, around the creek, on the lake, on the hill, on the mountains, camping out on the mountains. Those are the happiest memories I have. There was no phase in my life up to the time I was mature, married, a father that I didn't spend a lot of time with nature. My children tell me that I taught them the same thing, to be careful of nature, to take care of nature, and to enjoy it.

BEATTIE: You were, in 1954, co-recipient of the Pulitzer Prize.

PEARCE: Yes. And that year I went to Columbia University. The Pulitzer didn't mean anything.

BEATTIE: It didn't? It would to a lot of people.

PEARCE: Yes. I got a medal out of it and a handshake. I don't think I even got a raise. It was a big disappointment.

BEATTIE: What did you get the prize for, specifically?

PEARCE: Work I did on a magazine, on conservation, on strip mining. We got a strip mining law passed. I got a scholarship to Columbia. That was fun, living in New York. I bought my first Brooks Brothers suit. I'd heard about Brooks Brothers suits, so I went down and bought one. Good suit. Lasted for years.

BEATTIE: What did you do at Columbia?

PEARCE: Studied government. It was an American Press Institute thing, which is located there. It wasn't anything like the Nieman. The Nieman program, that's the greatest thing a journalist can do, in my opinion. I'd much rather have a Nieman than have a Pulitzer, or anything else.

BEATTIE: Still, it sounds good to have won a Pulitzer.

PEARCE: Yes, in your résumé. I'm not really in need of a résumé right now.

BEATTIE: Well, you also won The Headliner Award.

PEARCE: That didn't make any difference. I won all of the awards. Let's don't go through them all. They didn't amount to a hill of beans. Funny thing, I won a Nieman Conservation Award and it came in a manila envelope. I thought, "Oh, God, I don't have time to open that now." I put it away and forgot about it. And, maybe two weeks later, I opened it up and there was a check for a thousand dollars, I think, and a big certificate. I went in and told Jeff Vincent. He almost died.

BEATTIE: Can you comment on the changes you've seen in Kentucky, politically and socially, since you started writing?

PEARCE: We don't seem to have the caliber of men in the governor's mansion. We don't have men anymore like Earle Clements and Bert Combs. We've had a lot of businessmen, like John Brown and Brereton Jones and Wallace Wilkinson. Jones may turn out to be a good governor. And John Brown could have been. He was bright. He wouldn't work hard at it, in my opinion. He objects to that very violently. A very vain man. Combs, [Edward "Ned"] Breathitt, and Clements were men of great intellect. Earle Clements was a man of terrific intellect and great personal power, a forceful personality. He would have made a great president. Bert Combs would have made a fine senator. He made a great governor. We don't have that caliber of men anymore. And perhaps it isn't needed. Starting with John Brown, the focal point of power swung to the legislature. The governor no longer was instrumental in selecting the leadership of the legislature, the House, or the Senate. They selected their own leadership. The Legislative Research Commission was enlarged to be very influential in the framing of legislation. The legislature is much more powerful than it was in the Combs, Clements, [Albert "Happy"] Chandler days. I should have mentioned Chandler in that, too. Happy Chandler was a great personality, had a great deal of power and could have done a great deal more than he did, had he been of that character. Clements, Chandler, Combs—those were the big three, I think. Like everything else, the Kentucky government has become television-conscious, very much influenced by television. And the influence has not been good. Television has a tendency to corrupt and trivialize everything it touches. At the same time, I must say that I think that Kentucky Educational Television was one of the great things that Bert Combs did. He founded that. It keeps Kentucky in touch with itself. And none of the private stations will do that. They're there for the profit, like newspapers. Mary Bingham was probably the best thing that ever happened to this state. She's a great person.

BEATTIE: Do you still keep in touch with her?

PEARCE: Yes. I think Mary Bingham is one of the greatest people I've ever known and one of the greatest Kentuckians. We've got a lot of nice people in Kentucky. That has enriched my life. I like to sit down with James Still; he's funny.

I think Tom Clark is one of the finest people I've ever known. I'm so sorry that Bert [Combs] died; he was a great addition to my life. I loved him.

I find living alone very strange. Not entirely unpleasant; I do what I want. But I look forward to the rest of life with some trepidation. I sometimes worry about being alone all the time, no one to talk to, no one to exchange ideas with. No one to appreciate the wonderful me. I hate to deny myself to so many people.

January 9, 1993

In 1995, Pearce purchased a house on North Captiva Island, Florida, where he now spends six months of every year. Pearce continues to write, and in 1996 he won a Genesis Award for his newspaper columns concerning the environment. In the same year, Pearce discontinued writing his column for the *Courier-Journal*, thereby concluding his fifty-year liaison with the Louisville newspaper, but Pearce remains a weekly columnist for the *Lexington Herald-Leader*.

BOOKS BY JOHN ED PEARCE

Nothing Better in the Market. Louisville, Ky.: Kentucky Press, 1970.

The Colonel, A Biography on Harland Sanders. New York: Doubleday, 1982.

Seasons. Louisville, Ky.: Cherokee Press, 1983.

Divide and Dissent. Lexington, Ky.: University Press of Kentucky, 1987.

The Ohio River. Lexington Ky.: University Press of Kentucky, 1989.

Days of Darkness. Lexington, Ky.: University Press of Kentucky, 1994.

This Place Called Kentucky. Louisville, Ky.: Sulgrave Press, 1994.

Memories, 50 Years at the Courier-Journal and Other Places. Louisville, Ky.: Sulgrave Press, 1997.

AMELIA BLOSSOM PEGRAM

PEGRAM: Amelia Blossom Pegram, that's my maiden name, the name I use for writing, but some people also know me as Amelia Blossom House. I have my early works published under House, but anything new that's been published is under Pegram.

BEATTIE: Where and when were you born?

PEGRAM: Oh, when, I don't know. It seems like a whole century ago, a very long time ago. I was born in Cape Town, South Africa, and I'm hemming and hawing now because of my age. I was born in the spring time, and that's why my name is Blossom. Spring time in South Africa is October. I was born on the third of October, and there is again a discrepancy as to when I was born. There's three years' difference between my birth certificates, so I have two birth certificates, and that sounds kind of crazy, but one says '38, the other one says '35. So I have a choice of what I want to be on a particular day. It came about by record keeping in South Africa. When I first sent for my birth certificate they sent me one thing, and then when I had to leave the country, I needed another birth certificate for another purpose, and so they sent this other date, and I said, "Okay," you know. So I have two birth certificates.

My father was Henry Bowman-Pegram, and it's very strange that it's been hyphenated all along. We come from a family called Bowman-Pegram. My father's brother spelled it B-A-U-M-A-N-N. They were from England and came to South Africa. There was at the time, and I don't have the full details about which king it was who had an illegitimate son, but the son said, "I'm in line for the throne; I'm in line to be king of England." He was exiled, and with him he took his group of friends, and my father's family was part of that set, and they were given an area called Knysna in South Africa.

So my family settled there with Harkers, Prinsloos, and Davidsons. And this particular family that had the illegitimate son, he changed his name to Rex. He said, "People will always know that I'm of royal descent." So, the Rexes lived there. I just found that story very fascinating, and I didn't know it until George Bernard Shaw visited South Africa and spoke about that story when he was there. He spoke about how poor this whole group of people had become, and he spoke about where they had originated and what they had been and so forth. But my father's family was sort of back and forth from England; they did lots of moving back and forth.

My mother was Evelyn Minnie West, and again, very interesting. Her mother was German and Jewish, and her family was given land by Queen Victoria in a particular area for services during the Crimean War. And there are papers, you know. I remember, as a child, looking at this parchment and this pink Queen Victoria seal. Her father was from St. Helena, and his mother was an African from that particular eastern cape.

My father's mother came from Holland. Cape Town, South Africa, is such a mixture. The interesting thing about that is that, as you grew up, because of the racial situation in South Africa, you were always told you were half white. You would never say you were half black.

My father worked for the post office for many, many years. After he left the Knysna area where most people worked in forestry, he came to the Cape area and worked in the post office. And my mother, she was probably one of the most creative seamstresses, but she never worked outside the house. She did sewing for different people in the house. And she was a writer. She wrote beautiful stuff. She kept a journal, which I don't have now, and she wrote poetry and stories.

BEATTIE: Do you think you developed your love of writing from your mother?

PEGRAM: Well, it's not only from my mother. It was particularly from, I would say, my mother's side of the family, because there were other writers and, you know, we never had television and radio and, so, all during my growing up years, we spent the long winter nights reading to each other, performing, and writing little plays. The four of us—I have two sisters and a brother—we would write plays and put them on for each other; we had that kind of family entertainment. So reading and performing was part of my childhood.

BEATTIE: Your brother or sisters, do they write now?

PEGRAM: My brother, he does a lot of writing and performing and acting and that kind of thing. He's in England. A retired teacher. And my two sisters are really not into writing. My one sister in Canada, she's a very good artist, but she has been really one of these squashed people that marriage takes over, and their creativity just gets put aside. The other sister in England, she's into education, and her creativity comes out in really finding ways to work with each child in non-traditional ways. But reading is important to all of us. We read, we read, we read.

My father was not a reader. He was sort of more the outdoor person in the garden, and he fished, but he had the most poetic turn of phrase when he was talking. He would see things, he would describe things, but he just never put them down on paper. I have memories of things he would say in a very dry sense of humor, and it was very interesting to listen to him, so he was, in that way, an influence.

BEATTIE: What about your grandparents? Do you remember them?

PEGRAM: Well, my grandfathers had both died before I was born. My grandmothers I knew more. More my mother's mother, who stood about four foot ten and, boy, you never crossed Granny! And, when she spoke Yiddish, you knew she was *really* angry! But still, there was also the sense of storytelling listening to her, and she was just a very influential person in the whole family. Talk about a matriarch!

But my father's mother, when I got to know her, she was already very old, and it was more senility that I was looking at. Beautiful woman, but I was not her favorite. My brother was, so she didn't really have much time to talk to me.

But, in the African sense, there were other people. I had an uncle-in-law whose mother was like a granny, and I'd sit, and she sort of took the place of all grandmothers. That kind of extended family in Africa is very important. Extended family was everybody in the neighborhood, because the children all knew everybody was watching you in the neighborhood. But Ma Marroon was one that I would go and sit and talk to, and I loved talking to old people. I always enjoyed their very interesting stories, and this is what I got from my grandmother, too, when she was telling me about my uncles.

I had come across a picture of my uncles. It was my mother's family, and they were all dressed in dresses. And I said to my granny, "But surely there were boys, too? Where's Uncle Joe? Where's Uncle Bill?" And then she pointed out, "This is Uncle Joe, this is Uncle ..." all in dresses, and it was taken during the time of the Anglo-Boer War, and the little boys were dressed as little girls because the British soldiers were taking these little boys and putting them in little concentration camps to try and break the backs of the local people. So the boys were then disguised as little girls.

BEATTIE: I hadn't heard that before. Do you still have that photo?

PEGRAM: No. I don't have any photographs, because one of the things I had to do when I ran away from South Africa was to go with what's light. Then you look at what's a priority, and I haven't got a single photograph.

BEATTIE: What was your childhood like?

PEGRAM: When we grew up, it was very strongly British influenced, so our education was very British. We had a good diet of the Lake Poets and Shakespeare and so forth. We didn't get much of the South African scene at all. It was a pretty quiet, suburban life. I regard it as a very good childhood. You go back over fifty years, and it's memory—my mother used to say "memory-colored glasses." Your memory *does* color your recollection.

I went to a Methodist school and, of course, it was already segregated. It was already a school for colored children, and *colored* in the South African sense of the word means that you're all mixed, whatever that might be, of mixed-color descent. So I went to this Methodist school till I was in the fifth grade. I started school when I was very young. I was three years old when I entered school. I was always around the school and I always learned. I'd go visit and run messages for the principal, and I could read to him. I'd sit and read, and he said, "Oh, just go on down and enroll in school."

BEATTIE: Had your mother taught you to read?

PEGRAM: I think it's because of my siblings. They were reading and, of course, I wanted to do whatever they did. Apparently, I was extremely precocious and was really not afraid to get up and talk, much to the embarrassment of my other sister, the one next to me in age who lives in Canada and who is very quiet. She was always so embarrassed at my just getting up and talking.

The Methodist was the church school, and then the high school was the public high school where I had to go by train. Then, from there, I went to teacher training college and to a university. The training part of where you do the going to the classrooms and learning the education and doing those education foundation courses and educational psychology courses and all that, that is a two-year or three-year course. I was able to do the three years in two years, and then the B.A. degree is separate from that. So your teacher training is really five years. But you do your teacher training, and I wish Kentucky or this country would do what we did during the first three years.

Our system runs a little different from here. We start at the beginning in January, and we'll take that same subject through until December, and you do an exam in December. If you major, you will take your major subject for three years. Your minor, your second subject, you take for only two years. But I had to do history three years, because I failed it the first year. When we walked into the classroom this teacher got up and she said, "No colored person has ever passed this course on the first attempt." So we all went, "Oh!" And no matter what you did, you got a C. So my brother once had the audacity to say to her, "Dr. Vanderpool, could I please get a B for *black* instead of C for *colored?*"

Those were the conditions under which you operated, and you paid the same student fees and you paid everything, but you were not allowed in sports, and you couldn't go to any of the dances at the University of Cape Town. And I was the last of the people who were allowed there at the time. You know, we were there after the change, and we were allowed to finish our degrees but, after that, you had to go to the colored university. The University of the Western Cape was for the colored people.

BEATTIE: Going back from elementary school through high school, was English your favorite subject, or did writing emerge as something that you were especially good at?

PEGRAM: I think writing emerged quite early, because of this whole thing of writing plays, and writing stories, and writing poems, and writing notes to each other. What developed very early was letter writing. I had pen friends from all over the world, as a child, because I loved to get letters. I still love it. I think there was one magazine called *Girl's Friend* or something. It came from England, and they had names, and I just wrote to people all over, just to get those letters coming. Then, to family members, too, I'd write, because they were in other parts of the world. At night, my mother used to write, and night was our calming time when we would reflect on the day and write. I can remember writing very, very early on.

You see, I suffered a lot under English teachers, because my way of thinking was kind of different and, in elementary school, you know, you just do all the subjects, and you have to do your English and Afrikaans and well, it wasn't social studies then—it became social studies afterwards—but we had geography, and nature study, and biology, so one subject didn't emerge as dominant. But what sticks in my mind as far as English, we learned a lot of poems, because we did a lot of recitation. That, to me, was very important, because you really had to think what the poems said in order to recite the poems and get up and make them meaningful to people. Also, when you read a story, you had to be able to get up and tell that story. So the oral tradition was very alive.

BEATTIE: I understand that you taught in South Africa for—was it seven years—after receiving your B.A.?

PEGRAM: I started in 1955. My first class was at a place called Kennington Central, and it was supposed to be equivalent to our fifth-grade year. I had fifty-five children in the class. I remember going to teach with my bobby socks on. But I had children ranging from eleven to eighteen in the class, because people had to pay for their education, and it wasn't unusual for children to drop out, go and earn some money for the next year, and come back. Also, there was an exam they had to pass in order to go to the next class, so it wasn't that everybody got promoted. You had to know that body of work before you went on.

I had a lot of children from a squatter camp. You see, about these Cross-roads, a lot of it was called Windermere then, a lot of children from there were just living in tin shanties. It was really sad, and I think I earned the equivalent of about thirty dollars a month. Most of that money went back to the children in buying them clothing and fruit. It was really so sad. You had very few books, and you had your chalk and your blackboard. A lot of it was "chalk and talk" kind of education. You tried to really be innovative, but it was extremely difficult.

Then I went to a teacher training college where I worked in a lab school, and the kids who were training had to come and work with me. From there I went to Grassy Park High School to teach English, and from there I left South Africa.

BEATTIE: Did you prefer elementary or high school teaching?

PEGRAM: I really don't know. Each one has its own merits. In a high school you could engage quite fully with the children, and it was interesting from that point of view, because I was closer to their age, in a way, and I could think of a lot of things that they could do. Each level, they really have their own pluses and minuses. I enjoyed in the high school the discussions I could get into with the students. I taught only English, which is good, to be concentrated in one area, and I could do a lot of research along with my students.

BEATTIE: At the time, when you were teaching English, was it mostly British literature you were teaching?

PEGRAM: Oh, yes, exclusively. It was exclusively British literature. I don't remember teaching any South African. I got to know the South African writers once I got to England.

BEATTIE: You said you escaped South Africa and went to London. What brought this about?

PEGRAM: One of the things is, at the time, South African officials were wanting to change the syllabus. When I started teaching, blacks and whites had the same syllabus for the public exam. One of their philosophies was, "Why teach the black children things that they cannot aspire to, things that they cannot attain?" And that's how my brother lost his job, because he started a theater company for the kids, and I was asked to be part of writing the syllabus. And when you say, "No," you're in big trouble. And I refused to do this. My father, through his family connections, he was called by one of the Chief Inspectors who told him that I was in trouble. He told my father that either I comply or my family would have to decide to do something with me. So we spoke about it, and, this inspector, he said he could sit on the paperwork. He gave my father a month where he would sit on the paperwork in order to get me out. He advised my father just to send me to England.

BEATTIE: Was this a white inspector?

PEGRAM: Oh, yes. He was lenient because of my father's family connections. So that's how I got out. Then I had to go and get my passport and say that I was going on a holiday and that kind of thing, because black people, in order to get a passport, had to go for a police interview. So I went to this interview, and I had my return ticket and so forth, but also, you couldn't take a lot, because you were supposedly going on a holiday, and you weren't going to take all your stuff with you. So, guess what? I took my *Complete Works of Chaucer.* I mean, it was strange stuff that I would be taking with me. And I left the things that were really important. When you left you were leaving with the feeling that you couldn't come back. Not the feeling, the certain knowledge. It was two days before my departure that this inspector phoned my father and said, "I'm going to have to give up this paperwork, and we just hope that we can get the secretaries to delay it long enough for her to get out."

I went to England, and when I went back to South Africa for my father's funeral, I had to report to the police. Now I had a compassionate visa. I left in '63 and my father was buried in '67. And, of course, my father had been with us in England. He had just gone back to South Africa when he met with an accident. It was not nice, you know. Not until you were on that ocean, way out, did you feel relaxed. Even then you didn't, because you tried to avoid anybody who is too friendly. You suspected that they were wanting to know about you. It was because they've always told you that they have long arms, and they certainly *do* have long arms. I feel, finally, more at ease. I mean, they harassed my mother after I left. There was a lot of harassment of the family.

BEATTIE: It sounds as though you weren't really involved in politics.

PEGRAM: Well, no, but I did do protests, and we were involved with the sit-ins. There were other things. It wasn't just that, but that was the culmination. I think, had I not been involved in politics and had just said "No" to this, they would not have harassed me that much. But we had gone on protests and on boycotts. And the separate elections, we organized against those and we had public rallies and meetings, and we rode in white people's trains.

BEATTIE: How long was it after you left for England before you saw family members again?

PEGRAM: I left in '63; my other sister came in '64, because she had been arrested and got off on a technicality, so she took to the high seas, too. She was in a protest march and her banner, they said, didn't have an address posted or something, and she got off on the word *posted* because she said, "Well, *posted* means going through the mail." That's how her lawyer got her off, but then my father said, "No, put her on a ship. Send her out."

BEATTIE: What about your parents? You said your father had visited England before he died?

PEGRAM: Oh, yes, and my mother. They stayed with us in South London. My father came just at the end of '64. My parents had just returned in '67 when my sister had just gone back, because we still had a house in South Africa. They'd gone with the intention of just selling it and coming back.

BEATTIE: After your father died, did your mother stay in South Africa?

PEGRAM: No. They told me I needed to take my mother. It was very blunt. "You've got two months to bury your father. Take your mother back, because you won't be allowed to go back and bury her."

My brother could definitely not go back. My sister had married a white South African, which was sort of an immorality act.

BEATTIE: What part of London did you live in?

PEGRAM: South London, Stockwell. And I taught around there. I went to Guildhall School of Music and Drama, but I also did teaching and taught in Stockwell and, oh, at Norwood Girls School in Brixton.

When I first arrived in London, I went to stay with a family. My sister had been in England the year before, and she had gotten to know some people. So I could go and stay with that family until I got a job as a teacher and could get an apartment. Then, by accident, I met a cousin who had also run away from South Africa; I was in a hospital and there she was. People must have thought we were crazy the way we jumped up and down. Then we got an apartment together.

BEATTIE: You said you taught when you first got to London. How long was it after you arrived before you had your first teaching job?

PEGRAM: It was about a month. I did "supply teaching," which was very interesting. Substitute teaching. They call it "supply teaching" in England. The places I saw and the different kinds of children took me all over London.

Then I got a job at a church school, St. Philip's, in Lambeth, Kennington. It was near Lambeth Walk. England's schools were at that time "streamed," the brightest children in one class, and so forth. It was the whole thing of knowing what it's like to be an underdog and of knowing what it's like to be treated as an inferior. I had some kind of empathy with these children, and it was for me a joy to work with them because I always thought of what it's like to be always regarded as a second-class citizen.

I remember teaching at Stockwell High School Manor, Stockwell Secondary School, which is your high school here. They had thirteen tracks in that school; there were over two thousand children. I taught tracks eleven, twelve, and thirteen. We taught as a team, a great unit we had.

I started out with nine-year-olds because, in England, it's ages that distinguish school years, so you talk about nine-year-olds, ten-year-olds, and so forth, because you get social promotion by age. Then, at age eleven, British children have this big eleven-class exam, and then they get sorted out into children who are and who are not going into the academic stream. Then they have a thirteenth class just in case there are late bloomers among the eleven classes. Then I taught English as a second language. That was very interesting, because I had to keep my Greek Cypriots apart from my Turkish Cypriots. Then I taught English at the high school and also special education. That was interesting, really interesting.

In South Africa we belonged to Peninsula Dramatic Society, and we had put on plays and we had toured these plays, and we were great Stanislavsky people. I remember acting in lots and lots of plays in South Africa. So I think we were putting it on as good as any as I've seen at Actors [Actors Theatre of Louisville], because it was really incredible what sets they could build in a very limited space. We put on a lot of plays. This was also part of our educating the people politically. So we would put on things like *Lower Depths* or *Street Scene* or *Deep Are the Roots,* things that could then have a political message, too. We did Bertolt Brecht. We did a lot of Shaw, and we'd have discussions afterward. And I remember doing Jean Genet's *The Blacks,* and the police closing it down, the police walking on stage and closing our production because we had a mixed cast. The one advantage of the segregation was that, as black people, we got to act in … I mean, here we were doing Anton Chekhov, we were doing Brecht, we were doing Henrik Ibsen, we were doing Maxim Gorky and Shakespeare, and I could play in it. Then, when you get to London, "Oh, gosh," you know. "No, no, no. That's not the *black* part," you know.

And here in Louisville, oh, I mean, I have been *so* disgusted with the fact that Actors Theatre has *still* not done color-blind casting! Here you have *Anthony and Cleopatra* and not a single black person! And I remember in London going for an audition for *The Tempest,* and Jonathan Miller was directing. I kept going back and going back. I mean, when you've auditioned five times for a part, you really think, "Now, *this* is it," and then he said to me, "You're not black enough." And I said, "What?" He said, "Under the lights you don't look black, and the island people I want really black." I said, "Have you heard of makeup?" But I did a lot in England, professionally. I did stage work and radio. Radio was probably what I did most. For the BBC [British Broadcasting Corporation], we did different plays. We rehearsed on Friday and Saturday, and on Sunday we recorded. I recorded for

Foreign Service, for Africa Service, and I did some television—the Somerset Maugham series and soap opera.

BEATTIE: You were in films as well?

PEGRAM: Yes. I'm embarrassed to talk about this kind of stuff. One set was so funny. We were doing a thing called *The Body,* but it was very funny, because we just sat on these boxes for days on end. A Jonathan Miller production I think it was, too. It was that, basically, there's a cycle, so the newborn baby looks as wrinkled as a 100–year-old. It was a weird, weird thing. But one of the things that was really nice was *The Lion and the Jewel.* We did a film of that, and *Sweet September* was an interesting film.

BEATTIE: Were you hoping to get into acting full-time and leave teaching?

PEGRAM: I think so. I still enjoy acting, but I think I enjoy the stage probably the best. I really think there's a sense of the immediacy of the audience, and it's hard work. There's nothing glamorous about it; it's just darn hard work. But I still think about getting engaged with that script because, you see, in film sometimes you don't even see the whole script, and especially if you're doing a bit part, you come, and these are your lines, blah, blah, and you don't always see a whole script. Whereas in theater, you've got the play, you're discussing the play; it's more close to the literature. The same was true with the radio plays; at least we had the whole script, and went over it, so the radio plays I enjoyed doing, too.

BEATTIE: Were you writing any plays at this time?

PEGRAM: No. But some of my poems, some of my short stories, were being used in the radio reading. I was doing poetry performances with the jazz group called The Blue Notes. They did quite a bit of work in London and in Paris. Those guys have died now. *That* was an *era.* I don't know which direction I would have gone had I stayed. I left London in '72. I met an American soldier while I was doing some work in Germany.

BEATTIE: Acting work?

PEGRAM: Yes. Then I went to Canada, at first because my mother disapproved of this man. I went to live with my sister in Canada for the few months before I got married, and then I came to Kentucky because he was stationed at Fort Knox, and I never did move out of Kentucky. There's a lot of good things about Kentucky, and there's an amazing, amazing number of writers and visual artists, for the size of the place. I don't know if I'm just seeing one little side, because I haven't traveled around in the other parts, but I guess the biggest influence on my life in Kentucky has been Leon Driskell. Thank God for Leon Driskell. If I go to heaven one day and Leon's not there, then I probably won't think of it as being a heaven. There must be special stars in his crown one day. But not only did I suffer for my writing in elementary school; in high school, teachers asked, "Where did you copy this from?" Even in college I was told a black child was not supposed to be able to write like this. Leon Driskell was really one of the early teachers that celebrated my work, that believed and celebrated and accepted my voice. So he is an extremely special person, and I think that there's a lot of writers that will have to go back to Leon. In South Africa we have this greeting that says, "May you live a thousand years through the lives of those you've touched." I think Leon has got ten thousand years yet.

BEATTIE: When you came here in '72, did you live at Fort Knox?

PEGRAM: No, I didn't live on base. I lived in Radcliff, and that was a traumatic experience. I had never seen a trailer in my life, and here I was going into this house trailer, and I had the feeling that I had gotten onto one of those train carriages. I don't know if it's the same here, with the sleeping cars, but I felt as though I was on this train that I couldn't get off. And my mother came and she said, "He's put you in a caravan."

BEATTIE: Why did your mother disapprove of the marriage?

PEGRAM: Oh, she said it was because he was divorced, but basically I think he was too black.

BEATTIE: Too black?

PEGRAM: I think so. I think because you get the indoctrination over the years and years and years in South Africa that a dark skin is not of value. Also, my mother disapproved of the military. So there were a lot of reasons, but she pinned it on the divorce, because she believed I was living in sin. You marry a divorced person whose wife is still alive, then you are living in sin, and that's a Biblical sin, and so forth. She never did come to terms with him. She came over when Melanie [Pegram's daughter] was born, to be with me.

BEATTIE: What year was that?

PEGRAM: Seventy-four. And it was extremely hard, knowing my mother didn't approve. And also, educationally, my husband didn't have a college degree. He got it later, during our marriage, but she just felt that I had married beneath my station in life, whatever that might be.

But coming to Kentucky, I don't want to sound as if there is a fate, and that your life is planned ahead, and you have no free will and all that, but I think that a lot of times things happen for a purpose. You can make the right or wrong choice, but still, I don't think I would have grown as a writer had I stayed in England, because I think the acting might have taken over. I've grown as a writer here. I have grown more in the performance part of my writing, so I've been able to have the best of both worlds.

I got this job teaching first grade [with Fort Knox Independent Schools], and I'd always been scared of little children. But I learned on this job, and I had a wonderful teacher working with me, Shirley Jarvis, who now teaches in the four-year-old program at Fort Knox. What I did, how I got a job, was I went in and volunteered in the classrooms. Psychologically, it was very bad for me in the beginning, and I joined a woman's group, and one woman there whose husband was a doctor, she said, "You know, you need to talk," because I was getting these letters from my mother, and my family, telling me how horrible and bad I was. It was really awful. Then, as therapy, they really told me to go and do something in the classroom, to just get myself out of this caravan I was in. I did two things. I started doing part-time studying, and I went into psychology classes at Fort Knox before I did the M.A. degree.

BEATTIE: So you took some courses?

PEGRAM: At U of L [the University of Louisville program at Fort Knox], I did. I took things like abnormal psychology and general psychology. Then I came up to U of L [Belknap Campus] to do my M.A. in English and creative writing. And I did the volunteer teaching and then I did substitute teaching and then I got a job.

BEATTIE: What was your M.A. thesis?

PEGRAM: It was creative writing. I did poetry and short stories. I was working with Sena Naslund and Leon Driskell. Although Sena was chairing the program, I didn't work as much with her as I did with Leon. Leon loomed much larger, and I did other courses with him, like the Shakespeare courses.

BEATTIE: So you were finding a niche here despite having to live in the caravan?

PEGRAM: Yes, I was, and that was my salvation, because I was going out and I was meeting other people, and I wasn't tied to the army base, and I was never involved with that army wives' thing.

BEATTIE: And all this time you were commuting from Radcliff to attend U of L?

PEGRAM: Yes. Then we moved to Elizabethtown. We bought a house, and I moved out of the caravan and into a house. So I was commuting, and then I got my degree, and then I didn't even go to the graduation ceremony because, at the time, there was nobody in my family here.

BEATTIE: When do you do most of your writing?

PEGRAM: Any time. I'm a very undisciplined writer. I look at these people that every day set aside time to write, and I don't know if it's the whole idea of having, as a child, kept all those journals and not having one of them, but I'm not very good at journal keeping. I'm very sporadic. At one time I thought I was going to write letters to Melanie every day. I don't know. They're somewhere. Maybe one day when I've died, and she looks through all this stuff, she might find some things that I have written to her. What I tend to do is to carry things around in my head. I'll walk around and walk around so that, when I write, I might be at that typewriter for days on end, just putting down. I have not made notes or anything, but it's just there, you know. I become sometimes very distracted. People who are talking to me notice I'm not really with them because I'm sort of somewhere else.

BEATTIE: You have published short stories and critical essays. Will you discuss those and where they have been published?

PEGRAM: The short stories, well, the latest was in that collection they put together, *A Century of Poetry and a Century of Fiction,* I think it's called.

BEATTIE: And they are titled "Breaking the Silence" and "Raising the Blinds"?

PEGRAM: Umhumm. Then I have a book that's used on a lot of campuses,

Unwinding Threads, Writing by Women in Africa, published by Heinemann. In that book, Southern Africa is represented by Miriam Tlali, Bessie Head, Olive Schreiner, Nadine Gordimer, Doris Lessing, and me. There is another book called *Africa Today;* these stories have appeared in different magazines, as well. Then *Callaloo* has published some stuff, and so has *Presence Africaine,* which is English-French translations. I had some published in Norway, Denmark, and Holland. I sort of lost count.

But, being in Kentucky, I have been able to see parallels of South African life here. South Africa has equipped me for dealing with life here. The only thing I miss is the ocean. Oh gosh, how I miss *that*! When things go bad for me, I wish I could just be walking along the shore, sitting on a rock and having that spray up in my face and being able to climb Table Mountain [in Cape Town]. Not that I could climb it now; I probably would have to go up in the cable car. But that mountain and the ocean are the two things that I miss very, very much.

I'm also thinking of going into a new career, which may or may not happen, but I have started the process. I've had one interview; I have another one this month. I want to become an Episcopal priest. That's the process that I'm going through at the moment.

What amazes me about Louisville, Kentucky, is the number of really good visual artists in the black community, visual artists that have won international acclaim. The sad part of it is that the main stream—like the ballet, like the opera, like the theater—they are not recognizing the talent in the black community. In England, we used to refer to it as the Sunday Tea Ladies' Organization. There is an elitist thing going on. I wish that there'd be more multicultural stuff, because there is so much talent in this place that is just going to waste because, black actors, they don't have that money base to do anything. To me, the sad part of it is that whites can play any part, but blacks cannot, you see. I mean, Cleopatra could be a white lady, but a black guy couldn't go and play Marc Anthony, and Marc Anthony was probably a Swahili. I don't think that he would have been very fair-skinned to begin with, so the stage is wide open for white people, but not for black people.

BEATTIE: I know that you write book reviews for Louisville's *Courier-Journal.* How did that start?

PEGRAM: It actually started with writing an article about when Mandela came out of prison. A friend of mine works there, and she told the editor, "Oh, I've got someone who, I'm sure, will be able to write something about Mandela."

BEATTIE: Was this editor Keith Runyon?

PEGRAM: Yes. Then he asked me about doing book reviews. I said, "Sure." I read, anyway, so I might as well. I've enjoyed doing the book reviews, because you are able to read more critically.

BEATTIE: Will you discuss your poetry readings in this and other countries?

PEGRAM: Oh, that's been a joy, joy, joy. I do poetry readings with percussion. As I said, I started out in England with a jazz group, and that was great fun, but in South Africa I had worked with drums. And, when I came here, I sort of missed the drums, and I looked for a drummer, and I was sort of passed on from friend to friend to friend, and I finally got Abe Johnson, and there was an instant connection. He reads the work, and he immediately says to me, "I can drum on this," or "I can't drum on this." He'll read it and get the rhythm. It is just a marvelous high; he is able just to follow those words and respond in a particular rhythm.

BEATTIE: And your readings are almost always accompanied by percussion?

PEGRAM: I would like them always to be accompanied, so I won't say *almost* always. In fact, nowadays, I normally tell people I won't perform without the drums.

BEATTIE: How did that develop? I know you loved the performing plus the writing, but how did you decide to do your reading that way?

PEGRAM: In South Africa we had performed that way, so it was something that I had done before.

BEATTIE: And you generally dance to the accompaniment of the drums?

PEGRAM: Oh, well, as the spirit moves I will do a little dance, but I sometimes would have a dancer, separate, and at one time there were fifteen dancers at the Louisville Youth Performing Arts School, and they danced to my poetry, and they had the dance concert that year with poetry and drums.

BEATTIE: When did your divorce take place?

PEGRAM: In '85, or maybe from the day I was married. It took place during the thirteen years of the marriage, because my friends always tell me that it disintegrated from the start. "If I need an 'as' or a 'like' / to shape a poem/ of our marriage / let it be a grapefruit/ After I have discarded/ the bitter rind/ of my anger and regret/ I bit into the/ memory's meat/ bitter sour sweet/ our flesh on the/ bones of our daughter/ your smile in her eyes/ of brighter times/ sour the juice/ trickling with the/ sucking of each segment/ of our marriage/ bitter/ your inability to/ slake your lust/ on the grapefruit." That was "Segments," one of the things I just kind of wrote down, and "Woman Speak" is a poem that I have fun with, because in performance I do the zeroing in on a poor, unsuspecting, male, and it's called "Woman Speak": "tearing my skirts/ jumping the hedgerow/ racing barefoot through/ the brush/ ribbon ponytails flapping in the chase/ swinging exhausted through the gate/ flopping on the porch/ to catch a breath/ those were girl days/ now I have tamed my hair/ close-crop/ Thirty-six Ceed my breasts/ And sheathed my hips in pencil-slim skirt/ Step sedate/ Feet imprisoned in stiletto pumps/ And you come by/ say/ 'Girl, looking mighty fine./ What's happening, girl?'/ Five foot two frame stretched tall/ I heave my breast/ Toss my head/ 'Did I hear you call me, *Girl?*'" I have written a few poems lately for my mother and my grandmother, and that's all. In fact, the title has changed from "Woman Speak," and I can't recall the name of that—the title—now, because it is a Zulu name, and it has gone to the feelings and memories of a woman.

BEATTIE: Do you feel equally comfortable writing poetry and prose?

PEGRAM: I always thought that I would do prose, and I was never very sure of my poetry, and Leon Driskell convinced me of my poetry. I have this way of not finishing my sentences and so forth, when I write, and that's just my style.

BEATTIE: When you are reading your poetry, your voice has a very musical quality that really complements the poem, that brings out the meaning.

PEGRAM: And sometimes it's the rhythm that comes to me before the words. In *Our Sun Will Rise,* we have a little skip poem, you know: "Did you hear my mother cry ..." It's called "Soweto Jump Rope," and I have been always fascinated by these jumps and sing-songs. I had this little jump thing in my mind, and then we were talking one day of how the news gets spread, because some of the news in South Africa you could not put in the newspapers, and it was illegal to publish the names of people who were arrested. Yet everybody got to know the news, and it was in the songs of the children that the news went around, and that's when I wrote that little poem, "Soweto Jump Rope."

I'm in the third writing of a South African love story. It's based loosely on a true story about a priest in South Africa. But, again, you know how in writing you use the truth here and you transpose it to a different period? A lot of the incidents are all true, but in different settings. That's what all my work is about, really. I like to call it basically biographical and, yet, not biographical. Maybe *transplanted* or *transplaced* biography, because it is really you placing it in different places, so that a piece of a story that happened in Cape Town I might place in Kentucky.

BEATTIE: Would you comment on what you think the nature of creativity itself is?

PEGRAM: Oh, gosh, what I do, I really don't know. Giving birth? I am the kind of poet that is always pregnant with my next poem. I am pregnant with my next work, and then I give birth to it when it finally comes out. I think it's largely gift, I really do, because we are all born with separate gifts. My sister in Canada has the gift for drawing. When her pen goes to paper, it's to make a picture, whereas my pen goes with a picture of words. I need words for my picture, and she just needs lines for her picture. My sister in England, her creativity is when she sings and her voice comes out in a different way. Once you have that gift, it's how that gift is nurtured. My writing was nurtured all along.

June 8, 1992

Pegram cites her 1995 Kentucky Foundation for Women grant as "one of the most significant events" in her life, as it enabled her to return to Cape Town for the first time in thirty-two years. However, on her return journey, she lost with her luggage her research concerning the conditions of women in South African slavery. Pegram continues to publish in journals and magazines, as well as in such anthologies as Random House's *Daughters of Africa* and Heinemann's *African Women's Poetry,* just as she continues to perform her poetry throughout the United States and Canada.

BOOKS BY AMELIA BLOSSOM PEGRAM:

Deliverances. New York: Nubia Press, 1980.

Our Sun Will Rise. Washington, D. C.: Three Continents Press, 1989.

Echoes Across a Thousand Hills. Lawrenceville, N.J.: Africa World Press, 1994.

KAREN ROBARDS

ROBARDS: My name is Karen Ann Johnson Robards. I was born on August 24, 1954, in Elizabethtown, Kentucky. My mother is Sally Ann Skaggs Johnson, and my father is Walter Lee Johnson. My father is an orthodontist. He went to University of Louisville Dental School and to Eastman Dental Center in Rochester, New York. He's been in practice here [Louisville] for twenty-five years.

My mother comes from Green County. The Skaggs were the original longhunters who came over with Daniel Boone, and a lot of her family is still here. It's a very interesting family. My mother is my father's business secretary. My father just turned sixty, and my mother's fifty-seven. They met when my mother was in first grade. They've known each other all their lives. My mother lived in Glendale, and my father lived on a farm outside of Elizabethtown.

My maternal grandparents had a house in Glendale, and my mother just turned nineteen two days before I was born. She went back to her mother and father with me. And my father lived there, too. He was still in college at the time. We lived there for a year. Then my father got into dental school at University of Louisville, and we moved to Louisville, and my maternal grandparents moved with us. They kept me and my mother worked while my father went to school.

BEATTIE: What are the names of your maternal grandparents?

ROBARDS: It was Mary Katherine Leaha Skaggs who raised me. She was like a mother to me until she died when I was nine. My grandfather was Albert Leslie Skaggs. He died when I was four, on Christmas Eve. Had a heart attack.

Then my father's parents both died about twenty years ago, Sylvia Clara Higdon Johnson and William Otto Johnson.

As to my maternal grandparents, Kate was a teacher before she got married. I called her Kate. I was the only grandchild who did. Mom says that Pop, my maternal grandfather, used to tease her by teaching me to call her Kate. It drove her nuts, but I didn't know it. She was a schoolteacher, so she taught me to read and write when I was little. He owned a service station in Fort Knox. He was seventy when I was born; before I was born he was a farmer. He was a dentist for awhile, which I thought was interesting. My mother, she's the youngest of six children. And *they* all had a lot of children. My father is the second of six children, but two died in childhood. So, we have a large, extended family.

BEATTIE: What about brothers and sisters?

ROBARDS: I'm the oldest. I have a brother who is five years younger than I am. His name's Tod Leslie Johnson. He is the operating manager for Gannett [News Service] here in town. I have twin brothers who are younger than Tod—Bruce and Brad Hodges Johnson. Bruce owns Lawn Pro, which is a lawn care company here in town. Brad just got out of mortuary school and he's looking to buy a funeral home. They are seven years younger than I am. I have a baby sister, Lee Ann, who is fifteen years younger than I am. She just got out of Eastern Kentucky University, and she just got married. Everybody lives in Louisville, except my sister.

BEATTIE: What was your childhood like, and where did you live in Louisville when you moved here?

ROBARDS: When we first moved here, we lived in Valley Station. My mother worked. She was very young. My father was in dental school, so I was raised by my maternal grandparents. They thought the sun rose and set with me. Mom said they would carry me around on pillows. I never had an unfulfilled wish. Nothing bad ever happened to me. I was their precious darling. They both just catered totally to me. Then Pop died when I was four. That's one of my earliest memories. I can remember that because I just loved him dearly. I didn't see that much of my real parents. I saw my grandparents all the time. And I can remember he had a horror of funeral homes, so they had him in a coffin with a clear, acrylic cover. I can remember being very little and looking up and seeing him in that glass coffin and not understanding and thinking if they'd just lift the lid and let him out, he'd be fine. But, of course, they didn't.

Then I lived with my maternal grandmother until she died of cancer, when I was nine. Then I went to live with my parents and my three younger brothers. By that time, I was very much the oldest. My mother always worked, and I kind of raised the little ones. I'm very close to my family. We're all very close.

BEATTIE: What do you remember doing as a child?

ROBARDS: Babysitting.

BEATTIE: All your brothers and sisters?

ROBARDS: All my life. That's what I did. I chased children. I read books. I always read. I've always been a voracious reader. I wrote. I've been writing since I was about five years old.

BEATTIE: I remember reading in one of your books about your first writing being for your grandmother. Is that right?

ROBARDS: Oh yes, I wrote her a book. My mother still has it somewhere. I always wrote. You know, she was a school teacher, and that's kind of what we did. We read and we wrote. But I've always been a writer and I've always read. I've always had lots of animals, and I've always chased children. This is my whole life. There it is in a nutshell.

BEATTIE: Was that the first thing you ever wrote, what you wrote for your grandmother?

ROBARDS: No, I'm sure it wasn't. I mean, it's the first thing I remember.

BEATTIE: Did you first start writing before you went to school?

ROBARDS: It was before I went to school, because they didn't have kindergarten then and, as I said, I wrote that book at age five. I didn't start school until I was six, in first grade. I don't remember when I first started writing. But I could write at five and I could read at five. It was just such a natural thing.

BEATTIE: Were you read to a lot as a child?

ROBARDS: Oh, God. Mom said I used to drive Kate crazy. No matter what she was doing, I'd make her sit and read. She said she'd go through a hundred books in a day. My children are like that. They read and read and read and read.

BEATTIE: Do you remember the books you liked as a child?

ROBARDS: Ah, Nancy Drew. I was raised to be a southern lady. Well, I got hold of a book called *Ivy Anders, Night Nurse,* which must have been one of the early romances. Well, they kissed in the novel. I guess I was about eight or nine years old when I read it. I thought my mother was going to have a heart attack when she found it, so she gave me Nancy Drew. I was reading Dostoevski when I was ten. I read *Gone With the Wind* when I was ten—any book I could come across.

BEATTIE: What do you remember about your elementary school years?

ROBARDS: In first grade, I made straight A's. Of course I knew how to read and how to write, which helped a lot. In second grade, I made straight A's, except Mrs. Studerman had a falling out with my father, who was her son's dentist. So she gave me a B. I was so horrified that she took it back and she erased it and changed it to an A.

Well, after that, I didn't make straight A's anymore. I was a gifted child. Very gifted. But what I would do in class is, instead of doing the work I was supposed to do, I'd get my math book out and I'd get whatever book I was reading and hide it behind the math book. So, sometimes I missed the lesson, and people didn't always understand. It depended on the teacher. But I wasn't real popular with the other kids. I was a little different because I was a reader. I liked to do research papers. I always excelled in research papers. I was always in the school play. I was very good. A lot of writers are shy. I'm not shy. I'm very good at acting and getting in front of an audience. I did best in things where I was let alone to do my own thing. You know, read and write, that type of thing.

Well, let me go back to fourth grade first, because my son has this problem. I was so forgetful. You know, the absent-minded professor. This is me. This is my older boy, actually. Lucky for him, I've been there, so I laugh and I tell the teachers okay, I know where this child's coming from. But I was in the fourth grade. I used to forget my homework every day. I don't know what it was. I'd forget it. So one day she sent me home to get the homework. I got home early. I forgot why she sent me home, so I just stayed home. So she calls my mother about six o'clock, and says, "Is Karen *ever* coming back with that homework?" But, by sixth grade, I had a teacher named Mrs. Wise, and she was a very smart woman. I really liked her. We got along. They didn't have the gifted program as they have it now. It was just starting out. I guess this was the early '60s. They would have a psychologist come to each school and test two or three children that the teachers had selected as possibly being academically gifted. I was one of them that Mrs. Wise selected. Not because I had the best grades in class, because I didn't, but simply because I read so much. And it turned out I was extremely gifted, intellectually. So they put me in a special school in seventh grade. I can't even remember the name of it. I was only there three weeks. We moved to New York. My father had been a practicing dentist for seven years and had decided to go to orthodontic school in Rochester, New York. We went to Rochester and I went to junior high in Rochester, New York, for seventh and eighth grade. Then we came back and I went to Ballard for four years.

BEATTIE: In school, did English emerge as your favorite subject?

ROBARDS: I wouldn't say it was my favorite, really. It was the easiest for me. I always excelled in it, and I was absolutely the best in the class. I would say that my influence, as far as writing is concerned, was my grandmother. Absolutely. No doubt about it.

BEATTIE: Did you go directly from high school to college?

ROBARDS: Absolutely. You couldn't have kept me back. I was seventeen years old. My parents didn't want me to leave home. I left for college about the ninth of August. I wanted to leave a little early. Now you have to understand that my mother worked all the time. *All* the time. And I raised the children and kept the house. So I was real anxious to go to college. My mother did not own a dishwasher until I left for college, because she did not need one. *I* was the dishwasher.

So I left for college and loved it. I went to Western Kentucky University for two years. I met my husband three weeks after I got up there. Peggy Lutts, still my dearest friend—we've been dearest friends since we were little girls—Peggy and I were roommates, and we were walking, and it started to rain. At Western, there was a Dairy Queen over there behind McCormick Hall, which is one of the girls' dorms. We stopped in at the Dairy Queen, and we sat down. We ordered a sundae and these two guys came in. They sat down beside Peggy. One guy said to Peggy, "Oh, that looks good." She said, "Do you want a bite?" He took a bite. Well, this turned out to be my husband. I didn't see him that night. He didn't see me. But they drove us home because it was raining, and then his friend came down that same night, and I dated his friend for awhile. But the boy I eventually married kept hanging around and hanging around and, by Thanksgiving, we were dating. By January of the next year, this was 1973, we were living together. We've been together ever since. Twenty years.

BEATTIE: Did you finish college at Western?

ROBARDS: No, at the University of Kentucky. Doug [Robards's husband] was a senior when I got there. So he finished after my first year, and then he worked a year. Then he went to get his MBA at the University of Kentucky, so I finished at the University of Kentucky. I majored in journalism. I was there two years.

BEATTIE: I'm wondering why you majored in journalism instead of English.

ROBARDS: Because I knew I could get straight A's. I knew by then that I was a truly good writer. I did it as easily as breathing. I knew I'd make straight A's in journalism and I wanted to go to law school. It had not occurred to me to be a writer. Everybody I knew was a doctor, a lawyer, a professional person, and that's what I thought I would be. And, as I said, I didn't know any writers. I had no idea that people made their livings that way. I was going to be a lawyer. But in order to get into a good law school, I needed really good grades. So I majored in journalism, and I took a lot of advanced placement tests, so I really didn't have to work that hard at all. I got almost sixty hours of credit through advance placement tests. I'm really good at tests. And the rest of it—the actual hands-on writing courses—just came easily. So I ended up with a really high grade point average and, sure enough, got into the University of Kentucky College of Law.

BEATTIE: Did you work, while you were a journalism major, on the *Kentucky Kernel?*

ROBARDS: Oh yes, I worked on the *Kentucky Kernel.* I worked on the yearbook. In fact, I wrote so many of the articles for the yearbook that they made me use a pseudonym. I've got pseudonyms all over that yearbook. Just about every article in there is written by me, under a pseudonym. I was real prolific, and I liked to do it.

BEATTIE: Did you feel at all constricted by journalism?

ROBARDS: Just a little bit. They didn't have a sense of humor. I mean, it is so easy—who, what, when, where, why. So I'm sitting in the first journalism course. We had to write these stupid, dry leads. I was getting kind of tired of it, you know. So the professor had this one woman fall off a cliff. I started mine saying, "Suzie so-and-so should have watched that first step, because it was a doozy." The professor was not amused. I had to rewrite it. Hard news is a little dry for me. But it was a way to make good grades.

BEATTIE: Then you were sure that you wanted to go to law school?

ROBARDS: Oh, yes. There was absolutely no doubt in my mind. I was going to be the best lawyer that ever was: Perry Mason.

BEATTIE: You wanted criminal law.

ROBARDS: Criminal law, absolutely. Because I'm not shy, and I speak well. And I emote well. I had no career qualms at all. It's the funniest thing. From the time I was ten years old, I was going to be a lawyer. I had no doubts. I started to law school. My husband was working at Manpower Temporary Services in Lexington. I was in law school three weeks and I figured something out. I *hated* law school. It was all research. It wasn't talking, it wasn't even writing. It was sitting in class listening to these people talk about stupid stuff. There's no right or wrong in law. There are only precedents. But I was my parents' oldest child. I was the oldest grandchild on my father's side. I mean, everybody thought I was brilliant. Everybody thought I was going to be the best and the brightest. My cousins were looking up to me. My brothers were looking up to me. My entire, huge family was waiting for me to dazzle them. I hated law school, but I couldn't drop out. I couldn't do it. My parents would have died on the spot.

Well, I had never read a romance novel up to that point. I read everything, but I thought romance novels were beneath me. I wouldn't be caught dead reading one of those. Well, it was so stressful for me, figuring out that I had made this major career miscalculation, that I had to do something to relieve the stress. And there was a little used bookstore right around the corner from the University of Kentucky College of Law, and I started stopping in there on the way home. They had stacks and stacks of Harlequin romance novels. That's about *all* they had. I looked and saw that they were little, thin things. And I thought, "I can read that in about an hour. This is what I need, a little break." So I bought one or two. I read them. And they were really good. By the time three or four months had passed, I'd read every book in that store. That was the first time it hit me that I could do that.

So I was still in law school, still hating it, hanging in there. It may have been the first semester of my second year, I don't remember. I signed up for a graduate-level creative writing course with Ed McClanahan. It was the first real creative writing course I'd ever taken. And, for our class project, we had to write something wonderful. We had to come up with something publishable, something that showed our futures as writers. Well, there were about twelve people in the class. I wrote the first fifty pages of what turned out to be *Island Flame*. It was a romance novel, a historical romance novel. It was really good. The only problem was, Ed McClanahan didn't tell us that at the end of the class we were going to have to read our work aloud. So I got up and read the darn thing aloud. It took the whole class period, I think. It was a two-hour class. We had an hour to read and an hour to discuss. I got to the end, and the class laughed. There was this dead silence, then they all burst into laughter because it was a romance novel. That was very, very disheartening. I mean, I'm not used to people laughing at me. So, finally, Professor McClanahan stood up. "You know, Karen," he said, "you're a really good writer. But I'd like to encourage you to go into serious fiction." Well, that kind of made me mad. I stood up and I said, "Well, I'll tell you what. You write what you write. And I'll write this stuff, and let's get together in fifteen, twenty years, and see where we are." And the funny thing about it is, we ran into each other at the Kentucky Book Fair about four or five years ago and, sure enough, romances gave me my start. I'm not a romance writer now, officially. I am a contemporary women's fiction hardback writer. But I started out being a romance writer, and I'll never apologize for it. It was a wonderful step and some of those wonderful books got me where I am. And where I am is a good place to be.

BEATTIE: What about after you wrote that class assignment? How did your career take off?

ROBARDS: Well, after that, I was so demoralized by all the laughter that I packed these fifty pages up and didn't look at them again for a little while. Fortunately, my husband had his MBA by this time from the University of Kentucky in marketing. He got a job offer in Columbus, Ohio, from the world's largest research and development institute. We had to move to Columbus, Ohio. So that got me out of law school. I was going to go back to school at Ohio State, but I had a free summer where I didn't have anything to do. I thought, "I'm going to spend this summer and try to be a writer." So I pulled out my fifty pages and I was very, very methodical. I had a *Writer's Market,* which lists all the publishers and all the agents. I went alphabetically down the list. Well, Avon was the biggest romance publisher at that time, and they intimidated me. But I sent a copy of those first fifty pages to Bantam, to Belmont Tower, which is now Leisure, and to Ballantine, I guess to the first B's there. And, two weeks later, I got this little envelope in the mail saying that Belmont Tower loved the first fifty pages and wanted to see the rest of the book. This was wonderful. I mean, I was thrilled. There was just one little problem. There *was* no rest of the book. And we're talking about a hundred-and-twenty-five-thousand-word book. So I had a portable manual typewriter that my husband had bought me some years before. This was pre-computer. I mean, if you had an IBM Selectric, you were a big deal. I went out and I rented an IBM Selectric typewriter. I brought it home to our house that had four apartments in it. And I plugged it in, in the second spare bedroom of our little apartment there, and I locked myself in there and I wrote from eight o'clock in the morning until ten or eleven o'clock at night, every day, seven days a week, for six weeks. I wrote as hard as I could, as fast as I could, and as well as I could. By the time I got done, there were wads of paper up over my head, and I'm five foot seven. The only clear place in the room was a little path between the door and my chair and the table. The landlord had started peeping in the windows to see what I was doing in there, but I got it done. And I mailed it. And I prayed. Two weeks later, I got this skinny little envelope. Once you get to be a successful writer, you know that a skinny envelope means good news. So I got this skinny little envelope in the mail, and it was Belmont Tower, and they wanted to buy the book. Well, it was absolutely the happiest day in my life. I was a published writer. Well, *going* to be published. I was twenty-four, and the book didn't come out for another year and a half. But I waited to get rich and famous. It didn't happen. The book came out and I didn't get rich and famous, darn it. I'd been just sure that, with one book, you're going to be rich and famous. It didn't happen. In fact, I couldn't even sell them another book. They didn't want to hear from me at this point. They wanted to see how the book would do.

BEATTIE: When you got that first contract, did you go home and immediately start plans for another book?

ROBARDS: Yes, I kind of did. I worked on a sequel to *Island Flame,* because I was sure they'd want a sequel. I thought it was going to be a major bestseller. I think they paid twelve hundred fifty dollars for *Island Flame,* which isn't very much. They only paid me half of it, actually. I was going to have to get a job. So I did. I started working as an orthodontic assistant.

BEATTIE: Had you had any training in that?

ROBARDS: I worked for my father from the time I was a little girl. I'd been doing that since I was twelve years old. I can put braces on with the best of them. Yes, I knew how to do that. So I was making good money. But I was working from seven in the morning to seven at night. They were long hours. I was making about eighteen thousand a year, which was quite a bit back then, for that. And I kept waiting for the royalties to start rolling in, because they told me about royalties.

Then it hit me: "I'm not going to be a big, famous, successful writer off this." And they didn't want the sequel to that book, either. It was this real lowering feeling—like okay, I've got a book published, *now* what? And it hit me. I didn't have any time to write anymore because I had a full-time job. And it was really a draining full-time job. I thought, "Well, if something more is going to happen in this career, I'm going to have to do it. So I gritted my teeth, and I got a yellow legal pad, and every day I had an hour for lunch. I went into the restroom. The dental clinic had a four-stall women's restroom. I'd lock myself in a stall of that restroom, and I wrote what turned out to be *To Love a Man* in the stall of that restroom, longhand, during my lunch hours. I didn't tell anybody else what I was doing. All the people in the office thought I had major stomach problems. Anyway, I wrote *To Love a Man,* and as I said, nothing much happened with my writing career. Finally, Leisure did agree to buy the sequel to *Island Flame.* It was *Sea Fire.* Again, they weren't paying me anything. I mean, if I was making six hundred dollars a year off this, I was really doing well. And I thought, "This isn't working. This is not how this is supposed to work." *To Love a Man* was a contemporary. *Island Flame* and *Sea Fire* were historicals. The book I had written in the restroom, *To Love a Man,* was a contemporary and it was really good. It *still* is pretty good. It's one of the classics. I sent it to them. They wouldn't buy it because it was contemporary, and I was now seen as a historical novelist. I was typecast, okay? It made me mad. My life works best when something makes me mad.

So I got my little trusty *Writer's Market* out again. I turned to the authors' agents. And I'm very methodical. Shirley Burke was the first one I came to. I sent her the first fifty pages of *To Love a Man.* Well, she loved it. She absolutely loved it. She agreed to represent me for ten percent terms, and she sold it to Warner Books for a thousand times more than I had been getting to that point. Well, Warner didn't want to publish that as their first book of mine, and I still owed Leisure another book. So I did *Forbidden Love* for Leisure. They went bankrupt, and I was pregnant with my first child about this time. I remember that because they owed me seventy-five hundred dollars in August for *Forbidden Love,* and my baby was due in August. Being kind of new at the business, I went out and I spent a lot of the seventy-five hundred dollars on nursery furniture. Well, Leisure went bankrupt; I didn't get the seventy-five hundred dollars. The book came out and died. I think it had, like, two thousand copies in print because they went bankrupt. But the baby came. I still have the baby.

BEATTIE: And the furniture?

ROBARDS: And the furniture. He had a beautiful nursery. So I had three historicals with Leisure by that time. But I was now a Warner author, which was a whole different ball game. I mean, they were treating me like a big deal. It was my first taste of real success as a writer. And I published a historical with them, *Amanda Rose,* then *To Love a Man* six months later. *To Love a Man,* they printed more than five hundred thousand copies. It won every major award that year. *To Love a Man,* the one I wrote in the restroom, actually the funny thing about it is, I couldn't think what to write. I was sitting there on the toilet. *To Love a Man* starts in an outhouse, and that's why. But *To Love a Man* was the real launch of my career.

BEATTIE: What awards did it win?

ROBARDS: Oh, it won everything. It won Reviewers' Choice Award from *Romantic Times.* It won Best Contemporary Novel for 1985 from *Romantic Times.* It won a silver pin from *Affaire d'Coeur.* It won a Walden Books Award for bestselling new author. It won six or seven awards.

BEATTIE: So that was really the book that got your name launched as a romance writer?

ROBARDS: That was the book. And, as I said, they printed five hundred and seventy-five thousand copies, which was a huge printing for an unknown writer then. After *To Love a Man,* it's kind of all been uphill. I've never looked back since *To Love a Man,* which came out, I think, in January of '85. I've done so many now I've kind of lost track, but I think that's when it was published. They bought it a year and a half before that. I'm now up to book number nineteen. *To Love a Man* was number five.

BEATTIE: That's quite a lot of writing.

ROBARDS: Right. I write and I chase children and I read. My life hasn't changed a bit.

BEATTIE: Many romance writers published under pseudonyms, and you publish everything under you own name.

ROBARDS: When I first got into the business, Leisure wanted to buy all my books in perpetuity. Fortunately, I went to law school. I read the contract, and I wouldn't sign it. They also wanted me to use a pseudonym. I have never used a pseudonym, and I won't. It's my guarantee of quality to my fans. If it's got my name on it, it's the best I can do. I don't ever write junk. Every book I write is the best I can do. I'm really serious about it.

This last book I finished is really good, *Maggy's Child.* It will be out in January of '94. We started negotiating a contract in the middle of it. I kind of get into a trance state when I write. I don't even know my neighbors. I mean, they're used to me by now. They think I'm a little weird, but hey, I'm not there. And I couldn't get in that trance state during this contract. So, finally, I thought, "Okay.

I can do this now." I was four or five months late with that book, which I never am. It was simply because I had to negotiate the contract first before I could give that book my best. I get paid well, but I don't write for the money. I do my best. And there's something in me that has to do it. Every book I've written is good. I'm proud of every one. They're the best I can do.

BEATTIE: The settings of your books have ranged from colonial America to seventeenth century Ireland to Rhodesia to contemporary United States. How much research do you do for your novels to ensure that dress, manners, speech patterns, and the like are accurate?

ROBARDS: I do quite a bit. Actually, you have to remember, I'm a voracious reader. I read everything. I mean, all the magazines, everything. My little boy, they have a magazine subscription drive every year at his school. Well, I read all the magazines. I even read stupid *Business Week,* which is a really dumb magazine, because I always have to have something to read. I'd rather not eat than not read. A lot of this information is already stored in my head. You'd be surprised what little, odd snippets are up there. And they come out. So I don't have to do as much research, most of the time, as I guess a lot of people may have to. The hardest thing for me, when I first started out with historicals, was underwear. That's the truth. There wasn't a lot of research on underwear, and it drove me batty. I had these people getting dressed and getting undressed. I didn't know what was under their dresses. It was driving me nuts. Finally, I found out. That was the hardest piece of research.

When I wrote *To Love a Man* in the restroom, I could not do an awful lot of research in that restroom because there was just me and the toilet and the legal pad, right? I made it up. I made Rhodesia totally up as I went along. I made up the rivers. I just imagined myself there in Rhodesia. What would it be like? Then, when I got done, and I checked it all, I was right on the money. The river was even there where I put it. It was the most amazing thing. But, you know, you do a little research. You do the research that you need to do. I'm as accurate as I can be. I do what is needed for my characters. The great thing about it is you don't have to know any more than the character whose voice you are. So, depending on whose voice I'm in, my character may not know the name of that daggone road, either. I don't know the name of half the streets around here. So you don't have to know everything. You have to know what they ate, what the weather was like, what the names of the rivers are—if you're going to use rivers. But you don't have to know who was president unless you're going to mention it.

BEATTIE: I know you usually write from the point of view of your female protagonists. Have you ever written a romance, or wanted to, from a male's point of view?

ROBARDS: I go back and forth. My viewpoint goes back and forth. I am sometimes the female character. I am sometimes the male character. They each have their own voice. But write strictly through the male? No, I never have. And I doubt I ever would. I don't see any need to. As I said, I put both voices in there.

The most unusual voice I've used lately is in the Halloween anthology. Some publisher asked me to write a Dracula story for them. So I was a nine-year-old boy and I spoke in the voice of a nine-year-old boy, which isn't hard for me. He spoke from his voice, and it was fun. His parents adopted a little sister from Romania. He became convinced the little girl was a vampire. It's really a fun story. I enjoyed it a lot. Except he killed her in the end.

BEATTIE: Earlier, you talked about being typecast as a historical romance writer. So I'm wondering if you found that readers prefer your historical romances to your contemporary settings, or if you have found any difference in readers' reactions to your different types of work?

ROBARDS: Well, the funny thing about it is that I've done nineteen books now. Every one of them is somebody's favorite. You know, people have different tastes. Some people love my historicals best. Some people love my contemporaries best. My own personal feeling is that I am a really good historical writer, but there are a lot of really good historical writers out there. I think what I do totally best is what I'm doing now, this contemporary mainstream fiction thing. There's not a lot of us out there, and I am really good at it. I think this is where I'm going to make my mark.

BEATTIE: I've read that some publishers of romance novels dictate to their writers the exact nature and extent of each romantic action that must occur between characters in particular chapters. Have you experienced this?

ROBARDS: No.

BEATTIE: How much freedom do you have in writing love scenes?

ROBARDS: I have total freedom. Nobody has ever dictated to me. I don't believe they ever really tried. I've never had anybody tell me I need more love scenes or need fewer love scenes. I've never had anybody tell me what to write. In fact, I sell a book on the basis of a synopsis. Now I don't even sell a synopsis. I don't know what's going to happen until I start to write. So, when the editor buys the book, she gets about two paragraphs, three paragraphs, of a vague, general story, so she doesn't know what's going to happen, either. I mean, they have to take me on trust.

BEATTIE: They take you on past performance.

ROBARDS: Such restrictions belong more to category romances. The categories are like the Harlequins, which are a hundred and eight pages, usually. And Harlequin controls them. They're much smaller books, and they're what people think of when they're thinking romances. There is more of a guideline for them, because the editors know, or feel they know, what their readers want in these books, and their job is to give it to the reader every time. So the books have to follow more of a formula. I've never written under those constraints.

BEATTIE: You say that, when you start to write, you don't know what's going to happen.

ROBARDS: No idea.

BEATTIE: Since your books are so plot-oriented, that surprises me. You don't do any kind of outline? You don't even have a little sketch of what's going to happen?

ROBARDS: I have the best editor now. Damaris Roland is my editor at Delacorte. She lets me do my own thing. If you saw what I started out with, you'd laugh. It's about a paragraph. It's got my main characters' names, ages, and physical descriptions. But that's not written in stone. It always changes. My last girl started out being Ann and ended up being Magdalena. She started out being White Anglo-Saxon Protestant; she ended up being Hispanic. I write a general plot line, like hometown bad boy, convicted of murder, comes back to town, and what happens? Have you read *One Summer*?

BEATTIE: Yes.

ROBARDS: I thought Johnny might have done it. I wasn't sure. I didn't know. But I get into the characters, inside their heads, and they take me along. I mean, it's like I'm living the story through them. And it just happens. So, no, I never know. It's the whole creative process. I think that's why my books are so good. It's because there's a freshness there so they're not written to a plot written two years ago. I don't have any idea. I sit down. I give myself about three months, and I write a daggone book. And I make it as real as I can. So I experience all this.

BEATTIE: To what extent do you believe romance novels are also fantasy? And do you believe that any fantasy inherent in them is their primary appeal to women?

ROBARDS: Romance novels are fantasy in some ways. Of course, there's always the fantasy. Women tend to want to think that, at some point in their lives, some man is going to come and sweep them off their feet and take care of them forever. That is the ultimate romantic fantasy. And that, I think, is part of the appeal of romance novels. Having said that, I have to say that my heroines are very much their own women. I don't write wimpy women, you know, because I have to live through their eyes. And my men aren't wimpy, either. And my men aren't your classical heroes. I mean, I can't imagine Johnny Harris being a knight in shining armor. What I think fantasy is, is that there's this huge, true love that these people are going to experience together, and it's going to last a lifetime. We don't ever go twenty years past. We stop. Some of my characters, I don't think, would make it for twenty years. But it's this passionate, passionate love that everybody dreams of having just once. That is the fantasy. That absolute, incredible physical chemistry, this emotional closeness, this true love. *That's* the fantasy. And a lot of people don't ever have it. That's the fantasy right there. It's just this wonderful falling in love.

BEATTIE: Do you get fan mail from men as well as from women?

ROBARDS: Men as well as women. Not as many, but sure. There's a much smaller male audience. I think a lot of the males' problem is that the books used to have these very racy covers, and they're embarrassed to be seen reading them. My husband, as a matter of fact, used to travel a lot on business. He used to try to read my latest book on the airplane. Well, he got so many comments that he quit.

You know, like, "What are you reading?" "It's my wife's book." "Really?" "Yes, my wife's book." Probably thought maybe I just *owned* it, not that I *wrote* it. I think if there wasn't such a stigma of them being "women's books" that you'd have a lot more male readers. I've noticed with *One Summer* I had more male readers. If you get away from the covers, there's a good story there either way. I know I read Louis L'Amour. But see, there's not a stigma for women doing this. It's like schoolteachers. If there is anything that is strictly by women, for women, or woman-oriented, it's stigmatized a little bit in our society. It's the truth. That's why schoolteachers don't make as much money. Childcare workers make less than janitors and that's because it's a woman thing. Nurses. It's a women's ghetto.

BEATTIE: How do you believe your novels differ from those of other romance writers, or what are you attempting to do in your work that's different or that's most important to you?

ROBARDS: First of all, I don't consider myself a romance writer. I am a writer. My books have been romances up to a certain point. I am a writer. I can write anything. I'm only thirty-eight years old. Before I get done, there's no telling what I'll write, you know, because I'm a writer.

BEATTIE: Do you have any desire to write in another genre?

ROBARDS: Well, I'm a big horror fan. I keep telling my editor I'm going to write her a horrible romance, but she doesn't think that's funny. Yes, I want to write anything, everything. I chose romance to begin with because I thought it would be the easiest, best way to become a published writer and, sure enough, it was. But I don't feel that I am bound by it, by any means, except I have reached such a level of success as a romance writer that I feel a need to give my fans what they want, to a certain degree. As I said, now I'm writing contemporary women's fiction. But it has the romance element, too. It's got suspense. It's got romance. Got a little horror in this one, but it's a romance. Well, I was just getting started with *One Summer*. *Maggy's Child* is a little different from that. *Maggy's Child* is the one coming out in January of '94. Then I have, I'm calling it *The Dead Man* right now. I'm having the best time with *The Dead Man*. It's a little different, too. It's got a little horror in there. I really consider that I'm only getting started at this point. I'm at the point now where I'm almost free to write pretty much what I want, which is a wonderfully liberating thing. I'm really at a good point in my career, and I hope to get bigger and bigger. We'll see. The bigger I get, the freer I get. The freer I get, the better I think my books get, because you're not constricted by what other people expect of you.

BEATTIE: How free do you feel to make your heroines not beautiful, not attractive, according to contemporary standards?

ROBARDS: When I started out, Cathy, my first heroine, was gorgeous. Lisa, in *To Love a Man*, was gorgeous. Caitlin, in *Forbidden Love*, was gorgeous. Amanda Rose was gorgeous. Julia, in *Loving Julia*, was gorgeous. Clara, in *Night Magic*, was not. *Night Magic* won all kinds of awards, too. It's one of my favorite books. Clara, in *Night Magic*, was a lot like me. She was a romance writer. She's spacey as all get out. She was plump. Clara was not beautiful. I've had a lot of not-beautiful heroines since then. Susannah, in *Nobody's Angel*, one of my latest, was downright plain. She was short and square-faced and plump, and he loved her for the beauty of her soul. I mean *that*, to me, is true romance. If somebody just wants somebody because they're pretty, it's like wanting a present because it's got nice wrapping. You know, you're missing the point. It's this true melding of the soul. This guy fell in love with her energy. That's why I like "The Beauty and the Beast" story because she was able to see through that to the inner beauty within. That is true romance today.

BEATTIE: I would think that point of view would be more popular with more readers, anyway, because most people don't consider themselves perfect looking, even if they are fairly good looking.

ROBARDS: I've had real good success with it. You know, it just depends on my character. Some characters are beautiful. Some aren't. Just depends on who they are, where they are.

BEATTIE: I've noticed that with your heroes, too, that the men—and oftentimes the women, until they fall in love—don't think the men are particularly handsome. Or they make comments about not really liking the hero's looks almost until they fall in love, and then they see how handsome he really is.

ROBARDS: Well, it's inner beauty. To me, that's romantic. Outer beauty is superficial. Sometimes they are, sometimes they aren't, depending on how I'm feeling the day I write that character.

BEATTIE: What are you working on now, and do you have future books planned?

ROBARDS: I always have future books planned. Right now I'm working on *The Dead Man,* which I've had the best time with. It's a contemporary hardback, which is kind of a romantic mystery. And I just signed a contract with Delacorte for four more hardback contemporary women's fiction. In other words, I can kind of write what I want. I don't have any idea exactly what the books are going to be yet, but I will have, and they'll be good. By the time I get done with this contract, I'll have done six in a row hardback contemporary women's fiction. And I imagine I'll stay in that area for awhile, depending on the market.

BEATTIE: Have you stayed with the same publisher for awhile now?

ROBARDS: Well, I like my editor. The editor is the key. I've had some good ones, I've had some bad ones. I've had some that don't know what they're doing. You know, they get them right out of Harvard or something, and sometimes they can drive you nuts. Damaris Roland's been in the business a long time. She has enough sense not to change anything and to leave me alone. That's how I work best. My agent, Shirley Burke, died. I had her until she died. She was eighty when I got her. I didn't know it. It was all through the mail. So when she died, a while ago, I got Jay Acton, and the first thing I told him when I got him was, "Don't call me and I won't call you." If people are bugging me, I can't work. I don't want any input, I don't want any feedback, I don't want anything. Leave me alone, I'll write the book. That's how my editor is, and it works for me. I've been with them for four books now, and I'll be with them for four more, and then we'll see. I'd like to stay with this editor. But editors are sort of like musical chairs up there [New York]. They come and go.

BEATTIE: What are your work habits, and does anyone other than you read your work before you send it out?

ROBARDS: Nobody other than me ever reads my work before I send it out. There's just me and my computer. I used to work in my house when there was just my one boy. Since my three year old was born, and we got a nanny, there's too much confusion all the time. So I converted an outbuilding into my office. Just a simple little office—one room where I write, with a bathroom and little kitchenette. I get out there early in the morning, during the summer. I like to be out there by six-thirty, seven o'clock, and I'll work 'till, like, one o'clock. Then I have the rest of the afternoon to play with the children, because my children are my top priority. During the school year, my life revolves around my children. I take my older boy to school. He was in third grade this year. He has to be there at 8 o'clock. So then I come back and I go straight to work at 8:00, and then I'll work 'till two-thirty, three o'clock. I'm done by the time he gets out of school, and then I come in. I'm pretty religious about it. I mean, I'm out there every day, just about. It takes me about two-and-a-half to three months of hard concentration to write a book. It takes me about two-and-a-half to three months to psych into it. That's about four days a week. I don't work Wednesdays, because that's the day I spend with my little one, just he and me together. You know, I only do this mothering once. I'll be a writer forever.

BEATTIE: You say it takes a few months for you to think about a book. Does that mean you're not working during that time, or does that mean that you're finishing up something else?

ROBARDS: No, I'm not writing. See, that's what I tell my husband. This is God's truth.

I'm always working. I'm reading and picking up little bits of information. It's kind of a subconscious process of building these people and this book in my head. Sometimes, I don't even know how it's going to come out. I'll wake up in the middle of the night and say, "Oh, good idea!" But it's cooking. It's cooking in there right now.

BEATTIE: So you're setting and your subject matter will be dictated just by something you might be interested in?

ROBARDS: I tend to favor the South over the North simply because I'm more familiar with it. I tend to favor the East Coast over the West Coast simply because I'm more familiar with it. Not always, but that helps, because characters are so much influenced by their environments and, in order for me to get into it, I can't do something totally foreign to me. I guess I could, but it would be harder. They tend to kind of have to be filtered through my eyes.

BEATTIE: What about living in Kentucky? You're obviously a Kentuckian, but do you think even if your books aren't set here, that living here has anything to do with sense of place in your writing?

ROBARDS: To a certain degree. Of course, again, all my characters are filtered through me, so they all have a certain sensibility that I can't help. It's just you're a part of it, which, again, is influenced by my having lived all my life in Kentucky. I like to set books in Kentucky because it's a very little-used setting. People don't know much about the state. They think we're all a bunch of hillbillies here, barefoot. Truly, they do. When I first went to New York to meet my first publisher, I don't know what they were expecting, but it wasn't me. That's what she told me. She looked me up. She looked me down. She said, "You know, you're not what I expected at all." I mean, I had on a business suit. What were you expecting? They were expecting a hayseed.

BEATTIE: Do you work on a word processor?

ROBARDS: Yes. I got my word processor and my oldest boy at the same time. I thought that I could write faster on a word processor. I wrote, I guess, about eight or nine books on a typewriter, but I don't see how I ever did it now. I have an IBM clone, and I use Word Perfect 5.1. It helps an awful lot.

BEATTIE: Do you think journalistic training helped you in terms of your learning the importance of meeting deadlines?

ROBARDS: Journalism taught me to write to a deadline and it taught me to be precise, to say what you mean and to mean what you say and to use few words, if possible. And to never use a long word when a little word will do. I think it was real valuable, and I didn't even know it at the time.

BEATTIE: Do you think the act of constant reading was a better creative writing teacher than any creative writing teacher you ever had?

ROBARDS: The best creative writing teacher I ever had. You're not being taught; you're giving yourself pleasure. You're absorbing by osmosis. Writers are born, not made. But reading teaches you your craft subconsciously. You learn the words that make you laugh and cry and feel. And they're imbedded, and that's the way to learn it. I mean, I think reading is absolutely the most educational thing anybody can do. I really, strongly promote it. Anything. I don't care what they read. I don't care if they're romances. I don't care if it's pornography. If they're reading, they're learning how language works, and that's an educational thing.

BEATTIE: How do you think creative writing should be taught?

ROBARDS: You can't teach it. You can teach people to write a correct sentence. You can teach them to write a correct paragraph, but that spark, that creative spark that gives a work life, *I* couldn't teach it.

BEATTIE: What do you think the nature of creativity is?

ROBARDS: It's indefinable. You can't teach it. I'll use myself as an example. I write. I read. I paint. I like to create. I enjoy it. And I think it's an innate gift, like some people are good athletes. I'm glad I have it. My children have it. I absolutely see it in them. My husband's a great athlete. Creative he's not. It's just something some people have and some people don't. I have had more people tell me that they want to write books. They think they can. Everybody thinks there's a book in them. For some reason, book writing is very acceptable to everybody. They don't realize how truly difficult it is to create a real book. I mean a *real* book. Not three hundred fifty, four hundred pages, but a real book with life and characters and everything. They don't realize that it's a really difficult process. It's like the ministry, you know. Many are called, but few are chosen. It's just not something that everybody can do.

BEATTIE: Will you talk about your husband and your children?

ROBARDS: My husband's name is Douglas J. Robards, and he is from Madisonville, Kentucky. He worked for Battelle Memorial Institute for eight years in Columbus, Ohio. Then, when we moved back to Louisville, he started his own business. He does management consulting now. Twenty years, now, we've been together.

And I have a nine year old; his name is Peter Douglas Robards. Peter Douglas is the joy of my life. When he was born, I was twenty-nine, and I didn't have a nanny or any help. It was Peter and me. He would play under my computer when I wrote. He unplugged me once. I lost three chapters of *Wild Orchids*. But I didn't kill him. I never raised my voice to that child. I was so determined that what I did was not going to take away from Peter. Fortunately, he's a very good child, as I didn't ever raise my voice to him.

He has a little brother, Christopher, who is three. Chrissy is a different type of child. He's more independent than Peter. And, of course, I was older when Christopher was born.

I love Peter more than anything in my life. Peter never slept. Peter never slept more than two hours at a time from the time he was born until the time he was four years old. Never. He had ear problems, but we didn't know it at the time. They were never able to diagnose it. Peter couldn't hear as a little boy, but we didn't know it. Finally, when he was four, they diagnosed it. They put tubes in his ears and the child slept. I managed to write despite not sleeping. But I couldn't do it with Chris, too. I just couldn't do it. So we hired a nanny. Rose started working here when Chrissy was two days old. She takes care of him four days a week from nine to three.

BEATTIE: Is there anything that we haven't talked about that you think is important for people to know about you?

ROBARDS: I was first published at eighteen in *Reader's Digest*. I was working for my father, and was getting ready to go away to college. I was eighteen by the time it came out. It was a Thursday, and I was working in my father's office by myself, and I was reading *Reader's Digest*. The front of the magazine said, "Want to earn a hundred dollars? Do you have a funny anecdote?" or something like that. I thought, "Oh, what an easy way to earn a hundred dollars." I sat down at the typewriter there and I pecked out a little anecdote about my parents. I sent it in and I knew so little about the business of writing that I was positive that they were going to buy it, and I'd get this hundred dollars. I was sure of it. Had no doubt.

Well, daggone, I did. About a month later they sent a note saying they were going to publish it in the December issue. It was December '73 of *Reader's Digest,* and they sent me a check for a hundred dollars. I made the anecdote up. It wasn't true.

BEATTIE: Have you ever gotten a rejection slip in your life?

ROBARDS: No, I never have.

BEATTIE: That's a rarity among writers.

ROBARDS: I know. I've been so lucky. I mean, I'm talented. I'm a heck of a good writer. But I don't give that the credit. It's luck. I can't attribute it to anything else. I mean, everything kind of fell into place for me. I hit the market with the right kind of book at the right time, and once the first one sold, I just kept building on that.

BEATTIE: Do you have advice for aspiring writers?

ROBARDS: Read anything and everything. Backs of cereal boxes, I don't care. I don't think there's any writer alive who is not a reader. I don't think it's possible to be one and not the other. My second advice is to hang in there. You know, I was lucky. Lightning struck me. God smiled. I didn't get rejected. Every other writer I've ever heard of, ninety-nine out of a hundred, get rejected time and again. Taylor Caldwell is one of my favorite authors. I don't think she published until she was, like, fifty years old. Some of the books I loved were rejected, like, a hundred times. Some of the best writers are rejected hundreds of thousands of times, and this is part of a writer's life.

June 19, 1993

In 1995, Robards's family increased by one son, John Hamilton Robards, called Jack. Since 1993 Robards has focused exclusively on hardcover mainstream fiction, and all of her novels have appeared on the *New York Times, Wall Street Journal,* or *USA Today* bestseller lists. Her most recent writing honors include the following awards: Best Contemporary Writer, Career Achievement Award in Women's Fiction, Reviewer's Choice Award, and "Wally," Waldenbooks's bestselling novel award.

BOOKS BY KAREN ROBARDS:

Island Flame. New York: Leisure Books, 1981.

Sea Fire. New York: Leisure Books, 1981.

Forbidden Love. New York: Leisure Books, 1983.

Amanda Rose. New York: Warner Books, 1984.

To Love a Man. New York: Warner Books, 1985.

Dark Torment. New York: Warner Books, 1985.

White Orchids. New York: Warner Books, 1986.

Loving Julia. New York: Warner Books, 1986.

Some Kind of Hero. New York: Warner Books, 1987.

Night Magic. New York: Warner Books, 1988.

Dark of the Moon. New York: Avon, 1988.

Desire in the Sun. New York: Avon, 1988.

Tiger's Eye. New York: Avon, 1989.

Morning Song. New York: Avon, 1990.

Green Eyes. New York: Avon, 1991.

This Side of Heaven. New York: Dell, 1991.

Nobody's Angel. New York: Delacorte, 1992.

One Summer. New York: Delacorte, 1993.

Maggy's Child. New York: Delacorte, 1994.

Walking After Midnight. New York: Delacorte, 1995.

Hunter's Moon. New York: Delacorte, 1996.

Heartbreaker. New York: Delacorte, 1997.

The Senator's Wife. New York: Delacorte, 1998

Midnight Hour. New York: Delacorte, 1999.

JEFFREY SKINNER

SKINNER: I am Jeffrey Thomas Skinner, and I was born December 8th, 1949, in Buffalo, New York. My father's full name is Thomas Franklin Skinner. He was an FBI agent in the fifties and, after that, he worked for a time as an investigator for the Nassau County, New York, Board of Supervisors, and then he owned a business in Connecticut, a private investigative business and security guard agency. My mother's full name is Doris Ann Skinner, and she has at various times worked in my father's office with him and then been a homemaker.

William Donhauser, my maternal grandfather, was an interesting guy. He was a musician—a violinist—and when he was nineteen years old he was playing for Bing Crosby in the orchestra, and he had his own band for a while and was making more money at that age than all his family put together. I guess he was second generation himself—his parents came over from Germany—and his father and mother lived in a house, and I knew them briefly, my great-grandparents. He and his wife had two kids, and he quit music because it was a road kind of job. He was in vaudeville, basically, and he did a lot of traveling. His wife, my grandmother, just couldn't take it. So he quit and went to work for Bethlehem Steel. And that's always been sort of a negative example for me, because he gave up, I think, a lot, and I think he always missed it. He became a clerk at Bethlehem Steel. Every so often he'd bring out his violin at parties, and he really was fantastic. He could play anything.

My grandmother on that side, Vera Donhauser, had a Scotch-Irish background, and I knew some of her brothers and sisters who were farmers in upstate New York and in Canada.

Then, on my father's side, his parents, both of them, came from England on the boat in the early 1920s. They didn't meet in England, but they were both from England. My grandfather, I think, was from London, and my grandmother was from someplace in England not too far from London. They met and married, and they had three kids. My father was the youngest son, and then there were two other sons, and one sister, who's still alive, as is one of the brothers. So, I knew them and, when I was growing up in New York, I visited those cousins and those uncles and aunts.

My mother, Joan Schick is her name now, had two brothers who are somewhat younger than me. They came to Long Island because my uncle was an advertising person, and they lived with us for a while. I was very close to the cousins all during the time that we were growing up on Long Island.

I have one Sister, Jodie, who is five years younger than me, and she now lives in New Hampshire. She's married and has two kids of her own. There was enough distance in age between us—I think she's six years younger than I—and because she was a girl, I think, we weren't really close growing up. We had different friends. But we didn't fight, and we loved each other. She has a disease that is now in remission, called myasthenia gravis, and there was a period in my youth when she got sick that was very tense in the family, because it was sort of a mysterious disease at that point. But it's been in remission for a long time; she's led a normal life. We see her every other year.

BEATTIE: What sort of childhood did you have, and where was it spent?

SKINNER: It was peripatetic. We lived in a lot of different places. My father had quite a few different jobs before we finally ended up in Long Island, and when he was in the Bureau, the FBI, we moved around a lot. He trained at Quantico, like they all do, and so he was away a lot. We lived in Erie, Pennsylvania, for a period of time. I think we lived in four different places. So I remember a lot of moving around and difficulty making friends until we finally got to Long Island, when I was seven or eight years old, and we stayed there till I was in the middle of my junior year in high school. Then we moved to Connecticut.

I remember a pretty happy childhood. The growing up part, the part I remember best, is from age seven on, and during that period we were in Long Island, which was a booming community of mainly blue-collar workers and rising professionals, the World War II boom of fathers and mothers coming out of the war and starting over in the cheap housing of Levittown. It seems to me, looking back, that the idea of Levittown worked, for that period of time. It was cheap housing, there were millions of kids my age, and I was part of the baby boom.

BEATTIE: The original suburb.

SKINNER: It was an original suburb. And there were pools, you know. Levitt had the idea of having baseball diamonds and pools and football stands, and they were all used tremendously, and it worked. There was a real sense of community, at least in our part of it. I remember that, in summer, people would drift to each other's houses for barbecues all the time. There really was that extended family feeling much more than I feel now. Nobody visits in Louisville, that I know of, without calling and saying, "We're coming over," or "Can we come over?" People just dropped in then.

BEATTIE: I wonder how much of that has to do with the era instead of the place.

SKINNER: We're talking about the fifties and early sixties when there was a lot more trust. People had more time, I think. Nobody seems to have any time at all today to do things and, you know, things have to be planned.

BEATTIE: What about your early education? What was that like?

SKINNER: I went to a public elementary school for a year or so, and then my parents put me into a Lutheran school, which was near Levittown, called Trinity Lutheran. I went there until high school, and then I went to Long Island Lutheran High School. My parents really liked the idea of a church kind of school, and it was our church.

BEATTIE: Were both your parents Lutheran?

SKINNER: Yes. My father converted. He really didn't grow up with a religion. So my parents liked the way that school was run, they liked the moral atmosphere of it, and I think I got a decent education. One never really knows for sure, I don't think, but it had good teaching.

BEATTIE: Did any particular subject emerge as your favorite early on?

SKINNER: I liked science an awful lot and thought, for a while, that that's what I wanted to do, but I kept being stopped by the math part of it. I liked all of the experimental part and the theoretical part. I loved geometry, and that's about where I stopped. Everything after that was just totally opaque to me. I couldn't get it. But I liked that, and I did like reading. I have always read, and that has always seemed like a given part of my existence. I read early.

BEATTIE: Were you read to before you could read?

SKINNER: Yes. My mother says from the time I was an infant she would read to me, and she read to me constantly. And I read before I went to school, and that continued. But I never thought of that as any kind of career. It was just fun.

BEATTIE: Did you start writing in elementary school, writing that was other than assigned work?

SKINNER: No, that was something that just wasn't done in the fifties, you know.

BEATTIE: Especially by boys, I guess.

SKINNER: Especially by boys. I mean, I would have been a sissy if I'd done that.

BEATTIE: Do you recall any of your teachers?

SKINNER: The only one I can remember from elementary school is Miss Zelinsky. See, I remember her name. And I think the only thing that I recall about her is this warmth she showed toward me that seemed particular to me. I really liked her a lot, and she seemed to care about me. I was a very shy kid, so I must have been a trial for a lot of teachers, and she seemed to take an interest.

BEATTIE: What about your junior high and high school years?

SKINNER: I had a lot of problems. I entered school a year early because I was born December 8th, so I was always one of the youngest in my class. My mother told me that, when I was due to go to kindergarten, there wasn't a kindergarten nearby, so she put me into first grade. So I was a year or more younger than most kids. Developmentally, physically, I was that much younger, and I was a shy child, so I had a difficult time when I got to junior high. Before that it was no problem, but when all that pre-puberty stuff started to happen, I was pretty miserable, because it happened to me later than it happened to everybody else. I didn't like that at all.

Then in, high school, I just really withdrew into myself and kept reading. I was curious about things that I was curious about, but I had no interest in social activities, and part of it was the fact that I was shy, and I was not in the popular group. My sport was swimming, which, at that time, had no glamour whatsoever. So I couldn't be successful in that area.

Then we moved in the middle of my junior year of high school, which sort of made me give up entirely. I thought, "Oh, the hell with this; here I am, going to start all over again after I've just begun to make a certain group of friends." I just really withdrew and did my swimming and did my school work, and I played in the band and had some other geeky sort of activities.

BEATTIE: What sorts of things were you reading?

SKINNER: I loved Kipling's jungle stories, and I liked adventure stories, and I liked Sherlock Holmes quite a bit—that sort of Victorian, dense diction coupled with high intrigue and mystery and suspense and dark passageways.

I always liked English. But it was a breeze for me; I always got good grades in English without trying at all. I never had to really study, so I guess it was fun. But the fun part was reading what I wanted to read, and I would read what I had to read, and I sort of resented having to do all the other stuff. But I kept reading on my own, the whole time, and enjoying that a lot.

BEATTIE: What about after high school? Did you go straight to college?

SKINNER: I did. I went to Rollins College in Florida, and I chose that because I wanted to get as far away from my parents as I could. I was at Rollins from '68 to '71, and I had a really good college experience. That's when I really opened up and everything started to make sense to me, and I became more social, and I came out of my shell, and I found that there were things that I could be valued for and could like myself for.

BEATTIE: What was especially good about that experience?

SKINNER: Theater. I discovered acting and theater, and mainly what I did during my four years was a lot of acting in plays and directing and working in them and hanging out with the theater crowd. I discovered at that point I was some sort of artist, and it felt right from the beginning. I thought maybe I was an actor at that point. I still hadn't done any writing. But I knew that my destiny had something to do with art, for sure. So that was a revelation, and a good one.

BEATTIE: What about after college? Did you go straight to graduate school?

SKINNER: No, I didn't. I had majored in psychology in college and, at that point, parents were still telling kids—well, I guess they still are today, even more so—that you need a back-up, that if you're going to fool around with acting, you need to have some sort of real-live thing to do. So I was in psychology, and I could never fully commit myself to acting or the theater. I think it was because of that parental thing, but maybe there was some subconscious wisdom that it really wasn't the right art for me. But, in any case, I drifted after I got out of college until

'76, when I went back to graduate school in writing. And I did all sorts of jobs during that period. I worked for a while with a social psychologist who was trying to increase the sensitivity of policemen to minorities.

BEATTIE: What other jobs did you have?

SKINNER: I'm sort of ashamed to say that I wrote term papers for a while for college students. And I taught swimming, and I was, as I say, a swimmer in high school. I was very good. And I was a lifeguard for a period and the director of a waterfront at a summer camp. I put up groceries at an A& P grocery store for one period. I was a psychology graduate student at the University of Bridgeport— I did that for a couple of years—and I worked there. I had a job working for a psychologist devising a new introduction to the psychology program, and then I taught that for a while. I was a private investigator for my father.

BEATTIE: Did you ever think you would be teaching psychology? Was that your original plan, in graduate school?

SKINNER: I think the original plan was I wanted to be a researcher of some sort and/or maybe a clinician. I wanted to help people. So many people of our generation wanted to do something helpful.

BEATTIE: You were thinking of a career as a therapist?

SKINNER: Yes. See, my degree at UB [University of Bridgeport) was theoretical psychology. I didn't go for clinical psychology because I was more interested in ideas at that point, but I thought eventually I might become a psychologist and have a practice. But it was all very vague, and I was not a focused young man at all.

BEATTIE: What convinced you that psychology wasn't for you?

SKINNER: I started writing poetry when I was going to graduate school. I was about twenty-two, and I picked up a book of poems by W. S. Merwin. I don't remember now where I got it. Nobody gave it to me; I just found it somewhere and read it, and I was shocked and amazed. There was this incredible recognition of something. I was just terribly excited.

BEATTIE: And you hadn't really been a poetry reader before that?

SKINNER: No. I had been a psychology major in college, so I really took only the basic English courses and, you know, treated them the same as I did my high school classes, and I read no poetry during that time. No contemporary poetry was taught, as far as I know, at the college I went to. So, I just discovered it on my own. Then I went out and bought many, many more books of poems and started getting into it. Psychology diminished rapidly in its importance in comparison with what I was finding and discovering about language.

BEATTIE: Do you think that had anything to do with the fact that poetry, or really any genre, hits the truth almost better than psychology can? Psychology describes it, but literature reveals it?

SKINNER: Right. It did for me what literature, I still think, needs to do, which is to hit people. It hit me in body and mind at the same time, whereas psychology was an interesting parlor game up to that point, and an interesting cerebral exercise and manipulation of ideas that may or may not have any correspondence with reality. Poetry was undeniably bodily, and I couldn't believe that one could mix ideas and the body in such a manner. It seemed instantly much more profound. Then I started to write.

I got married when I was twenty-four, and I did it because I met this woman, my first wife. I auditioned for a show, a cabaret theater, which was going on in Norwalk, Connecticut, where I was living and going to graduate school. I was trying to do theater all through this time, on a part-time basis. The woman who was directing the show became my first wife. Elizabeth Orlowsky was her name.

BEATTIE: How long did that marriage last?

SKINNER: We got divorced in '81. I got married in '74 or '75, but it's a blur, because I knew from the beginning it was the wrong idea, and I can't believe, from this vantage, that I actually went through with it, although I wouldn't say anything bad about this woman. Elizabeth is a wonderful woman, and she has a lot of talent and spirit and intelligence, and we were just wrong for each other.

BEATTIE: What were those years like? What were you doing?

SKINNER: Well, in '75 we got married and, at that point, I had written quite a bit of poetry, and I was committed almost ninety percent to that. But I still didn't understand how one could do that. You know, I didn't have an English background, so I didn't know anything about it, really. I was writing, and I did take one course from Dick Allen at the University of Bridgeport in writing, and he said, "God, you're good." That confirmed me, but I didn't know what to do, and I guess from Dick I learned that it would be possible, maybe, to teach for a career. So that was in the back of my mind. And by 1975—I must have married in '74— Elizabeth and I were together, and we were having problems, even at that point, because she wanted me to get serious with my life, and she wanted to have a family, and I didn't know what I was doing. So I applied to graduate school in creative writing at Columbia University. And in '76 I went to Columbia for an M.F.A. degree and got that in '78. While I was doing that I was commuting into New York, and I was working part-time for my father to make money—investigative, security guard stuff.

BEATTIE: How was the Columbia experience?

SKINNER: It was fabulous. I really, for the first time, I think, used standard education in a way that was beneficial to me. Before that, I consider I got my education pretty much on my own, although I needed to be in an educational environment to get it. It pains me to say that now, because I have a lot of students who treat it the same way I did, and I get mad as hell at them. A lot of them don't read anything, yet they want to write, and that's hard for me to understand, because I was reading enormously, voluminously, all through that period. I just had to. But the Columbia experience was really good for me.

BEATTIE: Whom did you work with there?

SKINNER: You had two workshops a year, and I worked with David Ignatow, Dan Halpern, and Howard Moss. Philip Levine was my thesis advisor. Part of what Columbia offered were these high-powered heavy hitters.

BEATTIE: Did you work best with any one of those?

SKINNER: I worked best with Phil Levine, and he became a real important mentor to me. He was a real example of how to be a man who writes poetry who comes from a lower-middle class, working-class background and wants to have a family and write poetry in America. You know, an almost impossible goal, really. But he showed me that it was possible. I also got along really well with Howard Moss and liked him very much. And I know that he liked me very much, and we stayed in contact until he died.

BEATTIE: Did his being the magazine's poetry editor give you entree to *The New Yorker*?

SKINNER: Well, I was published in *The New Yorker* when he was editing. I haven't had success there since he's died, so I doubly lament his death.

BEATTIE: And what happened after Columbia?

SKINNER: After Columbia I thought, "Well, I've got my M.F.A. from Columbia. It's a big deal, and I'll get a teaching job." But no, there were no teaching jobs to be had in the late seventies, and I just didn't have enough publication credits, anyway.

BEATTIE: Had you been sending out poems for publication during graduate school?

SKINNER: Yes, I had, and I'd been getting publications at decent places like *Poetry Northwest* and *Mississippi Review*. And I guess I hit *Poetry* right after I got out of graduate school. I had two poems in *Poetry Magazine*. That was a big milestone for me.

BEATTIE: When you found out you couldn't get a teaching job, what happened?

SKINNER: Then I was married to Elizabeth, and she said, "You can't get a teaching job; now we *really* have to be serious. You're twenty-eight years old; go to work for your father, why don't you, full-time?" So I did, again being pushed, and not taking control of my own destiny. I did it in a passive/aggressive kind of way, and I regret it now, but it was what I had to do. So, I went to work for him. And, amazingly, I rose through the ranks rapidly. I mean, no one could have predicted it. I became office manager, then I became vice-president, and I was doing full-time business in Stamford, Connecticut. I had two hundred employees.

BEATTIE: Had you taken over your father's business?

SKINNER: No, I had taken over the Fairfield County operation, and he had operations in other counties around Connecticut. My operation was the largest one, and I was at the home office, but I was not doing the business as a whole. I didn't want to. My father was there, anyway, and that was what he did; he oversaw the entire operation.

BEATTIE: How long did this last?

SKINNER: Too long. When I was in it, I must say it felt like forever, and it taught me a lot. Again, looking at it from this vantage, I think everything had a reason, and that had a reason. But I was not really liking what I was doing. I mean, it was not what I wanted to be doing; I wanted to teach and pay attention to my art. But I was always writing at the same time.

On the positive side, working for my father gave me contact, on a day-to-day basis, with people who had no inkling of what literature could mean, just like most of America. I spent a lot of time and a lot of energy and a lot of my emotional, psychic life with people who were just like the rest of the country. It was no sheltered, academic, ivory tower. So I began to know something about the way those people think. *Those* people. I'm one of them, and I can never deny that, either. And I have, maybe as a result, a vast impatience for a certain kind of academic who sneers at what might be termed middle-class writing. I was taken to task in my own poetry for being a suburban poet, whatever the hell that may mean. And, you know, it was by somebody who was a suburban academic, and there's a certain self-loathing on the part of a lot of academics that makes them extremely willing to valorize, to use that horrible current word, somebody like William Burroughs. And the reason they do is because he's so far from their own life that that must be what real art is. They can't imagine that their own life has any art or spirit to it. I think that's a lie, and it's a dangerous lie.

So I think that I learned that every life, no matter what your class or what you do for a living, has the potential for art and has definitely the worth-whileness that any other life does. So I took material from that period that I would not otherwise have had contact with. I've written about business people, I've written about insurance agents, and I will do more of that. I've written about lawyers. I'm not stuck with writing about academics.

BEATTIE: Do you think it maybe also made you prize what you eventually earned?

SKINNER: Absolutely. During that time I had friends who were in academia, and they were always telling me, "Jeff, this is a tough life, academics." And I said, "Wait a minute. If you knew what I did, you wouldn't last forty minutes." And I got into teaching, and, you know something? I was right. It's better. You have your summers and you're doing something, even though we feel like we're banging our heads against the wall with students, sometimes. At least I talk about things that are close to my heart, whether they get across or not. I mean, try having that stuff close to your heart and not being able to say it to anybody for ten years.

BEATTIE: When were you able to break out of that job?

SKINNER: Well, I met Sarah Gorham at Yaddo in 1981. And, at that point, I was getting good at poetry. Attending Yaddo was my first experience at a writers' colony and my first experience being around a lot of artists.

BEATTIE: What inspired you to apply to Yaddo?

SKINNER: I don't know. I think Dick Allen told me about it as a possibility, and it sounded great to me, and I was lucky enough to get in. One of the advantages of working for my father was I could go to him and say, "I got this great honor," and I put it to him that way, and I still consider it that, "and I want to take two months off and go there." And he said, "Okay."

He covered for me, and I went there and met Sarah. At that point, I had been separated from my first wife, and Sarah and I hit it off. We left Yaddo together, lived together for a year, got married, had kids. And, during that time, I was getting less and less able to live this schizophrenic life of businessman/poet, but I was doing it.

My first book came out in '85, so that was a big milestone, a book of poems. And in '86 I said to Sarah, "I can't do it anymore; I have to stop." It was driving me nuts. So her father had a place, a summer place, in Lewes, Delaware, and he offered it to us for cheap rent, and we just chucked the whole thing without any job offer or potential to get a teaching job and said, "We'll take a year and spend some savings," and that's what we did. And I told my father and left.

BEATTIE: Going back to Yaddo, how did you find that experience, other than meeting Sarah?

SKINNER· I found it artistically really exciting, and it delivers on its promise to be a haven and a right atmosphere for production. Well, Sarah and I have been to Yaddo three times now, and each time I've produced much more than I ever would have under any other circumstances. It's idyllic. I mean, they take away the responsibilities of everyday life for you and handle them all, and they limit distractions and treat you like somebody worthwhile. It's one of the few places where an artist can go, a fine artist who's not commercially viable, and feel like, "God, I am doing something that's worth something in this society."

BEATTIE: Have you made professional contacts there that have been important to you, as well as made friends? I know Sarah said you got married there the year after you met, and that you invited to the wedding the same people who'd been with you during your first stay at Yaddo.

SKINNER: We stayed pretty close to Curt Harnack, who was the director of Yaddo at that time, and to some other people.

BEATTIE: Tell me about your first book, *Late Stars*.

SKINNER: The first book was written over a long period of time, as most first books are, and so it was very important to me, as it is for any poet, to get a first book. I mean, that's a validation that one can't really do without, and I was feeling antsy about it at age thirty-three, when it was accepted by Wesleyan University Press. So at that point I was thinking, "God, I've got to get this book out." I had that anxiety, that first-book anxiety, and I had been revising it year-by-year, making it stronger. It was a typical kind of story of a first book, and I felt that it was really ready at that point, and finished, and, luckily, it was taken at probably the exact right time. I would have preferred it to be published a year before, when it was a finalist at a few contests, such as at Yale. But it was fine the way it turned out. And I think, now, it's still a pretty good book.

BEATTIE: When *Late Stars* came out, what kind of reception did it have, and how did its publication change your view of yourself as a poet?

SKINNER: I was naive at that point, and I'd never heard Don Marquis's comment about first books of poems. He said, "Publishing a book of poems is like dropping a rose petal into the Grand Canyon and waiting for the sound." And, unfortunately, he's correct. But I didn't know that at that time, and I thought lots of things would change, and I would have some measure of fame, and I would get a job instantly. And none of that happened. It was well thought of by a lot of people; it was not particularly well reviewed. I did get a review in *Poetry,* which I was not happy with. So I got the first few stings of criticism on a professional level, and that was probably good for me, to get my feet wet with that. But it did validate my sense of myself as a poet, and Wesleyan is a superb press. Wesleyan is one of the best, so I was very happy to have that. That alone was enough to say, "This is what you should be doing," for me. I mean, I'm a stubborn person. I think any writer has to be incredibly stubborn and crazy, in a way, to keep going with this. And I had that, but the book helped me to go on.

BEATTIE: How was that year you spent in Lewes, Delaware, for you, artistically?

SKINNER: It was really a rich year. I wrote a lot. I wrote my second book, *A Guide to Forgetting,* in a short period of time, probably in two years. I wrote lots of the poems just before we left, and then a lot of poems when we got to Lewes. I wrote a lot in Lewes. We had that year off. It was a change. It was like a relief, a weight off my back, the weight of ten years of a job I didn't really care for, and I felt a tremendous freedom. And, artistically, I had freedom. The poems are marked, in my mind, as they advance artistically in that book, and it probably had to do with that release, or it had to do with my maturity. I was in my mid-thirties, which is a good time for a writer, generally, I think. I mean, you sort of start to come into your own. Writers, I think, mature later than other kinds of artists, generally, and I was beginning to have a mature art, and to have some sort of control over language. It was very exciting.

BEATTIE: Did you also win awards that year?

SKINNER: Yes, I think it was meant to be. It was a God-given turn of events the way things went, because as soon as we moved there, we had, as I said, no prospects for a job or anything after that year. We were going to use our savings. And here I was with two kids, no job, and one year. And that year I won the National Endowment for the Arts, which is a twenty thousand dollar grant. I won the National Poetry Series with my second book in '87. And, in '87, I got the job here [University of Louisville] based on all of the things that happened, as a result of that change. It was a risk that paid off enormously well for me and for my family.

BEATTIE: In your poem, "As the Women Sleep," you conclude "Doubt is my only hope/the strength of it." Would you comment on that?

SKINNER: Well, the lines before that talk about how you step from childhood thinking the isolation will end, or something like that. The poem is sort of a coming-of-age poem, in my mind, and you find that things don't change that much, that we are still isolate selves. And there's irony in those last lines, "Doubt is my only hope/the strength of it." The doubt that I'm going to remain isolate, that we are all in our separate universes and the hope that, behind that, there will be connection. In my work there's always been a sort of play between hope and doubt, and a fight in strong terms, I think.

BEATTIE: In the essay he wrote for *Kentucky Voices,* your University of Louisville colleague, Tom Byers, writes, "It is as a poet that Jeffrey Skinner spends long hours in surveillance, that he risks himself, that he explores the dark edges. These days when he goes on a stake-out, his life, more even than his soul, is what's at stake." Would you comment on that?

SKINNER: I was touched by Tom's essay, and I think he said things about my work that no one has said before, and I would like to believe what he said is true. As we get older, loss becomes a constant theme of one sort or another, and if one holds onto writing and one continues to believe in the power of writing, you're continuing to believe in invisibility, basically. Well, what *is* writing? Writing is code that goes on a page and then is recoded back into meaning by transposition, in C. S. Lewis's terms, in another person's mind. It's a totally invisible occupation, when you come right down to it. It doesn't even touch the material world, basically. I never thought that way before, but the stakes get higher, in a way, and I think that Tom is correct in stating that more and more is risked. When you're younger, I guess you're just so full of yourself, or I was so full of myself, that a sort of insanely confident arrogance carried me through. But I have much less of that as I get older, and more has to be carried by a sort of firm belief that what we do, in terms of books and writing and poetry, has some meaning and some weight in the world, and it's contradicted by everything we see around us. So, the struggle is harder.

BEATTIE: Byers also writes, in that same essay, that in your poetry the "combination of domesticity and daily love with the hope of escape from the limits of the self offers a suggestion that transcendence and grace may happen within rather than beyond the imminent world of human relationships." He writes that he believes that that is the core of your vision and that it is interestingly at odds with the standard tradition of American literature by men. Do you agree with that, and would you comment on that?

SKINNER: I do agree with that. I mean, Tom makes a good point that a sort of stereotypically male vision of transcendence in America has been carried through people like Thoreau or Emerson or Hemingway, in which transcendence of the self comes about through the leaving behind of domesticity or the everyday life and an investment of energy in things outside the self and the externals and on the road with Kerouac, or some leaving of home, because home is not where one finds the true self. And my vision is opposed to that.

BEATTIE: An inward instead of an outward vision? A different catalyst?

SKINNER: Yes, so I think he's correct.

BEATTIE: In what ways do you think your poetic vision complements, and also differs from, that of your wife, Sarah Gorham?

SKINNER: I think that, in some ways, Sarah shares that faith that the opening into transcendence is through family, through things close at hand. She says in one of her poems, "Mine is a peopled world," and that could have come from one of my poems, I think.

BEATTIE: You say in your poem, "Problems," "what an effort it takes to love,/so much of the self in the way,/ like a building that must be blasted to make the horizon visible." That reminds me of comments she made concerning her poetic vision.

SKINNER: Yes. I think we do share that. We look at spiritual work in similar terms. It's an interior job, it's an inner job, and it's not a matter of escape into some sort of alternate lifestyle or escape from roots. It's, rather, a turning back and facing and acceptance—in real hard terms, though—not easily, and not without question, and not without doubt. Maybe we're wrong, I don't know. That has got to be part of the poem, too.

BEATTIE: She made some interesting comments, when I interviewed her, about her poetic vision solidifying when she became a mother and after she got married, in terms of finding her own voice, a more feminine voice. Do you feel that your vision and/or voice altered when you married her, or do you feel that being married to a poet does something in terms of both connecting with another or with others, as well as with needing to separate and find your own voice?

SKINNER: I've not felt that marriage to Sarah has affected, in a direct way, my search for my own voice. I don't know what that means. I've felt pretty confident, since my first book, that I had some sort of voice and, for me, it was more of, as W. H. Auden says, "subject looking for form," and that was apart from her.

BEATTIE: I don't mean finding a voice in the first place, but changing or altering your voice in some way.

SKINNER: Well, what meeting Sarah did was change me, and since I believe every writer uses himself or herself as basic material, no matter how far their materials may seem to range from the facts of their lives, everything is autobiographical in the end. And my work and Sarah's work is more autobiographical than some others' work. So, the fact that I married a writer and I had children somehow deeply affected me, yes. I mean, you look at my second book and there's a series of sonnets to my daughters. So, just in terms of pure subject, that would not have happened otherwise. And I think that, again, as Auden says, subject and form come together in a very mysterious way that I can't articulate. I don't know how that happens; I just know that it does. So I may not have had the tone, even, or the lilt of the language, had I not had the experiences I did. And that, I think, is a very interesting matter. It's almost a matter of tone. It's not a matter of, well, you had a child; all those historical facts are not what makes it. It's that some new kind of access to language is opened up in you because of what happens.

BEATTIE: I understand that you, like your wife, have made some retreats to the Abbey of Gethsemani near Bardstown, Kentucky. What has that experience been like for you?

SKINNER: Oh, it's been very interesting for me. I've always read Zen literature and Christian mysticism, and I've read things like *The Cloud of Unknowing* for twenty years. That's always been a part of my reading. And there is some attractiveness—and it's probably true of a lot of writers, because we share a sort of solitary preoccupation with monks and religious orders that remove themselves from the world—if I have any romantic inclinations, it would be in that direction. So I went there and felt pretty comfortable, in an odd kind of way. Just that solitude. Just being near people who have committed themselves to doing work that's interior for the sake of God's universe, to put it that way—I don't know how else to put it—just being close to people who have that faith is a source of energy for me. And I believe it helps the world in a way that is, again, beyond articulation. So I like being there, just seeing those people, and being able to admire them for what they do, even though they're people. You know, they're not saints, they're just ordinary people for the most part, but they've made this commitment, and I like that. I think more people need to do that, just to commit to something in this world.

BEATTIE: When you're there, do you write?

SKINNER: I did. I have a journal that I've kept since I've been there. I've been, I think, four times, and I have not tried to write poems; I've just sat down and done impression- and journal-kind of entries and questionings and prose, and I have quite a bit of that material.

BEATTIE: Do you keep a daily journal?

SKINNER: No. I've never been able to.

BEATTIE: Sarah also told me how important an influence attending the Episcopal Church and finding, through that church and other sources, a sense of spiritual centeredness has been to her. Has formal religion or have other sources of spirituality been important to you in your development as a person or a poet?

SKINNER: I think they've been crucial. As I said, I went to Lutheran schools when I was a kid, and some of that obviously rubbed off. I mean, in some deep way, the fact that I was exposed to it younger . . . The poet Czeslaw Milosz has an interesting interview in which he talks about his early upbringing as a Catholic and how no one can believe, who interviews him, that he still has that faith. And he says, "Well, to some people it looks naïve, but to me the fact that there's a naïveté still to my beliefs is not discordant with the fact that I can think about philosophy and my experiences with Nazi Germany." He said, "To me, it's a different kind of naïveté. It's not a bumpkin innocence, it's a sort of affirmative naïveté." And I share that attitude and want to get back to that even more. I would like that. And yes, I did, like most of my generation, drift away from any kind of formalized religion from the middle of the sixties to the middle of my thirties. And then I came back to it, as a lot of people seem to be doing now, because I needed to. And it's been very important to me.

BEATTIE: Do you think that your writing is more visually oriented or more sound oriented?

SKINNER: I generally begin a poem with a line, and of utmost importance is the rhythm. I think that's what you're talking about. You're talking about the language and whether it has the right sound to it. And sound has to do with rhythm and meter and nuance. For me, my best poems happen when the sound is right and where what the poem addresses is also vivid and has the same coloring as the sound. I don't know if that makes any sense at all, but there are poems that I write that are just pure sound. And I have a good ear, so I can write a good line. I'm fairly graceful with that. But they can turn out to be stupid because they're not about anything. The poems that are my best poems are the ones that just happen upon a convergence of ear and eye. I don't know how that happens, but generally I start with a rhythm, and I can almost hear the rhythm or feel the rhythm, and I just have to fill in the words.

BEATTIE: That's what I meant by sound-oriented.

SKINNER: Yes, I think I am. And that's where I start with a poem. I'm not a subject-first kind of poet.

BEATTIE: Well, your lines are so graceful, that that's what I would have thought. I understand that writer Tess Gallagher selected *A Guide to Forgetting* for the National Poetry Series. Did she ever tell you how she responded to your poem, "The Good Story," that you dedicated to her husband, Raymond Carver?

SKINNER: Yes, she changed the last line.

BEATTIE: What did she change? What had the last line been?

SKINNER: It had been, "Till the last sweet word." She said, "Jeff, I think you mean, 'the last unsweetened word.'" And I said, "Tess, you're absolutely correct." There's a little tidbit for literary history right there. She actually told me that Ray Carver—I don't know if I should say this, but I don't think she would mind. She said that Ray really made the decision for her. She had liked three finalists' manuscripts, and, during their [Gallager and Carver] being together, they almost did everything very closely, tightly together. She told me that he tipped the balance and he said, "You have got to pick Skinner."

BEATTIE: That's nice to know.

SKINNER: It *is* nice to know.

BEATTIE: In your memoir, you write about your brief acting career, and you've talked about it. I understand you were a finalist in the Eugene O'Neill National Playwrights Conference for your play, *The Last Time I Saw Richard.* Will you discuss that play, and is playwriting a genre you'd like to continue working in?

SKINNER: *The Last Time I Saw Richard* I wrote when I was at Yaddo and met Sarah, in fact. I wrote the first draft there. Then I worked on it for a couple of years thereafter. In New York City I worked with a couple of people on the play. It's probably the best full-length play I've done, by far. And it's autobiographical, in a way, although nothing in it actually happened to me, but a lot of the feeling is autobiographical. It's about a guy who can't stand the work he's doing and wants to do something simpler and is sort of being slowly driven crazy by the press of commerce and wants to get out. But I never got it right. I think that theater, or drama writing, is a very difficult thing to do on a part-time basis, the way I've done it. One needs to commit one's self to playwriting totally, I think, because it's tough. One of the reasons that it's tough is that it's a collaborative art. A play is not finished until it's up on the boards and in the mouths of living, human people. And to get it to that point is really difficult, and you have to expend enormous amounts of energy. And, even then, you know, you're changing it all the time. It's just never finished. To do a play is so expensive and so time-consuming on the part of so many different kinds of people, but I would love to do more. I love the theater, and it's a good conjunction of my experience. But if I have a choice of what to commit myself to—prose or story or poetry or drama— I'm generally not going to pick drama, because of all those unknowns.

BEATTIE: What about other genres, like the short story or the novel? Are you interested in those?

SKINNER: I've got ninety pages of a novel written, and the short story that it started with was published in *Negative Capability* and was an honorable mention in their contest. And I've written other stories. I'm getting, just recently, into prose and writing stories. I'm very interested in it, and I want to finish this novel. It's an unknown to me. I've not done it before, so I'm anxious. I don't know what the hell I'm doing.

BEATTIE: Shall I ask what it's about?

SKINNER: The story that it came from involves a guy who has a daughter who's about six months old, and he gets divorced at that point. And it's sort of a custody battle. The novel is going to take off from the fact that his wife, who has custody of the child, is making it more and more difficult for him to see this girl, who he's more and more in love with. And I think it's going to the point where they're going to be pulled apart for good. But I don't want to say any more than that about it. And more and more of his energy—I mean, this seems to be a theme of mine—I find it poignant, the person who begins to feel a sort of drain or loss of meaning in the external world, and begins to see where real meaning and significance in their lives is collecting and then doesn't know how to hold it, to take care of it, to enhance it, because they have no experience. I find that a really moving, contemporary problem.

BEATTIE: I think your recently written "Memoir"—the grace of its language and its alliteration make it read almost like a prose poem. I also very much like the fact that it includes several different points of view or perspectives. Will you discuss that work?

SKINNER: As I said earlier, it's still under construction, in a way, so I'm not sure how it's going to end up. And there are things that I don't know about its structure and construction right now. But I'm glad you like the fact that it has different points of view; I probably will try and get more of that into it, or experiment with that, at least. It's a very experimental work for me, anyway. I don't know if it's going to strike other people as experimental. Yes, I like the different kinds of form and the way that it veers close to poetry and then goes more toward narrative and then goes more towards pure speech. And I like the fact that it's trying to mix all of those kinds of things and stay within an emotional range. I'm not trying to have a wide emotional spectrum. I'm trying to see how different kinds of speech and rhetoric can be applied within a narrow range.

BEATTIE: I also like the brevity of the chapters that are staccato and punctuated, mimicking memory itself. And your style also keeps your memoir from being limited by biography.

SKINNER: I'm not really interested in providing an overarching frame and evaluating and placing in context. I'm more interested in the way memory itself works.

BEATTIE: Well, each chapter works very well from the child's point of view, or even from the adult's point of view, with the adult looking back and commenting, but your memoir doesn't get bogged down in just the chronological correctness of anything.

SKINNER: I don't find that that's the way memory is. Memory's not chronological; *my* memory's not chronological, anyway. It is very jagged, and it is very shifting. I found that a lot of what people say about rewriting the past is really true, that there are versions of the past, and those versions can change very swiftly.

BEATTIE: What future work do you have planned?

SKINNER: I have the novel and I have this memoir, which is, as I say, not finished. So those are the two projects I'm working on. I just finished a short story about three weeks ago that I like a good deal, and I'd like to do more stories. It's funny, in prose it works a little differently for me. Now I have ideas for stories and I have situations and characters and themes, and my problem is opposite to the way I handle poetry. I don't know what the form will be; I don't know the tone I'm looking for. Generally, I start with tone or sound in poetry, and the subject will find itself, but now I have a subject seemingly looking for a tone. Maybe that's a difference between prose and poetry, and maybe it's just me. I don't know. It's probably ridiculous to try and generalize, but that's the way I'm finding it for me. I'd like to do plays, too, but I'm going to have to have just a boffo idea before I try.

BEATTIE: Will you talk about your method of composition?

SKINNER: Poetry I write with a pen and a piece of paper, and then I move to the computer. I almost never use a typewriter anymore. Prose—essays, the memoir, novel, stories—I write directly on the computer, basically. I've gotten into the habit, and it feels as comfortable as a pen does for poetry. I can't write poetry on the computer; it's too formal too quickly. And also, when I'm writing poetry, there's more freedom with a pen and a piece of paper, because you can scratch things out real quick, and the computer is not more effective, I find. But I like the way sentences sort of sink into concrete so quickly, or have sort of a blocky angularity, on the screen of the computer.

BEATTIE: It's interesting that you have an artistic way of looking at the process of composition.

SKINNER: Well, the way things look is important to my way of composition, for some reason. I don't understand that totally, but it is very important. When I'm writing a long piece, like when I was working on the novel, I found it necessary to work every day. I think that lots of writers have talked about the psychological gain of engaging the subconscious on a regular schedule, in so far as some of the work is done when you're not writing, if you return to it at the same time every day. I think that's ideal, but I don't do that. I mean, I'm not a really disciplined person, and I do tend to write in bursts. *A Guide to Forgetting* I wrote in a year, and constantly. Then I'll go for periods of time when I don't do anything, or I'll do lots of fragmentary work. So it's really hard to make a general statement about it. I never know, and it's something I'm constantly trying to figure out, what is best for me. All I know is that I have to keep going at it somehow.

BEATTIE: Do you work at home as well as at your office at the University?

SKINNER: Yes, I work in both places. Mainly at the office, recently, because Sarah is also a writer, and she works here at home quite a bit, so I don't get much time to work here, and I have an office of my own, so it's comfortable to write there. But I try not to make too many rules.

BEATTIE: You taught at Salisbury State College, right?

SKINNER: Right. I taught one creative writing course and three other courses, a regular load with my specialty being one course, which is the way things were done there. So I taught two sections of freshman composition, one literature survey, and one creative writing course.

BEATTIE: Given your experience teaching there, and your teaching now at the University of Louisville, how do you like teaching creative writing?

SKINNER: I love teaching creative writing. I think it's a fine thing to do with my life. I think it's what I need to be doing, what I'm supposed to be doing. I feel like I'm using myself in the best way possible for the good of other people and the good of myself.

BEATTIE: You don't resent it as time taken away from your own writing?

SKINNER: No. I mean, it *is* time taken away from my own writing, but one has to make money. No, I don't resent it. I enjoy it. I like it. It's fun. It's exciting. It's maddening. It requires an enormous psychic cost.

BEATTIE: How do you think creative writing *should* be taught?

SKINNER: With great humility. Great humility and lots of confidence that what you have discovered for yourself has some transfer, even though how that transfer is going to work one could never codify. But the enthusiasm and the desire and the love of writing somehow can become infectious, and that's what I try and exhibit for the students. I can also do very detailed looking at their work using my best judgment, which is twenty years of evaluating my own work, to their advantage. So, I don't buy the argument that creative writing can't be taught. But you cannot teach talent. You can teach technical things.

BEATTIE: Will you comment on what you think the nature of creativity itself is?

SKINNER: I think creativity is a much-abused term, myself. When I was banging around in my early twenties, I considered advertising as a career. So I went to a class at J. Walter Thompson Advertising Agency where my uncle worked, and the guy who was leading the class would routinely bring in these ad copy writers and say, "Now here's the incredible genius, the most creative man in America." And what creativity meant was, you know, "So get up and get away, you deserve a break today, at McDonald's." *That* was creative genius. Now, if that's creativity, then to me the word means nothing. And a lot of people use it, especially in education, it seems. You know, "we've got to be creative." Well, we don't. We don't have to be *creative*. I think that art is much more mysterious than the word *creative*. I think it's some mixture of gift and hard work. And the hard work is writing the bad poems, which I do, to get ready for the good poems. I have no idea what the relation is.

BEATTIE: This past year you won a fellowship from the Howard Foundation. How has that helped your career?

SKINNER: I've never liked the word *career*, because I don't understand what it means. I mean, it's going to be good for my records, and it's going to be good for what people give me in the future, and success builds on success in academia as well as in any other field. So it's great for that. It gave me a year off. I wrote the memoir, I wrote two stories, I wrote twenty pages of poems, I wrote a few essays. I did a lot of work that I would not have done had I not had that time. I wouldn't have even attempted the memoir, because I just don't do extended pieces when I'm teaching; I can't. So, it's meant a lot insofar as what I've been able to do.

BEATTIE: Has living in Louisville or teaching at U of L influenced your work in any way that you know of?

SKINNER: I'm slow. Things take a long time to sink in, and I think that I will become more of a Louisvillian in my soul as time goes on. In my third book, there are a number of poems that are set in Louisville. One of them is set in Creason Park, which I think is one of my best, "Late in the Afternoon, Late in the Twentieth Century." I think that's really one of my better pieces of work, and that came as a result of being here. So there are indications here and there, already cropping up, that the place is reflected in the work, and vice versa.

BEATTIE: You said you loved teaching creative writing; how have you found U of L [University of Louisville] as a school?

SKINNER: I've been really happy and pleased with the quality of my writing students. I think there's an amazing proportion of good writers at U of L. I don't know why, but there are. I taught at Salisbury State College and there wasn't anywhere near the proportion, and I've been to conferences, and I've judged contests. We have a really incredibly good percentage of talented, serious students here. So I'm very happy with the creative writing. Now, I don't know much about the general level of student, because I haven't taught many of those kinds of courses. I'd put our best students against any M.F.A.-program students.

BEATTIE: What about other writers here in the city or in the state? Are there any who have particularly influenced you or whose work you admire?

SKINNER: Well, two who I like best, and some of it is proximity, but I love Sena Naslund's work, and I love Leon's [Driskell] work. I think both of them are idiosyncratic masters, I really do. Leon's stories are like no other stories. And Sena's also. She's in a class of her own. They're superb. There's a good poet named Sarah Gorham, too.

May 21, 1992

Since 1992, Skinner has given readings in such places as New York City (Civic Center Synagogue), Salisbury State University (Maryland), Georgia Southern University, and Rutgers University, as well as readings in Kentucky, including Elizabethtown Community College, The Morton Center, and Morehead State University. Skinner has continued writing poems, stories, and plays. In 1996 his play, *Preexisting Conditions,* was a finalist in the Eugene O'Neill Theater Conference. In that same year he was awarded a seasonal Al Smith Fellowship from the Kentucky Council on the Arts. In 1997 Skinner was named the Frost House Poet-in-Residence, an honor that caused him, his wife Sarah Gorham, and their two children to live in Robert Frost's farmhouse in Franconia, New Hampshire, for the months of July and August. During their stay, Skinner performed a reading for the Frost House Writers' Conference and a reading for the town of Franconia on Poets' Day. Also, in the summer of 1997, Skinner taught in the Louisville, Kentucky, Writers for Racing Conference, and he and Gorham read at the Ropewalk Writers Conference in New Harmony, Indiana.

BOOKS BY JEFFREY SKINNER

Late Stars. Middletown, Ct.: Wesleyan University Press, 1985.

A Guide to Forgetting. St. Paul, Mn.: Graywolf Press, (National Poetry Winner), 1988.

The Night Lifted Us. (with Sarah Gorham). Monterey, Ky.: Larkspur Press, 1991.

Real Toads in Imaginary Gardens. (Instructional Essay). (with Stephen Policoff). Chicago: Chicago Review Press, 1991.

The Company of Heaven. Pittsburgh: University of Pittsburgh Press, 1992.

The Atlantic. (Chapbook, memoir). Whitsfield, Vt.: White Field Books Inc., 1993.

Last Call: Poems on Alcoholism, Addiction, & Deliverance (Edited with Sarah Gorham) Louisville, Ky.: Sarabande Books, 1997.

FREDERICK SMOCK

SMOCK: My name is Frederick Smock and I was born in Louisville in 1954. My mother's maiden name was Betty Bourne. Her father was a drugstore owner here in town, and she went to U of L [University of Louisville] and was an art major and was an artist all of her life. She got a master's in social work and did some work for a time with children, and had other jobs off and on, but primarily she was a housewife, although she's always painted. My father was also named Fred; I'm the third. He was a radiologist. He died two years ago, and mother's still alive.

BEATTIE: Did you grow up around your grandparents?

SMOCK: My father's grandparents—we didn't see them much, although they lived in town. I never knew my mother's father; he died long before I was born. But from the time I was born until I was five, we lived with my mother's mother and her sister. And then, of course, my father was gone all the time, either in medical school or working, so basically I was raised those first three years by three women, two of them quite old.

My mother's father was named Morton Bourne, and her mother's name was Mattie Bourne. My father's father was also named Fred, and his wife's name was Susan Smock. They were opposites in a lot of ways—both very sweet, you know. One was terribly thin, the other was terribly fat. They quilted. One hated to piece; one loved to. And one hated to quilt and one loved to quilt, so they meshed, in a way.

My mother's mother, Mattie, was very religious and very pretty and also very fragile. Even though she worked hard all of her life, she still seemed rather fragile, whereas Mattie's sister, Iley, was quite large and quite jovial and a wonderful cook. She did have a temper, but it only showed when a cooking project failed.

BEATTIE: Did you have brothers and sisters?

SMOCK: One sister named Sally, who's three years younger than me, and one brother named Brad, who's six years younger than me.

BEATTIE: Where did you live?

SMOCK: We moved first to a house out near Fern Creek off Bardstown Road. It was a stone cottage, and we rented that and rented a couple of other houses while the one we were building, just across the hill, was being completed. We finally moved there when I was, I guess, eight.

BEATTIE: What do you remember about your childhood?

SMOCK: It sort of splits. My early childhood, which was urban and living downtown with my grandparents—I remember just sort of playing street ball and being out on the street and roaming around the neighborhood and exploring. Then, suddenly, we moved to the country where we had neighbors who had horses and other animals, and there were lots of woods around us. So a lot of the time was just spent running through the woods and building treehouses and riding horses and playing sports. I was a jock when I was a kid and during my teenage years.

BEATTIE: Did you own horses?

SMOCK: My sister had a horse for a while. I never did. I wasn't that interested in them. I read a lot when I was a child. Reading and basketball were the two things I mostly did.

BEATTIE: What did you enjoy reading?

SMOCK: I remember one summer sitting by a window in the house and eating bowls of vanilla ice cream, reading *Gone With the Wind*. Took me all summer, but I read it. I don't know why I chose *Gone with the Wind*, but that was one.

BEATTIE: That's unusual for a boy.

SMOCK: It is. And it's a big, thick book. I might have been interested in the Civil War. I don't remember. But I remember reading a lot of short stories and history. I was interested in history at the time.

BEATTIE: Did your mother or father read to you much when you were a child?

SMOCK: No, my father wasn't much there. I don't really remember much of my father, but my mother read to us, and we always had books around. Reading seemed to be important to them.

BEATTIE: What about schools? When did you start school, and what was it like for you?

SMOCK: I went to a little church kindergarten not far from where we lived. Then, my first four years in grade school, I was at Fern Creek Elementary. Then, in the fifth grade, I entered the Advanced Program, which they had here in the county. So, in fifth grade, I was at a new school, Kennedy Elementary, where that year we were joined with the sixth grade. Then, for sixth grade, I went to Goldsmith. For the seventh grade, I went up to Seneca High School. I ended up graduating from Seneca High School in the Advanced Program.

BEATTIE: In elementary school, did you have a favorite subject?

SMOCK: I had a favorite teacher, who was my fourth grade teacher, who had red hair. I can't remember her name, but I had a crush on her, and she had a bookshelf where you could get extra credit for reading. I was always doing that, probably to impress her. That teacher was the one who nominated me for the Advanced Program. You had to have a nomination and pass a series of tests to get into it. But, as far back as I can remember, it was reading, English, and social studies that I liked a lot. I'm still not good at math and sciences. I'm very, very weak. I'm fascinated by them, especially physics, but I have to really concentrate to get anything out of it.

BEATTIE: Did you know how to read before going to school, or did you learn in school?

SMOCK: I think I learned in school.

BEATTIE: When did you start writing?

SMOCK: I had a journal that I kept when I was, maybe, ten. Then, when I was in high school, I went through a phase listening to music—rock and roll and folk music—that my sister was interested in. Bob Dylan and all those that I started trying to write song lyrics like. I probably wrote a hundred really bad song lyrics. So yes, I guess I was always scribbling something.

BEATTIE: You think the relative isolation of where you lived had something to do with developing your imagination?

SMOCK: I think it probably did, because going from the city where everything was sort of filled in around you, to the country where it was just woods and open spaces, I think writing might have been a way of dealing with it.

BEATTIE: What about favorite teachers in junior high or high school?

SMOCK: Several come to mind. One was a Mrs. Billingsley at Seneca, who was an English teacher and encouraged us to read and was very lively about reading. She was the first person who didn't make us memorize Browning, but made it come alive. Most important was a Spanish teacher, Susan Dunlap, who I had in Spanish all the way through, who was college level, and taught us as though *we* were college level. We spoke Spanish and she could fix us with a glare if we messed up or misbehaved. But she demanded the best out of us and, of course, we gave it to her. So she was quite strong, quite impressive.

BEATTIE: Did you go directly from high school to college?

SMOCK: Yes. I went to Georgetown College in Georgetown, Kentucky.

BEATTIE: What was that experience like for you?

SMOCK: It was good because Georgetown is a small college, and half of it is very Baptist and that half is almost invisible if you belong to the other half, which is liberal arts. And, you know, it has a very good student/teacher ratio. Good faculty. Interesting, smart people. And it's not so large that you get lost. It was very reassuring and encouraging and stimulating.

BEATTIE: Did you major in English?

SMOCK: I did, but not the first two years. I just took the requirements because I really didn't know what I was doing. I had gotten no help or advice on how to choose college. It was the time of the draft lottery, and that's what we were thinking about when the program overseer, whoever it was, came around to interview some of us seniors, who were tracked all the way through. Then, as seniors, we were asked where we were going to college, and we said, "Oh, it depends on our draft number, University of Kentucky or University of Toronto, Canada," if we wanted to evade the draft. So we really hadn't thought about it. Then, when I got to Georgetown, the first couple of years, I just took requirements. One day I was registering for my junior year, and I realized I didn't have anything left that I had to take. I suddenly had to decide what that should be, and I just took a bunch of English classes because that's what appealed to me. So I felt good that English was a kind of gut choice. I minored in Spanish.

BEATTIE: Did you write for any school publications, such as the newspaper or literary magazine?

SMOCK: Yes. I wrote for the paper. I had a column for the Georgetown paper, which was just my name, but spelled P-h-r-e-d, after, I think, a Communist character in the Doonesbury cartoons. Then I wrote for the campus literary magazine, which was called *Endscape*.

BEATTIE: What was your column about?

SMOCK: It was a humor column. I don't know how funny it would be now if I looked at it. It was topical. You know, news-of-the-day commentary—a sort of college man's version of Russell Baker, perhaps.

BEATTIE: Did you think, at the time, that you'd be working on publications in the future?

SMOCK: Yes, I thought I'd be a journalist, if I thought about it at all, which I didn't, much. But I guess, when I did think about it, I thought I'd be a newspaperman.

BEATTIE: You didn't think you wanted to teach?

SMOCK: Well, I turned toward that as I got through college, because suddenly college was over, and I had no idea what I was going to do, so of course I went to graduate school, with, I suppose, the idea of wanting to teach.

BEATTIE: You graduated from college in 197– . . .

SMOCK: Seventy-six. Yes, and then the next month, June, I enrolled at U of L in the master's program in American literature, which I took in '78 with a creative thesis.

BEATTIE: What was your thesis?

SMOCK: It was a collection of poems and short stories that I wrote under the direction of Sena Naslund, whom you've probably interviewed. She's a wonderful person. I think it was in Sena's workshop that I really got serious about writing. I had Bill Grant, kind of a cowboy professor, for the American Studies portion of it; then I had Sena for the creative side. She'd been through Iowa [The Iowa Writers Workshop], and she knew how to do workshops, and she knew how to encourage writers, and really, it was Sena who got me thinking about writing and reading poetry that would feed my own work, and not just poetry that would feed a critical paper, which was an interesting discovery to me.

BEATTIE: What poets did she get you interested in?

SMOCK: I don't remember the poets *per se*. We looked at the *Louisville Review*, obviously, which she was the faculty advisor for, and she had us read copies of *The Iowa Review*. I remember one issue that was an international issue with poets from all over the world, and it was just a real eye-opening thing to have this laid in front of you, and they were all writing very contemporary, hip poetry. Because, in the textbook, there's only, like, Bob Dylan, which is what I'd grown up with, and suddenly here are a lot of writers who are writing in that kind of imme-diate, visceral language that Dylan used. That kind of connected, too, for me.

BEATTIE: Did you ever work on *The Louisville Review*?

SMOCK: No, I didn't. I contributed to it, but I was a teaching assistant, and I guess most of my time was given to classes and to teaching and to what little writing I was doing.

BEATTIE: What did you teach?

SMOCK: Freshman composition. It's what everybody does. It paid for the tuition.

BEATTIE: How did you enjoy or not enjoy that, as the case may be?

SMOCK: Oh, I loved it a lot. I really took to it, I think, partly, because I was young and naïve and enthusiastic.

BEATTIE: Did you make friends in graduate school, or had you before, who were interested in writing as well? Were you ever a member of a writers' group?

SMOCK: No, not outside of the workshop. But we all hung out together. There was this whole group of Sena's students, and we all lived together down in Old Louisville, right within the same blocks, and we all partied together, and we saw each other a lot, and we didn't talk about writing a whole lot outside of class. There was so much else to talk about, and, I think, too, you know, at that age, you're interested in living and not in retreating.

BEATTIE: But was it a group of people fairly intense about their work? Did you share your work with other people, and did you edit each other's work?

SMOCK: We didn't edit each other's work, but we showed it around. There were people like Jane Olmsted and Bonnie Cherry and Michael Snyder and sev-eral others from that era down there who all still write, and we were all pretty intense about it. And we were all into being graduate students. I don't know whether we knew what we were going to do with it, but we just loved that kind of intellectual climate. I think they, too, had come from small colleges, where if you're of that bent, eventually you need more than the small college can offer you.

BEATTIE: What did you do after graduate school?

SMOCK: Well, I right away applied to a Ph.D. program. I got my master's and still didn't know what I wanted to do, so I applied to graduate school and wound up going to the University of Arizona in Tucson. I think I was going to be a college professor. But I got out there and was there a couple of months before I realized that I was totally burned out on school. I was thrown back into neo-classical literature, and I was just in a terrible funk about it. So I dropped out for a semester. I'd been going straight through graduate school, all the way through, and working.

BEATTIE: What had you been working on and where?

SMOCK: Well, in addition to teaching, I ran out of money, so I got a job that was sort of an arrangement on a judge's property in the East End of Louisville with another graduate student, David Bell, who was in law school at the time, and whom I'd known at Georgetown. We lived in this cottage in return for so many hours' work a week on the judge's estate. It didn't cost us money; it cost us time. So I was there for awhile—working, teaching, and going to school. When that ended, I went right out to Arizona, and just was in a real funk, so I dropped out. I wandered around a little bit and wound up back here in Louisville.

BEATTIE: When you came back to Louisville, what did you do?

SMOCK: I got an apartment in the Highlands, and I started teaching again as a part-time lecturer at U of L. Then I got a job. Carmichael's Bookstore had just opened in the Highlands, so I got a job there. I wound up working at Carmichael's five or six years, at least, really liking it. At the same time, I was teaching at U of L and just sort of hanging out. I mean, I had no sense of career, and I think it might have been because my father had always said that anything I wanted to be was okay with him, as long as I wasn't a career student. So I think I had subconsciously decided to become a career student.

BEATTIE: To spite him?

SMOCK: Father's *angst*.

BEATTIE: When you were teaching at U of L, was that still freshman English?

SMOCK: It began as freshman English, and then I started teaching some creative writing classes. It was a mix, the first few years. I'm still teaching there. I've been teaching there ever since '79, which is when I began.

BEATTIE: What caused you to stop working at the bookstore, and what did you do from there?

SMOCK: Well, at the same time that I moved back to Louisville from Arizona, Sallie Bingham had moved from New York after, I guess, ten or twelve years, to Louisville. And she, too, got a job at U of L, and we were assigned the same desk in the department and began taking messages for each other, and we eventually met and became friends. So, in '83 to '84, when she began thinking of selling her interests in the family business [The Louisville *Courier-Journal*], we were by that time firm friends, and I had been reviewing books for her at the *Courier*. I was still just kind of floating along, and we began talking about doing a magazine, and it dovetailed with her notion of creating a foundation. So, in '85, when she incorporated all of that, I was hired as editor of this new magazine [*The American Voice*] we were going to do together, and I was also hired as Secretary of the Board of Directors for what became The Kentucky Foundation for Women. So that was the very serendipitous beginning of our partnership.

BEATTIE: I was wondering how that came about.

SMOCK: Totally by accident, and I had no idea who she was when we met.

BEATTIE: Were you married at that time?

SMOCK: Yes, I'd gotten married. I think that was in '83.

BEATTIE: Whom did you marry?

SMOCK: I married Jackie Strange. She was born up near Cincinnati. She went to law school here, and we met through a volleyball group that played in the park. A lot of artists, like Julius Friedman and John Beckman, and writers and designers — artsy people — had a non-serious volleyball group going, and I played in that for a number of years, and Jackie was dating a photographer and came a couple of times, so we met over the volleyball net.

BEATTIE: Do you have children?

SMOCK: We do. We have two sons: Sam, who was born in '84, and Ben, who was born in '87.

BEATTIE: Do either of them look as though they might want to be writers?

SMOCK: Oh, yes. Sam has always written. He writes poems. A year or two ago, when my chapbook came out from Larkspur, Sam produced probably a dozen chapbooks of poems and stories, and he is very environmentally aware. He's very, very intense, very cerebral, and very, very winning. I mean, he's not an obnoxious, smart kid. He's a very lovable smart kid, which is a marvelous combination. Ben, I don't know. Ben is quiet and more like me. More reserved, I suppose. He keeps more to himself. It may be too early to tell.

BEATTIE: Does your wife practice as an attorney?

SMOCK: No, she is a headhunter. She has her own company and she finds lawyers for law firms, and she also does other referral work.

BEATTIE: Where do you live now?

SMOCK: We live in the Highlands, at the corner of Spring and Lauderdale Roads, not far from Douglass Boulevard.

BEATTIE: Back to *The American Voice*. Tell me how you think your editorial direction has shaped the magazine.

SMOCK: Well, when we began it, we were talking, Sallie and I, about all the people we liked to read. And they tended to be the French people, the ones whose books were hard to find and you had to root through little magazines to find them. So we began with a commitment to publishing new writers, daring writers, who just weren't getting published—people who were not John Updike. So it's been a constant kind of exploration—writing letters, reading, meeting people, trying to find the new, good writers. I guess that's always the editor's job.

Sallie's interest, of course, was in women's writing, and the magazine has always been primarily for women writers. I've had an interest in South American writing because of my background in Spanish, and also in Canadian writers, so we opened it up to a kind of hemispheric thing. Sallie was at dinner in New York with the critic, Frank MacShane, who's an old New York friend of hers, and they were talking about troubles we were having coming up with a name for the magazine. We thought of *Other Voices,* names like that. And Frank suggested, "Why not call it *The American Voice* and locate it centrally?" Which we did. So by calling it *The American Voice,* it *is* hemispheric, it *is* all the Americas. It *is* all the people who don't normally get published: Hispanics, gays, lesbians, young writers, old writers, beginning writers in their fifties, Latin American writers, Caribbean writers—the whole really exciting mix of writing that you get, you know, in any land mass this huge, that stands in some opposition to the canon, the American canon.

BEATTIE: Have you ever solicited writing from particular writers?

SMOCK: Oh, yes, all the time. We're always reading little magazines and coming across writers here and there, and a lot of my job is writing letters, corresponding with writers, and trying to find and encourage them.

BEATTIE: Are there a couple of pieces that you might say have been your favorites or real coups in terms of getting particular writers?

SMOCK: Well, we've published a lot of wonderful writers. One of my favorites, I guess, was an early essay by Isabel Allende. I'd been to New York and met her editor at Knopf, a man named Lee Goerner, who's now a publisher at Athenaeum, and he was squiring her around. This was just when she was beginning to get known. I'd met Lee, and we talked about her and my interest in Latin American writing, and he sent me this address she'd given to a small college where she talked about Latin America, and she described South America as looking physically, on a map, like a wounded heart. It made a beautiful essay. I was really glad to get that for the magazine.

We've had some wonderful successes with young writers. One, a writer named Fae Myenne Ng, we gave her her first publication for a story called "The Red Sweater." It came to us via Frank MacShane. She'd been a student of his at Columbia, and he had heard some of this story, which we published, and then which we nominated for a Pushcart Prize, which it won, and then it also got her admittance to a couple of writing colonies, which led her to her first book, which is called *Bone* and is getting wonderful reviews. So her career just kind of took off on publication in our magazine.

BEATTIE: Does Sallie Bingham still take an active interest in the magazine?

SMOCK: Yes. We still share manuscripts back and forth, and her moving away from Louisville has caused us to shift around in the way we do it, because we had always been here, and we both agreed on everything that went into it. I think we're shaping down now to a new system, working it out across the distances that separate us. But she still looks at magazines and she finds writers and she has input with me. I do all of the production of the magazine, but she and I usually share in the philosophical, editorial aspect of it, as well as in deciding what goes into the magazine.

BEATTIE: How is it working now? Do you send her manuscripts?

SMOCK: Yes, I send most everything from here. I send her manuscripts. Occasionally, she comes across manuscripts from writers and sends them to me.

BEATTIE: Are there ways in which you would like to see the magazine head in the future?

SMOCK: I'd like to do more Latin American work. We always publish Kentucky writers or artists along with writers from the rest of the hemisphere. I think that's good. It showcases them a little, and proves that we're just as good as anybody else. I'm pretty happy with it. I want it to get bigger and better, and I want its reputation to be more solid. Of course, I'm always learning, and I always feel like I'm way behind the curve. When you realize how much you, yourself, are dedicated to something, you also realize how much you have to learn.

BEATTIE: In terms of the editorial content, even though *The American*

Voice is a feminist magazine, do you or will you publish work that is not necessarily feminist in focus? I don't mean anti-feminist, I mean just somebody whose writing you think is wonderful, but the subject of the writing does not necessarily deal with feminism.

SMOCK: Right, we do. I think by *feminist,* we mean not only work that is pro-feminist, but also good writing that is not sexist, racist, classist, or ageist. Good work that usually is, in some way, political. I mean that really is our bent: writing that is connected to the social fabric and that involves politics. It involves social issues. We don't do much for the nature of poetry, or we don't do baseball poems. We don't do, I guess, a lot of things that are sort of totally divorced from the arena of politics or social issues. It really is pretty much an activist literary magazine.

BEATTIE: Has it received acclaim nationally?

SMOCK: We get really good reviews from library journals, small tracts—the other magazines that do reviews that are very positive.

BEATTIE: What is the magazine's circulation, approximately?

SMOCK: Right now, it's about two thousand. And we have won awards. I guess, in eight years, we've won five Pushcarts, which I think is a pretty good number. The only magazines that win that quantity tend to be those like *Paris Review* and *Antaeus.* But I don't put much stock in that, because prizes are often politically motivated and very capricious awards, so it's nice for us and it's nice for the writers, but I don't measure our success by that.

People seem to like the magazine. We have a lot of renewals, and the subscription base is always growing. I know other magazine editors often look to us when they're trying to answer a design question or something, so little things like that make me feel good about it.

BEATTIE: Are there other magazines, nationally, that you think are competitive in terms of trying to do the same or similar types of things, editorially?

SMOCK: No. There are what are called feminist journals, but they don't publish men. They are not really for a wide audience, and they sometimes inadvertently create a ghetto of women writers so that they give each other publication and some notice, but they don't affect culture at large. What we're really about is creating a beautiful magazine that passes into the culture of art that which is feminist. Well, I say that, and now I have to contradict myself by saying that magazines like *Grand Street* and *Antaeus* and now, certainly, *The Kenyon Review* with Marilyn Hacker as the editor—any literary magazine that is that serious that's devoted to excellent writing, and that is that advanced intellectually—is also going to be feminist in most ways. So there's a point at which all of that sort of converges. Those magazines are for enlightenment, and feminism is a part of that.

BEATTIE: I'm sure you have been asked numerous times about how you, as a man, find being the editor of a feminist magazine. Do you think your position is something that most people see as positive, as sort of an endorsement of just what you were referring to, in terms of incorporating all of society into the feminist point of view of the magazine?

SMOCK: I don't know what people think. We get a few questions about it, but in my correspondence with really the hardcore feminist editors, like the people at *Trivia Magazine,* it's a very warm relationship, and so I think probably, yes, they're open to that. And Sallie and I work together, and I also have a wonderful woman writer, Christina McGrath, who is a reader for the magazine. So a lot of our support is women. I'm just one man among several women and together we do the magazine.

BEATTIE: I just wondered if you had had any difficulties in your role.

SMOCK: I've had several women poets who have objected to my editorial suggestions on their work. It has only happened three or four times, I guess, since the magazine began, but there were women who took my suggestions as a sexist thing, that I, being a man, could not understand what they were after. And maybe they were right. You know, it's possible that I *did* miss it. But any editor can miss any writer's point of view, and certainly it keeps our eyes open.

BEATTIE: How do you feel about writers calling themselves women writers or African-American writers or whatever descriptor they may choose, instead of just writers? And do you think this is something that is important to our time because of exclusion, in the past or even now, or do you think such labeling is sort of ghettoizing in its own right?

SMOCK: I think if they call *themselves* African writers, then it's empowering. If they are labeled by the people African writers, then it's dispiriting. So I think whatever they choose to do is right.

BEATTIE: In your view, what has the Kentucky Foundation for Women done for Kentucky women?

SMOCK: Oh, I think it's done a tremendous lot. I think Sallie, by her example, has empowered lots and lots of people in little ways—and in big ways too—that sometimes we're not aware of. The Foundation, of course, has given away, I don't know what the latest figure is, around five million dollars in grants to individuals. So that's five million dollars going to individual artists for their own use. And I think that is wonderful, and it's a kind of groundswell of change. Also, the fact that the Foundation is here and exists and it's just for women artists, that changes the cultural cityscape as well.

BEATTIE: Your poetry has appeared in a number of prestigious literary journals, including *The Iowa Review, The Kentucky Poetry Review,* and *Poet and Critic.* When did you first start writing poetry outside of graduate school? Or was your writing continuous from graduate school on? And how would you characterize your poetry?

SMOCK: Well, I've always written. I've never been able to separate it. I would describe my poetry as lyric poetry, I think. It's image-driven. It's short. Maybe the best term, and this is the way that somebody else put it, is that my poems tend to be little epiphanies.

BEATTIE: They strike me as heavily influenced by haiku and by Wallace Stevens-like austere elegance.

SMOCK: I remember, in graduate school, being really affected by Emily Dickinson.

BEATTIE: Who are your favorite poets or who are poets that you think most influenced you?

SMOCK: One writer, who's not a poet, is William Saroyan, who I think is marvelous for the feeling that he gives to writing. Poets? It's hard to say. I love the ancient Persian poet, Rumi, whose poems are very brief, like mine. The other Chinese poets, Tu Fu and Basho, certainly. I like the French poet, Rene Char, the Provencal poet. Other Europeans, like Nina Cassian, an exiled Romanian poet. Actually, in this country, I just read so many of them that it's hard to know. Mark Doty is a wonderful poet writing now. I really like Jim Baker Hall's work, a Kentucky poet.

BEATTIE: Are there Kentucky writers whom you particularly admire?

SMOCK: Aleda Shirley, who's no longer a Kentucky writer, I like her. I've always liked Wendell Berry. I think he's a wonderful person and writer. I've always read him.

BEATTIE: In 1991, Larkspur Press published your book, *12 Poems,* in a limited edition of four hundred. Will you comment how the publication came about and on your poetry in the book?

SMOCK: Gray Zeitz was doing a few chapbooks at the time and asked me if I wanted to send any poems to him. So I kind of looked around. I never really thought about collecting them in a book. I'd been writing and writing and writing, and suddenly the idea of a book was intimidating. So what I did was just pick the dozen or so best poems I thought I had. And, looking back at it now, they really are each very different from each other in a lot of ways. So I don't know if I have a style or not but, for me, I found that each poem seems to demand it's own shape and have its own direction. If I try too hard to impose myself on the poem, it doesn't work. It ends up falling flat. So each of my poems tends to be a little bit different from the other.

BEATTIE: In the beginning of your book, you quote Czeslaw Milosz's theory that, "… poems should be written rarely and reluctantly, under unbearable duress and only with the hope that good spirits, not evil ones, choose us for their instruments." Is that how your poetry is written?

SMOCK: Yes. I might be covering my own lack of production. I really tend not to be very prolific. I write all the time, and I write a lot, but if I had to tell you how many good poems I've written in my life, it'd probably be five or six that I think are worth anything. The good poems only come so often.

BEATTIE: Are you your own best critic, do you think?

SMOCK: I think so. And I publish poems of mine that I don't like. Or it happens after the fact. So I think I am.

BEATTIE: I wonder what you think the nature of creativity itself might be.

SMOCK: Where does it come from? Well, it's not intellectual, I'm pretty sure of that. I think it's intuitive, visceral. It comes churning up out of the guts and the heart, and I think the only effect that the brain has on it is just that the brain is able to channel it. There has to be some kind of passion in it, some talent, or some ability, but I think feeling deeply is the only one necessary thing to creativity. Without that, you get pretty phrases, but no real meaning. So I guess just feeling deeply is where it comes from. I guess everybody is going to have a different explanation for creativity, and it does come out of individual circumstances. It probably is a similar thing to everyone, and yet how it arises is going to be different.

My father took off when we were young, and his and mine was a totally dysfunctional relationship. I mean, it was really the only blot, I guess, on my childhood. You know, the absent father who, our whole lives, we were going to be rejoined to him, and that was his promise to us. When we found out as young adults that, in fact, he had had a relationship and was married to this other woman, it all collapsed. So there is that pain, and there is that, I think, sense of trying to set things right somehow. There's a problem with trying to impose too much order on chaos, because I think a little chaos is good. It's also, you know, just the pain of mortality and loss that, as you become adults, you realize is the true shape of life, and you have to deal with that. You have to come to terms with your own limitations and your own losses, and I think creativity is a way of dealing with that. I would hesitate to use the word *therapy,* only because that word itself is becoming cheapened, and I don't think that writing is a cure, which *therapy* seems to imply. I think writing is short of a cure, but I think it is a way to deal with it. It still leaves you with the loss, but at least you've done something with your hands in the meantime.

BEATTIE: Jim [Baker] Hall said that he thought most great writers had one story to tell, and all of their individual books are a retelling of the same story over and over and over until they get it right. He said a few geniuses, such as Proust and Faulkner, had two or three stories.

SMOCK: That's probably true.

BEATTIE: So, he said, creativity's never a cure, but is the getting closer to an understanding. Or at least that's the effort. I enjoyed reading your essays, especially "Anonymous: A Brief Memoir." It's quite poetic, and I'm wondering if you view yourself primarily as a poet or if you enjoy writing in several genres?

SMOCK: I've tried writing novels. I wrote a couple of really bad novels in my twenties, and I realized I was a poet, if I was anything. The essays I love to write, but they come rarely, too, and they tend to be that kind of poetic prose, I guess. I like "Anonymous," too. It's modeled on a woman ... I knew her a long number of years, who was not an artist, but she was artistic, and she had a huge house up in Glenview that was kind of tumble down. I spent a lot of time there, and my mother lived there for awhile. It was kind of a second home, and the place was just massive. Everything was just huge. The dogs were huge. The house was huge. The rooms were huge. So it was this whole world, and when I started writing about that, the idea of calling it a memoir of an anonymous woman writer—that just seemed to be a good place to set it, and she seemed to be a good person to model it after.

BEATTIE: Is that published anywhere, or will it be?

SMOCK: Not yet. It's at a magazine called *American Literary Review.* They're doing a special issue on the American essay in all of its various forms. They're reading it now, but it's unpublished at the moment.

BEATTIE: The piece you did, the essay on family heritage …

SMOCK: "Armorial Bearings?"

BEATTIE: Right. Do you think that was part of your dealing with your father's desertion?

SMOCK: I think so. And through him, the whole notion of lineage. Yes, you know, on my father's side is this ancient family with a coat of arms going back to a prince of Holland, and on my mother's side, they claim to be descended from King Bruce of Scotland, who ran the English out. Bruce is one of the family names. So I was looking back along these lines as though there's some greatness there that is supposed to ennoble us, and more often it's a cover. It's there to pounce upon if you feel inadequate yourself, and I think you have to reject that. That's why I love the quote, and I can't remember who said it, that there is honor in having good ancestors, but the honor belongs to them. You have to create honor for yourself.

BEATTIE: Is there a writing project you'd like to tackle more than any other?

SMOCK: I love the form of the memoir. I'd love to write a memoir when I get older. But right now, I love turning out a nicely fashioned essay. I also like turning out a poem. For a number of years, I've felt driven to write a long poem. I thought that was necessary. The one long poem I was ever able to write was "The Ballad of Externals," which is in the *12 Poems,* and that was an exhausting poem, which took two years to do. I realized then that my form is the brief lyric, and I'm happy with that.

BEATTIE: I was wondering if you'd discuss your writing habits.

SMOCK: Sometimes I write here [Smock's *American Voice* office]. This is a wonderful space, and this office is very nice, with its windows and the views. And I think Sallie, by creating the Foundation the way she did, made sure that it's not a pressure cooker. It's a very liberal environment, and we can set our own hours. We're all project driven, so we can take a few minutes here and there to do other things, if that sustains us. But mostly, I write at home, usually at night, after the boys are in bed. I'm just too busy. My wife works, and her job is more demanding, it seems, at times, than mine is, so I find myself doing a lot of the cooking and childcare and homework and baths and all of that, which I love to do. So I write when everybody else is in bed.

BEATTIE: Do you write with a word processor?

SMOCK: No, I can't. I'm a Luddite. I can't do anything on computer. I write with a pen on scratch paper, and then I'll type it up. But no, I'm not a computer person.

BEATTIE: Do you write most nights?

SMOCK: No, I probably try to write three or four times a week, at least. But it varies widely how much time I'm able to give.

BEATTIE: Do you think your writing depends in any way on sense of place? I mean that in a limited way, either as the home or the room that you're writing in, or, in a more expansive sense, the state of Kentucky. Does Kentucky enter into your writing in any way?

SMOCK: I think not, really. It's bound here, and it's centered here, in a lot of ways. I know when I'm writing where things are happening, and it's often here. But it's not been terribly important for me to locate it here.

BEATTIE: Is yours more of an interior landscape?

SMOCK: It is an interior landscape, and I also don't want the limitations that that location can sometimes give. It's quite nice to be a Louisville writer or to be a Kentucky writer. But the place is not the essence of what I'm about, so to locate it in the writing would be to give that too much prominence. There's something else going on that's the real subject of the poem.

BEATTIE: You say you taught creative writing some. Do you still teach it?

SMOCK: Yes, now I teach only creative writing—usually the upper-level classes now, as they are available. I also started a course, which I've done once, and I think it's gong to come up again, which is a graduate course on the history of the literary magazine in the Twentieth Century. So I'm just doing one class a term at U of L right now.

BEATTIE: I was wondering how you think creative writing should be taught.

SMOCK: Gosh, there's so many theories and battle lines drawn. I like Wallace Stegner's view, the workshop idea. There's a problem with teaching young writers, and that is they don't have much to say yet. I'm frustrated in my classes, trying to get something profound out of them. So what I try to do, especially since most of these students are going to be young, is I've tried to get them to think about writing seriously. I try to get them to develop their writing habits, their attention to their skill, and their editing abilities, so that as they get older, and as they have things to say, they will also have the words to say them. Teaching young writers is going to be an incomplete task. You always have to wait for them to age. Jean Cocteau, the French artist, said that it takes sixty years to make a man, and then he's good for nothing but dying. But I think it takes a while to make an artist.

May 11, 1993

In 1995, Smock received an Al Smith Fellowship in poetry from the Kentucky Arts Council. The journal Smock edits, *the American Voice,* celebrated its tenth anniversary, and an anthology of poems from its pages, *The American Voice Anthology of Poetry,* was published by the University Press of Kentucky in 1998. In the spring of 1997, Larkspur Press published his book of poems, *Gardencourt,* and, that fall, Smock began dividing his teaching between the University of Louisville and Bellarmine College. He now teaches at Bellarmine College, exclusively, and he reviews books for Louisville's *Courier-Journal.* An excerpt from Smock's unpublished novella, "Anonymous: A Memoir," is scheduled to appear in the anthology, *Kentucky Voices. The American Voice* ceased publishing with issue No. 50, and in its place The Kentucky Foundation for Women inaugurated a literature program that sponsors a journal of regional writing, *The Hopscotch Annual,* which Smock co-edits.

BOOKS BY FREDERICK SMOCK

12 Poems. Monterey, Ky.: Larkspur Press, 1991.

This Meadow of Time, A Provence Journal. Louisville, Ky.: The Sulgrave Press, 1995.

Gardencourt: Poems. Monterey, Ky.: Larkspur Press, 1997.

Frank Steele

STEELE: I am Frank Pettus Steele, Jr., and I was born in 1935 in Tuscaloosa, Alabama.

My father's name was Frank Steele, Sr. He was a hardware salesman in Tuscaloosa. And my mother was Zeila Stovall, originally, and she was a piano teacher in Tuscaloosa. I don't have any brothers or sisters. My grandfather on my mother's side was James B. Stovall, who was a Presbyterian minister and superintendent of schools in Bibb County, Alabama. He died in 1917 in an accident, and my grandmother had the job of raising her five children, four daughters and a son, alone on a sort of pension she got after the accidental death. And, oh, they grew up and became teachers and home economists and social workers and various things.

On the other side of the family, my grandfather Steele—whom I didn't know, he died when I was four—was a tax collector in Bibb County, Alabama. His wife, my grandmother, Effie Elizabeth Fowler Stovall, was a school teacher until she married him and began to have children. I think that was her third marriage; she had lost a couple of husbands, and he had lost a wife or two. In this particular marriage she had five sons and a daughter. They were people fairly prominent in the community, and they became things like hospital administrators.

BEATTIE: Do you remember particular incidents or anecdotes connected to them and your childhood?

STEELE: On the Steele side I remember Uncle Wallace, who became Secretary of Agriculture for the state of Alabama. One of the things that he sort of communicated, without many words, to me was how much he loved the land. I really felt that strongly, and that has entered into me in some kind of way so it's in my writing. On the other side of the family, an aunt is Ruth Stovall, who was for many years State Supervisor of Vocational Home Economics for Alabama. She was somebody who gave me a lot of guidance in my early years and teen years when I hadn't the slightest idea who I was or what I was meant to do or anything. I was an only child, so I needed a lot of guidance.

BEATTIE: What do you remember about your childhood?

STEELE: I'm not sure I really had a childhood. What happened was that I went to the movies all the time, when I wasn't in school. I just had a tremendous, absorbing, nostalgic interest in everything about movies that goes back to the age of six.

BEATTIE: Do you ever consider, as a career, something related to the movies?

STEELE: Oh, yes, sure. I wanted to play Tarzan when I was about nine. I was sure that I would. It didn't happen, somehow. But actually, I've been in a movie or two. I was in a movie with Elvis Presley, whom I knew in the service. It was a movie called *The G.I. Blues.* Terrible film. But I was an extra and did some stunt work in that film. I was in the army at the time, and some of the guys who just happened to be in the right place at the right time got to be in the movie. So I did fulfill that ambition a little bit. I made ten dollars a day and took a trip up the Rhine River in Germany with my wife and had a wonderful time.

BEATTIE: Did you think your going to so many movies as a child helped with your interest in literature or fiction?

STEELE: It sort of complemented it. The time that I wasn't in a movie house, I was in the public library reading, oh, thousands of adventure books and things, you know. But I wasn't all that literary. Actually, I was much more interested in athletics when I was a kid. I played a little football in high school, and basketball, and I was convinced that I should be a coach of some sort, and I majored in that stuff when I went to college. I started out as a physical education major. It wasn't until about my third year of college that I switched over and became an English major, and that's because I had a really inspirational teacher named Stephen Mooney, who was a poet and was very helpful to me. He began to show me that literature wasn't all that bad, really. I had hated the stuff in high school, except for just adventure/escape kind of literature.

BEATTIE: What was your early education like, and did any particular subjects emerge as favorites?

STEELE: I liked softball a lot as a subject and, mainly, elementary school passed without incident. It was fun, I enjoyed it, and nothing much happened. Those first six years went by, somehow. I started school a year early, I think, because my mother wanted to get me out of the house. She was teaching piano and having to travel to schools and various places and was having to get people to stay with me. I was a very mediocre student. I got by, but I was completely undistinguished and relatively lost. I was asking people for advice: "What do you think I should major in?" And they would say, "Well, business, of course. Every fool knows that." And somehow, I never could take business. But I could imagine coaching, so I started in to do that.

BEATTIE: So, you wanted something with adventure?

STEELE: Oh, yes. I went to the University of Alabama, which is in Tuscaloosa. It was right out my back door, so I just walked out the door and went to college. I entered school in 1952, and it took me a long time of deciding on majors and dropping out for a while. I went off and actually taught somewhere for a year in the middle of all that, on some kind of emergency teaching certificate. Then I came back and completed my work, and then I went into the army because I was drafted. I think I finally graduated with a bachelor's degree in 1960. It took about eight years to get me a degree. I didn't know who or what I was. It took me a long time, and there was a wonderful girl that I kept going with and chasing all over the country. It was awfully difficult, for me, to be deeply in love for the first time and confused about what I wanted to do, switching from one thing to another, taking opportunities that came up. I just sort of wandered around until I finally graduated.

BEATTIE: And this English teacher you referred to, how was he influential?

STEELE: He was thrilling to be in a classroom with. If I was bored, or had just eaten and was too full, I went into his classroom and suddenly my mind came alive. I didn't know there *was* a mind in there, even. But I would go out of his class just dizzy with complicated thoughts that led to other thoughts, layers upon layers of thoughts. That was just a wonderful awakening for me. Then I discovered that he actually wrote poems, and he showed some of them to me. And that was a marvelous discovery for me, that somebody actually alive wrote poems. I thought only people like Longfellow had written poems. Stephen Mooney was a terrific teacher. He was a person who could just do anything. He could compose music, build houses, paint, write poems, teach. Just a really social kind of individual who stayed around in my life. He was really a mentor. He left the University of Alabama and went to the University of Tennessee and sort of issued a summons to me to come there and do some graduate work. So I did, and I took a doctorate at the University of Tennessee. Prior to doing my doctoral work, I had taught in Chattanooga for four years at a private military high school, and during that time I went on and got a master's at the University of Chattanooga, because it was right out the back door. Stephen Mooney also had moved around a lot. He was at the University of Tennessee at Martin, and he said, "Come on over and finish your doctorate and we'll start a poetry journal." So I did, and we started the *Tennessee Poetry Journal* in 1967. It became pretty well known. A cousin of mine named Ben Thomas was the third editor. So it's sort of all in the family.

BEATTIE: When you were teaching at the military school, did you enjoy teaching?

STEELE: I had a wonderful time at Baylor School. I was teaching English. I had about five classes a day, and I coached. I fulfilled that ambition in the afternoon. I didn't have any choice because every teacher coached. I coached all the things that I had had courses in as an undergraduate, plus some things that I had not had courses in. They gave me a textbook and said, "You will be the driving instructor."

BEATTIE: Did you think then that you would want to continue teaching?

STEELE: Yes. It hadn't occurred to me that I was going to teach until I met Steve Mooney, but I made him a kind of model. He was an excellent teacher, and I gradually came to see that I'd rather teach than coach. He put me in touch with what was going to last me for the rest of my life.

BEATTIE: Was it when you met Stephen Mooney that you started reading literature?

STEELE: Yes. I read books that he pointed out, and those books led to other books. I entered into a kind of life-long reading program. I'm still in it.

BEATTIE: You mentioned having been in the army. What time period was that in relation to your teaching at that school?

STEELE: That was in 1958, before I even had a bachelor's degree. It was pre-Vietnam and post-Korea; I was sort of between wars, yet the draft was still going on. I think I may have gotten drafted because of low grades. I was in Germany for about a year and a half. I took all the army battery of tests and tested out pure clerical in every area. People like that were always sent either to the infantry or to heavy-truck driving school. So, I wound up being able to drive everything that doesn't have tracks, and I knew that that wasn't exactly what I wanted to do with those two years. So I went AWOL one Saturday morning. I commandeered a jeep and drove to Frankfurt, Germany, and walked into the public information office, which put out a newspaper, and invented myself a newspaper background in America, which was totally fictitious. I said that I would just be ever-so-happy if they would transfer me out of heavy-truck driving into public information, which is where I thought I belonged. I managed to survive, somehow. Nobody ever checked on my background, fortunately. In those days nobody checked. It was the wonderful thing about the late fifties; you could get away with anything. I did things in those years that frighten me to think of now. That was a wild, strange time of being twenty-three years old.

BEATTIE: You said you knew Elvis Presley then.

STEELE: Yes, we went through basic training together at Fort Hood, Texas, and I knew him slightly. Then, when I was in Germany, putting out *Spearhead,* the newspaper for the Third Armored Division, Elvis would come in occasionally to do a poster for the crippled child for that year or some other public information activity. It was while we were all there together that the army decided they would allow Paramount Pictures to come and film background scenes for the movie to be released after Elvis was released from the army. There's a kind of byzantine logic that the army follows. The logic is that "We can't allow Elvis to appear in the film, because that would give a bad impression to the people back home. Therefore, we will select a double for Elvis, also in service, but he doesn't matter because he's not famous. And we'll use him in the background scenes. We'll use Third Armored tanks, material, guns, everything, and we'll write the whole movie off as a training exercise." That was their logic. And our PIO [Public Information Officer] leader was the technical advisor for the film, so everybody in the office who worked on the newspaper got to be in the movie.

BEATTIE: Did you ever know Elvis Presley well enough to have a conversation with him?

STEELE: Yes. I had to release things to the national media about Elvis. *Time* magazine would call and ask how Elvis was doing, and this would be at ten o'clock in the morning. The preceding evening we would have had an alert in the German woods at three o'clock in the morning, and we would all have driven out on country roads and played soldier. "The Russians are coming," *that* game. "They're coming through the gap and we have to prepare." So we went through training exercises. I remember riding in a jeep with Elvis somewhere far off in the misty German woods, at four o'clock in the morning, and Elvis would say something like, "This ..." and then he'd let out a string of truck-driver expletives, which he knew because he'd *been* a truck driver, and it all ended with "army." He hated the army thoroughly. It was costing him millions of dollars a year to be in the service, but he was doing it. So when *Time* would call the following morning after we got back from the alert, I would say, "Private Presley is doing extremely well. He's a well-adjusted soldier. He's very happy and proud to be serving his country. He's a normal soldier who works in the motor pool every day and ..." I went on and on like that. It was not true at all.

BEATTIE: Was this when you started to invent fiction? Was your work on the newspaper in the army the first writing you did outside of academic writing?

STEELE: I think it was. I may have written a few little would-be poems, which I have suppressed long since. But I suspect that that was the first thing that even remotely resembled professional writing I'd ever done.

BEATTIE: The discipline of the writing you had to do as a journalist, do you think that helped your writing?

STEELE: I'm sure it did. It taught me how to be economical, how to get things said in a hurry, how to load sentences with information that was necessary and exclude information that was irrelevant. And it taught me how to do things fast. There was always a deadline. I got to the point where I could make writing move, if nothing else.

BEATTIE: Did you have to teach yourself journalism, or were there people who helped you?

STEELE: A little of both. By that time, I was a fairly apt student, especially around writing. I'd been to college and had had a lot of writing courses of one kind or another, and I liked writing. I also just looked at what other people were doing and imitated it as well as I could.

BEATTIE: Did you ever contemplate journalism as a career?

STEELE: I had thought about it. I forgot to mention this, but part of my wandering in college was, at one point, I had the idea that I was going to be a journalist, and I took some courses in that, so I did have a little background in it. I was interested in the idea of being a foreign correspondent, or something romantic like that. But by the time I had had two or three journalism courses, I was pretty sick of it, because I went into a journalism course and the professor said, "Well, I can teach any fool to write, it's very simple." And he told me about the inverted pyramid principle and other things like that. It's all a matter of simple mechanical rules. By the time I'd done that for fifteen minutes, I was getting a little weary, because I knew that writing was more than that. So I got out of journalism and into English.

BEATTIE: When did you meet your wife?

STEELE: I met her in Steve Mooney's class. She was his star student.

BEATTIE: You got a lot out of that class.

STEELE: I *did* get a lot out of Steve Mooney's class. And my future wife and I began to go together, and we married just before I went into the army. I took her with me over to Germany, and we lived off-post.

After I came back from Germany I still had the job of graduating from Alabama. So I spent a summer there finishing up course work, and then moved to Chattanooga, and I had four years of preparatory school teaching at Baylor. Then my wife and I went to Knoxville, where Steve Mooney had moved, and I did a doctorate there and taught at Webb School of Knoxville for three years. Then I went to UT [University of Tennessee]-Martin for one year. After that, I came to Kentucky. I seem to be moving North.

BEATTIE: What was the subject of your master's thesis?

STEELE: Carson McCullers. I did something called "The Manipulation of Character Types in the Work of Carson McCullers." I studied her fiction. It taught me something that I had not known, which is what it's like to do something fairly lengthy. I had never done a long piece of writing that was seventy-five pages or so. All my papers were fifteen pages, and I was used to batting them out in two or three hours. But I learned a little something there. Then, when I came to the dissertation, I learned even more, because that turned out to be four hundred pages. That was an edition of Tennessee poets that I assembled, really a kind of anthology I had intended for high schools, an anthology of modern Tennessee poets. I had an introduction to each one and a bibliography. I was still thinking high school at that point. It remains unpublished and probably always will, but it got me a doctorate, so I was happy. It was a combination of the old Fugitive poets, John Crowe Ransom and Donald Davidson and people like that, with more recent southern Tennessee poets.

BEATTIE: Most of the Fugitives had left Vanderbilt by the time you were there.

STEELE: They had all gone, except for Donald Davidson, who remained down there so that Jim Wayne Miller could study with him. No, that's not really true, but he was the only remaining Fugitive; the others all went North.

BEATTIE: Had you decided in college that American literature was going to be your primary area of study?

STEELE: I was completely indecisive about everything, but Steve Mooney said that American literature was where it was at. So I wrote that down and decided that I would get into American literature. And I did, pretty much.

BEATTIE: When you were in graduate school, what was your wife doing?

STEELE: She was teaching piano, privately. There's an echo in my life, or something, I don't know. My mother taught piano, and I married a girl who had a major in English and a minor in piano. But she gave piano lessons privately, and studied piano for those years that I was in graduate school. Also, we had two children, who were growing up, so there was a lot of responsibility there. Carolyn was born in 1960, and Nancy came along in 1962. Those are the two daughters. Later, when we went to Martin for the year, Peg took off to Murray State University and completed a master's degree in English, which she had always wanted to do. So, she has her master's and, like me, she teaches at Western Kentucky University.

BEATTIE: After you received your doctorate, what did you do?

STEELE: Looked for a job and found one at Western. I have been there ever since. I'm verging onto retirement, or beginning to think about it, anyway.

BEATTIE: And when you were hired at Western Kentucky University, what were you hired to teach?

STEELE: American literature. But a little bit of this, and a little bit of that. I taught whatever I was told to teach. After about a year, the director of freshman English left and went to Georgia, and they made me acting director of freshman English. I don't know how I fell into that. But they approached me and said, "Would you like to try this for a while?" And I said, "Well, sure, why not?" I got into that and became director of freshman English and stayed in that for thirteen years.

BEATTIE: I wanted to ask you about your publishing career. You talked about having written a couple of poems before going into the service. Was that during college?

STEELE: Yes. I had done a little bit of writing; I'd taken some creative writing classes at the University of Alabama and had begun to write poems. I had had one or two published in some little Methodist magazine. Then, when I got to the University of Tennessee, I had some work in the Tennessee creative writing magazine for students. I won some kind of prize, and I think there was money involved. I think I won fifty dollars for a poem. Oh, I was thrilled out of my mind. I thought, "The future looms, and I'm bound to succeed. I'm the next James Dickey." I thought that for a while. I mention Dickey, because he was probably the most prominent figure around in the sixties. He was *the* southern poet at that time. But I went on and began to write more and more poems, in addition to teaching, and to try to place them here or place them there, and I was not very successful at all. But that developed, little by little. And after Mooney and I began the *Tennessee Poetry Journal,* it became a little easier somehow, because I got to know people all over the place. And when you get into that, the world of poetry, it *is* a world. It has politics and weather and all kinds of interesting things. There are meetings that occur all over the place, and people come to the meetings, and you gradually get to know who they are and what's going on.

BEATTIE: You talk about getting into the world. What did that involve for you?

STEELE: One day I received a letter from Ted Kooser, whom I'd never heard of. He's a Nebraska poet. He wanted some of my work. He had seen it in some magazine, so I sent him some, and he put it into his own magazine. Later, he did a whole series of books and got to be very well known all over the country. He's a good poet. He's an insurance executive, of all things—vice-president of an insurance company, like Wallace Stevens. We've developed a friendship and have corresponded over the years. That's just one example. I got to know Michael Cuttihee, who edited *Ironwood* for a long time. He wrote to me and asked for something, and so I sent it, and things just sort of coalesced. I haven't published in the *Atlantic* and the *New Yorker* and *Harper's*. I mean, mine has not been that kind of career. But there is a sub-culture world of poetry that's pretty vital, that's just really going on like blazes, over all the country.

BEATTIE: How did you select the first places you sent your poems?

STEELE: I would hear by word of mouth what was good and what was not good, and what I must have on my shelf. I couldn't live another minute without it. I knew that I had to have *The Sixties* that Robert Bly was editing in Minnesota, because if you didn't have that, you weren't even alive in the sixties. That was one of the main directions that everybody's thinking was going. So I got that. I never published anything there, although, after Robert Bly stopped publishing *The Sixties,* he did accept a poem of mine for a journal that he was going to entitle "The Seventies." It never came out.

BEATTIE: Did you start doing poetry readings in the sixties?

STEELE: Yes. The first reading I ever gave was in '69. I read at SAMLA [Southern Association of the Modern Language Association]. It was the first poetry reading ever given at SAMLA, as a matter of fact. It was in Atlanta, and I think I read very badly. But still, that was a reading. And I've had a few since then, here and there.

BEATTIE: What about poetry workshops or conferences? Did you start going to those in the sixties?

STEELE: Yes, I have been to a lot of them. I've been to a lot of places all over the country, studying creative writing in one way or another.

BEATTIE: As a student or as an instructor?

STEELE: I have not taught much at those things. One that's been pretty steady for me has been Robert Bly's conference. I've been to his Great Mother Conference, which moves all over the country, and has been going on since 1974. I started attending that regularly in '81, and have been to ten of them or so. It's an interesting and wild and fruitful sort of experience. Bly will always pick a little YMCA camp somewhere far out in the wilderness. It's always trouble to get there. He thinks that's very important, that you should have some difficulty arriving at the conference. If you just simply fly there, then he thinks that you're probably becoming more infantile as you travel. But if you have to walk and carry a suitcase a certain distance, then you're becoming more adult as you travel.

BEATTIE: I guess he could have his conference at the Altanta Airport and fulfill all of those requirements.

STEELE: Well, it's not rustic enough, though. But you get out there and, by golly, William Stafford or some major kind of figure in poetry will be present, or some psychological thinker like James Hillman or Marian Woodman. There'll be some wonderful people who are the honchos in that conference. My wife, Peg, is now one of the conveners of that conference, and she has been for the last year. There are a lot of musicians, there are a lot of painters and a lot of poets. A lot of Jungian psychologists will attend Bly's conferences. And to see those people mix with each other in creative ways is a kind of exciting experience. It's sort of avant garde. We'll talk about something at the conference, and three years later it'll come to the attention of national people. I mean, they'll begin to get the word. It's a little advanced.

BEATTIE: Have you found that inspirational for your own work?

STEELE: Oh, yes. I always do a lot of writing out in the woods. But I also do a lot of writing at home, or at the office, or wherever I am.

BEATTIE: I wanted to ask you about your poetry magazine, *Plainsong.* When was that founded, and how did it come about?

STEELE: Well, it's a sort of a culmination of activity. One of the things you do, if you fool around with creative writing classes and you teach creative writing, is that you get involved with writing groups, not only ones that have your students, but also just people in town who write. Peg and I have been in several of these. She runs a little group called The Capitol Arts Writers in Bowling Green, and they're just community people. Some are from the university and some are not, and we meet and share work, and we've been doing this sort of thing for a long time. In '79, we had a little group at the house, and somebody said, "Well, what about Kentucky magazines? Are they any good?" And somebody else said, "Well, why don't we find out? Why don't we write a really bad poem as a group and see if we can get it published?" So we did that. I wrote a rhyme and we passed it around, and there were some rules to this activity. One was that everything about this poem had to be bad; it could have no redeeming features at all. Secondly, it could not make any sense; it had to be totally incoherent. Thirdly, it had to have some literary echoes in it, just little touches of famous styles. With those three rules in mind, we passed it around and everybody wrote a little part, and at the end we assembled it, gave it a title, and we made up a name of a poem out of all of our initials. I was given the job of sending this around to Kentucky magazines. We found out what those publications were, and I thought, "Oh, Lord, this will take forever." But it was a prank. So I sent it off to one of the leading Kentucky magazines right away, and within two weeks it was accepted. It was actually published. We decided then that maybe it was time for another magazine in Kentucky.

We did decide to start *Plainsong* in '79, and we didn't know what to call it. Peg is the one who named it, and we were always a little bit worried about the title, because it sounds kind of Catholic. Plainsong is used in the Catholic church, and we were afraid that it might be taken as a Catholic magazine. But I checked with some Catholic friends of mine, and they said they didn't think it would matter very much. We liked the idea of plainness in writing, and song is a kind of hope that you have if you're a poet. So, it's an aspiration, sort of. But we like poems that are clear and not decorated with too much rhetoric—straightforward poems, usually short ones. There are not many journals that are champions of the short poem. But we decided that we would be. Not haiku, but poems that are about twelve lines long. So our journal has a lot of white space around the small poems. Occasionally, we'll take a longer poem, but not very often. Peg and I are *Plainsong*'s editors, and also Elizabeth Oakes, who is the Shakespeare teacher at Western, and also a poet. The three of us together have been the editors, and we've worked very smoothly together. Occasionally, one will champion a poem that the other two don't much like, and either will or will not persuade the other two editors to take the poem. We've published about fourteen issues. We've got another one cooking. It was supposed to be published twice a year, and was, for several years. We were lucky enough to get some NEA [National Endowment for the Arts] grants to support it. We had two of those to help support the magazine in the middle eighties. Since then, such financial support has become irregular. *Plainsong* became a kind of annual, but I think it's been more than one year since it's been published now. We put out an issue when we have an issue ready. Submissions come from Australia and Japan and Germany and England. We have submissions from Oregon, and a lot of work comes from California and New York and Kentucky.

We'd like to publish more Kentuckians. Any time we get something from a Kentuckian, we look at it with a very special interest. If we can put in a Kentucky poet, we will. To some extent, *Plainsong* is still flying under Steve Mooney's flag. The motto for the *Tennessee Poetry Journal* that we worked for years ago was to bring those on the outside in, and to send those on the inside out. We like that same mix. We're happy to put in big-name poets, and they're always very generous about sending their work, but we also like to feature unknown people from nearby, if we can. And that's a kind of hope. There's a strong sense of place in this journal. It's a magazine that likes to explore what place means in writing, not just in the South, but in other regions as well. Kentucky is interesting, in terms of its writers. We've been talking here a little bit about my having gone far away, and I've done that. Kentucky writers seem to be people who mainly stay fairly still. Wendell Berry goes off somewhere to the university, but then he comes home, and he stays in Port Royal and lives there. And what happens is that people come from all over the country to visit Wendell Berry and solicit his opinions. Guy Davenport is visited by people from far away. Kentucky becomes a place where other writers from other places come to to see the writer. When Gary Snyder came to give a reading at Western, he just happened to be in the area because he wanted to visit Wendell Berry and get his opinions on things. They're close, in some ways. It's just a strange sort of phenomenon. There's a rootedness about Kentucky writers.

BEATTIE: I'm wondering what Kentucky writers you may especially admire, or for whose work you have an affinity?

STEELE: I think Wendell Berry is clearly the leading poet in Kentucky. I mean, by far, by leaps and bounds. There's not another poet who is the equal of Wendell Berry today. There are a lot of poets in Kentucky. A lot of them are gifted, talented, bright, very successful. And then there's Wendell Berry. He's just done marvelous work, and not just in his poetry, but in his fiction, and in his essays, and with his interest in the environment. He's a person with a broad base and a lot of depth.

I've admired Gurney Norman, James Baker Hall, James Still. There have been many of them. I've seen a lot of their writing. Jim Hall is a friend of mine, as is, of course, Jim Wayne Miller. There are some younger ones coming along. Sallie Bingham is a friend of mine, and is very, very special in a lot of ways. She's made a tremendous contribution, I think, in Kentucky. Kentucky is a place with a lot going on. An interesting phenomenon I've observed not only with Kentucky writers, but with poets, especially, across the country, is that their lives are becoming more important to them than their work. I think that's the direction of the future.

BEATTIE: Do you feel this way about yourself and your work?

STEELE: Yes. I don't have everything based around my writing. I do a lot of writing, but I suspect that that's not the most important thing I do. If I publish, that's a fairly casual thing to me, more and more. I think, probably, my teaching is more important to me than my writing, ultimately.

BEATTIE: Do you teach creative writing?

STEELE: I teach creative writing. I have classes in American literature. I have composition classes. We teach four classes a term at Western. And, with the recent budget cuts, we never have a course-load reduction anymore. We're fairly active in the classroom. We grade a lot of papers. But, I like the teaching. I continue to enjoy students, even after all these years. If I get into a classroom and I have students, I'm usually pretty happy.

BEATTIE: How do you think creative writing should be taught?

STEELE: In a kind of friendly, encouraging way. I have a class now in editing and publishing, which has both undergraduate and graduate students. Teaching is a kind of a mystery. It's a greater mystery than writing. I don't know how people do it at all. I can't begin to describe how it happens, but I know that it's possible to do it well. I've sat in other people's classes that were brilliantly handled, and I've had a few lucky moments of my own in the classroom. I don't know how to describe teaching creative writing. Probably what we do at Western is more motherly than it needs to be. Then what happens, sometimes, is that students will go on and graduate, and they'll go off to graduate school, and they may succeed there as well, but they run into some thorniness somewhere. If we've been too motherly and tender and encouraging, they may lack a kind of toughness that they'll need later. I'm trying to correct this problem.

So, one of my tactics has been to reintroduce some old books that have to do with self-knowledge in tough situations. I'll put these into creative writing classes, or anything else. A book like Conrad's *Heart of Darkness,* which is hard for students to read, but it points exactly toward the need to know yourself. I'm putting back in *The Sacred Shadow,* and I'll use Bly's book on the shadow. He has a book about self-knowledge, the need to get to the bottom of one's own mystery. It's a book that writers need to know about. I may teach a little Carl Jung; somehow, that's important. If the psychology department wants to get after me and say I'm not qualified, they can always do that.

BEATTIE: English, I keep telling my students, is philosophy and psychology humanized.

STEELE: You bet. That's exactly the combination.

BEATTIE: Anybody who can do literary analysis is not too far from human analysis, I think.

STEELE: I agree with that. America's a dangerous place. There are a lot of programs in creative writing, more and more. There's tremendous interest in writing all over the country now, and that hasn't been there forever. Twenty years ago we had one lonely creative writing course in our program, which was for an elective. But we put in a minor in writing, and then a major in writing, and now we have graduate work in writing, and that's fairly typical of what's happened all over the country, I think. When Peg began the Capitol Arts Writers' Group, people just came out of the woodwork all over the community and joined us.

BEATTIE: Was that the first writing group in the community?

STEELE: Oh, I think there have been others. There are a lot of literary clubs in Bowling Green. But I was amazed at the number of young people, older people, middle-aged people, who just want to share their work and do some writing. That's encouraging to me. I've heard from many other writers I'm in touch with that this is happening elsewhere, as well. I can't help seeing that as good. It may be that some people are writing as a form of therapy. But writing *is* a kind of therapy. It's a sort of healing. It has a dimension that's healing.

BEATTIE: What do you think the nature of creativity itself is?

STEELE: In this country I think that it's for the purpose of survival. I think that writing is some kind of survival tactic. It's probably true of American literature as a whole. I think Nathaniel Hawthorne gives you ways to survive, if you read him carefully. And everybody's interested in that. T. S. Eliot's *The Waste Land* is about how to survive World War I.

BEATTIE: You say it's a survival tactic, but do you think it is something people are born with, or something only certain people need to or *can* acquire?

STEELE: No, I think everybody's got some creativity. Something usually kills it off around the seventh grade; I don't know what. Probably some way it's taught in school or something, but everybody's got some. And if they can ever find some way to enter the world of writing and literature, then it's easy to get hooked on it. And once you get it, it becomes one of the things you do.

BEATTIE: That's interesting. You think that people are born with creative instincts and that everybody has them, and that such instincts may leave. What

I've heard other writers say is that some people are born with it, and some people are not, and that those who are not can be taught a certain amount of creativity.

STEELE: Well, there are people for whom language is difficult or frightening. An awful lot of people are scared to death of words.

BEATTIE: Some of the people I have interviewed, such as Jim Hall and Gurney Norman and Leon Driskell, talk about creativity as something that fills a lack. They've called it a lack or a gap or a hollow.

STEELE: That's almost Freudian thinking. In my own experience, I try to keep my writing close to daily life. It's a way of trying to think through what's happening in the feeling area. When trauma comes, it's a way of dealing with that, but not always. It could be something not at all traumatic. It could be something just interesting in itself. It could be an object. It can be something from the natural world that is worth holding and thinking about. There's something that comes from the natural world that's a part of some healing thing. I don't know how this works, exactly. But if you pick up a pine cone and you look at it carefully and begin to describe it, your life will attach itself to the pine cone. The same will happen if you look at a potato for a long time or a piece of quartz or a seashell or anything that's an object that's from the natural world. There are vibrations that come from that activity that would not come if you were holding a Coke can. It's very large, very mysterious, and probably goes back to Emerson and Transcendentalism and all that business, which has been neglected for a long time. But if there's a change in the current of thinking, we have been an ironic century for a long time, and the shadow over poetry in our century has been T.S. Eliot's shadow, which was not interested at all in the natural world. You can feel a change all over, not exactly a back-to-nature movement, but a reawakening of some kind of interest in the environment and ecology and getting in touch with the earth in some important kind of way. Wendell Berry is full of this in his writings. His whole ethic is connected with uses of the earth, with the proper uses and with uses that are improper. That seems awfully important to me. So anyway, when I'm writing, I'm writing about what's going on in my life, and a lot of it is casual. I mean, it's not earthshaking or a statement of some aesthetic principle. That's not what I write.

BEATTIE: But do you feel that you are driven to write?

STEELE: It's like being right-handed. I looked at my hand when I was twelve years old, and I thought, "That's a male hand. I must be a male." And I accepted that. It was okay with me. Writing is doing the thing that the hand does. It's perfectly natural to me, and I guess I could try being left-handed, but I like being right-handed. There's a kind of acceptance of the self gradually, without being too tortured about it, and writing enters into that, too, in some way. I happen to be white. I would have more problems if I were black or Indian or Asian.

BEATTIE: So, in other words, being a writer is not something you feel you ever chose to do; it was just something you finally recognized was a fact about you.

STEELE: It took me a long time. I still have some leftover PE-major interest. I can't go to the basket anymore because I'm too old, but in a line of poetry I can feel that turn, and I know I'm going to the basket. And it's the same feeling, except that it turns into language. Having coffee water boil in the morning can be the subject of a poem. Anything can. I always write every morning, and sometimes it's absolute drivel. There's nothing, and that's okay with me. I just let it happen. And sometimes something will rise up and make itself into a poem. I'm always writing early in the morning before I'm half awake. My feeling is that there are two worlds; one of them is this one, and the other one is the other one. There's this one and the other one, and the other one goes by several names. It's religious and philosophical and aesthetic and psychological. It has heaven in it and glorious ideas and truth and wonder. I think that the two worlds are joined, and the way to get to that other one, call it by what you want to, is through the physical. I think the key thing starts with the body. It's a body thing that begins what I know about as poetry. It always goes out from some center that's physical. And that's why maybe the athletic thing comes back to me even now that I'm 800 years old.

BEATTIE: Several writers have mentioned to me that they have a real, physical hurt when they have a need to write but don't do it, and they say that pain only goes away after they have written.

STEELE: Hemingway was fond of saying, "I write to get rid of it." It comes into the mind. If you don't write, it hurts. And you have to get rid of it. It's a kind of venting, and that's true with a lot of people. I don't think that's quite as true for me, because there's not that urgency about it. See, it's okay with me if I write for five mornings and nothing emerges. I can write for two, three weeks and have it not be anything that I ever want to preserve, particularly. It's just writing. Some people read the newspaper early in the morning. Some people watch television early in the morning. Peg often will get up and play the piano early in the morning. And I get up in the morning and write.

BEATTIE: Is that the first thing you do when you get up?

STEELE: Practically.

BEATTIE: Before breakfast or anything else?

STEELE: Yes, I fill a blank paper with some words. It may be a dream I remember having, or parts of a dream, something that comes to me from a long time ago, or something someone said yesterday.

BEATTIE: Is there any particular amount of time or number of pages?

STEELE: I always have to go to school, so I'm up early. I'm talking six o'clock, 6:15. It is a kind of discipline. I would be lonely if I didn't do that. And I'm never lonely. If I get my writing done, then that's over for the day and I can go on and have the day.

BEATTIE: Do you do this every day of the week?

STEELE: Yes, unless I'm sick. But sometimes, even when I'm sick, the writing will hit very strange, if I'm taking medicine or something. I don't know what goes on, some chemical thing that enters into the writing, too.

BEATTIE: Do you write in long hand?

STEELE: Yes. Peg has a computer, but she's a fiction writer as well as a poet. Prose seems to go awfully well on the computer. Dangerously well. I mean, you get into it and suddenly you become enormously gabby. That can happen. But I don't know many poets who write on the computer. I can type pretty quickly and fluently, and yet I would never type while composing poetry. I want the feeling of the pen on the page, and it has to be a pen that I can feel the tread of on the highway. I don't want these little Flair felt pens that are so light. I want to really feel what's under me. But that's for the early morning writing. Later, I don't care. I can also do the computer a little, or write with a pencil or anything; it doesn't matter. I can think about completing a poem on the computer, once it's in some sort of form. But before it's in a form, the computer would kind of terrify me.

BEATTIE: I feel the same way, but I think it's because I feel a computer is sort of introducing a foreign element into something that's a very personal process. It almost destroys the intimacy of composition.

STEELE: Yes, intimacy is good. There is a feeling. It's like solitude. Golly, it's almost as if someone else were there. And, in a way, someone else *is* there. I don't know whose voice that is that gets onto the page. It's not the one I use in class, and it's not the child, either. It's some voice I have come to know as the one I use when I'm there with a blank page of paper in the morning, early. It's an inventive voice, I'm sure. And I'm pretty happy with it, at this stage.

September 23, 1992

Steele, who, since this interview, was selected as the first William E. Wood Professor at Western Kentucky University, has retired from his full-time professorship, but continues to teach part-time. His William E. Wood project consisted of editing and publishing two anthologies from work that had appeared in *Plainsong: The Valley Beneath Words* and *Quiet Music*. Steele now devotes as much time as possible to writing, editing, and publishing.

BOOKS BY FRANK STEELE

Poetry Explication: A Handbook with a Glossary. Taylor, Tx.: Merchants Press, 1964.

Walking to the Waterfall. Martin, Tn.: Tennessee Poetry Press, 1969.

Poems. Lincoln, Ne.: Three Sheets Press, 1972.

The Salesman. Lincoln, Ne.: Three Sheets Press, 1988.

The Valley Beneath Words: The Best of Plainsong (editor). Bowling Green, Ky.: Plainsong Press, 1995.

Quiet Music: A Plainsong Reader (editor). Bowling Green, Ky.: Plainsong Press, 1995.

MARTHA BENNETT STILES

STILES: Martha Bennett Wells Stiles is my name, and I was born March 30, 1933, in Santiago, San Juan, which is in the Philippine Islands. My mother was Jane McClintock Bennett Wells, and my father was Forrest Hampton Wells. He was a naval officer until he retired, when he got interested in teaching people who couldn't read to read. My mother was a Charlestonian [South Carolina], and my great-grandmother was also from that part of the country.

I'm the second child. I have three sisters and one brother. One sister is older, two are younger, and my brother is younger. My father was born in Booneville, Indiana, which was the town nearest the farm of my paternal great-grandfather. His mother was a Chase. His father was from southern Indiana and, when he married my grandmother, he made that his hometown since he was an orphan by that time and she wasn't.

My mother's parents, I did, of course, know. My grandmother was Susan Dunlap Adger Smythe Bennett of Charleston, South Carolina. Her husband was John Bennett of Chillicothe, Ohio, who moved south for his health, and having married a Charleston girl, made Charleston his home. He was a writer. In fact, he's being inducted into the South Carolina Academy of Authors on March 20th, which is nice.

BEATTIE: What did your grandfather write?

STILES: Oh, he wrote various scholarly things, and he wrote children's books. He wrote *Master Skylark*. It's the most famous children's book that he wrote. He wrote *The Doctor to the Dead,* which was a collection of gullah folk tales, African folk tales.

BEATTIE: Do you remember him?

STILES: Oh, dearly. I adored him.

BEATTIE: Do you think your writing has anything to do with having been around him or having been influenced by him?

STILES: Yes, I imagine that a child whose grandfather is writing children's books grows up realizing that that's something that one can do. There were a lot of jobs I could have held, happily, that never crossed my mind. But writing for children, I knew that was there, because Grandfather did it.

BEATTIE: What was your childhood like?

STILES: Well, if I were a novelist, I would write about it.

BEATTIE: Have you?

STILES: Not much. One reason I write children's books is that writing in that genre preserves the family's privacy. I think my family likes its privacy, and my writing children's books reassures them. Also, I am very reserved, and there's nothing that one writes about for children that I'm uncomfortable writing about.

BEATTIE: Where did you grow up?

STILES: Well, I had my first birthday on the ship coming home from China, so I don't remember the Orient. I grew up in Virginia.

BEATTIE: What part of Virginia?

STILES: Tidewater. Isle of Wight County. I grew up on a so-called farm. I guess it was a farm. We had sheep, and I sheared and butchered and milked goats and all that. We had dairy goats and sheep and bees and pigeons and an orchard, and we lived on a fifty-foot bluff. The river was seven miles wide in front of the house. It was a beautiful place to grow up. Farm children, particularly if their fathers are naval officers, are kept busy, which has its good and its bad aspects. I didn't have time to develop my talent. I really would as much have liked to be an illustrator as a writer. But you can write in snatches better than you can paint in snatches, and you don't need money or space for writing. For painting or drawing, you need paper and you need pastels or water colors or brushes. You need a place to store all this stuff. You need to be able to do it when the light is thus-and-so. To be a writer, you can do it on one end of the table, and I did, once I started writing, which I didn't until I was married.

BEATTIE: What was your early education like?

STILES: I went to Smithfield, which is five miles from what was then my home. I rode the school bus to the elementary school and walked across the street. There was the little school and the big school. Neither exists anymore.

BEATTIE: Did you have a favorite subject?

STILES: Oh, English. Well, I liked drawing very much, and my second grade teacher let me draw on the blackboards all I wanted to. The big thing in first and second grade is trying to teach people to read and write, and I learned to read quickly because my father taught me before I started school, lest I be ruined in school, because in school they weren't teaching phonics at that time. He felt that you would never learn to read if you didn't learn phonics. So I knew how to read already, and printing was easy for me because I just copied. I couldn't write. I have dreadful handwriting to this day, probably because I skipped a grade. I was enough ahead in class that the teacher let me read all I wanted while she was trying to teach my classmates to read, some of whom probably had parents who couldn't read, and many of whom came from homes with no books. So nobody noticed that I couldn't write worth diddly squat and that I didn't know the multiplication tables. They said, "Oh, she's so far advanced, let her skip," and I did. I don't think it was a good idea. I learned the multiplication tables as a sophomore in college, and I definitely suffered in between from not knowing them. I hadn't the foggiest idea how to learn them.

BEATTIE: Were you read to a lot at home?

STILES: Oh, yes. Both my parents read to us.

BEATTIE: When did you start writing on your own?

STILES: After I was married. I wrote what I was required to write for school. Then, sometimes in class, when I was bored, I would start writing jingles. My grandfather, of course, always thought they were marvelous, and they were *not* marvelous.

BEATTIE: What was high school like for you?

STILES: Miserable, socially. Nothing mattered except did a boy ask you out. Or did a boy give you a ride in a car. Or did a boy buy you a Coca-Cola. None of these things happened to me in high school, and every year I thought, "It might happen *this* year." I tried this and that, all irrelevant, and oh, I felt ugly and disagreeable and despicable. And I *was* ugly and disagreeable. I had no idea that I could fix all this by just smiling and speaking to people. But, when I got to college, everything was marvelous. Brave new world. Never had another moment's trouble.

BEATTIE: You said you worked for a year between high school and college. What did you do?

STILES: I was a telephone operator. I didn't leave home. I graduated when I was sixteen, and I had no money to go to college, and my father had informed me that I was to be a nurse. I didn't wish to be a nurse, but that's what he said, so I assumed I was to be a nurse. I was very anxious to leave home. I was very anxious to get out and go to Norfolk General Hospital, and the administrators there said they would waive the requirement that I be, I forget how old, and permit me to begin my coursework at sixteen. But my parents concluded that I was not mature enough, and they were quite right. I thought, "Well, one house is not big enough for three adults, so I've got to get a job. I've got to get out of here." My father was retired. He was at home twenty-four hours a day, and I thought we'd quarrel, and then, I thought, the sky would fall. I mean, the idea that I would shout back at my father, I didn't imagine *what* would happen. It was just abysmal. Like in my book, *Kate of Still Waters.* She doesn't imagine what will happen beyond this terrible disaster. It's just the abyss. So, I thought I better get a job. I would ride my bicycle five miles in to the telephone company, and ride my bicycle out five miles so my mother would give me lunch, and I wouldn't have to pay for it. I would ride my bicycle back five miles. It didn't do my weight a bit of good, and it didn't make my legs strong. Anyway, I saved all my money because my family kindly didn't cause me any expenses.

BEATTIE: The father, in *Kate of Still Waters,* does he have any of the characteristics of your father?

STILES: Well, there's one little speech in that book that *is* my father's speech, the speech about the helpless sheep. That speech was in there, and my editor at Macmillan, Judy Whipple, a nice woman, suggested certain cuts, and that was one of the cuts. So I cut it. Then, I just could not rest, having cut that speech. It just had to go back in, and I'm glad it went back in. I wanted to be helpful, that's why

I wrote those books. I wanted to help compulsive children like me who think in terms of the abyss. Failure, that's the end. I wanted my character Kate to learn this. Then I wanted to show the effect of strain on the family.

This was not the case with my family. My mother didn't get a job. My family didn't grow apart, but *Kate of Still Waters* wasn't my idea. My husband said, "You should write about the farm crisis because, nowadays, most people don't live on farms. You are in a minority as a book writer who lives on a farm. You understand these problems, and most writers don't. You should write about this." This was in the middle of the farm crisis. I was suffering just as much as anybody else in the farm crisis. We were feeding more hay in August than we normally feed in January. You don't normally feed any hay in August. It was hard. I heard a woman on the radio. She was someone who counseled children who were having trouble in school. She lived in the farm belt, and she was saying it's hard here because the children are coming to school tired. They're doing more chores at home because the father has taken a job off the farm, or the mother has taken a job and she hasn't had a job since the children came, and the children are not getting their homework done the way they should. They're tired and they're also worried because their parents feel anxiety, because maybe the mother's bringing in more money than the father. The parents are wondering how they're going to meet the payments, and this translates into strain between the parents, and that frightens the children. Are they going to break up? What's going to become of this family? I thought, "Oh, man, I know I should write this book. I should write this book and try to be a little bit reassuring." Just as in *Sarah the Dragon Lady*, I have Mrs. Demeter say, "Well, how many more years are you going to be living at home in this difficult situation?" You know, children think home goes on forever. They think, if they're being pushed around at home, that's life. Years seem so long to children because they have had so few. I mean, if you're twelve, then two years is one-sixth of your life, and if someone says to you, "Well, don't worry, it's only two more years," the child is thinking, "One-sixth of my life." That's a long time. Two years is a long time. It's hard to get across to a child how very few years remain in a difficult family situation, and a lot of children need to be told that, although I'm sure they can't absorb it. If you're an alcoholic's child and some social worker tells you, "Work, work, work, and get out of here," I don't know that they take much hope from that, but maybe one will. It was for people like that that I wrote *Sarah the Dragon Lady*.

BEATTIE: I think what is also so good about *Kate of Still Waters* is that it's not just a book written for children or adolescents who grew up on farms; any child of that age under any similar psychological circumstance can relate to the book.

STILES: I'm glad you say that. That's very reassuring and comforting and flattering. Obviously, the milieu was the farm, but all parents are going to scrap sometimes, and it's not the end of the world, and quarelling can be for this reason and that reason.

BEATTIE: Back to your schooling. What made you decide to go to The College of William and Mary? Had you decided you didn't want to be a nurse?

STILES: Oh, I never wanted to be a nurse. As a result of working, after about one paycheck, I toted up and I went to my mother and I said, "A year of this would be a year of college." She said, "Oh, I wondered when you'd realize that." I thought, "Well, if you did, why didn't you tell me?" I just put all the money in the bank. I used that for a year of college and, after that, I worked and had scholarships. I got a UDC [United Daughters of the Confederacy] scholarship.

Well, as to why I went to William and Mary, I could afford it. I would have liked to have gone to the University of Virginia, but they didn't permit women students. Unless you were a nursing student, you couldn't go there, and I didn't want to go to a girls' school. I wanted to date. I wanted to get married and have children. That was my life's ambition. Well, I wanted to graduate from college. I was absolutely set on that. But then I wanted to get married and have children. That is what I wanted to do. And I wasn't going to any girls' school, and my shortage of funds meant that going to a state-subsidized school like William and Mary was open to me, and it was a good school. When I transferred to the University of Michigan, I didn't have to work a bit harder to get the same grades. We were academically challenged at William and Mary. Attending school there was a brave new world, as I said. I loved it.

BEATTIE: What made you go from William and Mary to Michigan?

STILES: Well, as the drunk said when he woke up in traction, "It seemed like a good idea at the time." Michigan had a lot to offer. I was a chemistry major, and we simply didn't have the number of chemistry courses I wanted at William and Mary. But the University of Michigan paid off in other subjects, also. For instance, English. I very much liked my English teachers. I had never had, in my life, an English teacher who enriched the reading the way mine did when I got to the University of Michigan. My idea of an English class had been, "Fine. We're all told what to read and we all read it, and my opinion is as good as anybody's." It didn't occur to me that the professor knew more about what we had just read than I did, because I had read it, too. Unfortunately, I was a chemistry major, but for electives, I took English, and it was wonderful.

BEATTIE: So you just knew, in Virginia, that the University of Michigan had a reputation for being good?

STILES: No. At William and Mary, I had a professor named J.T. Baldwin, and he had been on the staff of the University of Michigan. My freshman year, I took his botany course. So I wasn't a chemistry major when I entered college. I made that decision later. Baldwin was very dear to me. He was our son's godfather. I'm mentioning that to indicate a special place he occupies in our hearts. When it was decided that I should look around, he wrote the President's [of the University of Michigan] assistant, Frank Robbins, who was a friend of his, and said, "Would you take her? She has five A's, and she is supporting herself." Robbins went to the Dean of Women and said, "Would you take her?" The Dean of Women said, "I will take her if William and Mary's Dean of Women telephones me and asks me to." You see, it was past time to ask to come. I came in February of my sophomore year. In other words, I went for a year and a half to William and Mary, and it was too late to apply. In fact, I missed orientation and that was very serious for me. Anyhow, the Deans of Women spoke to one another, and they put me on the train. Weeping. I had never been homesick in my life, but I learned about that my first semester at Michigan.

BEATTIE: Did you get scholarships at Michigan, as well?

STILES: Oh, yes. Not the first semester. My father went to the bank and borrowed the money to get me through that first semester at Michigan, because now, of course, I was paying out-of-state tuition. My expenses went up enormously when I transferred. But my father went to the bank and borrowed the money, and I paid him back, but he never charged me interest.

BEATTIE: So your parents were supportive of your transferring?

STILES: Oh yes. My mother was always supportive, and my father . . . anytime I was annoyed with my father, I would remember: "You owe him; you owe him because he didn't even want you to go to college. He wanted you to be a nurse." He backed me because he saw it was going to make me happy.

BEATTIE: And what was your plan in terms of majoring in chemistry? What did you think you would do with the degree after graduation?

STILES: I went to work for duPont. I wanted to support myself. I wanted to eat. I had no aptitude for chemistry whatsoever, but I was an extremely hard worker. I do have some aptitude for logic. In analytical trigonometry, for example, I was very good. I was very good because it was just cold, firm logic. But so far as having any scientific aptitude, if I had remained a chemist for three hundred years, I never would have had an original idea, I'm sure, in my life. Never. To be a research chemist, you have to be as creative as to be a poet. And I lack it in that field, that spark. I think, in any art, you can get so far on learning the logic and working, and then from somewhere that you can't identify comes something that propels you across an empty space. I think it's just a question of your particular brain, of what's in there, of what you are like genetically. I have students who ask me extremely pedestrian questions: "How do you construct a scene?" They want a manual. I look at them; I haven't the foggiest idea how to give them a manual which will enable them to follow one, two, three, four steps and construct a scene, because I don't do it that way. I just write down what I think is necessary of what I am seeing, and later I see that I have put in a lot that wasn't necessary, and I try to take that out. Later I reread it, and it's published already, and it's too late, and I see that there's stuff in there that wasn't necessary, and also that there were things that I was seeing, and so assumed the reader was seeing, and the reader wasn't seeing them at all.

BEATTIE: You met your husband at the University of Michigan. What was he doing there?

STILES: My senior year, he came as a post-doctoral fellow. He was working for my advisor, as a matter of fact.

BEATTIE: In what field?

STILES: Chemistry. I knew he was coming before he came, and he helped me with my German and my organic chemistry. We met in September of '53 and we married in September of '54. I worked for duPont until I married. duPont was in Richmond, Virginia. I had accepted that job before I was engaged to my husband. So, when I arrived and told them that I was engaged and was going to quit in September, they were a bit disturbed.

BEATTIE: When you married, where did you live?

STILES: In Ann Arbor. My husband joined the faculty of the University of Michigan in 1955. Prior to that, he'd been a post-doc, looking for an academic job.

BEATTIE: How long did you live there?

STILES: Until 1977.

BEATTIE: And what brought you to Kentucky?

STILES: Horses.

BEATTIE: Was this something that had been an interest of both of yours for a long time?

STILES: No. His.

BEATTIE: Did he retire, then, from teaching?

STILES: No, he took a leave of absence for a year, and at the end of the year he took a leave of absence for another year, and at the end of that year he resigned. He was a lot too young to retire. He hasn't retired yet, as a matter of fact.

BEATTIE: How have you liked Kentucky?

STILES: Oh, everyone likes Kentucky. Kentucky's very kind to writers. Very helpful. Gracious. The Frankfort Arts Foundation, are you familiar with the work they do, the books they publish and the contests they sponsor, and the encouragement they give and the speakers they sponsor? The Kentucky Arts Council does more than giving these Al Smith Fellowships, which I'm very grateful to have received. It sponsors residencies in the schools, which I took advantage of.

BEATTIE: Actually, you won college prizes, didn't you, for poetry, and then for essays?

STILES: Well, come to think of it, when I was at William and Mary, I worked on the college literary magazine and, at the end of my freshman year, it turned out that there was a prize or scholarship given to the student who had contributed what the committee decided was the best work that year. They gave it to me—probably because I needed the money. I don't think my work was so hot, but I got the money. It was the James Bryant Hope Memorial Scholarship, and I was glad to have it. And, let's see, at the University of Michigan, when I was in school, I didn't have time for writing. In fact, I never set foot in the library, hardly.

BEATTIE: When did you make the transition from chemistry to writing?

STILES: When somebody else was willing to feed me. Chemistry was a job; writing was for fun. So when I moved into a two-room apartment and didn't need a job, and even the yard was looked after by the maintenance man, then my husband went downtown and bought me a second-hand typewriter for eighty-six dollars. We put it on one end of the table. We extended the table full-length, and there I worked. When we had company for supper, we carried the typewriter in and put it on the bedroom floor.

BEATTIE: What did you first start writing? Was it children's books?

STILES: Yes. Well, yes and no. The first story I published was in *Humpty Dumpty Magazine.* Then I was working on a story which eventually became *The Strange House at Newburyport.* What I did was take a course from John Muehl at the University of Michigan and work on assignments for his class. I didn't publish an adult short story—in fact, I didn't publish again—after the story in *Humpty Dumpty Magazine,* I didn't sell another thing until January, 1959, when I published a story in the *Virginia Quarterly Review.* I can't remember whether I wrote that for John Muehl or not. I must have, because I kept on going to him. First to him and then to Allan Seagar, and, somewhere in there, to Robert Haugh. Eventually, I was able to take a summer course from Joyce Carol Oates.

BEATTIE: What about your publishing history? You published first children's books and short stories, as well as articles. Was it a conscious choice to begin writing children's literature for the reasons you stated earlier?

STILES: In the first place, I wasn't ambitious, and, therefore, I didn't have a plan. I was doing something to have something to do until the babies came, and it pleased me to have something to do, which I was going to be able to continue after the babies came. This was something which could be done at home. So I never had a game plan. If I had an idea that appealed to me, then I would write that. If that was a humorous article for *Esquire,* or a travel article for the *New York Times,* or a story about a duck who had to get ice skates because the pond was frozen, or a story about a girl who has to cut the head off a newborn kid, then I wrote that. It was not the wisest way to get ahead, but I didn't know I was going to want to get ahead, because I didn't know I wasn't going to have children. If I had known I wasn't going to have children, I would go back and choose one.

BEATTIE: I'm particularly interested in the social commentary in your young adult books, which ranges from the personal, in such books as *Sarah the Dragon Lady* and *Kate of Still Waters,* to the universal, in such books as *Darkness Over the Land* and *The Strange House at Newburyport.* Of course, all of these books deal with concerns that are personal *and* universal, no matter what the dominant theme, and that seems to me to be one of your real writing strengths, seeing and revealing the complexity of human concerns. What would you say your major concerns are in writing?

STILES: Complexity. I want children to understand the complexity of moral questions. That *is* one of my main interests. If I could state things concisely, I'd be an essayist instead of going on and on with fiction. But take *Darkness Over the*

Land. I grew up during that particular war, World War II. The propaganda was that the Germans did the perfectly unimaginable things that were done because they were German. I couldn't believe that, because I grew up in a household which very much appreciated Mozart and Tilman Riemen Schneider. I mean, the creche figures were made in Germany, and the various members of the family had been to Germany and brought back pictures and so on. Anyway, I just very much appreciated German culture. So I knew when I went to Germany that I was going to spend that year trying to figure out . . . I had my own theory about how it had happened there, which was wrong. What I concluded when I was there was that those things could have been done anywhere. I tried to make this plain in the book. I think the important dialogue is the one between Mark and his brother. When Gottfried comes back he says, "I can't be Abraham anymore. Too often there was no goat." That was very important. But the conversations that they had over the little chest that came with their Huguenot ancestors, isn't that where Gottfried talks to him about what happens once the war starts?

BEATTIE: I believe so.

STILES: Once the war starts, people will do anything. At each point, the choice that you're offered is this or this. People will always choose self-preservation. And bit by bit, in any country in any way, at any time, anything can, inch by inch, happen. Which is why you have to be so careful. All of us have to be so careful. But yes, you see, we had been brought up on no complexity about that war at all. The enemy was evil and we and our allies were virtuous. And, if you remember, there is very little fiction in that book. I mean, the bad deeds attributed to this country and that country are not made up. None of them are made up. Somebody asked Jerzy Kosinski, who wrote *Painted Bird,* "Is this autobiographical?" He said, "The bricks are real, but the wall is mine," and this describes *Darkness Over the Land,* doesn't it? I didn't make up any slanders.

BEATTIE: Your choosing to write that novel from the point of view of an Aryan German child as opposed to a Jewish German child isn't the typical delivery.

STILES: Absolutely. Nobody had considered *his* moral dilemma. It's very easy to write from the point of view of the child in the occupied country. It's very easy to write from the point of view of the Jewish child. He knows right from wrong. But I wanted the reader of my book to ask himself, "What would I have done in Mark's place?" An honest child would reply, "I don't know." We were brought up to think that good people did good things and always knew what was the good thing to do. There's a great deal of children's literature put out like that. Children aren't confronted by moral complexity. I don't think they're learning it, and it's because it's not dramatic. It makes for much more drama if it's quite clear in the book which is evil and which is good.

BEATTIE: Maybe not external drama, but it makes for much richer internal drama.

STILES: Well, that's harder to write and harder to get across, and it's not as dramatic. Introspection is not as dramatic as shooting the villain.

BEATTIE: Possibly not, but since I've always been fond of it, I go much more for that.

STILES: Well, that's lucky for people like me. I wish more readers shared that attitude. I think teachers are very anxious to teach children to be good and noble and brave and strong, so they like to give them books which encourage children in that path. It's easier for the child to grasp that idea if it's very clear in the book who is good and what is the path. Life isn't going to be like that, and I think such teaching turns out monsters. You get things like the Red Guard. You get things like the people who bombed the University of Minnesota building and killed the man who was doing research at night because they were opposed to war research. You get people who think that moral questions are easy and that they know the right answer and that they should destroy evil and that they know what is best. In *The Strange House at Newburyport* . . . you see, I was brought up in the South, and I thought that the North had had the proper attitude about slavery. When I was in the North doing research for that novel, I found that the preachers in the pulpits were preaching against people who disrupted property rights. It was a rare northerner who was opposed to slavery. Plus, the way they treated the children in the cotton mills in New England was worse than most slaves got treated in the South.

I grew up believing what I was taught, that it was a good thing for this country that the English settled the United States rather than the Spanish or the Indians, and that the land was taken from the Indians because the Spanish and the Indians were so cruel. But, to my horror, I discovered what the English brought with them. There weren't many ships, and they really needed to bring all sorts of things with them, but they brought things like thumbscrews. When you start reading about people being hanged, drawn, and quartered because they wanted to blow up Parliament, you discover that we are just as violent and just as cruel as anybody else. And I wasn't taught that. I was taught that problems should be resolved on the basis of that which was right and that which was good.

There's a dialogue in my novel, *One Among the Indians,* that is very important to me, though it doesn't take up a blink, between Pocatowah and Tom, about how shall this fighting be resolved. How shall the ownership of the land be resolved? Tom is embarrassed that the English are taking land, and Pocatowah says, "Well, it was a prophecy, and it's true. It was a prophecy in our tribe that a tribe would come from the East and destroy us. There was a very powerful tribe to the east of us, and my father, Powhatan, rose in the night and descended on this village and killed them all—man, woman and child—in their sleep. Otherwise, they would have come and killed me, and it was my father's job to keep me from being killed. That was his job. It was his job to protect his women and children and people." So he said the purpose of this fighting was not to resolve who is right. It's to resolve whose descendants are going to occupy this land—yours or mine. It's heartbreaking. It gave me a headache to realize it.

Tom was my ancestor. So my hands are somewhat tied with what I could have him do. I had to rely on historical records. Everything that has surfaced has been published that concerned Jamestown, because it was the first colony. Pocatowah, I was a little bit freer with, because all I know about Powhatan's children is that he had forty, twelve of whom were boys. One of whom was Naumuntauck, if I remember correctly, and he's the one who died in Bermuda, and Tom was the hostage. That's when Tom had to get out. Pocatowah, of course, was fictional. I don't even know the names of any of the other sons.

BEATTIE: Even in *Sarah the Dragon Lady,* you point out, both from Sarah's point of view and from each parent's point of view—from all three points of view—the annoying things about the others. But, also, you emphasize the fact that nobody is right or wrong in the situation.

STILES: Well, you *can* be wrong. You *can* be right. The conflict, it isn't because somebody else is wrong; it's because *you* have a conflict. Where is the time going to go? Are you the center of this house or am I? Am I going to have to sacrifice this for you? Are you going to sacrifice that for me? You have to arrive at a *modus vivendi.* Everybody has to.

BEATTIE: Since the 1970s there has been more emphasis in children's and in young adult books on contemporary issues, and on writing from politically correct, if you will, points of view, on discussing problems that are societal as well as personal. But I don't see a lot of emphasis on showing the complexities that you're talking about.

STILES: I want to show children complexity. I desperately do, and I work very hard to do that.

BEATTIE: I'm most impressed with the manuscript of your adult novel, "Cold Mountain." Will you discuss that book and the research you did for it? Where did the idea come from for writing it, and what are you hoping to accomplish?

STILES: You're going to be disappointed with how it came about. I read about Eytam Patz, a child who was kidnapped and never returned. He was a New York child, but his fate hit me very hard because I lost my only child. He died. I decided I would write about that kidnapped child, but I wanted to write about the strain it puts on a happy, well-adjusted, satisfied family to have something really severe happen to one member. My friend, Anne Rogers, who is the Bourbon County public librarian, said to me once that her work caused her to read that, statistically, it was a real blow to a family to have anything happen to one member. She said it can be a defective child, it can be a deaf child, it can be a dead child. Well, this information just stunned me, because it wasn't about to break me up from my husband. If your husband is bleeding, you don't kick him. If I was throwing up, my husband wouldn't divorce me. You take care of the person who is hurt. You lose a child, you desperately hurt. So we tried to take care of each other. So, withdrawing from a grieving partner was something that was a new idea to me, and I thought about it. I think two things came together; the impact on me of this woman's dilemma, with a child gone—I wanted to write a book about the strain on the family, and I was going to tell it from her point of view because that's definitely easiest. I am a woman. I wanted to show the parents together and then being pulled apart by the tragedy and then shifting their shoulders, getting the load adjusted, resolving to bear it, and coming back together again. This was the book which I had in mind. I was not writing about the child, the kidnapping. I was writing about how this marriage was almost broken up and how the husband and wife brought it back together.

I worked and I worked and I worked. I resolved at one point in the writing it would be too hard on a young woman, which is what I figured my audience would be, to read this book and not find out what happens to the child. So I sat down and tried to think, "Well, where is he? Where did he go?" I thought, "He left to go to school." You may have noticed *this* farm is the farm in the novel. It just made it easier. He got as far as the mailbox, certainly. Nobody's going to snatch him up between here and the road. So, all right, he got as far as the mailbox. The boy is standing in front of the mailbox, killing time until the bus comes. The mother's entire story, which means the first thirty-three chapters, is told by her standing beside the fence on that August night and, therefore, it's written in the past tense. But then her son's story begins standing beside the mailbox, and there's no reason not to write it that way. In the course of writing this book, I experimented, alternating chapters so that you knew where he was quite early. There was more third person when I first wrote it, because there were things that I wanted to say about Ruth that broke the mood that she should have been in. I tried to deal with that by taking those words away from her and putting them into third person. Not much of that remains because I eventually realized that where it really belonged was out of that book.

BEATTIE: When did you start writing "Cold Mountain?"

STILES: 1980. I worked on it steadily for three years. After that, I would revise it and set it aside and revise it and set it aside. It spent two years sitting on the office floor. I had sent it to my agent, but then I wrote her and said, "I want to put some more in. Send it back." That's when I put in the snake-handling. That's when I put in the shooting.

I have a very Victorian style. I remember, once, when someone said, "Now, what have you read?" I began telling him, and he said, "Child, you're a period piece." Of course, Faulkner has the same long sentences I do, and I think he does because he was like me, although a generation older. He read the same things I read. My sentences seem quite normal to me, and my convoluted style and my backing up to things seems quite normal to me. My husband gets so angry.

BEATTIE: Is he a critic of your work?

STILES: Oh, he's very smart, and he's very helpful, but I'm not the kind of writer he best likes. So he's apt to be quite harsh and discouraging, so far as reading something and saying whether he likes it is concerned.

BEATTIE: He reads the manuscripts before you send them off?

STILES: Often, but not always. Often, he'll start reading something and say,

"I won't read anymore of this." When he started reading *Kate* [*Kate of Still Waters*], and the scene of the lambs and their dead mothers steaming in the moonlight, he put it down and said, "No little girl will read anything so painful. *I* will not read anything so painful." On the other hand, he loved *Sarah the Dragon Lady.* But what he's useful for is good advice. That is, he, for instance, said with *Kate,* "Start *Kate* with a chapter in which Kate can triumph. Let the children get to know her and like her before you hit them with dogs eviscerating lambs and their mothers, or they'll put it down and not go on." I am always torn when I get this kind of advice, but I took that advice. I started with a chapter in which you could get to know Kate and in which she could be successful. I can't just take Martin's advice without question, because he doesn't read girls' books. He doesn't know about *Julie of the Wolves* or *Island of Blue the Dolphins* or books like that, and he really wants to protect little girls. Little girls don't want to be protected. Well, *some* do.

BEATTIE: We're not living in a society where people are very protected, whether they want to be or not.

STILES: Not for five hundred thousand years has it been safe to be a child. Children are at risk in every generation. Always, they have been, and they know that. You may think children are honest and kind and sweet, but if you're having to go to school with them, you know they could kill you.

My husband also gave me my computer for Christmas. Oh, it's been helpful. A long book like *Cold Mountain,* which is more than three hundred pages, and which I revised and revised and revised, I just couldn't do what I'm doing without that.

BEATTIE: What are your writing habits?

STILES: When I was a faculty wife, I wrote for hours every day, and I tried to be on a schedule. I recommend that. I'm a morning person, so I got to it as early in the morning as I could and worked a minimum of X hours. But if it was going well, then I kept on, unless we happened to have company for dinner. I mean, if the ox is in a ditch . . . as a farmwife, my life is not quite like that. But I try to write a certain number of hours every day. I usually can't. But I try, and sometimes I can. But, as you see, work is getting done, and books have been published.

When I moved to Kentucky as a farmwife, and realized I had less time now, I made two or three changes. The first was I stopped writing historical fiction, because that takes so long. One way to compensate for having less time was to set myself a task which required less time. I wrote contemporary stories and I placed them here. I also thought, "Now it is time to learn to compose on the typewriter," which I had always heard recommended, so I made myself learn that. Now composing on the computer is more or less like working on the typewriter, but not quite. It has advantages and disadvantages. I very much like having more in front of me at a time than I can have in front of me at a time on the computer screen. It's also helpful to make your mark on a piece of paper so you retain what you used to have. So there are disadvantages to having a computer, but it surely is a help when you suddenly need three copies or five copies, and it surely is a help when you want to see how it would be if you suddenly decided to move three pages from chapter thirty-four to chapter one.

BEATTIE: You've also published a dozen short stories in magazines, as well as magazine articles. Will you discuss those?

STILES: In 1967 my husband bought a horse, and I had never been to the horse races until 1966 or 1967. I found out after we bought this farm, my father told me that his father had always had a box at the Kentucky Derby. I had no idea of that. This had never been mentioned. There was no interest in horses. My mother learned to ride as a toddler in front of her grandfather, but that was social riding. I don't imagine she'd ever been to a horse race until my husband and I took her. So horses were really foreign to me and didn't immediately grab me, either. I thought, "Well, if this is what my husband's interested in, then I better get interested in it." So I thought, all right, the thing to do was to try to write something about horses. I started in easy with an article on the collection of sporting art, the Woodward Collection, at the Baltimore Museum of Art. My husband was doing some work at Johns Hopkins University. My husband was extremely helpful to me with the articles I was writing for *The Thoroughbred Record.*

BEATTIE: When he first bought a horse, did you keep it here in Kentucky?

STILES: No, we kept it in Michigan, which wasn't satisfactory. The stallions are here. The auctions are here. The vans are here. The blacksmiths are here. The vets are here. All those things were inferior where we were. This was the place to be.

BEATTIE: Have any writing prizes that you've won been particularly meaningful to you?

STILES: All. All. All. I get so discouraged. The Al Smith Fellowship I won was for excerpts from "Cold Mountain."

BEATTIE: Of what does that prize consist?

STILES: Five thousand dollars, and that's a lot of money. You send in anonymous submissions of X pages, and out-of-state judges, different ones every year, read these and rank them. They take submissions from fiction writers every other year, along with choreographers and poets and I forget what-all. There were two hundred and fifty applicants, as I recall. Fifteen prizes as I recall, the year I won. Five, if I remember correctly, for fiction. So, you see, you're competing with apples and pears. I was glad to get this encouragement for this manuscript, but, believe me, back in '86 when I won the hundred dollars from the Frankfort Arts Foundation, that prize was so encouraging. I came home and wrote five short stories, because that award said, "You can write," and I didn't have a lot of evidence that I could. So I'm just immensely grateful to those people in Frankfort [The Kentucky Arts Council]. They've given me two of their prizes. Then, there again, they judge poets one year, and fiction the next year. When I had won the first prize and then the next one, the next year came along and they were trying to discourage me from entering, and I said, "Yes, I'm going to enter." They said,

"Well, would you be a judge?" I said, "You don't pay the judges." "Well," they said, "will you be a judge if we paid you what we give as a prize?" "Oh, yes," I said, "I'd love that," and I enjoyed the judging. I've always enjoyed judging.

BEATTIE: You've also taught creative writing in numerous school and university settings, as well as at writers' conferences throughout the country. How do you like teaching creative writing, and how do you think it should be taught?

STILES: Those are very difficult questions. I really like teaching literature. I really like being confronted with an audience to whom I can say, "Read this." I really like reading them things that I think they'll like having been made aware of. I like talking to them after they've read something, and saying to them, "Why do you think the author did this? And do you see, in these three stories, that the author used the same technique to induce you to enter the same state of mind?" That is a lot of fun. I don't mind giving line-by-line criticism, in a writers' group of friends, listening to someone read a story and saying, "Maybe you could do this with it. Maybe you could go there with it." That's fun. When a student says to me, "How do you do this? How do you do that?" I'm usually in pain. I feel I'm failing them.

BEATTIE: Where do you think creativity comes from?

STILES: Someone said, "If I knew where my ideas came from, I'd go live there." I don't know. Sometimes it's a voice. Sometimes it's a very clear picture. Sometimes it's deliberate. An analogy occurred to me many years ago. You were locked in a room and the building's on fire, and there is absolutely no way out. Will you spend your last hour running around screaming? Or will you sit down at the typewriter and write a story? This is essentially the situation we all are in. We're all going to die. Essentially, we are all locked in a burning building and there is no way out. So are you going to spend the time beating your brow, or shall you sit down at the typewriter and write some stories? I'm filling my time, because otherwise I'd scream. I'm not a calm person.

BEATTIE: But do you think the writing you do, the creative work, satisfies the need that some other type of work would not?

STILES: I got awfully bored in the analytical laboratory, I can tell you that, which I had not anticipated. I was bored to death in short order, which astounded me.

I don't mind farm work. I don't mind cleaning stalls, because you can think while you're doing it. But to be an analytical chemist, you have to pay attention. Once I learned it, then I was bored, but I had to pay attention to it. Now I can work in the garden all day and think and think and think. And I am *not* bored; I am very happy with it. I've been very lucky that my husband has supported me, and I haven't had to be bored. I haven't been bored very much in my life. Very, very little time have I spent either lonely or bored.

BEATTIE: What advice would you give to beginning writers?

STILES: Do something else. Because you'll never be happy. You'll never be satisfied with your own work. You'll never be satisfied with the recognition. You'll never be satisfied with the money.

BEATTIE: But you wouldn't give writing up now, would you?

STILES: Oh, heavenly days, no. I am very upset when I'm not writing now.

BEATTIE: Do you feel driven to write?

STILES: I don't know if *driven* is the right word, but I just want to do it, and I'm annoyed when I can't. I get out of sorts and cross and depressed and anxious. Writing is what relaxes me. I don't know that this is necessarily because I'm a born writer. I don't think I *am* a born writer, but it is the thing which, because I have been doing it so long and because I'm so interested in it, I can be absorbed by. Therefore, it rests me. This does not argue genius; this argues interest. I am very interested. I am sufficiently interested in writing that, when I am writing, I can detach myself from all these other things and, therefore, it is what rests me. I'm trying to account for why I get headaches and stomachaches and cross and snarly and feel abused and anxious when I can't write. I don't think it's because genius burns. I think it's because nothing else is absorbing me that way, and I feel discontented and anxious to get back to it.

February 27, 1993

Stiles's most recent work is the young adult novel she had been wanting to write since the Toyota Plant came to Georgetown, Kentucky, fourteen miles from her home. She states that this convergence of different cultures intrigues her, especially as the two groups concerned were so recently at war with one another. Stiles states that her own immediate and extended family's experiences in the Orient contributed to her interest, but that having completed her manuscript's second draft, she sees the book's theme is "all of a piece" with *One Among the Indians* and *Darkness Over the Land*. The book's working title is "Looking Ahead." Stiles changed the title of her manuscript, *Cold Mountain*, to *Lonesome Road*, which was published by Gnomon Press in 1998.

BOOKS BY MARTHA BENNETT STILES

One Among the Indians. New York: Dial Press, 1962.

The Strange House at Newburyport. New York: Dial Press, 1964.

Darkness Over the Land. New York: Dial Press, 1966.

Dougal Looks for Birds. New York: Four Winds Press, 1972.

James the Vine Puller. Minneapolis: Carolrhoda Books, 1975.

The Star in the Forest. New York: Four Winds Press, 1979.

Tana and the Useless Monkey. New York: Elsevier/Nelson Books, 1979.

Sarah the Dragon Lady. New York: Macmillan, 1986.

Kate of Still Waters. New York: Macmillan, 1990.

Lonesome Road. Frankfort, Ky.: Gnomon Press, 1998.

Island Magic. New York: Atheneaum, 1999.

RICHARD TAYLOR

TAYLOR: My name is Richard Lawrence Taylor. I was born in Washington, D.C., September 17th, 1941. My father, Joe Howard Taylor, who is deceased, was born in 1905 and died in 1974. He was a native of Kentucky. He was a practicing lawyer until his death. My mother is still living. Her name is Dorothy Dey Taylor. She lives in Louisville, Kentucky. She is now eighty years old.

I have a brother, who is two years younger than I, Douglas Taylor, who practices law in Louisville. I have a sister, who is two years older, Treva Duffy Taylor, who teaches in the gifted program in the Louisville public school system.

Probably the relative who had most influence on me is a wonderful woman who was sort of a distant cousin, who was very close to the family, named Lucy Spurgin. She was for some time the principal of the Cochran School in Louisville, but she also had a farm off what is Lime Kiln Lane, where my father also had some land. My earliest recollections are spending time with her and spending time on that farm. She had a sister named Edmonia Spurgin. The Spurgins were from Eminence, Kentucky, and Edmonia was a first-rate cook who refused to cook on an electric stove. I can remember vividly a cast-iron coal stove in her kitchen. She died before I was ten, but I can remember her making elaborate, heavy, country meals with multiple dishes, lots of vegetables, always, and meat and a cobbler or a pie of some kind. She was the cook, and Lucy, her sister, was a sort of business woman who ran the farm. Both of them were spinsters, and they were really remarkable people.

I had a very normal childhood. I grew up in Crescent Hill in Louisville, Kentucky, very close to the Baptist Seminary, on Pleasantview Avenue in a middle-class neighborhood. I attended a public school, Emmett Field School, which is located adjacent to the Louisville Waterworks. I then attended J.M. Barret Junior High School, and then, finally, Atherton High School.

My uncle lived with our family, and he had a great—probably more than my father—love of language, which affected me at a very early age. For instance, from the time I was in junior high school, he was a person who revelled in language to the extent that he was always popping big words on my sister and my brother or on me, and he got us interested in the language at an early age to the extent that we were keeping word lists. About the time I went to high school I decided that language was something that I had a real interest in. At that point I was interested in language mostly through literature and poetry, but I see him as a kind of seminal influence. My father was a learned kind of person, but not terribly given to storytelling, and he did not have any great flair for literature. Though he did have, and I owe this to him, a great interest in history, in family history and in what the old people he could remember were like, and in what growing up in the country was like. Those memories of his were very vivid and have always played a role in my thinking and development.

BEATTIE: Did your mother read to you when you were a child?

TAYLOR: She did, and I'm sure we read the standard children's books. My literary development came much later, and it came primarily through, not a teacher in the strictest sense, but a person with whom I grew up.

He is a remarkable person and he did become a teacher. He is deceased now. His name was David A. Orr, and David and I grew up together. We went to dancing class together and we were in the Scouts for a time together. We were constant companions and, in high school, David was an omnivorous reader. He later taught philosophy at the University of Louisville, and he never really completed his dissertation at Northwestern University, but he was probably the most remarkable teacher that I had the privilege to know. David was constantly, particularly in high school, saying, "You really ought to read this," or "You ought to try this." So, I had the benefit of years of tutelage under a person who was probably better read than most of his teachers.

BEATTIE: You dedicate one of your books to him, I recall. And you believe that he, more than anyone else, shaped your literary sensibilities?

TAYLOR: I would say so.

BEATTIE: Do you think he gave you the impetus to write?

TAYLOR: I would say yes to all of those things. David took an interest in my writing and encouraged me to do it, but was constantly opening up myriads of possibilities for other people. His interest in literature played a very important role with me, particularly, as I went to college. I can remember, for instance, his getting me to read John Thomas who, in 1958 or '59, had an effect on me. I can remember his getting me to read the Beat poets, Ferlinghetti and Kerouac and Ginsburg. I think the two of us, in high school, were pretty much rebels, and what academic interest I had was pretty much outside of high school and pretty largely through his influence.   •

BEATTIE: Before you got to college, do you remember having a favorite subject, or did you ever write outside of school assignments?

TAYLOR: Yes, I started writing fairly early, and I can remember one experience in particular with writing a terrible, terrible, terrible poem—the kind of poem that, I guess, all of us interested in writing write—one of those poems that is governed more by dim recollections of Edgar Allan Poe and a kind of gushy pre-eminence of feeling, over any kind of control. I can remember writing a poem like that and taking it to my English teacher, Mrs. Moran, and Mrs. Moran, in a very polite way, sort of discounted it. She didn't come out and say, "This is a terrible piece of work; you really should pursue some other field," but I can remember at that point her negative reaction probably had a positive effect, because it made me want to write something that was acceptable, something that was better.

BEATTIE: Do you remember how old you were when you started writing?

TAYLOR: I would have been about sixteen or seventeen when I started writing seriously. I can remember having kept word lists for years and reading quite a lot. I had a job in high school where I was a delivery boy for a drugstore, and I had access to books pretty easily through the drugstore. I could read anything I wanted there, and I was always reading something when I wasn't on the job.

My interest in reading came parallel to school, not through school. My English classes were not really strong in cultivating an appreciation for literature. That was, I know, part of the goal, but it was more a question of reading so many units, covering so many authors, in a superficial way. So, most of what I read I read outside of high school, and probably—as much as anything—as an act of youthful rebellion.

But I always read. I guess, from the time I was in junior high school on, I was a pretty avid reader. I remember vividly reading the work of Joseph A. Altsheier. In fact, I've managed to come on some of his books recently; he is long out of print. My interest in the frontier grew a lot from his rather tame, in retrospect, rather stiff-but-always-interesting accounts of two young boy scouts— not Boy Scouts, but scouts who were boys—in the frontier setting in Kentucky during the period of the Revolution and after, during the Indian Wars. I think that had a vivid impact on me. I know my interest in Girty came out of reading a Kentucky history which was part of the curriculum at that time, I think in the fifth grade, reading about Daniel Boone, Sue Mundy, and [Simon] Girty.

BEATTIE: Did you go directly from high school to college?

TAYLOR: Yes. I graduated from Atherton High School in 1959. I went to the University of Kentucky where I majored in English, graduated in 1963 as an English major, and worked there with the campus literary magazine. At that time it was called *Stylus*. Bobbie Ann Mason graduated a year or maybe two years ahead of me, and I can vaguely remember having at least one class with her. There is a rather interesting writer from Western Kentucky University who was an English major at the time, Joe Survant. Joe and I were in classes together, and to this day we share an interest in writing. Wendell Berry had left the University at that time, as had Gurney Norman and Ed McClanahan.

From UK in 1963 I went to the University of Louisville, where I worked on a master's degree for a year in English. I graduated in '64, and I was not certain what to do at that point, so I was persuaded by my father to go to law school for the next three years at the University of Louisville Law School. I had a rather not-what-you-would-call-extensive law practice, in either duration or intensity. I clerked in law school for my father's law firm, and practiced nearly two months before giving up the practice of law. When I decided that I was not going to practice law, my father was very understanding. I don't think he had wanted to be a lawyer. He'd always wanted to be a landscape architect and, strangely, found out he couldn't draw.

So the first job I could find after abandoning law was teaching English in a small junior college in Morehead, Mississippi, called Mississippi Delta Junior College. I taught there for a semester, in February or late January of 1968. I had a master's degree then. I taught there, finished out the school year, and was put onto a job at another junior college in Mississippi, called Northwest Mississippi Junior College in Senatobia, Mississippi, about forty or so miles south of Memphis. I taught English there for a full year, and that next summer I took some graduate courses at the University of Mississippi, having decided that if I were going to follow teaching as a career, I really needed to get a doctorate. I came back to the University of Kentucky in the fall of 1969; I then became reacquainted with the University of Kentucky, which had, of course, undergone enormous changes between 1963 and '69, changes not only in size, but in orientation. It was a much more cosmopolitan campus. At that time, I encountered people like Wendell Berry. I knew him first through his writing, which at that time was very, very hot stuff, and I also met Ed McClanahan, with whom I had some connection through the Department of English where I was a teaching assistant and he was a professor or a visiting writer. Wendell was still teaching there at that time. Guy Davenport was probably the major influence on my own graduate studies, and certainly a major influence on my writing. I took several courses under him and, eventually, did my dissertation under him.

There was a very vibrant writing scene at the University of Kentucky in the late sixties. There were a couple of literary magazines. It was there I met Gray Zeitz, who is probably the finest letterpress printer in the state, as well as what I call a kind of natural poet. He is the head of Larkspur Press in Monterey, Kentucky, which, of course, is just up the road. People like Gray Zeitz, and a little later, Jonathan Greene, helped create a kind of literary scene at the University, most of it centering on the literary magazine, but then that gave rise to spin-offs. People like Gray were producing their own literary magazines, such as *Handsel,* and were later, of course, publishing books. This was when I was in graduate school, when I came back to UK in about 1969 through about 1974. Before I completed my dissertation, however, I was writing poems right along in graduate school, and I was lucky to work two years with the Kentucky Arts Commission as a Poet in the Schools.

The arrangement was one where there was a recognition, first of all, that teachers in the program were not primarily teachers, they were artists. And because we were regarded as artists, there was a certain amount of time set apart from our schedules to permit us to write. So, as a consequence of spending two years working with poetry in the schools, I had a schedule that would permit me to teach maybe three days a week and have free time two days a week. My wife and I, at that time, lived outside of Lexington in Athens, Kentucky, in a rented farmhouse, and I would come back from these teaching stints and write pretty seriously.

It was at that time, too, that, through the Kentucky Arts Council, which was the Arts Commission at that time, I was asked to put together an anthology of student writing, which was eventually published by Larkspur Press and printed by the Kentucky Arts Council, called *Cloud-bumping*. That would have been during '73 and '74. In '75 I came to Kentucky State University where I've taught since.

BEATTIE: Back to your undergraduate days. Were you writing on your own at that time?

TAYLOR: I was, and I was publishing as often as I could be accepted in *Stylus* literary magazine, and that went straight on through my undergraduate years.

BEATTIE: Did you work as an editor on that magazine?

TAYLOR: I actually did. I have the vaguest recollection of working as an editor or co-editor on the magazine, probably for at least a couple of years.

BEATTIE: Were you sending any of your work out to publications beyond the university literary magazine?

TAYLOR: By the time I came back to graduate school, I was sending my poems to a number of places. In the late sixties, small magazines were beginning to come into their own, and many of us regarded those as an opportunity as well as an alternative to the more legitimate and proper literary outlets. So, I was sending more poems to magazines like *Small Farm*. There was a wonderful magazine out of Illinois called *Apple*, published by a guy named David Curry, who was very encouraging. I might send him six poems and he might accept one, or none, for that matter, and send back a note critiquing the poems and making suggestions, all of which were very, very supportive, and which reinforced young writers like myself.

BEATTIE: When you left the University of Kentucky and went to U of L to do your graduate work, what was your main area of concentration studying English?

TAYLOR: My interest has always been American literature, primarily. I did an M.A. thesis on Truman Capote's *Other Voices Other Rooms*. He fascinated me and, again, it may go back to his exploration of the affinity or the connections between poetry on the one hand and prose on the other. He was one of the writers who, at that time, including James Agee, had an enormous influence on me. I think now if there is a book or a writer who made an impact on me at that time, it was James Agee. Not so much his fiction, which is *A Death in the Family*, as his wonderful, impassioned account of sharecropping in North Alabama in the 1930s, called *Let Us Now Praise Famous Men*. That work affected me emotionally, but it also fascinated me. The photographs, for instance; I've painted most of the photographs from that book. Agee's prose, I thought and still think, is some of the finest written that I've encountered and that has been written in this century.

When I came back to the University of Kentucky for my doctoral work, I decided that I wanted to be a poet, and I read all the poetry I could find. Guy Davenport—I won't characterize him as a poet, though he is—his influence on me was his knowledge about poets.

BEATTIE: And your dissertation was?

TAYLOR: I read every poet I could get my hands on. I would go to the stacks in the library and look up the 811's and the 821's, and dig up particularly contemporary poets. One who impressed me greatly was James Wright, and early on I conferred with Guy Davenport, who agreed to be my dissertation director. I asked him about the advisability of doing a kind of critical analysis of four books of James Wright, and he said, "Sure, do it." It always struck me as interesting that they both have the same birth year, 1927. So, I did this analysis of James Wright's work, not a particularly penetrating analysis, but it did put me in contact with his poetry and with his connection to Robert Bly, who greatly interested me as a critic or as a great promoter of new ways of looking at poetry. Probably the most influential anthology that I can think of in recent years is a wonderful little anthology by Robert Bly in which there are some James Wright translations, I believe, called *The Sea and the Honeycomb: a Book of Tiny Poems.* None of the poems are over three or four lines, and they are from a number of cultures over the world, including some Japanese poems and others. They had an enormous influence on me because they showed me a new rhetoric, a new insight into what the possibilities for poems were. I still go back to that book and always find something new and vital in it, so that connection with James Wright and Robert Bly was extremely influential. A number of other poets also influenced me at that time: William Matthews, for instance, James Tate, Robert Haas, as well as Denise Levertov and, certainly, Sylvia Plath. Strange that a male should be so affected by her, but she is remarkable. Another writer who has influenced me and who has recently been accepted in the literary canon is a wonderful writer named Lorine Niedecker, who is, in my view, one of the most interesting poets of our century. She is sort of a twentieth-century version of Emily Dickinson—not a recluse, but a very original, vital voice.

BEATTIE: Aren't you influenced by A.R. Ammons?

TAYLOR: Greatly. I'm interested in poetry that in one way or another reflects on nature, and I think of that A.R. Ammons line, "In my backyard is more wordage than I can read." I think there is some truth to that. We are so ignorant about what goes on around us, whether it's naming what's in our front yard or simply seeing things that we, too often, miss. I forget who said this, but I also like the line, "Art is sort of perfected attention." It seems to me that poets like James Wright, like Lorine Niedecker, get us a kind of perfected attention. They look at things very carefully.

BEATTIE: You referred to you and your wife after graduate school. When did you meet and marry your wife?

TAYLOR: I met my wife-to-be in about 1970. She was a graduate student at the University of Kentucky in Childhood Development. We have three children. We dated and married in a house that two or three of my friends and I were renting at the time at 636 East High Street. Afterwards, we were fortunate to rent what is really a tenant house on a big farm on Gentry Road in Athens, Kentucky, during the time I worked in the Artists in the Schools' Program, at which time I was still completing my dissertation.

BEATTIE: Do you find that literary models are helpful for people who are not readers themselves, or who have had little familiarity with literature, when you are teaching people to write?

TAYLOR: I do. I still believe that art is nemesis. Art is essentially a process of imitation. Show me any poet worth his salt, and you get a clear sense of that poet's aptness by finding out what poets that poet has read, not because those poets produce an influence on him. But show me a poet who doesn't read other poets—and too many young poets don't—and I'll show you a poet who is not really developed.

BEATTIE: You've been teaching creative writing on the college level for some years now. How do you think creative writing should be taught?

TAYLOR: Most of the creative writing I teach now is fiction, and I believe very strongly in starting with the anatomy of an art form—exploring that, learning the essentials, doing something with language in a creative writing course. I work from an anthology, but my students also read John Gardner's very fine little book, *The Art of Fiction*. We also tie that in with the old standby, White and Strunk's *The Elements of Style*. The best part of any writing course, it seems to me, is giving students a forum in which to present their work and bounce their ideas off other members of the group. So, part of it is creating a supportive environment in which that can occur. At the same time, it is important that I give a very careful reading to the students' work, and that I make comments—not just generalizations, but specific comments, upon both problems in the writing itself, as well as technical or structural problems, problems of characterization or whatever, in the drafts that are submitted. I hope our own poet, our own voice, in some ways is a response to or a summary of all the voices we've read. But before we've read those voices, it seems to me, we're not fully aware of the array of possibilities that are there. "Great poetry requires great audiences," Whitman said, and you have to be the audience before you can be the poet, it seems to me, so reading is vital for people who want to write.

BEATTIE: How did you get your job at Kentucky State University?

TAYLOR: I was sending job applications out, and the first job offer I got, not the only, but the first one I got, was at Kentucky State. I got one to Transy [Transylvania University] about two weeks after I'd accepted the one at KSU. Like a number of other graduate students at the time, I was completing my dissertation and looking for a job. I wanted to stay in the state; I like very much living in the state. So, Kentucky State became the place, and I've been there now—I think I've just completed my nineteenth year. By and large, it's been a positive experience.

BEATTIE: What were you originally hired to teach?

TAYLOR: As I remember, I was teaching a lot of elementary writing courses. I came in as an instructor, and taught some students intermediate English, but early on I was given some opportunity to teach introduction to literature courses and then survey courses, then the full array of American literature, which is what I do now.

I enjoy the creative writing. I don't often get to teach it. Probably the thing I most enjoy teaching now because of the challenge—and I've come to it relatively late—is a course offering called Integrative Studies, a sequence of Humanities courses which each student is required to complete. I teach one beginning with Greek culture and another which picks up in the seventeenth to eighteenth centuries with political philosophy. I enjoy that because it's cross-disciplinary teaching, and it ties in with my teaching experience in Governor's Scholars where I've taught since about 1985.

BEATTIE: Governor's Scholars is the program for outstanding Kentucky high school students that takes place in the summer?

TAYLOR: Right, and this year, for the second year, I'm serving as dean of that program, this year on the Northern Kentucky University campus, last year on Murray State's campus. One of the things that attracts me to that program is that it is the optimal situation for a teacher. I regard myself essentially as a teacher. I'm a writer, too, but I don't separate the two. But the teaching experience in that program is having an enormous effect on me, on my feelings about learning as well as on my learning itself. Working with capable and innovative and creative teachers who are given every opportunity to do things differently to make things new is something that all of us need in order to stay on top of our feelings about the profession. My primary pleasure as dean comes from selecting the people who teach and from facilitating their teaching.

BEATTIE: Has your wife been working outside the home throughout your career?

TAYLOR: When we moved to Frankfort she had a job in the Attorney General's office. Then she had a job at a bookstore, which is what got us interested in going into the book business.

BEATTIE: This was not the bookstore you own now?

TAYLOR: No, there was another bookstore, the prior incarnation of our bookstore. It was literally called The Bookstore. It was in Fountain Place Shops, which are, in fact, what is now the Cocktail Lounge of the Holiday Inn Capital [Plaza] Hotel. In 1981 we moved to an old storefront on Broadway in part of an effort to revitalize downtown.

BEATTIE: How did your bookstore business, Poor Richard's, come about? Now, I assume the title is both a play on your name and Benjamin Franklin's *Poor Richard's Almanac.*

TAYLOR: Yes. The name came through our friend, David Orr, when we were brainstorming names. He said, "Well, if worse comes to worse, you could always call it Poor Richard's," which is what it ended up. I don't have too much connection with the bookstore. I'm interested in old books, and we sell books— new and old books—and I have an abiding interest in antiquarian books. I suppose getting into the book business was both my wife's and my way of supporting our own book habits.

BEATTIE: When did you get into the business?

TAYLOR: Nineteen seventy-eight we started, and what we did was buy out a bookstore that was going out of business on that site I mentioned in the Fountain Place Shops. We are now in our second decade.

BEATTIE: Your wife, primarily, works there, but how have you managed to handle that, plus teaching, plus writing?

TAYLOR: I do a lot of juggling. I'm not in the bookstore usually over fifteen minutes a week. I go to some book sales. I've had some more involvement in the past, organizing books and setting up shelves, but my wife is really the prime mover there, and we tend to say jokingly, although truthfully, that the place tends to prosper to the extent that I'm not connected with it. We call ourselves a comprehensive bookstore, comprehensive in the sense that we do put an emphasis on literature. We draw the line at Harlequins. I will not ever carry Harlequin romances. People comment that the store is very much a product of individual taste, and my wife is pretty much the big influence there. We like to think of ourselves as sort of a personal bookstore where we give people full service.

BEATTIE: Concerning your own writing, what interested you in the characters about whom you write?

TAYLOR: I tend to be attracted to, I don't want to say simply outlaws, but to those who in some ways are misfits. They don't quite fit in. I confess to an abiding interest in violence, perhaps because it's so antithetical to my character. Anyone who knows me will tell you I'm the most unviolent person that they know. I abhor violence, and yet there is this fascination with people who are violent themselves, as was Simon Girty, as was Sue Mundy, whom I've written about. I guess I'm interested in something about what it is that provokes violence in people.

BEATTIE: Would you talk about your publishing career?

TAYLOR: Well, we were talking earlier about small-press publications, and there were a number while I was in graduate school. My first collection of poems, called *Bluegrass,* which Gray Zeitz published as his first book in Larkspur Press in 1975, that book is a collection of, probably, I don't know, fifty, sixty poems, mostly relating to the experience of a city boy who took to the country and discovered the country and nature. The second book is *Simon Girty,* which was published initially in one form of the manuscript in Leon Driskell's *Adeena.* The work was not completed then. I did some more work on it and asked my dissertation director, Guy Davenport, to read it, which he very graciously did, and to suggest some place I might send it. He suggested Turtle Island Foundation, a small press publisher in Berkeley, California. I sent it and I was very surprised and pleased that they accepted it for publication. It was a letterpress publication in an edition of about a thousand copies.

At that point, Jonathan Greene at Gnomon Press was interested in doing a collection of poems. I put together a new collection, some of which came out of *Bluegrass,* my first book, and combined them with newer poems. They were printed in 1979 in a collection called *Earth Poems.* From that time I was interested, in fact, for nearly a period of ten years, in Marcellus Jerome Clark. I did an enormous amount of research. I have boxes of it now, and still haven't unraveled all the loose ends in his life. Among the places I went to research him—in addition to Special Collections and Louisville's Filson Club and the Historical Society—was the National Archives in Washington. I got a little research grant to go there. In fact, part of *Girty* and much of *Sue Mundy* were written as a result of two creative writing fellowships I received through the National Endowment for the Arts—one, I think, in 1976, and one in about 1985. That second grant, among other things, permitted me to go to Washington and spend some time in the Archives, where I found transcripts of court-martials of people who were guerrillas with Marcellus Jerome Clark—Sue Mundy—and there were literally hundreds of pages of handwritten trial transcripts. My legal training helped some, but I was able to glean from those a lot of the details of his life, and ordinary people's reactions to these guerrillas. A lot of that I was able to put into the book. Considerable parts of it have been published in a number of places, and many of them in *The Journal of Kentucky Studies.* As a book, it is yet to be published. That's a project I've put on hold in the last couple of years, though I come back to it from time to time.

Two years ago I was asked to write a book for the New Readers's adult literacy series through the University Press of Kentucky.

BEATTIE: What was your experience like writing *Three Kentucky Tragedies,* and what was it like writing for the New Books for New Readers Series?

TAYLOR: First of all, I believe very much in the need to promote literacy in the state, and I had read and taught a couple of the books in that series to new readers, in one or two libraries. When I was asked to write one, I originally thought about doing something with Cassius Clay, but so much had been written about Clay. So, to myself, I said, "If I were an adult who was just learning to read, and I wanted to look at something in Kentucky history, what would attract me?" I naturally led upon that wonderful story that four or five novelists, including Robert Penn Warren, had used as the grist for their novels, the so-called Beauchamps Tragedy, which occurred here in Frankfort in 1825, one of the most celebrated murder cases of the era, about which, incidentally, Edgar Allan Poe wrote an unfinished Senecan tragedy. Well, that attracted me, because it had a kind of dimension for a love triangle, and it was steeped in Kentucky history. All of that appealed to me greatly, because of its melodrama and sensationalism, I confess.

Secondly, I was very much taken with Boyton Merrill's book *Jefferson's Nephews,* which, to my thinking now, is one of the most interesting monographs on any subject in Kentucky history. It's much more than just a tale about an unfortunate murder of a slave by a Virginia transplant. To me, it's a book that gives a kind of portrait of the era, particularly of Livingston County, of that region of the state, in the first two decades of the nineteenth century. The third story moved more towards a kind of collective tragedy, and the book was called *Three Kentucky Tragedies*. I decided to write on the Battle of Blue Licks. I knew about the experience of Daniel Boone, who lost a son there and, of course, I tied in to Simon Girty, who was also at that battle among the British, who had made the foray into Kentucky in July and August of 1782. That interested me, so the real test became translating that history, abbreviating that history, into something that was readable in terms of the language, as well as readable in terms of the events. I tried to accurately portray events without oversimplifying them, and I found that to be a great challenge. I found it very difficult to write as I was supposed to on about an eighth-grade reading level, knowing that among the readers would be someone who was going to put that manuscript to the test. It made me become much more deliberate and much less venturesome with the language.

BEATTIE: Did you work with some of the new readers in the process of writing it?

TAYLOR: I did. I worked at the Thornhill Community School in Frankfort. There were a series of sessions where I worked with new readers, and I would give them a portion of the manuscript before our sessions, and then I would get their reactions. I found it extremely helpful and a lot of fun.

BEATTIE: In talking about the New Books for New Readers Series, how did you get involved in writing a book for that series?

TAYLOR: I'd worked on the Humanities Council. I'd been on their Board for several years, and when Ramona Lumpkin was the director, she set up a committee to do the groundwork for that series. I was on that committee and was asked, initially, to write one of the books. Unfortunately, the book was to have been written the year that I got a Fullbright and went to Denmark. At the end of the process, the person who was directing the project, Phyllis MacAdam, asked if I was interested in working in the libraries with some new readers, and I did that, and then she said, "Well, we're going to do another book; would you be interested in doing one?" I said, "Sure." She said, "Well, think about what you'd like to do, and come back to us with a prospectus." That's how I became involved.

I think Kentucky was really at the forefront, at the vanguard, in creating this concept of new books for new readers. So I think, probably, the project itself has had some national impact.

BEATTIE: You mentioned getting a Fullbright and going to Denmark. When was that and what did you do there?

TAYLOR: In 1989, my wife, three children, and I went to a remote part of northern Denmark to teach American Studies and, as much as anything, to answer questions about the U.S. political process. It was a wonderful experience. I found myself living in one community and teaching in four communities. I taught at two teachers' colleges, as well as two gymnasiums, and the gymnasiums are for the thirty-five percent or so of Danish students who elect to go to the university. All of these students spoke English. All Danish students study English from the time they are in what they call the fifth class. I had a wonderful time going from school to school. I got to do some traveling. I got to do a critique of American Studies books used in Danish high schools. I got to travel to Sweden, where I gave a talk on current American literature. I used Kentucky literature—Wendell Berry and Ed McClanahan, Bobbie Ann Mason—to discuss American literature before the fiftieth session of the Swedish Teachers of English. I got to go to Finland where I did a paper critiquing Danish readers in English. Denmark, to me, is like Tolkien land. It's the land of the hobbits, the armchair adventurers of whom create a kind of storybook.

BEATTIE: Did you get an opportunity to write on your own while you were in Denmark?

TAYLOR: Some, not a lot. I keep a journal—I've kept a journal for probably the last twelve or fifteen years—and I did a lot of reading. I did a lot of traveling. I was always on the go; it was very difficult to sustain the time you need to really do serious writing.

BEATTIE: What do you think distinguishes your writing, or what do you hope to achieve in your work?

TAYLOR: That's such a very difficult question. I'm not sure what I hope to achieve. I hope to become a better writer. In the last year I've been interested—and again, this is sort of a Davenport influence—in the idea of working on opposing plots, sort of alternative writing about one event that happens to have occurred two hundred years ago, and a contemporary event, and looking at the resonances and connections between those things. I am interested in experimental writing, I suppose, as much as for any other reason, because I have great difficulty writing in a kind of conventionally well-plotted, carefully framed, mode of expression. I just cannot do that.

BEATTIE: In *Simon Girty* you have a variety of forms for each chapter or each section.

TAYLOR: That's right. I guess I'm interested in frontiers not just literally, but frontiers in the sense of the place where conventional writing ends and experimental writing begins. That fascinates me. I guess another way of saying that is that I'm interested in the points at which prose and poetry meet. I feel like a kind of suppressed poet who is writing in a prose medium, and prose is more my medium now than poetry.

BEATTIE: Since you have written a couple of books of poetry, as well as novels, do you feel obligated to categorize yourself as a writer of a particular genre?

TAYLOR: No, I don't think most people are interested either way. I'm content to think of myself as a catch-as-catch-can writer. One of my greatest pleasures, though, is having something on the burner all the time. During this last year when I'd been tied up with things at school, and teaching with Governor's

Scholars, one of my great pleasures has been coming back to a computer disc and working with a manuscript which grew pretty much in its own way. I've never had so much fun writing, and, if writing is not pleasurable, I'd just as soon not do it. I am a consummate perfectionist. I say that in a negative sense, because I work on things too long and too hard. This Sue Mundy novel I've been fooling with for ten or twelve years now—I should really come to a point where I'm finished with it. That's why I was so happy to move on to this piece that's called *Sons of the Pioneers,* which has occupied me just lately. It's more than a short story; it's about seventy pages long, and I've just derived more pleasure from writing that. It's basically about people discovering where they are and who they are, and the effects the past has upon each of us.

BEATTIE: Have you ever been interested in writing nonfiction?

TAYLOR: I thought about doing a biography of Jerome Clark, and I may, at some point, do that. Of course the *Three Kentucky Tragedies* is supposed to be nonfiction. I'm not at all interested in criticism. I am very interested in history, and one of the projects I'd like to take on at some point is editing a collection of early travel accounts in Kentucky. That still fascinates me. What did the state look like to the first people who came here? That's been a biding question. I see my own bent more towards fiction because, this may sound strange, but I found writing poems requires an enormous amount of energy for a very little return on that energy. By return on that energy I mean satisfaction; I need something that's more protracted. Robert Penn Warren said that the novels of Kentucky ought to be found in its courthouses, and I take that to be quite true.

BEATTIE: Will you tell me about the publication of *Shackles?*

TAYLOR: It wasn't really a collaboration with George C. Wolfe at all. I worked for years with the Frankfort Arts Foundation, usually every year as a judge, except those years in which I tried to submit something, and *Shackles* is just a compilation. George had a section from one of his plays, and I just had an excerpt as part of a contest, a fiction contest. Part of *Sue Mundy* is in there.

BEATTIE: You have two books of poetry, *Earth Bones* and *Bluegrass.* I'm wondering if you could talk about those?

TAYLOR: Sure. Those books, particularly *Bluegrass* and, later, to some extent, *Earth Bones,* grew out of our experience moving out of Lexington into the country. And, though I had been around in the country all my life, I'd never really lived outside city limits. I don't think now I could ever live in a city again. One of the things I appreciate about this state is its rural beauty, as well as its rural folkways. Those books of poetry grew out of that experience of moving to the country and starting to look at nature with an eye that aspired to be an educated eye. I now see many of those early poems are sort of exercises in perception, in looking at things, in acknowledging them, and then in some way transforming them into something new. That's basically, I guess, the process of poetry. There is this very simple grounding in physical reality that somehow, at some point, must step beyond that and approach some sort of metaphysical or spiritual truth.

BEATTIE: I wanted to ask you about sense of place in your writing.

TAYLOR: I'm not so sure that the history of this house is so much what attracts me, as is living in the country and living in an old house where you sense not a ghost, but where you are aware that, just as with the earth, we are generations that come and go. This house is sort of my exercise in the project of preservation, and we'll be working on this house the rest of my life. I've just broken two wrists in the process of working on it, and this house will be here, I hope, for my kids, just as I hope this area, this part of the state, will remain essentially as it is. I worry a lot about urban development, urban sprawl. I worry a lot about our transition from a farming economy to whatever economy we are entering now. I worry about those of us not learning to read our backyards, and I'm convinced that that is at the root of many of our ecological, as well as other, social problems. A lot of this is straight Wendell Berry; we are a kind of mobile society. We've lost our grounding quite literally, and, somehow, we need to get back to that and, as Berry suggests, it's going to come through communities.

I like to be a part of this Frankfort community. Living in Frankfort is a joy. Living outside of Frankfort is maybe a greater joy, because you can always step out of it, but the people I know in this community, through school and through the bookstore, have been enriching. Our state history, much of it is unrecovered; it's an untapped gold mine for a fiction writer.

The kind of social breakdown we are currently witnessing, those matters concern me a great deal. It ties into my interest in teaching, and to my involvement in the Governor's Scholars Program, which is one of the real bright lights in education in the state. It's such a pleasure working with people who are not only gifted, but with people who are willing to take risks. It seems to me that all of these things tie in—the teaching, the writing, the interest in the past.

May 20, 1993

In 1995, Taylor received an Al Smith Award, and in that same year he collaborated with a group of Kentucky and Indiana writers, visual artists, and a composer on an exhibit and catalog of works interpreting marriage, "The Marriage Project: A Midlife Perspective."

During the Fall of 1996 Taylor experienced his first sabbatical in twenty years of teaching. He spent that semester researching, interviewing, and writing a text to accompany a series of photographs by Louisville photographer Adam Jones that was published in 1997 as *Palisades of the Kentucky River.*

Taylor's 1998 publications included an essay, "Guineas and Griddlecakes," in L. Elisabeth Beattie's *Savory Memories,* and a collection of poetry, *In the Country Morning Calm,* published by Larkspur Press.

Currently, Taylor, along with John Downs and Viola Gross, is conducting an oral history project concerning the life and times of the Dennis Doram family, an influential and prosperous family of nineteenth century Danville free African Americans, and in 1999 Taylor was appointed Poet Laureate of Kentucky.

BOOKS BY RICHARD TAYLOR

Taylor, Richard. *Bluegrass*. Monterey, Ky.: Larkspur Press, 1975.

Taylor, Richard, editor. *Cloud-bumping: A Collection of Poems by Students in Kentucky Schools*. (For the Kentucky Arts Commission). Monterey, Ky.: Larkspur Press, 1976.

Taylor, Richard. *Girty*. Berkley, Ca.: Turtle Island Foundation, 1977.

Taylor, Richard. *Earth Bones*. Frankfort, Ky.: Gnomon Press, 1979.

Taylor, Richard. *Three Kentucky Tragedies*. (New Books for New Readers Series). Lexington, Ky.: University Press of Kentucky, 1991.

Taylor, Richard. *The Palisades of the Kentucky River*. Englewood, Co.: Nature Conservancy and Westcliffe Publishing Co., 1997.

Taylor, Richard. *In the Country Morning Calm*. Monterey, Ky.: Larkspur Press, 1998.

MICHAEL WILLIAMS

BEATTIE: What is your full name?

WILLIAMS: Michael Leon Williams. I was born in Louisville, Kentucky, on December 17th of 1952. Carl Leon Williams is my father, and he was a high school physics and math teacher, and then he became a principal at Fort Knox Independent Schools and ended his career, retired, as assistant superintendent there. My mother is Mildred Booher Williams, and she was a teacher in Fort Knox Independent Schools. She taught everything from elementary school to high school English, and she ended up as a reading consultant.

BEATTIE: Did her teaching of English have anything to do with your interest in it?

WILLIAMS: I suppose that it did. She did encourage me in story reading, and she made a lot of books available to me, and that's always a good start for a writer, I believe.

BEATTIE: Do you recall your grandparents?

WILLIAMS: Yes, as a matter of fact, my paternal grandfather died when I was about eighteen, and the rest of them lived up until about three or four years ago.

My maternal grandfather, S. P. Booher, died in 1984, and I remember an awful lot about him and my grandmother. He was a grand storyteller, and he recalled everything back from the 1880s to the present, and he was filled with stories. I think, of all of the family influences on my development as a writer, that might be the most profound. I think that listening to a good storyteller can tell you an awful lot about the internal storyteller.

BEATTIE: Was that grandfather a Kentuckian?

WILLIAMS: Yes, he was. He was born in Clinton County, right on the Tennessee border. He lived in Clinton County all his life. We visited them more than they visited us. He could not stand to leave his farm for more than a couple of days. He figured that it would all just go to shambles. We would go down and visit on holidays, usually once every six weeks, and the other times of the year and in the summer, when I was a kid, I would go down there for extended periods.

BEATTIE: Do you remember the types of things you did while you were visiting?

WILLIAMS: I would play in the barn a lot. I had older cousins there. I was the baby of the family by some ten years, and so they were all very indulgent of me. I had older cousins who would build fortresses in the hayloft out of bales of hay, and I can remember leaping very dangerously from the highest part of the hayloft to a lower level and playing and having a great time and listening to my grandfather's stories and walking through the fields with him and pulling tobacco worms off the tobacco leaves and getting the great distinction of stepping on them.

I can remember doing lots of things with my grandmother, who was, I think, in a lot of ways, even more of an intimate companion than my grandfather. I confided a lot in her, and, the things that bothered me, I could tell Mamma about. She would solve things.

BEATTIE: That's what you called your grandmother?

WILLIAMS: Yes.

BEATTIE: What was her real name?

WILLIAMS: Mertie Elma Guffy Booher, and she despised her first name, Mertie, so we never called her that.

BEATTIE: Do you have brothers and sisters?

WILLIAMS: No, I'm an only child.

BEATTIE: What about the grandparents on the other side of the family?

WILLIAMS: The Williams grandparents were fine, upstanding people. They were a little bit stern, and the best thing about visiting them was the bevy of cousins that would be around, and there were a lot of cousins my age. As a matter of fact, there were five boys within four years of one another, and I was right in the middle of those. They were a lot of fun, and that was the thing I looked forward to.

BEATTIE: Where did they live?

WILLIAMS: Some lived in Louisville and some lived in Cumberland County. My grandparents lived in Cumberland County, which is right next to Clinton County, in the south-central part of the state. They are both very southern in the state and much closer to Nashville than they are to Louisville. Grandfather Williams was a farmer for a while. He worked as a ferryman on the Cumberland River. He did various kinds of jobs. I don't remember his working all that much, because he had retired by the time I was of an age to really remember anything.

BEATTIE: What about aunts and uncles? Did they play a very big role in your life?

WILLIAMS: My Aunt Ruby Nell, who is just absolutely wonderful and just a little bit eccentric, played an important part in my life. When I was visiting my maternal grandparents in Clinton County, very often I would hang around with her, and we would go to various places. She was there, it seemed to me, just to show me a good time. I had lots of pleasant memories of her and of my Aunt Nora, who is my dad's sister, and of my Aunt Hazel, who is my dad's youngest sister. It's a very complicated family, in that my Aunt Eileen on my mother's side, her oldest son married my dad's youngest sister, so I have cousins who are first cousins on one side, and who are first cousins once removed on the other, and it's this elaborate weaving of the family. So, it was a pretty close-knit extended family, and, yes, the aunts and uncles played a role in that.

BEATTIE: What was your childhood like?

WILLIAMS: I have lots of memories. We lived in Valley Station, in southwest Jefferson County, and my parents taught, as I said, at Fort Knox. I spent quite a bit of time when I was very small in the nursery school system and in kindergarten at Fort Knox, and then I was sort of commuting, like my parents were. My memories of childhood are, for the most part, quite pleasant. We lived on a sort of working-class block right off the Dixie Highway where a lot of the parents were my parents' age and, consequently, a lot of the kids were my age, and I grew up around ten to fifteen kids. We had very elaborate, imaginative games that we played with one another; those kind of things I remember quite well and quite fondly. I don't think I was ever as secure as I would like to have been, and I don't know what the consequence of that was, but I think that happens to a lot of kids. Childhood can be a frightening time in a lot of ways, too.

BEATTIE: Where did you go to elementary school?

WILLIAMS: Medora Elementary, which is at the corner of Deering Road and Dixie Highway.

BEATTIE: Did you have a favorite subject in your early years of school?

WILLIAMS: I liked reading, and I liked writing stories.

BEATTIE: Do you think it was because your mother read to you?

WILLIAMS: I think that was part of it. There was also a librarian down in Fort Knox, and when I would visit my parents—I started reading when I was two years old—she would provide me with all kinds of books. I can remember my mother reading to me some, but I was reading books for myself by the time I was about two years old—a lot of wide, indiscriminate reading. My parents told me that I started reading the name brands of products in the Winn-Dixie supermarket. I don't remember, of course, learning how to read, but all of a sudden I'm there spelling *Cheerios* and *Zesta Saltines* and *Seven-up,* and that came as a surprise to my parents.

BEATTIE: When you got to school, were you bored when everybody else was learning to read?

WILLIAMS: I was so afraid that I would be unpopular for being able to read that I hid it. I remember this; I hid it for a couple of months, and the way that I was found out by my classmates—I think the teacher knew, somehow—was the teacher circulated something that you were supposed to take home saying, "Any children who haven't had their polio shots should do this," and, of course, I could read it; nobody else could. And I said, "Well, I'm so glad I've had my polio shot."

BEATTIE: Were you popular or unpopular for that?

WILLIAMS: They tell me I was popular. I perceived myself as not being as popular as some of my teachers thought I was, but my parents tell me that I was. I think that we have two different versions of history on that.

BEATTIE: Do you think being an only child led you to develop your imagination more, in terms of playing by yourself and inventing games?

WILLIAMS: Yes. I don't see how you could avoid that. You're left to your own resources, you know. You have a relatively early bedtime, and your friends are gone. There were no brothers and sisters to play with.

BEATTIE: What sorts of things did you enjoy reading as a child?

WILLIAMS: I had a series of junior classic books which were not like Classic Comics or anything, but they were children's versions of some of the classics, and I can remember getting a copy of the *Odyssey*, which was basically the story of the adventures of Ulysses written at about the sixth- or seventh-grade level. I remember getting that down, and I loved that dearly. I loved Greek myths. I must have read Edith Hamilton's *Mythology* a dozen times in my elementary school years.

BEATTIE: So, the things you liked were densely plot-oriented?

WILLIAMS: Yes, and also, even then, very magical. I liked the elements of magic that, at that time, could take me away from my daily surroundings. I went to Valley High School, and I went to Valley High School, also, for junior high. The thing I remember the most about junior high was that we were on double sessions at that time, and I went to class from about, I think, 1:30 in the afternoon till about 8:00 at night.

BEATTIE: Was that because there were so many students?

WILLIAMS: There were so many students. My seventh grade composition teacher was wonderful. She was a woman named Grace Baker, who still lives in the Valley Station area, and who had a real talent for making literature come alive. We acted out Shakespeare plays in class. We went to see things. We went on lots of field trips to see theater, to see movies. She had a way of making the classroom very interesting, and it was right up my alley, because I loved the stories and she was masterful at presenting stories.

My other memories of middle school are, like a lot of other people's memories of that time, unpleasant. You know, that's the time where you hate everybody, and you hate yourself the most. Ms. Baker was the bright spot in that dark time.

BEATTIE: Were your interests mostly academic, or did you have sports interests or extracurricular involvements?

WILLIAMS: I was a baseball player, a first-baseman, an outfielder for a while. I pitched a little bit, but I could not hit anything. But I was a very good fielder, and a fairly fast base runner, so I had some talents to offer the team. I really enjoyed that, too, and quit that around age fourteen when I injured my back and, with that injury, we discovered that I had a mild case of spina bifida. I've got two bones missing at the base of my spine.

BEATTIE: What was high school like?

WILLIAMS: I had Ms. Baker again, who also taught in the high school. A man named Herb Condor taught me Humanities. He died three or four years ago. And a woman named Mary Theobald taught a creative writing class, and a man named Reason Newton was a math teacher I liked, despite the fact that math was not that interesting to me. I remember those teachers well. I remember feeling very much not a part of the high school community around me. This was in the sixties, and I think that it was a time when politics, in a lot of ways, polarized people. And my politics were a little bit far to the left of my classmates', and it made for some tension and some hostility. I was glad to get out of there, despite the fact that there were some good teachers. My family didn't share my views. They were encouraging when I wanted to go to New England for college, because I think they knew that there would be a good education where I intended to go. Miss Theobald, the creative writing teacher I mentioned, had mentioned Middlebury College very adamantly. I think she thought that they had a program geared especially for writers at Middlebury.

BEATTIE: Did she know about Bread Loaf Writers' Conference?

WILLIAMS: She knew about Bread Loaf, and she was getting that mixed up with the regular school at Middlebury. It turned out that, indeed, I *did* get a good background in writing at Middlebury, but I went up there, as it turns out, thinking that it was going to be like Bread Loaf, and it wasn't. It was a good, solid, liberal arts education. It was better for me than had it been specifically focused, like at Goddard where, at the time, you just picked out your curriculum.

BEATTIE: What kind of writing instruction did you receive at Middlebury?

WILLIAMS: I was mainly interested in poetry then. I wrote a lot of poetry. I studied under a fellow named John Conrad, who is an American literature scholar. He wrote *The American Landscape,* and I studied with a fairly prominent New England poet, Robert Peck. I attended the Bread Loaf Writers' Conference.

BEATTIE: Was that as an undergraduate?

WILLIAMS: As an undergraduate, on two occasions, on scholarship.

BEATTIE: That's fairly unusual, isn't it?

WILLIAMS: Yes, it is. It didn't hurt that the Bread Loaf Writers' Conference was connected to Middlebury. At the same time, there were a lot of Middlebury students who applied and did not make it. I guess I was a really pretty good undergraduate poet. My first piece was published in *The American Review,* while I was at Middlebury, and that's sort of unusual, too, for somebody who is twenty years old. I didn't write much fiction then, and I wasn't altogether that much interested in fiction. That came along much later.

BEATTIE: Did you think, at the time, you would be a poet?

WILLIAMS: For a while I did. I can't really tell you why I ended up not continuing to write poetry. Something happened, and I looked back, and I hadn't written poetry in a year or two. Part of what happened was graduate school; it was not as pleasant an experience as my undergraduate experience.

BEATTIE: Did you go directly from one school to the other?

WILLIAMS: Yes.

BEATTIE: Where did you attend graduate school?

WILLIAMS: The University of Rochester. Renaissance literature I studied for a while. I went there because Anthony Hecht was the poet-in-residence there, although they didn't have a creative writing program. I studied Renaissance literature, primarily, and Anglo-Saxon literature.

BEATTIE: And you received your master's degree in Renaissance literature?

WILLIAMS: Yes. I didn't have a thesis for the master's. I took a comprehensive exam. I worked for a while on a doctoral dissertation on Christopher Marlowe, and set it aside, and it just reached the point that I decided that I wanted to do something else. There is that joke, you know: How many graduate students does it take to screw in a light bulb? One, but it takes him eight years. I didn't want to get into that. There were other things in front of me, and even the most capable graduate students seem to have these prolonged careers in writing dissertations. Also, I don't think I was quite ready for it then. I think I was ready for a break from school. I mentioned I'd gone straight from high school to college, and from college to graduate school.

BEATTIE: How did you find working with poet Anthony Hecht?

WILLIAMS: Anthony Hecht is a very skilled poet, and I think that, just in the interest of decency, that's all I'll say. I really do admire his work. I worked with him for a while, as well. He was a reader as my dissertation progressed.

After my stay in graduate school, I came down to Louisville and in, I guess it was 1992, Teri [Williams's first wife], who was then in Florida, went up to Rochester on a National Endowment for the Humanities summer scholarship to study Geoffrey Chaucer, and she studied under a man named Russell Peck, who had been my English professor there, so she and I had this connection.

BEATTIE: How did you meet your wife, Teri?

WILLIAMS: We met in the Writing Center at the University of Louisville. She had been teaching at Fort Knox, of all places—this is years after my dad's retirement—but I had these childhood connections with Fort Knox. She had been there, and she had resigned from Fort Knox, because she wanted to get her master's in Humanities, and, at the same time, she began teaching part-time for the Writing Center, as I was, and we met, and the rest is history. This was August, 1986, and we got married in August of 1987. She is a year younger than I am.

BEATTIE: You came back to Louisville from the University of Rochester. What brought you back here?

WILLIAMS: I just wanted to get out of Rochester at that time. I guess, in the final analysis, I was tired of being a student. I came down here and began to work part-time at U of L [University of Louisville], and that job became a full-time job for a couple of years. I was a full-time lecturer at U of L, and this period lasted from 1978 till 1982. I taught freshman composition. I taught Shakespeare, and I taught the advanced essay classes. I did a little bit with modern poetry, then, too.

BEATTIE: Was this your first exposure to teaching?

WILLIAMS: I had taught two semesters at the University of Rochester as part of my student teaching assistantship. It was very different from one place to the other. The students were very different people. In Rochester they were mostly northeastern prep school products, and here, of course, it was mostly mid-southern public school. Each set of students had just a lot of different cultural assumptions, and I found that I liked to teach both places for different reasons. I felt much more attuned to the students here, and I still do. But it's kind of interesting to teach people that you're not attuned to, as well, where you have to stretch a little bit, and you have to make some kind of real effort to understand where they're coming from, instinctively.

I found that students here [U of L] are really bright and eager and capable, so we can make up for loss of time, we can make up for gaps in their backgrounds. You know, I had that myself when I went to Middlebury. I felt myself three or four years behind the other people in my freshman class. But if a student is fairly sharp and applies himself or herself, it's not that much of a gap to make up.

BEATTIE: You said your teaching here at the University of Louisville became full-time for a couple of years. Since then, you've been teaching part-time, is that correct?

WILLIAMS: No, what happened was they had a series of budget cuts at the University in the early eighties, roughly comparable, I guess, to the budget cuts that they've had more recently. It was '82, and I was twenty-nine years old, and I thought, "Here you are, you are twenty-nine years old, and you never really had a stable job. It's about time to forget academia for a while and go out into the business world and see what you can do." So, I went into publishing for about four years, in various capacities. I worked as an editor, and then came back to the University of Louisville, basically because I really missed teaching.

BEATTIE: Where did you work as a publisher or as an editor?

WILLIAMS: At TSR. I was a games editor there. They are the people that make the game Dungeons and Dragons. I worked on checking the math on those games and on cleaning up the writing, on making sure the game directions were clear enough that bright ten- to eleven-year olds could follow them. I left TSR and then joined another company, which was a starting-up company. I did a lot of the same kinds of things. This was all in southern Wisconsin—Lake Geneva, Wisconsin. I lived there, which is fifty to sixty miles from Chicago.

BEATTIE: When did your interest in fantasy and science fiction writing begin?

WILLIAMS: It was a goodly portion of what I read as a teenager. I read all those Mars stories, the things which are wonderfully bad.

I told you about injuring my back. Well, in that summer, when my back was first injured, there wasn't much I could do. I really couldn't even be active. I just had to sit around or lie around, and one of those older cousins of mine gave me a copy of Tolkien's *Lord of the Rings* and said, "You might enjoy this; this is a big, long book. You can sit down with it and enjoy the reading." And it was transforming. I think that was the work that really made fantasy a central part of my interest. I read it and said, "I would like to write something like this."

BEATTIE: When did you start writing?

WILLIAMS: I wrote things from childhood on, and I guess I really decided I wanted to write around the time of reading Tolkien. So I wrote as seriously as a high school student can write in the last couple of years of high school. I took a creative writing class in my junior and senior years, too, and showed my writing to my teacher. She was the one who suggested I go to Middlebury.

BEATTIE: You talked about having your first published poem in *The American Review*. How did your publishing career, your writing career, take off from there?

WILLIAMS: It didn't. I had several other poems published over the next five or six years, and then I didn't publish anything again until, I guess it was 1985. I basically wasn't doing any writing, and at that time I had stopped working with TSR, and they started the Dragonlance series with Margaret Weis and Tracy Hickman doing the initial Dragonlance novels, and I went up to Tracy in the parking lot—we had apartments about a block away from one another—and I said to him, "So, would you like some poems for the books?" I said, "The one thing that I never did like about Tolkien is I thought that his poems were kind of wooden, and so it would be nice to try my hand at doing something pretty good for your books." And he said, "Why, yes, and," he said, "I'll talk to Margaret." And so Margaret used to slip me little checks, and I would write them a poem, and, as is the way with the Dragonlance books, my poems became the property of someone else. But that's how I got into publishing. That was about '84 or '85. Then I began to publish with some of their anthologies, and then I guess it was in '87 that they called me and asked if I wanted to try a novel for them, and I said, "Sure." And they said, "Send in an outline," and that was *Weasel's Luck*.

BEATTIE: You've also published under a pen name, a pseudonym, in *Amazing Stories*.

WILLIAMS: Yes. I was Bubba Fletcher. Bubba has become a sort of myth around the University of Louisville Writing Center, less now than he was three or four years back. He is a visionary redneck, basically, who is a paranormal advisor, and he sees all of these things like flying saucers. He maintains what he has is preserved cryogenically under the football stadium.

BEATTIE: Do you still write under that pseudonym?

WILLIAMS: No. I've only done that with a couple of pieces.

BEATTIE: Since most of your published writing has been what some people call genre fiction, I'm wondering if you think that that is fair terminology, or if that limits your readership.

WILLIAMS: You know, it was really interesting. Teri and I were over in England in the summer of '91, and we went into a pub in Canterbury where we had a lengthy conversation with some graduate students in postmodernist literature there. And it was a surprise to me that they took in stride that I was primarily a fantasy writer; they thought that was great, and they were talking to me like they would talk to somebody who would be considered more "literary." I think that the distinction seems to be one in this country more than elsewhere. I guess everything is genre literature in some way or another; you know, academic fiction is genre literature, in the sense that it does adopt certain conventions. I think I've found being termed a fantasy writer limiting only if you try to do something that sort of bends the genre in some way or another. I have a manuscript that is a surrealist historical novel, and sometimes editors have problems with knowing where to place that, because they, too, think in genre terms. Sometimes I think that you have people who are inventive enough to see that certain things slip out of the boundaries of genre. In a lot of ways, some of the fiction that they call genre fiction hasn't developed its critical audience yet. There is some interesting critical and scholarly work going on now, but I think that you will probably find a few years down the road that reading, at least among students, would be a little bit more discriminate. I agree there's a lot of schlock being written, passing for fantasy. There is a lot of schlock passing for academic literature, too, you know. It happens in everything.

BEATTIE: Would you talk a bit about your books?

WILLIAMS: I think the creation of the world is what interests me the most, making that the background through which the characters move. I mean, I enjoy meeting the characters as they come into play in the books, obviously, but I believe that it's being able to draw on all kinds of things that I know—or that I want to know about—that interests me most. I'll go and research things if I don't know enough about something, or Teri will help, certainly; she knows a lot of other types of things. She knows all the things that are worth knowing, and I know all the rest, basically; that's what it comes down to. But I find that the whole process of putting together that world and making it both wondersome and plausible is a lot of fun for me. I find telling the story of a quest of conflict—those big, older, mythological versions of the stories—are really more fascinating to me than more realistic stories, which strike me as a little bit more tentative. I'm not tentative, as a writer. The realist story is much more quiet, I guess, and much more muted, and relies more on subtleties, although I hope there is some subtlety in my books, as well. But I like the way that they imitate the great stories of the Western world and the great stories of the ancient world.

BEATTIE: What I enjoy most about your books is their humor.

WILLIAMS: Thank you. I think it's a distinguishing part of my books. A funny story is when the editor was talking to Teri and me when we were getting ready to write *Before the Mask*. He said, "Now, this is going to be a part of our Dragonlance series, so it should be dark and somber," and he said, "None of that characteristic Williams' humor." Well, that's like tying one hand behind your back for me, but we managed to work together and, I think, make a very convincing book. But that's going to be totally different from a lot of the things that you've been reading where there is more humor.

BEATTIE: What would you say you have done or are trying to do in your books that is different from so many fantasy novels?

WILLIAMS: I like to think that they do deal in some way or another with big ideas, with great issues. *Weasel's Luck,* for example, deals with the thorny issue of what it means to be good, and that's a very simple and basic concern, but it's also a very universal concern, and it deals with questions of belief. I hope that my growing spiritual sense informs these books as well. I guess the thing that distinguishes these books from some of the other things that I have read in the field is that unique combination of theme and plot. Some writers will come at their stories from the thematic standpoint, and some come more as storytellers. I think that the balance of both of those elements distinguishes my books from, certainly, a lot of the less-effective stuff in the fantasy field. I like to think that my books do treat important issues.

I was basically floating somewhere between agnosticism and atheism for the first thirty-three to thirty-four years of my life. That includes my childhood. And, in the last five or six years, I have become Christian, and it is a very interesting process for me to bring that vision to the process of telling these stories. It's a tough thing to do, because as a Christian writer you don't want to be preachy. I have found that to be sort of a failure in C. S. Lewis's work. I find it a little bit didactic. But you want to tell as good a story as possible, and you want to be as thorough a storyteller as you can, at the same time as you're presenting a vision of the gospel.

BEATTIE: When you say you've become a Christian, are you talking about having joined a church?

WILLIAMS: Yes. I am Episcopalian. I attend St. Matthew's Episcopal Church in Louisville.

BEATTIE: I know that you have collaborated recently with your wife, Teri, on at least one novel.

WILLIAMS: Teri has been really instrumental in a lot of the novels; I think increasingly so. I think we balance the power. She is writing the Prologue and the Epilogue. Those are solely her work, and we just decided that it has reached the point that in a lot of the work, since she is doing so much of it, why not give her proper billing?

The collaboration is a very interesting process. What you've got to do, first of all, you've got to have somebody whose abilities you respect, and also, somebody whose industry you respect. Those things have to be there, and if you have that, collaboration works very, very well—much like a marriage in a lot of ways. There are a few little things that you need to do to set down ground rules; you need to know when to set aside the business, and it makes it very tricky, being married and collaborating. So, what Teri and I do is, we set aside specific times when we are working, and then when the workday is over, we go back to other aspects of our life. I guess that works more naturally if you are collaborating with somebody who you don't live with, and I've seen it work very well there, but I've seen married couples where it's been a disaster. For Teri and me, it's been a very smooth process. Since we are collaborating more extensively, we're circulating a project now among several publishers for a series where we will collaborate. I'm also circulating one where I will write the novels solo. So I'm trying to do both.

BEATTIE: What writing are you working on now?

WILLIAMS: Two projects. Without going into too much detail, we're working on a swashbuckling series of books, complete with pirates and New World exploration—fantasy—and we're trying to see if there's an interest in publishing these. Myself, I'm working on a series of books set in the nineteenth century, with their backdrop a strange combination of English Romanticism, the Industrial Revolution, and the American Civil War, although they won't be necessarily going by those names.

BEATTIE: Do you do any kind of market research to see what historical subjects, as well as futuristic types of subjects, are popular with publishers, or do you just write what you feel like writing and then, if it sells, great?

WILLIAMS: I write what I feel like writing, and we have a good agent who can tell you when something will definitely not wash.

BEATTIE: When did you get your agent?

WILLIAMS: Nineteen eighty-eight.

BEATTIE: So, it was after your first novel?

WILLIAMS: Yes, after the first novel. I wish I'd had an agent for negotiating *Weasel's Luck*. I didn't get as good a contract for that book as he has been able to get me and, ironically, *Weasel's Luck* has always been one of the better-selling of the books.

BEATTIE: How did you obtain your agent?

WILLIAMS: His fiction appeared in an anthology along with mine, and one of the editors at TSR said, "Scott Siegal is also an agent, and he's quite good. So, why don't you give him a call?" That editor said, "You're getting to the point that you need an agent," and I gave him a call, and we settled things over the phone. He said, "Sure, I know your work; I'll handle it."

BEATTIE: He is in New York?

WILLIAMS: Yes, he and his wife run an agency, Siegal and Siegal, Limited. A lot of his principal writers are fantasy writers.

BEATTIE: Speaking of people who write fantasy, who are the ones writing now whom you particularly admire?

WILLIAMS: Oh, boy! I like Gene Wolfe. There's a series of four books of his called *The Book of the New Sun,* which has, I think, really some superb writing. I like a lot of the stuff that was written earlier in the century, of course, such as Tolkien. There is a book called the *Crock of Gold* by James Stephens, an Irish writer, which is just splendid. I like a lot of Latin American novelists.

BEATTIE: Do you mean current Magical Realists?

WILLIAMS: Yes, yes, Magical Realists. I love Gabriele Garcia Marquez and Isabelle Allende.

BEATTIE: I'm wondering what your opinion is of the controversy about the Dungeons and Dragons Games that arose, probably a decade ago, when it came out in the media that some adolescents playing with the game would then go out and commit crimes.

WILLIAMS: Well, to be brief about that, the way I see it is that in almost all these cases, when something like that happened, the young person was very troubled to begin with. Dungeons and Dragons is a game for bright kids. Bright kids are almost always by nature in this culture troubled, because there is a streak in this culture that mistrusts them, I guess. I think that to blame suicides, to blame crime, to blame those kinds of things on Dungeons and Dragons, it's almost dangerous, because what it's saying is that there is one hard-and-fast solution for a very, very complicated issue. And I don't know what to blame for it, but I don't think that Dungeons and Dragons is the whole story, and I don't even think it's the partial story, in a lot of these situations. I think it's just a manifestation of that same kind of loneliness and that same kind of sense of being not a part of things that is so prevalent among young people in our time. That's one of the things that I try to address in my books, too; I try to be pretty aware of the fact that middle school kids are reading my books.

BEATTIE: You've talked about your writing habits in relation to collaborating with your wife. What about writing yourself?

WILLIAMS: In this particular field, fantasy, it's been my experience, at least, that I have a contract very often before very much of the book is written. And, as a consequence, I have a due date. So when I have a schedule laid out in front of me, I am really pretty organized. I'll get up at about four in the morning and sneak around the house, trying to keep the dogs at bay so that Teri doesn't have to wake up, and I work until eight or so when we start getting ready for school. I do this every day, four to five hours early in the morning every day, and I find that the regularity of that schedule is really productive when I'm doing it, because you get hungry at certain times of the day. You get inventive at certain times if you can establish that rhythm, if you're doing it long enough.

BEATTIE: Do you find that you're producing a certain number of pages, usually?

WILLIAMS: I try for 1,500 words, six or seven pages a day. I'm not saying that all of what I write daily will be kept.

BEATTIE: Do you write on a word processor?

WILLIAMS: Yes, I wouldn't be without one now. They're so much better than typewriters.

BEATTIE: How quickly, then, do you find yourself finishing books? You seem to be producing them rather rapidly.

WILLIAMS: They have varied from eight months to, well, this most recent book the collaboration with Teri, *Before the Mask,* took eight weeks.

BEATTIE: Eight weeks for a novel?

WILLIAMS: Yes, eight or nine weeks.

BEATTIE: That's impressive.

WILLIAMS: Yes. It's sort of necessary, in that it's our principal source of income. I'm part-time at the university; Teri is part-time at the university. This is the job.

BEATTIE: Do you have contracts now for a number of future writing projects?

WILLIAMS: We're on the brink of something.

BEATTIE: I see. And do you usually have several contracts at once?

WILLIAMS: It varies. I've had periods of time, and we've had periods of time, where there's a gap of several months without a contract, but it's no big deal, you know.

BEATTIE: At this point in your career, does it go both ways, in terms of you suggesting novels to editors and editors suggesting novels to you, as well?

WILLIAMS: Yes. It goes both ways. It started out with more. *Weasel's* was sort of an exception. I had a very free hand at deciding what *Weasel's* would be about, but a lot of the earlier projects were suggestions by the editors.

BEATTIE: And do you tend to think in terms of series when you think of books now, instead of in terms of single volumes?

WILLIAMS: Yes. I think trilogy all the time. It's just almost like a conventional form.

BEATTIE: Sounds more profitable to think that way.

WILLIAMS: It is. It is.

BEATTIE: And what about revising? Do you do that as you write, or do you do that after the fact, or both?

WILLIAMS: I do both, really. Very often I wait to see what the editor says. I'm fortunate to work with some editors who have some good suggestions. But when I'm working by myself, I'll have my five or six pages of the day, and then as I begin the next day, I usually revise the last two pages that I've done. It puts me into the swing for the day to come. When Teri is working with me, that's a little bit of a burden taken off me, because those pages, at the end of the day, will go to her.

BEATTIE: I've interviewed writers who have said that they'll have a general idea about a book when they sit down to write, but they're always surprised at what happens, plot-wise, as they create. I would think with the type of novel you write, that is so intricately plot-oriented, you would have to have a more concrete idea of exactly what's going to happen than some writers might. Do you?

WILLIAMS: Well, we generally have an outline, and it's generally written in some detail. You've got to have the sense as a writer when something else, more powerful, occurs to you to follow that, and to be surprised, to depart from that outline and then pick up the pieces, to go back and readjust and pick up the pieces as you go.

BEATTIE: This is perhaps a strange question to ask someone whose work is set in places about as far removed from Kentucky as it could be, but in terms of sense of place, does living in Kentucky, do you think, influence your work in any way?

WILLIAMS: Yes, the sense of place comes through very often in the voice. One of my characters in *Weasel's Luck* speaks not dialect, by any means, but a genuine Kentucky syntax, on occasion. I think my affinities to the landscape are Kentuckian. I like the landscape around the Ohio River Valley, and I think that very often that kind of thing enters into my work. My first impulse is to set books in terrain very much like the terrain with which I'm familiar.

Kentucky history passes through some of my books in some ways. Certainly a lot of Kentucky kids that grew up around the same time I did were interested in the Civil War, and I was especially interested in what happened in this state. And that's entering into the new project that I'm working on, and it entered into the surrealist, fantasy, historical novel.

BEATTIE: Could you ever envision setting a fantasy novel in Kentucky?

WILLIAMS: It's possible. Anything can happen in Kentucky, so why not?

BEATTIE: What do you think the nature of creativity may be?

WILLIAMS: Well, if God created us in His own image, part of that image is the continued state of creation out of nothing or the continued state of renewal, the creating of the new out of things that are old. And I like to think that God did create us in His own image, and that when we do create we're doing it, as I think George Herbert talked about, in humble imitation of the Father.

BEATTIE: Do you ascribe to any notion of creativity coming out of a need to understand or come to terms with negative feelings or traumatic experiences?

WILLIAMS: Yes, I think it comes out of all of those things, as an act of grace. With some people, it's a need to understand. But far less important than what provides the initial spark is what emerges from that, which is sheer grace.

BEATTIE: You've talked about what you're working on now; what about future work? Do you have things in mind that you would like to do, or is there one work that you would particularly like to write more than anything else?

WILLIAMS: I have two things in mind for the foreseeable future. One is a story about an Irish saint, and the other is a story about a group of traveling players who come to American shores in the seventeenth century. Both of them are a combination of historical novel and fantasy.

BEATTIE: But the characters you are referring to in these were real?

WILLIAMS: Yes. If the book works out the way I foresee it now, it will find its way into various, actual, historical situations, and the Irish saint is, yes, very real.

BEATTIE: Have you contemplated writing anything that isn't fantasy, other than poetry?

WILLIAMS: Not at the moment, no, because I think that the elements of the fantastic are really important to the kinds of things that I want to treat. When you strip aside the whole necessity of saying, "Is this realistic, does this correspond to life as I understand it?" you get the reader to make that particular leap of faith. And when you make one leap of faith, you can move into other leaps of faith, and that's, in a lot of ways, what my fiction deals with: questions of faith.

January 16, 1993

In 1994, Williams divorced his wife, Teri Patterson, and married Rhonda Needy of Louisville, Kentucky. Since then he has continued to teach part-time at the University of Louisville and he has become the step-father of two "remarkable teenage boys." Williams's novel, *Arcady*, was nominated for several awards, the most notable of which was the 1997 Nebula.

BOOKS BY MICHAEL WILLIAMS

Weasel's Luck. New York: Random House, 1988.

Galen Beknighted. New York: Random House, 1990.

Sorcerer's Apprentice. New York: Warner Books, 1990.

The Forest Land. New York: Warner Books, 1991.

The Oath and the Measure. New York: Random House, 1992.

The Balance of Power. New York: Warner Books, 1992.

Before the Mask. (with Teri Williams). New York: Random House, 1993.

The Dark Queen. (with Teri Williams). New York. Random House, 1994.

Arcady. New York: Roc/Penguin, 1996.

Allamanda. New York: Roc/Penguin, 1997.

INDEX